KU-080-108

The History of Irish Book Publishing

By Tony Farmar

The Legendary Lofty Clattery Café
A History of Craig Gardner & Co.
Ordinary Lives
Holles Street
A Brief History of Clé
Heitons: A Managed Transition
Godliness, Games and Good Learning
Believing in Action
Patients, Potions and Physicians
Mater Private
St Luke's: A Haven in Rathgar
Privileged Lives
The Versatile Profession

The History of Irish Book Publishing

Tony Farmar

Foreword by Fergal Tobin

First published 2018

The History Press
The Mill, Brimscombe Port
Stroud, Gloucestershire, GL5 2QG
www.thehistorypress.co.uk

British Library Cataloguing in Publication Data.
A catalogue record for this book is available from the British Library.

ISBN 978 1 84588 894 7

Typesetting and origination by The History Press
Printed and bound in Great Britain by TJ International Ltd

The Headmaster picked up the book. 'Ah,' he said. 'A book! Turn to page (i).' They turned to Page One.

'Ah, no' he said patiently, 'Not Page One, Page (i). And tell me who are Faber and Faber? Is he, they, one man or two men or perhaps Mrs and Mr Faber? Is he or they this book's author? And is a person who makes a book a bookmaker? What does ISBN mean and how should I say it? Is © a friend of the author? Is the book dedicated to him? Who are Butler and Tanner of Frome? What is a preface, an epigraph? This Foreword … need I read it? Can only William Shakespeare own a folio? Does a quire need a conductor? Can one catch a colophon by too heavy reading late at night? And spell it?'

He went on and on. My class's ignorance was utter. Finally he pronounced sentence. 'You don't seem to know much about this book. And I haven't got as far as Page One.'

My pupils looked reproachfully at me.

J.L. Carr *Harpole & Foxberrow General Publishers* (Kettering 1992) p.1

Contents

Acknowledgements

Books were Tony Farmar's vocation. He was my dear companion in marriage and publishing, and I was fortunate to be closely involved in all of his writings, but especially in this history which absorbed him for so many years. He had completed the main text, including the chronicle, by September 2017, when his illness made a final revision impossible. That task, the preparation of the text for The History Press Ireland, and the compiling of the picture sections, fell to me. Inevitably, queries arose which would have been easily resolved had Tony lived. Most have been answered by reference to his notes and extensive library of books and papers on all aspects of publishing, but there undoubtedly remain a few gaps.

Tony was grateful to Ronan Colgan of the History Press for commissioning the book. He was happy to know that Conor Kostick would contribute editorially as well as writing a final chapter on the recent period. Conor's input has been invaluable. Special thanks are due to Una MacConville and Nick Maxwell of Wordwell, publishers of *Books Ireland*, for their help with the illustrations.

Among Tony's notes was a draft list of the people he wished to thank for their assistance, particularly with the chronicle. It reads as follows:

For information, correction and steering, thanks to: Jeremy Addis, Seamus Cashman, Harold Clarke, Joe Collins, John Davey, Kieran Devlin, Maria Dickenson, Mary Feehan, Michael Gill, Brian Gilsenan, Samantha Holman, Clare Hutton, Sinéad Mac Aodha, Philip MacDermott, Jane Mahony, John Manning, Robin Montgomery, John Murphy, Hugh Oram, Ivan O'Brien, Michael O'Brien, Gerry O'Flaherty, Cian Ó hÉigeartaigh, Susan Rossney, Catherine Rose, John Spillane, Pat Staunton, Brian Sibley, Mary Stanley, Peter Thew, Robert Towers, Fergal Tobin, Jonathan Williams.

Thanks are also due to the following for permission to reproduce illustrations: *Books Ireland*, *The Bookseller*, Brandon Books (O'Brien Press), Cló Iar-Chonnacht, Dundalgan Press, Eason's, Gill Books, Mercier Press, Colin Smythe.

Anna Farmar, October 2018

List of Tables

Foreword

By Fergal Tobin

Ireland was a latecomer to the print revolution, as to so many other things. Gutenberg invented printing by moveable type in Mainz in 1454; yet Maurice Craig, in his classic *Dublin 1660–1860*, states that 'anything printed in Ireland before 1700 can be classed as "rare"'. Among other things, this helps to account for the failure of the Reformation in most of Ireland. Crucial to that enterprise was the translation of the Bible into the vernacular. But the earliest Irish language version of the New Testament did not appear until 1603. The Old Testament was not translated until the 1680s. The contrast with Wales is instructive: as early as 1563, the process began with the passing of an Act for the Translation of the Bible into Welsh.

It is no harm to be reminded of these delays, as Tony Farmar does in his opening chapters. They constitute a superb *tour d'horizon* of the book publishing scene in Ireland before 1890. He hurries his narrative to that point, the better to concentrate on the quickened environment that followed, for reasons that he sets out cogently in the introduction. Still, that scene-setting survey of the industry before 1890 is an education in itself. Anyone reading it – including people who consider themselves possessed of some knowledge of the subject – will learn much that is new or that is located in a fresh context.

This book is the product of prodigious research. The references and bibliography alone stand in evidence of that. To take one page at random: the notes include an article from the *Linen Hall Review* of 1987; two references to a dictionary of commerce published in London in 1839; a quote from the French eighteenth-century encyclopaedist Denis Diderot; and a dictionary of members of the Dublin book trade from 1550 to 1800. This has been a labour of love.

Tony was a publisher by avocation and an historian by inclination. He was a champion of one of the most neglected corners of publishing: that dealing with commercial history. It is interesting that we have an Irish Labour History Society but no equivalent society or journal to record the development of commercial and professional life. Tony himself wrote a number of commissioned works in this area, in particular a history of the accountancy profession in Ireland. Even in this unpromising territory he extracted nuggets: the number of accountants in Ireland grew by an astonishing 83 per cent in the short few years from 1996 to 2012. In the latter year, there were 27,116 accountants in the country. The equivalent figure for Roman Catholic priests and nuns was 6,729. It tells you something, that.

It is therefore little surprise that he was commissioned to write the history of his own trade. He was the obvious choice. He had the requisite skills. He brought to the task an almost amateur enthusiasm, but there is nothing amateur about the result, as those of you now holding the finished product in your hands can see for yourselves.

You'd know that he had been a production man. Many publishers are uninterested in the mechanics of typesetting, printing and binding. They see their role as gatekeepers – choosing what to accept and what to reject for their lists – and as financial brokers, putting up the risk money to allow the raw text see the light of day in the bookshops. Tony was more than alert to these primary impulses – as the text of this book makes abundantly clear – but he simply could not help himself from his several *excursus* into the technological changes that underpinned the developments in the trade.

These diversions have the great merit, however, of locating a small national industry in its wider technological and mechanical context. All the more so when rendered, as here, with lucidity and authority. He was an enthusiast – that shines forth on every page – but he was a knowledgeable one: he knew whereof he writ. By extension, it also meant embracing a significant part of British publishing, because Irish publishing could not be sensibly surveyed in any other context. The natural boundary of a publishing culture is linguistic, not political. Ireland shares with Austria and Wallonia what Tony always referred to as an 'over-mighty neighbour' and for the same reason: a shared language.

This left the small, vulnerable world of Irish language publishing in an isolated position, as the development of the business coincided with rapid Anglicisation and increasing literacy in that language. Yet in the later chapters of the book, he gives this subset of the Irish trade its due, recording its quietly heroic survival against all odds. Indeed, one of the more heart-lifting things at the Frankfurt Book Fair over the years was to see Irish language publishers not just present but doing rights deals.

Irish publishing is both national and regional. It is national in the sense that we can conduct a public conversation on matters that are of intense interest to us but not to others. This accounts for the preponderance of Irish interest non-fiction on Irish publishers' lists. As Tony points out, when the literary agent Jonathan Williams established his agency in Dublin in 1986, he quickly found that about 75 per cent of his list was in non-fiction. Moreover, for Irish publishers the Irish interest angle is as important as the non-fiction.

Take the case of Micheál Ó Muircheartaigh, whose autobiography was a tremendous bestseller. Imagine a commissioning editor in a London publishing house trying to convince sceptical colleagues to take this on. Nobody had ever heard of him (unless there was someone Irish in the room) and no one could even attempt to pronounce his name. The editor might try to explain that this guy was the Irish equivalent of John Arlott or John Motson. You can imagine the scornful laughter. Yet an Irish publisher, with a knowledge of the local (or should that be national?) culture not only took it on but actively pursued it by commission, and got his reward. There are things in Ireland that fly beneath the British radar, thank goodness.

There is one other aspect of this regionalism that is disturbing. I have long been struck by the number of Irish interest titles that speak only to one side of the border or the other. I recall one enormous bestseller in the Republic which hardly caused a ripple in the Northern Ireland trade. It was not alone in that. Ironically, the end of the Troubles has accelerated that trend. At least books on those dismal events found a market north and south – and also overseas.

The emphasis on non-fiction is organic: it arises out of the nature of the national industry itself. But it also allowed Tony to remind readers that publishing everywhere is heavily reliant on this genre. The excessive prestige granted to literary fiction and *belles lettres* is all very well for literary editors and reviewers: it is not a luxury available to most commercial publishers. As he loved to quote Stanley Unwin, a publisher's first duty to his authors is to remain solvent.

Sadly, as he points out early in this book, the history of book publishing in Ireland 'is littered with bankrupts'. It is a risky business anywhere, with more hit-and-miss hunches than most publishers will own up to. The Hollywood screenwriter William Goldman famously said: 'Nobody knows anything … Not one person in the entire motion picture field knows for a certainty what's going to work.' Well, up to a point, Lord Copper. As with the movies, so with books; but no publisher will survive for long backing guesses and hunches that are not better more often than those of a dabbler. The problem is exacerbated in a small country with a sometime exiguous capital base and a public that does not buy books in huge numbers.

The myth that the Irish are a nation of book buyers, disproportionate to bigger countries, has been one of the comforting lies that we have told ourselves. Tony deals with it here once and for all: it was a particular bogey of his for years.

This wonderful book will neither be challenged nor superseded for a long time, if ever. It is not a social history of modern Ireland but it does cut a very generous slice of that pie. The books we read and produce – and the changes of fashion and vogue that inform the trade – are mighty straws in the wind. This book should be read by anyone who is curious about Ireland, past and present.

Tony Farmar has not lived to see his book in print. He died, before his time, in December 2017. He was working on it until his final illness and was happy to know that Conor Kostick would write the final chapter. Tony and I were friends for over twenty years. He succeeded me as President of Clé (now Publishing Ireland) in 2004. For years, we lunched together about once a month in the snug embrace of La Cave, the wine bar on South Anne Street. He was the most wonderful man. Rather than gloss that remark with a welter of adjectives, I urge you instead to read and enjoy this product of his many talents.

Fergal Tobin
May 2018

PART ONE

Introduction

Studying the History of Book Publishing

> Books reach every aspect of our culture, interpreting the past and the present, anticipating the future, carrying necessary information, portraying life as it was and is and can be imagined. All kinds of books do this, and all kinds of publishers have opportunities to exercise judgement on quality – on the effect of what they publish, for books do have effects, both good and bad. If a publisher runs his business well, he has greater opportunities to favor quality, to distribute it widely, and thus to contribute something worthwhile to mankind.
>
> Herbert S. Bailey Jr, *The Art and Science of Book Publishing*[1]

This book describes the history of the Irish publishing industry. For reasons that will become clear, it mainly covers the years from 1890, though there is a sketch covering the period from the very first book printed in Ireland, in 1551.

The most common modern approach to the history of book publishing is as an adjunct to literary studies. This point of view thinks of publishing merely as the method by which literary texts get into the hands of readers. As the librarian and scholar Mary ('Paul') Pollard put it, 'I suppose the most compelling reason for the study of any book trade must be its function as a centre of publication where writer and publishing agent meet and the primary decision on the writing's worth is taken.'[2]

This literature-focused study of book history finds particularly interesting the way technical features of the publishing process can significantly affect the final text. The physicality of the book, its design and construction, its patterns of distribution, sale and use, are thought of as incidental. Focus falls on, for instance, how early typesetters normalised illegible scripts, thus producing textual variants; or how the finances of the trade insisted on the bloated size of the three-decker novel; or how the physical demands of the bootrade underpin the reluctance to publish short stories, or generally books too short to support a spine. These are classic examples, but some 'normalisation' (specifically editorial and presentational) is absolutely typical of the way publishers mediate between writer and reader.[3]

The almost sacred glamour allotted to fiction, poetry and *belles lettres* by this group of book historians is very much of our time. An historian critical of this approach has noted how, unlike in previous centuries where ideas (theological, philosophical, historical, political, economic) conveyed prestige:

> The genres of fiction, poetry, drama and literary criticism tend to be privileged over other kinds of writing. [Those] who write books in those genres are seen as the new cultural heroes of the age of print; the professional literary author is exalted as the paradigm of modernity; and figures in the book trade are rendered worthy – or not – on the basis of their contribution to those authors and their works.[4]

The opportunities in international publishing have for generations ensured that Irish literary authors have looked overseas, typically to the highly developed London market, to place their books. This is often deplored – as for instance in the 1840s by William Carleton (an exception), who described it as equivalent to absentee landlordism – but is difficult to gainsay.

In his discussion of the 1950–60 outburst of world publishing, the French sociologist Robert Escarpit distinguished between functional books and literary books. The latter he took for statistical purposes (though aware of the extreme leakiness of this because of local classification practices) to be equivalent to Class 8 in the Dewey classification. According to UNESCO statistics some 23 per cent of books published were in this literary class, a proportion that varied according to economic and political factors country by country. Economically developed democratic countries tended, not surprisingly, to publish a higher proportion of literary works.[5] Irish publishing history (like the publishing history of most countries) has been largely concerned with the 80 per cent or so of functional books that addressed intellectual, religious, political, education and practical matters with a sharp local focus and not so much with *belles lettres,* which inevitably found their way to the metropolis. When Jonathan Williams set up his plate in 1986 as Ireland's first literary agent he found that three quarters of his work was with non-fiction.[6]

The high estimation for the proportion of publishing designated as literature is a recent phenomenon and perhaps has a gender element. In his study of the catalogues of eighteenth-century Irish private libraries (all from male owners) Richard Cole found that 'the library owners apparently preferred works of discursive prose, works represented by such genres as lexicography, history, biography, and the essay … it was not simply novels that the library owners did not buy in large numbers, but other examples of belles-lettres such as poems and plays.'[7] For these there were numerous private circulating libraries open to the public, such as that run by the well-known publishing family of Hoey, then of Skinner Row, Dublin, who advertised in 1737 'a large collection of Histories, Romances, Novels, Memoirs etc.' that could be rented.

In 1963, a six-man (sic) editorial committee for the magisterial 1963 catalogue *Printing and the Mind of Man: The Impact of Print on Five Centuries of Western Civilisation* selected several hundred titles to represent the impact of printed books. They certainly included creative literature such as Homer, Virgil, Dante, Shakespeare, Cervantes, Defoe, Goethe and Walt Whitman, but the great bulk of the 424 titles chosen were clearly 'non-fiction', starting with the Gutenberg Bible, via Boyle, Berkeley, Kant, to Darwin and Einstein. Likewise, compiling a list of thirty-two 'books that define Ireland' in 2014, Bryan Fanning and Tom Garvin included only five works of fiction (and no poetry).[8]

There are other approaches to the history of the book, however, and they were often equally instrumental. Few admit to finding the book publishing process interesting in itself, as others might find the building of a railway or the metamorphosis of a caterpillar. In *The Coming of the Book* (1958) the founding fathers of the modern discipline, Lucien Febvre and Henri-Jean Martin, took a long sociological point of view, as befitted distinguished members of the Annales school.[9] In *The Reading Nation in the Romantic Era* (2007), William St Clair argued that the real importance of book history is the light it casts on mentalities. 'By mentalities,' he writes, 'I mean the beliefs, feelings, values, and dispositions to act in certain ways that are prevalent in a society at a particular historical and cultural conjuncture, including not only states of mind that are explicitly acknowledged but others that are unarticulated or regarded as fixed or natural.'[10]

In this spirit, we can consider the relative impact on Irish mentalities of two Macmillan authors, W.B. Yeats and James Carty (an educational author who worked in the National Library of Ireland). Generations of Irish secondary school pupils, who never willingly read a syllable of Yeats, imbibed (and still unconsciously reiterate) their approach and ideas about Irish history from the four volumes of Carty's *Class-Book of Irish History*, including, notoriously, the failure to mention either the Catholic Church (as such), or Kitty O'Shea, and the judgement that Patrick Pearse was 'one of the noblest characters in Irish history'.[11]

What Publishers Do

Either by leading, or by channelling, or perhaps only reinforcing public interest and taste (with drums and whistles), book publishers, like broadcasters, significantly shape the understandings, the knowledge base and the 'beliefs, feelings, values, and dispositions to act in certain ways' of their readers: in short, their mentalities. The long history of censorship testifies to this, for no one censors what does not matter. The shaping can be quite subtle. Thus even an unpretentious almanac, once the most common book in most people's hands, contains a purposeful ordering, an expression of a world view. One of the very earliest Irish almanacs, for instance, was issued in Waterford in 1646 in strong support of the Confederate Catholics. As well as saints' days, details of the rising and setting of the sun and monthly observations on farming matters (when to sow, graft, reap etc.), there is a tendentious Chronological Table showing various events in the 5,092 years since the Creation. These include: 'since Lutheranism, Calvinism and such like heresies arose in Germany, 128 years', 'since the virtuous and holy Queen Mary of Scotland was beheaded in England, 46 years' and 'since the Happy Union of the Catholics for the defence of His Majesty, 5 years'.[12]

What Publishers Actually Do

If writing is labour-intensive (as it undoubtedly is), publishing is capital-intensive. This suggests that publishing is a business rather than a craft or profession. Herein lies the paradox of publishing. It certainly is a business, but only up to a point. For the community, the value of a publisher does not lie in profits, but in the contribution his or her gatekeeping, encouragement and investing has made to authors and texts. Most publishers are driven by a didactic urge to contribute more than capital and technical expertise to the books they publish.[13]

There is, however, a lasting vagueness as to what publishers actually do. Perhaps this is because the role of stand-alone publisher, unconnected with either printer or bookseller, was a relatively late emergence. In rich countries such as France and Britain, as the publishing process became more complex, this new role was a phenomenon of the early nineteenth century. In Ireland this conjunction came much later.

Carol Haynes described the emergence thus in early nineteenth-century France:

> The primary role of the *éditeur* was not to manufacture or to sell the book himself. Rather it was to finance and coordinate the production and distribution of a book by others. The work of the *éditeur* involved procuring funding from subscribers, financiers, notaries, merchants, and other members of the book trade (who, given the difficulties of obtaining loans from banks, remained the main source of credit); acquiring or commissioning work by authors and artists, to whom he offered increasingly detailed contracts; overseeing the writing and illustrating of manuscripts; obtaining a supply of paper; coordinating the activities of engravers, printers and binders; marketing publications, by means of subscriptions, catalogs, prospectuses, reviews, and eventually advertisements and posters; and distributing products via wholesalers, commission agents, and retailers … the *éditeur* was defined by his role in investing capital both financial and human to create literary commodities.[14]

Most Irish publishers, on the other hand, remained until the 1970s associated with printers: Gill finally abandoned its print shop in 1966, but Dolmen retained its equipment to the end, as did Talbot, Browne & Nolan and Duffy. Irish University Press was closely associated with its Shannon printing plant.

But what, then, do publishers actually *do*? The four main functions are:

Selection: deciding what to publish, the 'primary decision' referred to by Mary Pollard, is the most important thing publishers do. This is where publishers sometimes stimulate, sometimes channel or sometimes merely follow public interest. Often this is referred to as gatekeeping, with overtones of cultural control and even censorship. But there are usually many gates: history is full of stories of authors papering their rooms with rejection slips before finally making good.

Idealistic would-be publishers have often started with a determination only to publish work of the finest literary quality (as declared for instance in 1905 by Joseph Hone, the director and financial backer of Maunsel; in 1967 by Michael Smith with his short-lived New Writers Press; and in 2015, by a new Irish publisher who announced that 'the only thing we want to publish is brilliant fiction.'[15]) Unfortunately, literary masterpieces are rarely bestsellers, at least initially. Since history (and daily experience) tell us that sales are unpredictable, the common way to stay afloat is to publish a balanced portfolio of books, with successes balancing failures. 'Literary' houses that do nothing else rarely survive for long without patronage or some other income source. Long surviving Dublin firms such as Gill, Duffy and Talbot each balanced fiction and poetry with education, religion and politics. Macmillan's Irish schoolbooks balanced its Irish playwrights. Even Leonard and Virginia Woolf's Hogarth Press, with its origins in the most refined Bloomsbury circles, alternated high literature with social or political analysis. This balancing act is not a chore: from the point of view of mentalities (and sales), an excellent reference book is a match for a second-rank poet.

Processing: this general term covers the technical engine, driving the production of books from the acquisition by contract of the appropriate publication rights, through editorial shaping and refining, the arrangement of illustrations, print and cover design and the commissioning and overseeing of the physical processes of typesetting, printing and binding. These technical skills, especially those relating to editing, are hard for self-publishers to replicate.

For much of the nineteenth century it was common for publishers to accept the outside reader's judgement and send the manuscripts straight to a printer for setting, layout and printing, often with little or no detailed in-house scrutiny. The process was quick – exemplified in Edna Lyall's 1889 novel *Derrick Vaughan: Novelist* in which the author completed his first novel in September and it was published in three volumes in November.[16] Anthony Powell remembered from his time at Duckworth in the 1920s that 'an author might be thought exigent if, delivering a manuscript in August, he expected the printed book to be in the bookshops by October, but, in practice, such optimism was rarely disappointed.'[17] In her history of Methuen, Maureen Duffy claims that it was the delays and hold-ups experienced during the Second World War that accustomed the trade to think of nine months as the normal time from receipt of manuscript to bound copies. From the second half of the twentieth century, publishers' in-house staff took on more pre-publication tasks. It became clear that there were advantages throughout the publishing house in specialisation, in the honing of skills to particular kinds of publishing. Thus the sensitivity appropriate to literary fiction or poetry floundered when presented with the organisational problems of a large textbook; the technical requirements of children's book editing and illustration were not easily transferred to academic history, with extended narrative, maps and footnotes in multiple languages. As in editing, so in design and production, where specific appropriate technology and materials could be refined. In marketing, specialising in an audience reaped dividends. Buyers of books, not generally sensitive to publishers' imprints, looked to Gallery for poetry, and The O'Brien Press or Wolfhound for children's books (and would look askance at poetry, however well-meant, emanating from a house specialising in true crime).

It is in the processing core that the many conventions of book production are considered. For example, a new biography could in theory be any length from 10,000 to 1.5 million words and any size from A6 to elephant folio. But since the eighteenth century (before the Internet loosened things), virtually all were more than 70,000 and less than 150,000 words and printed on Royal or Demy sheets, octavo, and the trimmed pages measured 9¼in x 6¼in or 8½in x 5½in. Printers expected this, the reviewers expected this and the booksellers' and buyers' shelves were constructed for these sizes. Of course, no one was forced to follow the current norms; for instance we might decide to produce a children's book in three bulky volumes (*The Lord of the Rings*) or, as the French do, to put the contents at the back of the book, do without an index and run the title up rather than down the spine – but the beaten path is always easier.

Marketing, selling and distribution: how publishers make the potential reader aware of the book and, by various distribution processes, make it physically possible to buy the book. This includes cataloguing, managing the house's presence on social media, outreach to bibliographical services such as Nielsen, promotion and advertising of the frontlist, management of backlist, book exhibitions and non-trade presence, distribution, negotiating with retailers (discounts, special placings, etc.), transportation and book storage, including pick, pack and despatch. This is the most arcane area of the trade and in many respects the hardest work. The key relationships with review editors, retailers and librarians can take years to evolve. Book warehouses are not glamorous places, but if inefficiently run can undermine the whole effort.

The crucial technical breakthrough was the invention of automated publishers' binding in the 1820s, which came into Ireland in the 1850s. Before then, says Charles Benson, 'books were usually sold in sheets or with paper wrappers'.[18] Booksellers often employed binders in the shop to meet customers' needs. Edition binding on more or less elaborately blocked cloth evolved over the century, with colour-printed jackets, blurbs, standardised pricing and (much later) ISBN coding, taking the marketing out of the bookretailers' hands and into the publishers'.

Finance: Carol Haynes put the organisation of finance at the centre of the emerging role of publisher. Here, too, specialisation has its impact. The cash-flow requirements of a five-year educational series are clearly different from those for a high-advance, quick sales, would-be bestseller, or a low-run academic book which, though expensive to edit and typeset, will, perhaps, continue to sell for years.

The supremely practical Stanley Unwin, doyen of the British publishing business until his death in 1968, said that the first duty of a publisher is to remain solvent, because a bankrupt publisher (whose first step on to the path to collapse is usually marked by failing to pay royalties) is no good to readers, writers or anyone else. He was, however, far from proposing that solvency or profit should be the only objective of a publisher. He stressed the duty of solvency because in his day it was so often forgotten. Now, as André Schriffen and others have complained, current conglomerate publishers frequently show the opposite failing.[19]

Digital and web-enabled self-publishing have tempted many people to wonder if publishers should join buggy-whip manufacturers in the halls of history. This misses the point that the practitioners of the four functions are in a continuous learning relationship over many titles between writers, readers, the enablers (booksellers, librarians, reviewers) and themselves. Like good bridges, good publishers *last,* until they become part of the heritage of the nation.

Irish publishing history is, alas, littered with bankrupts. To identify only the best-known names: William Figgis of Nassau Street, insolvent in 1812; William Curry, described by Charles Benson as 'the major Irish publisher in the 1820s and 1830s', bankrupt in 1847, on his own admission 'due to overtrading'; also Curry's one-time partner James McGlashan, whose interests were acquired by M.H. Gill in 1856; the feckless George Roberts of Maunsel was rescued by an indulgent compensatory committee after the firm's premises were destroyed in 1916 and the company limped on until 1926; his contemporary, Martin Lester, was sunk by overenthusiastic publication of a memorial volume to Michael Collins and Arthur Griffith; Liam Miller's Dolmen Press had to be rescued several times before succumbing on his death in 1987.

The cases of Maunsel and Dolmen raise a question: is it not enough to produce some timely or beautiful books? Given the books produced, should anyone care that the managers of those two houses were at least incompetent businessmen and perhaps worse? Did not the unpaid authors enter the arrangement with open eyes? Is longevity an overriding virtue? After all, the best-known publisher in Irish literary history published only one book – but it was James Joyce's *Ulysses*.

The missed opportunity is the answer. Imagine the contribution to Irish mentalities a reasonably well-managed local publishing house on the lines of Faber or Allen & Unwin might perhaps have made in the 1930s, 1940s and 1950s (particularly if Protestant, and so not inclined, like M.H. Gill, to become ultra-Catholic).

Why Focus on the Twentieth and Twenty-First Centuries?

The main focus of this book is on the period since 1890. There are four reasons for this.

The first reason is the enormous increase in readers, the beginning and end of book publishing. Publishing flourishes where there are plenty of active, curious readers with enough leisure and money to afford books. It was only by the end of the nineteenth century that anything like widespread literacy was achieved in Europe and this, of course, profoundly changed the environment in which publishing was carried out. In an extraordinary, continent-wide phenomenon, during the second half of the century the ability to read more than a small amount moved from a guarded privilege of the rich to a rapidly growing majority skill. In country after country, the customary old-style illiteracy (previously assumed to be necessary to keep the lower classes in their place) dwindled in the decades up to 1910. Among the easily measured cohort of army recruits, illiteracy fell in the Austrian Empire from 65 per cent in 1867 to 22 per cent in 1894; in Italy from 59 per cent in 1870 to 10 per cent in 1910; even in Russia it fell from 79 per cent in 1874 to 32 per cent in 1913.[20] In France, 55 per cent of conscripts were illiterate in 1828, by 1910 it was 4.5 per cent.[21] In Britain, the proportion of people reporting themselves illiterate fell from 53 per cent in the 1841 Census to 6 per cent in 1891. In Ireland, 33 per cent of the population in 1851 reported that they could read and write and a further 20 per cent could read; by 1901, these figures had climbed to 79 per cent reading and writing, 7 per cent reading only.[22]

Edith Newman Devlin, who became well known in the 1970s and 1980s for her series of extra mural lectures on literature in Queen's University Belfast, described what the transition meant to her:

> I soon cracked the great code, which men and women have devised for talking in print to each other over space and time; I had made the huge intellectual leap which is called 'reading' ... I would never be quite alone again.[23]

As every reader knows, when the skill is learned, reading becomes a habit and an appetite crying to be fed. Alberto Manguel wrote:

> Once I had learned my letters I read everything, books, but also notices, advertisements, the small type on the back of tram tickets, letters tossed into the garbage, weathered newspapers caught under my bench in the park, the backs of magazines held by other readers in the bus.[24]

Reading becomes a new channel of experience, full of entertainment, consolation and possibility. Readers long to spend time and money on this habit, and of course writers are happy to oblige. F.S.L. Lyons proposed that 'without this revolution, the foundations of the modern Irish state could not have been laid.'[25] He could reasonably have made a much wider claim.

The second reason is the great increase in the number of books being published. This of course follows directly on from the growth in literacy, combined with general economic development. The huge majority of books ever published have been published since 1890. In August 2010, Google estimated that the entire corpus of published books consists of some 130 million works.[26] It further believed that as many as 80 per cent of these are still in copyright, by which, following US law, it meant published after 1922. The cultural critic Raymond Williams captured the newness of widespread book reading in Britain when he wrote (in 1962): 'a majority public for books was probably first achieved in the 1950s, by comparison with a majority public for Sunday papers by 1910 and for daily papers by the end of the First World War.'[27] UNESCO calculated that there were some 250,000 titles being published worldwide in the early 1950s, 400,000 a year ten years later and perhaps a million by the 2000s (this number being complicated by digital editions). This unexpectedly late flowering of books generally is a worldwide phenomenon and is true also for Ireland. (See the Appendix where an estimate is made of the number of books published in Ireland since 1551.) Book publishing is thus an old craft suddenly transformed by new conditions and, despite digital rivalry, still expanding beyond recognition.

The third reason for focusing on the post-1890 period is the series of changes in book law, production technology and market practice that took place at the end of the nineteenth century as commercial and market opportunities developed. Their 'combined impact changed radically both the size and nature of the print culture', as book historian Simon Eliot put it. He instanced specifically the changes affecting the British scene (in which of course Irish writers and booksellers were immersed and Irish publishers more or less reluctant participants):

> [...] the development of the new journalism (in both newspaper and magazine forms) and the mass circulation papers of the 1890s; the expansion of the syndication market in the provinces, the Empire and the USA (particularly after the Chace Act of 1891 gave non-US authors copyright protection); the emergence of the literary agent; the founding of the Society of Authors, the Booksellers Association and the Publishers Association; the rapid growth of public libraries; the decline and collapse (in 1894) of the three decker novel; the development of cheap paper-covered reprints at sixpence or less; the enormous expansion of printing capacity represented by the large web-fed rotaries; the coming in the 1890s of the hot-metal typesetting machines.[28]

Cumulatively these changes set the scene for the publishing world of the twentieth and twenty-first centuries.

The fourth reason for the period of focus is that a great deal of recent book scholarship has opened out the pre-modern period in Ireland. This includes two monumental directories covering members of the book trade from 1550 to 1850, and several valuable books. Most of these, like the core text, *Printing and Bookselling in Dublin 1670–1800*,[29] centre on the activities of Ireland's age of piracy in the late eighteenth century, when the trade profited from the failure to extend the 1709 Copyright Act to Ireland and happily published and exported undercut editions of numerous Enlightenment classics to Britain and America.[30]

The major structural shifts described above radically differentiate the publishing world that Goldsmith and Burke, or Sheridan Le Fanu, Charles Kickham and Samuel Lover knew from that inhabited by Yeats, Gogarty and Moore. It was a different world. The period since 1890 has been extensively covered from the point of view of the great literary names from Yeats and Kavanagh to Heaney, but hardly at all from the point of view of publishing as such. It seems sensible therefore to concentrate on that period.

1

The Long History of Books in Ireland Before 1890

The very first book set in movable type and printed in Ireland was Edward VI's *Book of Common Prayer*, produced in 1551 by the King's Printer, Humphrey Powell, from his premises in Dublin Castle.[1] Twenty years later, the first book printed in Irish was a Reformation catechism. These were clearly colonising acts and were not the harbingers of a vibrant book trade. In fact, as historian Raymond Gillespie puts it, 'the history of the Irish printing press in the late sixteenth and early seventeenth centuries is, in the main, a story of inactivity. On the basis of surviving evidence, it appears that the bulk of printing was for government.'[2]

The devastating Cromwellian wars of the middle seventeenth century and the small number of English speakers limited demand for printed books (Irish language publications stuck largely to manuscript until the twentieth century). Even if there had been demand, supply was severely restricted: for 130 years only one officially licensed printer/bookseller was allowed to work in Dublin. The licence granted in 1609 to Powell's successor, John Franckton, gave him a complete monopoly over the Irish book trade (imported or otherwise) and forbade anyone else to print, bind, publish or sell books. Even during the 1640s and 1650s when the political situation allowed propaganda presses to set up in Kilkenny, Cork and Waterford, 'such provincial printing,' writes Gillespie, 'was of relatively short-term significance.'[3]

In the middle of the century, writes Mary Pollard, William Bladen 'was the only printer in Dublin and for most of his thirty-odd years the only bookseller'.[4] In theory the print monopoly continued until 1732, but in practice it was challenged in 1680 by Joseph Ray and, despite protests from the patentholder, the Privy Council adopted an Irish solution by recognising the monopoly right but doing nothing to enforce it. Joseph Ray became official printer to the City of Dublin and the Dublin Philosophical Society. He was described by Mary Pollard as 'an energetic and obstinate, perhaps pig-headed, fighter [whose] determined opposition to the King's Printer's monopoly was of immense importance to the Dublin book trade, resulting as it did in freedom to expand to match the growth in population in the eighteenth century.'[5]

From 1618, an 'Irish Stock' group of London booksellers specialised – not very successfully – in exporting books to Ireland and, under licence from the King's Printer, a few booksellers did import books. In this way London print came creeping into the eastern counties, much as British television was to do in the 1950s. But it was not until 1670 that the Guild of St Luke gave legal status and self-control to the stationers of Dublin (as the bookseller/publishers were then called, revealingly). Oddly, the Guild included also two quite different trades, the cutlers and the painter-stainers. By 1686, 'the piping time of peace' had allowed the five initial stationer brothers of the Guild to expand to thirty-five, though this number included binders, book printers and lawyers with booksellers as such.[6] There was some local publishing. Raymond Gillespie classifies the 229 titles published in Ireland between 1681 and 1685 as follows: 76 indigenous titles, 106 reprints (mostly of books originally published in London) and 47 official publications (statutes, proclamations, etc.).[7]

The mix of business of one of the largest of these booksellers, Samuel Helsham, can be identified from a few pages that survive of a day book covering 2 March to 16 May 1685. The eight pages record sales of sixty-three titles and numerous small stationery items such as pens, different paper products, wafers and legal forms. The books Helsham sold were mostly, as Mary Pollard puts it, 'Protestant devotional works and sermons, school and university textbooks, and topical pamphlets – news, trials, speeches, elegies and other substitutes for newspapers'. Perhaps three quarters of the books he sold were printed in England, 20 per cent in Ireland and 5 per cent on the Continent.

Helsham sold to fellow booksellers (at 25 per cent discount off retail price) and, it seems, supplied the country market via chapmen or pedlars. He also published on his own behalf, notably a textbook of logic by the Provost of Trinity and Helsham regularly took shares with fellow booksellers in publications.[8] In much of the country things were less organised. Book historian Vincent Kinane writes:

> The retail supply of books in provincial towns would have been through merchants who included them in their stock; a rung below were village shops selling cheap literature, and lower still were the travelling chapmen. This was the pattern for provincial bookselling well into the 19th century … a good example of a merchant-cum-bookseller in the 1790s was George Hynes, who sold groceries, wines, hardware, flax seed as well as 'every article in the stationery and bookselling way' at his shop in High Street [Galway]. He also operated a circulating library from there and an auctioneering business from Kirwan's Lane.[9]

Nineteenth-century travellers, such as Thackeray, who claimed they could not find bookshops in the Irish countryside were only half right.

The Dublin Scuffle

A vividly recalled episode of the late seventeenth century illustrates the conditions of the trade of the time. In 1698, English publisher and bookseller John Dunton brought over a large consignment ('ten tun', he claims) of some 600 titles to sell in Ireland.[10] This was an experiment he had tried a few years earlier in Boston, and at first all went well. Dunton set up a viewing room in the upstairs parlour of Dick's Coffee House in fashionable Skinner Row (now Christchurch Place). Here he held two successful auctions of various books published in England since the Great Fire of 1666. Members of Parliament, clergy, lawyers, academics, lords and ladies attended. But the local book trade was not happy with this invasion and one sourly described Dunton's list as 'a parcel of trash'. Dunton tartly responded with the assertion that there were in Dublin fifteen or sixteen men 'who feed upon Books, without being much the wiser for what they contain'.[11] One of these, Scotsman Patrick Campbell, managed to take over Dick's Coffee House before Dunton could organise his third auction and obliged him to decamp to a coffee house in the High Street, not at all so attractive a venue. Bad feeling flared between the two booksellers, with angry letters and with legal and physical threats, all vividly described by Dunton in his book *The Dublin Scuffle*. Dunton also printed an amorous letter to him from 'Dorinda', supposedly the wife of a Dublin citizen. Dunton records himself as sternly rejecting the 'wanton embraces' of this 'lewd woman', with many a moralistic comment, in his prolix way. Was this, as he hints, a put-up job, an attempt by the Irish book trade to discredit the incomer?[12]

The auction sale of books, a technique of which Dunton was an early adopter rather than pioneer, became a standard retailing device in the eighteenth century. It was frequently used to clear stocks of slow-selling titles and the stock of deceased booksellers. The last substantial such auctioneer was William Gilbert in the 1770s. He changed course to medical publishing and bookselling in the 1780s, taking his apprentice Robert Hodges as partner in 1800.

The First Copyright Act

Not long after Dunton's foray, the world's first copyright Act was passed in London. Referred to as the 'Act of Anne' dated 1709, this gave the author (and crucially, by extension, the bookseller/publisher) security for fourteen years, once renewable. Oddly, this Act was not extended to Ireland, so Irish booksellers were able to continue their established practice of reprinting London-published books. Why was the Act not extended to Ireland? Perhaps, writes Mary Pollard, because of the exiguous size of the Irish industry:

> In 1709 in Dublin, there were not more than perhaps ten printers at work; almost all of them were without capital and were starting from scratch, and scratch it was, with type that had seen years of hard usage, frequent changes of hole-and-corner addresses and an unexplored market. Though the sudden increase in activity in the last years of the seventeenth century was marked, and expansion continued with no loss of momentum, the results were minimal in comparison with the volume of book production in London.[13]

Initially, it was thought that Irish booksellers were entitled to export books thus reprinted to London and the respectable George Faulkner famously published a four-volume edition of Swift's works on that basis. This practice was definitively forbidden by a supplementary Act of 1739.

According to the law, it was perfectly legal to reprint any title from British originals, so long as no attempt was made to export them. Although Irish publishers were regularly denounced in London as 'pirates', there was no piracy so long as they did not attempt to sell the books outside of Ireland – for instance to London, to Scotland or, increasingly in the late eighteenth century, to the American colonies. Of course it was galling for the London publishers to have their markets in Ireland undermined for titles such as Pope's *Essay on Man* or Fielding's *Tom Jones* and, in 1752, *Amelia*, for which of course they had paid the authors. And it is as difficult for us as for eighteenth-century Londoners to imagine that, if, for instance, modern Irish publishers were legally allowed to republish British bestsellers such as *Fifty Shades of Grey* or the *Harry Potter* series in Dublin, copies would not somehow seep illegally into the lucrative British market. There is no question but that Dublin booksellers ruthlessly selected 'virtually all new books with a sales potential' from the new London publications. A study published in 2005 showed that there were Dublin editions for a carefully chosen 38 per cent of them.[14]

Whether with the local or a wider market in mind, London originals were usually reset in Dublin in a smaller format (octavo rather than quarto) and with more words per page. To achieve cheapness the re-publishers were also able to exploit three local advantages: they paid no copyright purchase fees to the author; production costs were less in Dublin, especially wages of compositors and printers; and both paper and binding leather were cheaper because of lower import duties.[15] Dublin-published books were produced very quickly and had a reputation for poor print quality, not always deserved.[16]

The Eighteenth-Century Business

The Irish book trade in the eighteenth century was highly varied. The old stationer's business had widened. From the beginning of the century, printed matter was becoming an everyday item. An early example of this occurred in the great Presbyterian doctrinal row of the 1720s which generated as many as fifty titles contributing to the debate. Crucially, it was noted that print and preaching carried equal weight in disseminating opinion.[17] Even so, as late as mid century a local author described Dublin as 'a pitiful place for disposing of books';[18] there was enough business to make it possible for 'stationers' to specialise in printing, in bookselling or in bookbinding, though no one was yet just a publisher. The leading booksellers of the day were George Faulkner of Essex Street (in what is now Temple Bar) and George Grierson, also of Essex Street, who died in 1753. The Catholic booksellers clustered round Cook Street near Christ Church. Most of the books sold were published in Britain, though there was importation also from France and the Netherlands.

Publication was undertaken by bookseller/printers such as George Faulkner, who, as we have seen, published Swift. To keep the presses busy, these men very often published newspapers as well. Another such bookseller/printer was James Hoey of Skinner Row, who would sell locally published books and a considerable importation, mostly from London. In Mountrath Street (which was off Charles Street West, near where the Four Courts were to be built) printers and booksellers specialised in products for the so-called 'flying stationers', who sold news-sheets and ballads in the street. Most booksellers, not just those in a smaller way of business, sold stationery and perhaps also medicines. By the end of the century, bookselling was commonly combined with patent medicine and lottery sales, but there were those who sold books as well as being wine merchants, stockbrokers, haberdashers and pawnbrokers.[19]

A snapshot of the books published in 1750 gives a clear image of the output in mid century. It was almost all in English: even for a Catholic audience, little was published in Irish. Welsh speakers in Wales and, to a lesser extent, Gaelic speakers in Scotland were better supplied.[20] Here, as a pioneer bilingual almanac put it, 'not one in 20,000 can either write or read their own language even though they can write English. No Shopbook was ever kept in that tongue, nor any agreement for a bargain written down, nor a receipt given, nor a letter written by the Post.' It was a matter of newspaper record when a sermon was preached in Irish in St Patrick's Cathedral in 1758.[21]

As usual, the new books of the year predominantly featured religion and politics. Several bookseller/printers had already published editions of the classics including Horace, Terence, Virgil and Juvenal. Powell published over forty titles in 1750. Isaac Watts's *Divine and Moral Songs for Children* (the locus of the classic, 'How doth the little busy bee') was re-issued at sixpence halfpenny for 72 pages. *The Book of Common Prayer* was issued by the King's Printer George Grierson.[22]

In the 1750s, Hoey printed *The Censor*, supposedly written by 'Frank Somebody', but in fact by the political sensation of the day, Charles Lucas. Over the previous decade, Lucas had engaged in a high-profile series of rows both with Dublin Corporation and the British House of Commons. Lucas was popular with the people of Dublin for his attacks on corruption in the government of Dublin and his advocacy of parliamentary independence for Ireland. In 1749, he and his publisher James Esdall were summoned to appear before the bar of the Irish House of Commons accused of promoting sedition and insurrection. Esdall went into hiding. Lucas was condemned to Newgate Prison but escaped to London. Esdall's wife Ann was later questioned by the House. The hectic atmosphere of the day can be judged by the fact that *The Censor* and other of Lucas' writings were condemned to be publicly burned by the Grand Jury, and the Chief Justice publicly warned the members of the Guild of St Luke against printing libels. Esdall died in 1755 and was succeeded in the business by his widow, Ann, as quite often happened. His young son William was apprenticed in 1763 and later took over the business. Many years later, in 1795, Ann (then aged 77), in distressed circumstances due to the death of her son, was obliged to seek the charity of the Guild.[23]

On the practical rather than political side, Powell published Sylvester O'Halloran's pathbreaking *Treatise on the Glaucoma* and Joseph Leathley a major new edition of Bolton's *Justice of the Peace for Ireland* (the longest book published in the year, which came out at 892 pages over two fat volumes). Leathley was coming to the end of his career (he died in 1757). Other substantial books of the 1750s were John Hill's *Arithmetic in Theory and Practice* (525 pages) and Campbell's *Present State of Europe* published by George Faulkner (528 pages), its first appearance in book form. Charles Smith's *Antient and Present State of Cork* was published by J. Exshaw of Cork-hill, who also published the reference book, *The English Registry* and several reprints of books by the philosopher George Berkeley, including *The Querist*.

There was crime: for instance, the account of the 'inhuman and bloody murder' of Colonel Bloodworth and his wife, published by Robert Wilson of Cook Street. He obviously found crime paid, for he had published in 1749 an account of a 'most horrid barbarous and bloody murther' by Captain Freney and his gang in Waterford and, in 1752, 'An account of the barbarous murder and rape of Mary Carty'. During 1750, George Faulkner published an account of the trial of Captain Edward Clark for murder in a duel.

Augustus Long of Essex Street, printer of the *Dublin Gazette*, published Shakespeare (including two different editions of *Romeo and Juliet*) as well as plays from other writers such as Addison, Farquhar, Cibber, Congreve and even Voltaire (in French). Long hoped to develop this interest with the *Playhouse Journal*, 'to treat the merit and demerit of dramatic writers and performers', but it seems that only one issue ever appeared.[24]

Total print/publication activity in Dublin (which includes official and legal documents such as Acts, proclamations, etc.) rose in the first quarter of the eighteenth century, peaking in 1725, then declined for some twenty years before hitting a plateau of some 250 items a year between 1752 and 1783, taking off again in the 1780s in a burst of activity.[25] Historian Richard Sher summarised the activity as follows:

> During the second half of the 18th century Dublin prided itself on being the second city of the Empire – the standard reference the *Eighteenth-century Short Title Catalogue* shows that Dublin was surpassed only by London. Producing 14,000 imprints between 1751 and 1800 just beating Edinburgh. In the 1780s Dublin produced 2,800 titles (as compared to 25,000 from London).[26]

If the eyes of historical comparison were not dazzled by English publishing, this might seem a reasonable performance. In the Scandinavian countries of Sweden, Norway and Finland, for instance, it was not until the late nineteenth century that any kind of a publishing industry developed.[27] Some of the Irish titles were of course reprints from previous London editions. Provincial centres in Ireland were not active, though they became increasingly so as the century progressed: Belfast produced 798 items of all sorts in the eighteenth century, of which three quarters were in the second half; Cork produced 702 items with two thirds in the last quarter of the century. Lesser centres such as Limerick, Waterford and Galway produced no more than 200 items in the whole century.[28]

ESTC all items published in Dublin 1700-1800

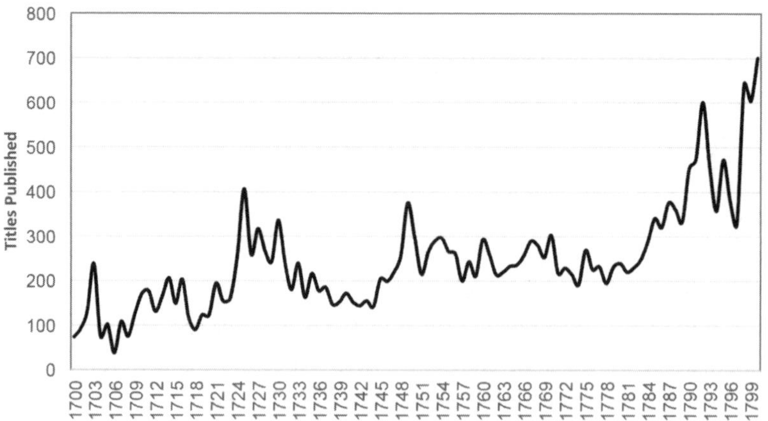

The Nineteenth-Century Business

At the very beginning of the century the surge of activity of previous decades came shuddering to a halt. The extension of the British Copyright Act to Ireland in 1801 revealed how important the dubious trade in reprinted books had been. The extension was, as Charles Benson put it:

> [...] ostensibly intended to put the publication of books in Ireland and Britain on an equal footing as far as the law was concerned, [but in practice the Copyright Act of July 1801] had the effect of entirely undermining the basis on which the Irish trade had developed in the preceding century. The surviving publishing business was, over the succeeding forty years, the object of dismissive comments which deplored both its lack of variety and its quality.[29]

Sadly, it seems that while concentrating on the reprint business, Dublin publishers had failed to cultivate local talent and so when the legislation changed, there was no traditional relationship with local authors. By contrast, publishers in Edinburgh had not fallen into this trap.

Typical of the negative comments was Robert Walsh's lament in the *History of the City of Dublin* published (in London) in 1818. He commented:

> Besides the injury the trade has sustained, great numbers who formerly were in the habit of reading are by this Act interdicted from doing so as the books which once, by their comparative cheapness were within their means of purchasing cannot be procured. The printing business is therefore confined to devotional and moral tracts which are paid for by charitable societies for gratuitous distribution – to printing handbills and playbills – to some half-dozen newspapers, and to one or two middling magazines which can scarcely maintain an ephemeral existence.[30]

He attributed some of the blame to the trade itself: 'It is true that there is no encouragement for literary exertion in the Irish metropolis, because the cautious Dublin bookseller will run no risk in publishing an original work, however great its merit. It must first appear in London, or not at all.'[31] To underline the point, Walsh listed sixty-six newspapers and periodicals which had been published since 1700; by 1818, fifty-four of them were extinct. The 'melancholy instance' of the 1816 *Dublin Examiner*, then the most recent attempt to establish a critical and literary periodical similar to the *Edinburgh*

Review, which lasted only a few months, simply underlined the 'low state of literature in a country which, while its talents contribute largely to enrich literature abroad cannot support at home one single periodical publication.'

In 1833, the *Dublin Penny Journal* noted:

> The only town in Ireland which has at all kept any pace with the literary stir of the last thirty years is the spirited town of Belfast. In the way of book-printing until lately Dublin has been woefully behind, when considered as the metropolis of the kingdom … there was never anything produced which could be at all compared with the London and Edinburgh printers until within these few years during which Mr Cumming, the Messrs Curry and others have set a praiseworthy example of energy and spirit.[32]

William Carleton complained of the consequence of the lack of local publishing in his 1842 preface to *Traits and Stories of the Irish Peasantry*: 'Our men and women of genius uniformly carried their talents to the English market, whilst we laboured at home under all the dark privations of a literary famine.' Ireland's 'native intellect', meant for 'home consumption', was instead exported, while Ireland was 'forced to subsist upon the scanty supplies which could be procured from the sister kingdom'.[33]

The situation was not, however, all 'literary famine'.

One of the publishers named by the *Dublin Penny Journal*, John Cumming, flourished between 1808 and 1850. Cumming owed his introduction to the trade to the famous eighteenth-century Catholic publisher Pat Wogan, whose partner he briefly became.[34] As well as publishing on his own account, Cumming was the sole Irish agent for the radical British publisher Effingham Wilson, whose list included Tennyson, Bentham and Disraeli. He was also Irish agent for the English poetry publisher Moxon, publisher of Browning, Wordsworth, Lamb and Hood. Towards the end of his career, Cumming took his employee Clement Ferguson as partner, Ferguson paying the substantial sum of £5,000 for the privilege. At the time the business was making £2,500 a year. Unfortunately, the difficult trading conditions of the late 1840s were too much for them and they went bankrupt in 1848.[35]

The publisher William Curry was a major rival to Cumming in the 1820s and 1830s, particularly with the novels of Charles Lever and Samuel Lover. The firm opened for business in 1824 and in 1830 Curry joined with the driving Scots publisher James McGlashan, who had been trained by the Edinburgh publisher Blackwood. The partnership was dissolved in 1845, but not before they had become a power in the Dublin literary world, with a connection based around their *Dublin University Magazine*. McGlashan and Curry set up separate publishing houses, Curry going bankrupt in 1847 and McGlashan in 1856. McGlashan was clearly an effective publisher, though described by one author as 'capricious, autocratic, tight-fisted in business matters and also somewhat unscrupulous'.[36] The university printer, M.H. Gill bought McGlashan's bankrupt business in 1856 and renamed his firm McGlashan & Gill.

McGlashan was closely involved in the affairs of the Dublin Booksellers Society which ran from 1830 to 1846.[37] They operated both as a conger (a group sharing the publishing rights and costs of agreed titles) and as a trade regulator. The Society shared responsibility for publication of editions of 1,500 copies and standard texts of 1,000 copies. With respect to regulation, at almost every meeting of the Society it was stressed that there should not be more than 10 per cent discount (allowed to retail customers) and that only on books of 15*s* or more.[38] The question of discount was to become increasingly vexed until the trade accepted publisher-fixed book pricing at the end of the century. In July 1832, James McGlashan proposed 'that the Booksellers Society of the city of Dublin give no encouragement to any bookbinders who are, or may become booksellers or to any printer who may become a publisher.' This attempt to encourage stand-alone publishing houses had no chance in Irish conditions and for 100 years or more virtually all Irish publishing houses maintained connections with printing firms.

Other publishing highlights were found in the activities of James Duffy (1808–71), the great publisher of the middle years of the century. Duffy began his career as a book pedlar and made his first coup when he bought up in the country the Protestant Bibles which had been so energetically distributed by various Bible societies and which Catholics were discouraged from reading. He sold these profitably in Liverpool.[39] Aged 30, he set up his first shop and printing works in Anglesea Street, publishing his first title *The Life and Actions of Robert Emmet* in 1838, signifying a Catholic nationalism that was to be his hallmark. Then he embarked on his Bruton series of 'thrilling tales of robbers, battles, adventures and the like at the low price of two-pence each'. In 1843, James Duffy commenced a long relationship with the Young Ireland movement, starting with the publication of Charles Gavan Duffy's anthology of nationalistic ballads, *Spirit of the Nation*. The general collapse of commerce in the famine years very nearly caused his bankruptcy, from which, legend has it, he was rescued by a last-minute loan from a neighbour. Duffy moved to Wellington Quay in 1846. In subsequent years his list contained books by John Mitchel, Thomas Davis, James Clarence Mangan and Daniel Madden.

From July 1845, Duffy began his Library of Ireland: monthly volumes at 1*s* each, printing, it is said, 'several thousand copies' of each. They were available in various binding styles and comprised a serious list of literary works, essays, history and biography from names such as Thomas Davis (several volumes), Gavan Duffy, William Carleton and Thomas D'Arcy McGee. In 1849, he launched Duffy's Cottage Library described as 'a series of delightful Catholic tales by the most eminent American writers'. Published as monthly volumes at 8*d*, they embodied a traditional, cosy Catholicism that fitted in well with nationalist feeling. 'Duffy went on,' writes Charles Benson, 'to become after 1850 the major Irish publisher.'[40] With a fleet of magazines such as *Duffy's Hibernian Magazine* he employed over 100 people in Wellington Quay. He also opened an office in London in 1860 and it was on a visit there that he broke his leg, hastening his relatively early death.

Although Charles Gavan Duffy, in his autobiography, rather grandly referred to James Duffy as 'a man of shrewd sense and sly humour but without cultivation or judgement in literature', there is no question that Duffy provided Catholic nationalism with a valuable, cheap and reliable channel for their cause. The verdict of the *Dictionary of Irish Biography* adds: 'by the number and popularity of his productions and their formative influence on Catholic popular opinion, he can be considered the most important Irish publisher in the middle decades of the nineteenth century.'[41]

Another enterprising Irish publisher, Simms & M'Intyre of Belfast, was producing books that were ideal for the railway market. This Belfast printing and publishing firm began in 1797 after Simms was thrown out of work when the printing plant of the *United Irishman* newspaper was wrecked by loyalists. By 1820, Simms & M'Intyre had five titles in print. As it expanded it published traditional tales such as *The Seven Champions* and *Reynard the Fox*, but also a broad range of books designed to be widely distributed throughout the northern counties, to appeal to both Catholic and Protestant tastes. In 1847, the firm's second generation launched its Parlour Library, consisting of whole works of fiction priced at 1*s*. This was at a time when even a cheap reprint series was priced at 6*s* and new novels were published at 31*s* 6*d*. Described by Michael Sadleir (bibliographer and managing director of Constable book publishers) as of 'sensational importance as an innovation in cheap book-making … its immediate and overwhelming popularity transformed it in a few weeks from a local Irish speculation into an international property of great value.'[42] By 1853, the series exceeded 100 titles and was sold to a London agent.[43]

The cost structure of this kind of publishing is analysed in the Victorian compendium of commercial principle and practice that is McCulloch's

Dictionary of Commerce (1839). The setting, printing and stitching of 500 copies of an eighty-page pamphlet would cost approximately £25; adding £10 for advertising gives a total publishing cost of £35. Importantly, nearly 10 per cent of this would be taken by the government in the form of paper and advertising duties, part of the so-called 'taxes on knowledge' that became such a *cause célèbre* in the 1850s. McCulloch assumes a sale of 475 copies (after free copies to author, libraries, etc.) at between 2*s* and 2*s* 6*d* a copy, giving a revenue of £51. The balance of £16 he describes as 'profit to author and publisher', a not unreasonable 31 per cent of sales.[44]

In the eighteenth century the great French encyclopaedist Denis Diderot had stressed the precariousness of the book business, writing that 'out of every ten ventures, one is successful – and this is already a great deal – four make ends meet in the long run, and five show a final loss.'[45] McCulloch repeated the message:

> On a late investigation into the affairs of an extensive publishing concern it was found that of 130 works published by it in a given time, 50 had not paid their expenses. Of the 80 that did pay, 13 only had arrived at a second edition; but in most cases that second edition had not been profitable. In general it may be estimated that of the books published a fourth do not pay their expenses; and that only one in eight or ten can be reprinted with advantage.[46]

Behind the literary swings of fashion, there was as ever a steady amount of serious factual publishing in education, law, science and theology. Prominent among the publishers of these titles was the last incarnation of a bewildering series of firms run by the Hodges family. It all started with William Gilbert, who set up in Crow Street in 1760 and in 1780 took Robert Hodges as his apprentice, later partner.[47] In 1800, the firm became Gilbert & Hodges. Then there was a new partnership of Hodges & McArthur formally from 1815, but who 'had conducted the business of Gilbert & Hodges for several years'. In 1828, Hodges & Smith took over the business of Hodges & McArthur. They moved to Grafton Street in 1844. Up to 1864 they had been described in a rather old-fashioned way as 'Booksellers to the University'; in that year, in a belated recognition of the separation of the businesses of bookseller and publisher they become formally 'Publishers to the University'. By 1869, the firm had become Hodges Foster and was still at 104 Grafton Street. Ten years later, in 1878, it became Hodges, Foster & Figgis, finally ending up as Hodges, Figgis & Co. by 1882.[48]

The Hodges firms became official booksellers to Trinity College Dublin and to the Queen's Colleges of Cork and Galway. They established a speciality in academic, informational and legal titles. In 1844, for instance, they advertised a 'long list of law books published by them'. Between 1876 and 1900 they published nearly 500 books, a rate of more than twenty a year, considerably more than their nearest rival, M.H. Gill (as McGlashan & Gill became in 1876). Another firm which was to build up a substantial factual and educational list was Thom's, whose principal Alex Thom (1800–79) had come from Scotland in 1820. He took over the firm in 1824, gaining the Post Office printing contract and in 1844 began the long series of directories, law reference and educational titles.

The founder of M.H. Gill was one of the most prominent men in the nineteenth-century trade. Michael Henry Gill was born in 1794, the son of a United Irishman who seems to have converted to Catholicism from his family's original Presbyterianism.[49] Michael was apprenticed to the Printer to the University in 1813 (aged eighteen or nineteen). He became a partner of the Printer Ruth Graisberry (widow of the former Printer Daniel Graisberry) in 1827 and managed the college business (mostly publishing classics and textbooks). In 1842, Ruth Graisberry died and Gill was formally appointed Printer to the University. Under his management the press gained an increasing reputation for the quality of its printing. In his sixties Gill took a great step by buying the copyrights and stock of the bankrupt James McGlashan, establishing a new firm called McGlashan & Gill. He ran the university press in conjunction with his new business, and established a wide commercial connection with British publishers such as Murray, Bentley, Hurst & Blackett and Routledge, explaining in the 1850s to the newly founded Macmillan company, then still in Cambridge, that 'our business is exclusively with the Trade ... we would be very happy to enter into an arrangement for the supply of your books to the Irish trade.'[50]

In 1876, Gill was in his 80s, and took the last big decision of his career, to give up the university printing and, with his son Henry Joseph, to establish his family printing, publishing and bookselling business as M.H.Gill in Sackville Street, where it was to remain for more than 100 years. Under Henry's guidance, writes Vincent Kinane, 'nationalist and Catholic (sometimes stridently Catholic) literature came to dominate the firm's lists'.[51]

Then there was the huge export of books originally prepared and published by the Irish Commissioners of National Education (the replacement from 1831 of the Kildare Place Society). Because they were both cheaper and editorially better than anything available from British publishers, they sold in their thousands into English and colonial schools. Nearly half a million copies of the reading lessons series were bought in England in the 1840s, amounting to half of the market; a similar proportion was achieved with the elementary arithmetic titles. So marked was this success that in 1848 leading publishers John Murray and William Longman remonstrated with the Prime Minister Lord John Russell, complaining of unfair competition, in that the Irish Commission of National Education was in effect a state-sponsored body. Lord John did very little in response, though a compromise was patched up. The grievance was only resolved when in 1861 the British authorities changed their syllabus, so the Irish books were no longer suitable.[52]

Another, similar triumph was with the copybooks initiated by the Irish philanthropist Vere Foster. These were devised and first published in 1865 (following, so it was said, a grumble from Lord Palmerston about the quality of his officials' handwriting: certainly Palmerston allowed his name to be used in the marketing).[53] Initially printed in Dublin (by Forster & Co. in the machinery department of the Dublin Exhibition in Earlsfort Terrace), the series originally consisted of thirteen separate titles, all on good-quality paper, graduating from simply strokes and curves to the well-remembered sententious proverbs ('He that cannot bear a jest should not make one' and 'Property has its Duties as well as its Rights'). Their stunning instant success necessitated a move to more professional print facilities, and the choice fell on the great Belfast firm of Marcus Ward. Foster kept the sales to the Irish National Board of Education in his own hands, while the three Ward brothers handled the extensive sales to the English-speaking world.

In connection with the copybooks the ever-enterprising Foster had established a 'National Competition in Writing ... open to pupils of either Public or Private Schools throughout the British Empire'. (He also sold his own ink, specially designed inkwells, a copybook protector and blotter, and Vere Foster pencils.) The extent of the copybook sales was revealed by the range of competition entries, coming as they did from India, Burma, Malta, Australia, Jamaica and the Cape of Good Hope as well as Ireland and Britain. By 1876, according to the Master of the Rolls, 'the annual sale of copy-books was around four million'. At 1*d* per copy (and some were 2*d*) this gives a turnover of some £17,000 a year, making it probably the most successful publishing exercise ever undertaken in Ireland. Had Vere Foster possessed anything of a publisher's gene, that would have served very nicely as the cash cow backing a fine firm.

By this time the series had expanded from simple black-only copybooks to a wide range including elaborate drawing copies, some in full colour. These were printed by the cumbersome process of chromolithography, which used large flat stones (imported from Germany) as the print surface. One stone was required for each colour: not CMYK (cyan, magenta, yellow and black) but one for brown, one for green and so on. One of Vere Foster's images for copying, a bunch of flowers, required as many as thirty-six stones. The actual printing was done from working stones, which deteriorated quickly on use so a set of 'mother stones' was needed.

Unfortunately, the enormous success of the firm and the vast sums of money involved caused the Ward brothers to quarrel.[54] Vere Foster stuck to his friend John Ward, who was bought out of the firm. Foster then sold the rights in the business for John Ward for a mere £3,000, but the two remaining brothers refused to return the litho stones, which they threatened to wipe clean of the images. They also advertised a spoiler brand of Marcus Ward copybooks. In 1878 Foster and Ward sued Marcus Ward & Co. for the return of the stones. They won the case and an appeal.

John Ward, however, did not set up his own firm as had been planned and the copybook franchise was sold to the Scottish educational publisher Blackie, on condition it established a factory in Dublin. Blackie established a dedicated factory and publishing department in Talbot Street. By this time the range of copybooks numbered over 150 separate lines.

But despite these successes, over the century, Irish book publishing continued in thrall to what was happening in Britain, which in practice meant what was happening in London. In the 1850s, one ordinary Protestant reader recorded his expenditure on books and periodicals. John Findlater (a young partner in the grocery firm) subscribed to the *Illustrated London News*, *Punch*, Dickens' *Household Words* and the *Economist* (all relatively new publications: the oldest, *Punch*, being barely 10 years old). He bought some novels, including *The Inheritance* (Louisa May Alcott's first novel), *Jane Eyre* and *The Christmas Carol*. A keen gardener, he bought Joseph Paxton's *Calendar of Gardening Operations*, which went on the shelf with *The Christian Treasury*, *Marriage – why so often unhappy?*, a *History of the Russian War* and *The Home School*, all published in London. The only Irish publication was *Saunders' Newsletter*.[55]

In the catalogue to the first Irish Industrial Exhibition of 1853, the writer John Sproule commented:

> In the publishing trade London is the head quarters as well as the great mart where the bulk of the trade is carried on. In Edinburgh and Dublin new works are produced not in any way inferior to those got out in London, but the number so published is inconsiderable, and even of those the great trade is done in London.[56]

It was largely, he believed, a matter of sales volume: 'books in small circulation must be sold at a comparatively high price to defray the expense of publication.'

In their *Guide to Irish Fiction*, Rolf and Magda Loeber recorded the consequences of the centripetal force: 'after the Union, the Dublin publishing industry declined in contrast to publishing houses in London … [this] encouraged Irish authors to become literary "absentees" and leave Ireland for journalism, translation and other literary work in London.'[57] This trend steadily accelerated during the century so that in the 1890s, '656 works of Irish fiction were published in London compared to 28 in Dublin.'[58] The overwhelming strength of the metropolis was not peculiar to the book world, but was experienced throughout the economy. As the railways carried Manchester goods to the farthest islands off Connemara, and young women discarded their red petticoats in favour of factory-made frocks, Ireland was steadily becoming economically and culturally integrated into the British sphere. Irish manufacturers struggled to re-create the nascent pre-Famine industrial economy. In 1884–85, a House of Commons Committee on Industries (Ireland) explored their difficulties.[59] Witness after witness told the Committee (which included such well-known names as Charles Parnell, Colonel King-Harman, Justin McCarthy and W.H. Smith, who the following year was to transfer his business in Dublin to the local manager Charles Eason) how in so many towns there had been more or less thriving industry before the Famine and now there was none.

In Bandon, for instance, a population of 14,000 serviced linen, woollen factories and two large cotton mills until 1826, when 'the country became flooded with English manufacture.'[60] In Birr, one witness averred, 'they had a large production of combs, brushes and hats, they had two distilleries and two breweries … of these there remained but one distillery.' Leaders from industries spanning pin- and spade-making to carriages and even flour milling, reported declines over the previous forty years, usually as a result of competition from England. Occasionally, of course, as the Committee heard, the wounds were self-inflicted. There was the tragi-comedy of complacency and incompetence leading to the collapse of the Cork butter industry, or the second-generation Malcolmsons from Portlaw, Co. Waterford, who wholeheartedly but disastrously backed the South in the American Civil War.

Could this trend be reversed? In a formidably detailed report of 1,100 pages the Committee came up with a series of causative factors, although, alas, no solutions. Among the causes adduced were the banking sector's reluctance to invest in Irish industry, the pricing structures of the railway system which favoured bulk-buying English shippers, the lack of technically-oriented education, the impossibility of bucking laissez-faire orthodoxy with differential tariffs, and the pervasive social aspiration to professional rather than industrial status.

Deepest of all, thought Sir Robert Kane, was the Famine:

> which shattered the confidence of the people in themselves, and broke down any spirit of confidence and energy they had, and they had a great deal of it before then … at that time there was very much more tendency to industrial enterprise than there has been since.[61]

By the 1890s, at least in the writing and publishing arenas, some portion of that old confidence had returned, and the Irish Literary Revival was under way.

2

The World of the 1890s

We have seen that there were combined technical and market upheavals which made the 1890s a watershed in publishing history. More fundamentally, affecting writers and readers alike, there were also deep structural changes in European culture.

In the narrow perspective of Irish history, the 1890s have been seen as the time when the death of Parnell (in 1891) brought to an end nationalists' hopes that Home Rule was close at hand. With the political sphere now considered something of a dead end, an upsurge of nationalist cultural activity took place. As F.S.L. Lyons put it, the disappointment at the failure of the promise of the 1880s 'provided an opportunity for nationalism to become, for a time at least, cultural rather than political. Literature, as the main channel of this cultural nationalism, began to seem suddenly more central, more relevant.'[1] This rather mechanical view was certainly how W.B. Yeats argued the point. He was conscious of a new Europe-wide spirit and saw an opening for a series of renovations of Irish culture (of which, of course, he was to be the leading light). Thus in December 1891, barely months after Parnell's death, Yeats and others launched the Irish Literary Society in London, following this with the foundation of the National Literary Society in Dublin in May 1892.

In the wider world, fundamental social and ideological change was brewing. At the end of the nineteenth century a series of scientific and social innovations amounted to a root and branch dismantling of old ideas in Europe and this was eagerly picked up by young intellectuals in Ireland. It had begun some years before, when Darwin had delivered a blow to the Victorian sense of self. 'Many readers', wrote a reviewer in 1889, thirty years after the first publication of *The Origin of Species*:

> will recall the shock the doctrine that man was descended from the brutes gave to all of us. It had the fascination of a horrible repulsion. It seemed to mock at poetry, mock at art, mock at the charm of womanhood, mock at religion, mock at everything the idealist's soul had previously cherished. There seemed to be no possibility of reconciling idealism with such a hideous reality as this. Thousands of thinkers passed through this ordeal.[2]

Under pressure, the old certainties were slipping, while the British 'greats' who had sustained the old ways died: George Eliot (1880); Trollope (1882); Matthew Arnold (1888); Ruskin (mental collapse in 1888); Browning (1889); Newman (1890); and the great booming voice of the era, Tennyson, in 1892. Only Herbert Spencer (1903) and the Queen herself (1901) made it into the new century. Like the great glaciers 10,000 years ago, which, having carved Ireland into hills and valleys, just melted away, these eminent Victorians left the earth, which, relieved of their weight, opened to all sorts of new growth and creativity. As one writer put it: 'the revolution profoundly affected the way people thought about the world and themselves ... [working to] batter, crush and eventually undermine social structures, moral norms and traditional ideas that had existed for centuries'.[3] And then came the Great War.

Everything seemed to be changing: the uncomfortable but unavoidable Modern loomed. The relations of men and women (in the home, in work, in sex, in sport) were dissected, as was the status (or perhaps death) of God and religion; in advanced circles the latent hypocrisy of bourgeois values was exposed and sexual prudery scoffed at; social and economic change exposed the political relations between rich and poor. Political and economic thinkers assaulted the doctrines of imperialism, natural class leadership and even free trade. The purpose or need of art was challenged as the Kodak camera, first marketed in 1888, became a commonplace creator of images. (As it happened, in France, Dégas, Monet, Toulouse-Lautrec and Renoir all produced their best work in the 1890s.)

In Vienna in the 1890s, Sigmund Freud developed a vision that seemed to many as hideous as Darwin's, 'disturbing the sleep of the world', as Freud put it. The Enlightenment's central value, the calm controlling mind, was, he said, in reality hag-ridden by unconscious horrors, often of an incestuous nature.

In this decade, Freud hovered between a theory that neurosis was caused by repressed memories of molestation in extreme childhood (the oddly named 'seduction theory') and the equally speculative Oedipus complex. For a society so self-conscious about sex, this focus was either squalid, or, for some, irresistible and accepted as a profound post-Christian reality, an attack on the last taboo. The waning of religious belief among intellectuals had in fact laid them open to new and bleak psychological horizons. In his 1899 work *The Interpretation of Dreams*, the key features of Freud's melodrama of the unconscious were first described and his instinct-driven, pessimistic view of human life began its extraordinary career.[4]

The 1890s were the 1960s of their century. The journalist and bibliophile Holbrook Jackson wrote that the 1890s, 'was so tolerant of novelty that it would seem as though the declining century wished to make amends for several decades of intellectual and artistic monotony.'[5] The poet Richard Le Gallienne (reader to one of the leading radical publishers, the Bodley Head) argued in his 1925 memoir *The Romantic '90s* that:

> Those last ten years of the nineteenth century properly belong to the twentieth and far from being 'decadent', except in certain manifestations, they were years of immense and multifarious renaissance ... all our present conditions, socially and artistically, found a more vital and authoritative expression than they have since because of the larger more significant personalities bringing them about.[6]

'Bliss it was in that dawn to be alive', as Wordsworth put it about another such period.

At the same time some of the novelties of the 1880s began to ferment: in transport with the safety bicycle and the motor car (which first came to Ireland in 1895); in communications with the web rotary press, cinema, radio, the phonograph and the telephone; in war with the machine gun; and in trade with the proliferation of branded goods and the importation of grain and frozen meat from Australasia and the Americas. Nothing, it seemed, not even The Book, was off limits. At a British booksellers' trade dinner in April 1892 the historian and anti-Parnellite Home Ruler, Justin McCarthy, referred to the prophecy that the phonograph would soon extinguish the book trade by substituting little cylinders for books. When placed in a machine these would recite the author's book in his own words.[7] He was not in favour of the possibility. In 1893, William Morris used the same prediction to push his own objectives, declaring: 'while there was still a chance, [we] should try and produce a few specimens of what was really good printing.'[8] There is no record that the Yeats sisters, in founding the Dun Emer Press a few years later, were affected by so apocalyptic a vision.

The safety bicycle, with pneumatic tyres from 1889, was about to have stirring effects, on female mobility and an investors' frenzy in 1893 on the Dublin stock exchange pushed prices in bicycle and tyre shares up 300 per cent. In 1894, Pope Leo XIII gave permission for Catholic clergy to cycle around their parishes ('the more willingly,' he declared, 'as the real inventor of the velocipede was the Abbé Pranton in 1845.'[9]) The development of the typewriter opened up possibilities for women's employment (Guinness bought its first in 1893). A poor telephone connection with London was established also in 1893. By 1900 there were fifty-six telephone exchanges in Ireland. From 1897, the Rotunda was used for 'moving picture' displays. There were new approaches to food: a vegetarian restaurant opened in Grafton Street in 1891. Even the staid *Irish Times* was caught up in the mood – in that newspaper the simple word 'new' was used 60 per cent more often in the 1890s than in the 1880s.[10]

Late-Nineteenth-Century Book Publishing

In the development of a national publishing industry local and international factors twist together. We have seen how the surge in book publishing in Ireland in the late eighteenth century was facilitated by the anomaly in copyright law. In the nineteenth century, publishers in Belgium and Austria took advantage of similar loopholes before they were closed by the 1886 Berne Convention. Just as the surge in literacy was a Europe-wide phenomenon, however, so too was the increase in the number of books being published (see Table 1).

Table 1. Number of new book titles published c. 1840, 1870, 1900 in UK (inc. Ireland) France and Germany

Country	*c. 1840*	*c. 1870*	*c. 1900*
UK (inc. Ireland)	2,900	4,600	14,500
France	6,000	8,800	15,000
Germany	9,000	14,000	24,000

Sources: UK: S. Eliot, *Some Patterns and Trends in British Publishing 1800–1919* (London, 1994), pp. 121–3; France: T. Zeldin, *France 1848–1945* (Oxford, 1977), p. 352; Germany: D. Sassoon, *The Culture of the Europeans* (London, 2006), p. 634. *Note*: Like so many book trade statistics, these figures should be taken as indicating trends rather than exact quantities. See the discussion in Eliot, op. cit. pp. 8–13.

Considerably the largest European publishing country by the end of the century was Germany, with 23,908 new titles and editions in 1898.[11] Its industry was also the best organised, with the Borsenverein sales clearing house based in Leipzig, which was founded in 1825. British book trade professionals were wont to cast an envious eye on so well managed a system. In 1894, William Heinemann set out the wonders of the German system in an attempt to stimulate faltering attempts at unity by the British trade.[12] Thirty years later Stanley Unwin described the Borsenverein as 'the most complete organisation for book distribution which exists anywhere in the world.'[13]

The scale of the difference between the German and British industries was exemplified by the fact that when, in 1906, Dent published the first fifty titles of the Everyman series, the German equivalent, Universalbibliothek published by Reclam, had more than 4,000 titles in print.[14] Reclam's sales reveal an open European or international mindset. Although Goethe headed the sales lists, non-German titles were prominent: between 1877 and 1942, 6 million translations of Ibsen's plays were sold and 6.4 million of Shakespeare's. Dickens did well (1.5 million copies) as did Plato, Mark Twain and Oscar Wilde (441,000 copies).[15] The Tauchnitz series of English language books published in Leipzig for Continental travellers reached its 2,000th volume in 1881. To Tauchnitz's credit, it had from the beginning paid the authors, which it was still not yet legally obliged to do.

In France, the tight controls on printing and bookselling imposed by a Napoleonic decree of 1810 were maintained until the 1860s. One such control demanded that a printer or bookseller hold one of the very limited official licences for each locality as a requisite to running such a business.[16] Paradoxically, this stimulated the growth of the much more volatile standalone book publishers, a new function not mentioned in the decree. Production increased accordingly: 'around 6,000 titles were printed in 1828; the figure had risen to 15,000 by 1889 and grew to about 25,000 by 1914.'[17] The number of copies sold had risen more than equivalently, driven upwards by experiments in cheap book production in the 1830s and 1850s by the firms of Charpentier and Levy. These were stimulated, it has been argued, by vigorous Belgian pirates undercutting French prices. Cheap books evidently encouraged reading, for travellers marvelled at public displays of book reading: 'In every hand there is a book!' wrote the Wild Irish Girl Lady Morgan in her survey, *France 1829–30*: 'Enter into the rudest porter's lodge of the simplest hotel, in the remotest quarter, and you will find cheap editions of the best authors.'[18] This was evidently far from her experience in Dublin.

A severe crisis reaction to overproduction of books struck in the 1880s. The depression which hit the French publishing industry in 1890 lasted until 1910 or 1911. It is suggested that the increasing use of serials from top authors in French newspapers contributed to the slump in book-buying – 'why should a reader buy books when he can get news, opinion and first rate literature for 10 centimes?' asked one French bookseller.[19] Whatever the cause, the slump left the wreckage of many firms, large and small, which had fallen before economic forces and conditions which they could not master. It left also a generation of 'frustrated aesthetes', of men who had entered the 1870s and 1880s with high hopes for careers as authors and critics.[20] It has even been speculated that the frustrations felt by some of these men turned into the passionate anti-Semitism (perceiving the publishing industry as largely run by Jews) exhibited in the Dreyfus scandal (1894–1906) and later.

Though its output appeared to contemporaries as prodigious, the United Kingdom's publishing industry (14,489 titles in 1898, including a small number of books published in Ireland) was only reasonably prolific: its great period of growth, financed by the sales of schoolbooks to the Empire, was just starting.

In every one of these countries, however, the growth figures for book publishing were swamped by the growth both in circulations and the number of publications of newspapers and periodicals. This was the great age of print. There were, in 1889, some 2,500 newspapers in the British Isles, including 500 in London alone, not to mention 650 London-based periodicals. 'Even these,' wrote one guide for would-be writers, 'do not exhaust the exceedingly numerous channels outside newspapers waiting to be filled with literary work.'[21] The four great newspapers published in Paris reached by 1910 some 3.6 million sales per day between them, a level never since attained. In England, the *Daily Mail* reached 1 million copies a day by 1899, and in 1902 the Irish journalist and MP T.P. O'Connor launched *T.P.'s Weekly* which sold a staggering 200,000 copies on the first day of publication and cruised thereafter at 250,000 a week. (The production and publishing were in the hands of the Waterford-born publisher Edmund Downey.)[22]

In Dublin in 1909, there were 8 daily newspapers, 34 weeklies, 38 monthlies and 6 less frequent periodicals.[23] At the same time, increasing numbers of English newspapers, magazines and 'light weeklies' of all sorts clattered into the market. C.S. 'Todd' Andrews' father was no doubt something of an exception, but multiple readership must have been common. As Andrews wrote of him:

> He was not a reader of books, Jules Verne and Arnold Bennett were the only writers I heard him talk about, but he made up for any deficiencies in that regard by his enthusiasm for newspapers. *The Independent* [before it disgraced itself with its reporting of the 1916 Rising], *The Freeman's Journal* were bought every morning ... and on the way to work my father bought an English paper and in the evening the *Evening Telegraph* and sometimes *The Herald*. He bought the *New Statesman* ... and on Sundays he bought *The Observer*. He took the *Irish Worker* and *The Leader* as well as Griffith's *Nationality*.[24]

He evidently did not buy any of the thirty-five or so periodicals devoted to short stories and articles, ranging from the *Strand Magazine* (from 1891 the home of Sherlock Holmes) to the self-conscious *Yellow Book*.

The penetration of the Irish market by British print started with the young, as the republican Andrews reported, reflecting on his boyhood before the Great War: 'from the comics we read, *Chips*, *Comic Cuts* and later the *Magnet* and the *Gem* and the *Union Jack*, we absorbed the correct British imperial attitudes.' Other, less decorous, fare from England included the 'bloods', 'shilling shockers' and various police news publications. Andrews's lifelong nickname comes from a character in the *Magnet*, Billy Bunter's home base.

Adult publications from England such as *Titbits*, *Photo Bits*, *Pearson's Weekly* and *Lloyd's Weekly News* are all referred to in *Ulysses*. In his history of M.H. Gill, J.J. O'Kelly quotes a statement from Bradbury and Evans that 12,000 copies of *Punch* were imported into Ireland every week by W.H. Smith (which became Eason's in 1885).[25] By 1912, as the *Daily Mail* pioneered new distribution methods, bringing the paper into the Dublin streets by early morning, barrister William Dawson noticed it was 'becoming as common a sight to see the man in the tram with a London morning paper as with a Dublin one'.[26] Like fast food, they were well-distributed, cheap and tasty.

The New Conditions of the Book Business

As the market evolved, there occurred in the 1890s a series of changes that reset the conditions of book publishing for the whole of the twentieth century. At first glance they might seem no more than technical matters, affecting only those professionally involved. But as always happens when the conditions of the book trade change, both writers and readers were affected by new norms.

With the background of rising literacy, technical change and a new willingness to spend money on reading materials, four key changes occurred in the British publishing business in the 1890s. These were: the opening out of the new fiction market; the establishment of a publisher-fixed book price regime (generally called resale price maintenance, or, in 1900, by the British book trade, unintuitively, the Net Book Agreement); the development of international copyright, notably by the Berne Convention, and in the US, where the Chace Act at last extended copyright protection to non-Americans in 1891; and the settling of book production technology for the next seventy years with the automation of typesetting through the development of hot metal machines combined with letterpress printing.

Opening Out the Fiction Market

The London-based book trade magazine *Publishers' Circular* reported that some 67,000 new books were published in the 1890s. The top six Irish publishers produced just 600 titles, with the most prolific being M.H. Gill with 189.[27] Of the London titles just over 31 per cent (i.e. 20,000 books) were in the fiction and children's category. The next largest set was the non-fiction catch-all 'geography, biography and travel' at 12 per cent.[28] The triumph of fiction represented a marked cultural shift. In the early-to mid-nineteenth century, religion had represented roughly 20 per cent of titles and history claimed 17 per cent. Social sciences accounted for between 17 and 20 per cent, leaving literature (i.e. fiction, poetry and drama) claiming a share of between 20 and 24 per cent.[29]

The importance of fiction in the publishing/reading mix focused attention on the highly structured – even bizarre – way new novels were brought to the British market. Following a model initiated by Walter Scott's publishers in the 1820s, new novels intended for a middle-class readership (i.e. excluding reprints, railway books, shilling shockers, chapbooks and similar popular vehicles, as well as serials) were first published in three volumes at a standard price of 10*s* 6*d* per volume. Physically, the three volumes were quite small – perhaps 7½in x 5in (i.e. no bigger than an A size paperback) – but they were absurdly laid-out with a standard 300 fat-margined pages of 22 over-leaded lines per page, eight or nine words to the line, and plenty of blanks, in forty-five chapters. At barely 200 words, a page contained less than half the text of a typical modern book.[30] Three-deckers were also long books, between 150,000 to 200,000 words (a modern literary novel is comfortable with 60,000, though blockbusters are much longer and some literary novels are very long). Authors such as Somerville & Ross, for example, struggled with this demanding formula: their first book, *The Irish Cousin*, is only two volumes and their second a single volume. Only with their masterpiece, *The Real Charlotte*, did they manage as many as 150,000 words. They seem to have been more at ease with the 8,000-word stories of *The Irish RM*.

The price, equivalent to more than €150 in today's money, ensured no member of the public actually bought these books. Instead they borrowed them from commercial lending libraries. What's more, this conventional price, which bore no relationship to cost, impinged on other books, which consequently tended, as Matthew Arnold pointed out at the time, to be much more expensive than their equivalents in France. Arnold called the system 'eccentric, artificial and unsatisfactory to the highest degree', and he excoriated it as 'a machinery for the multiplication of bad literature and keeping good books dear.'[31]

The key to why this odd arrangement lasted so long was in the power of the circulating libraries, most famously Mudie's, which could buy as much as the whole first edition of a new book. Even though the library demanded at least 60 per cent discount, what it paid was often sufficient to cover the publisher's costs and contribute to overheads in one deal.[32] For authors, too, the system provided some comforts, though at a cost. As a character in Gissing's 1891 novel about the literary life put it, the three-volume novel was 'a triple headed monster, sucking the blood of English novelists', but fear of the future pressed on less well-known writers: 'it is a question of payment. An author of moderate repute may live on a yearly three-volume novel ... but he would have to produce four one-volume novels to obtain the same income.'[33] In 1894, *The Bookseller* mused that if the three-decker was no longer published it would be harder in the future for young unknowns to make their mark, because of 'the lessening quantity of inferior fiction'.[34]

The libraries, with their enormous power over this central sector of publishing, used the high price of books to encourage consumers to become subscribers and the three volumes to persuade them to take out the more expensive multi-volume subscription. At best, the three-decker form constituted a kind of test marketing: if demand held up (the 'one in eight' that McCulloch's *Commercial Dictionary* instanced) the new novel would be produced for the public in a series of diminishing formats (assuming the sales kept running) priced successively at 10*s* 6*d*; 6*s*; 3*s* 6*d*; 2*s* and finally, for railway bookstalls, 1*s* or even 6*d*. At worst, the bloated three-decker encouraged bland productions 'in which the good end happily and the bad unhappily', for, as Miss Prism remarked, 'that is what fiction means.'[35]

At the same time, afraid of losing custom in a world quick to censor, the libraries insisted that nothing was to be published that, as Dickens' Mr Podsnap put it, would 'bring a blush into the cheek of the young person.' (In this instance, commerce did freely what the Irish State had later to establish a statutory Censorship Board for.) In France, novelists such as Zola, the Goncourt brothers and Flaubert, were increasingly exploring previously taboo subjects, but the buyers for Mudie's and W.H. Smith held the line, ensuring a uniformly bland outcome. In his ironic lament for the format, Kipling wrote, 'we asked no social questions, we pumped no hidden shame/we never talked obstetrics when the little stranger came.'[36]

Irish publishers did not produce three-deckers – the Loebers have identified nine such published before 1856 and none afterwards – but if Irish writers wanted to be published in London (and most of them did, producing 656 titles – mostly by one-novel writers – in the ten years of the 1890s alone), they were obliged to address the conventions.

By the 1890s, however, the format was under pressure. Authors such as George Moore not only chafed under the stringent physical demands of the format but complained bitterly about the increasingly irrelevant moral code (notably in his 1885 pamphlet *Literature at Nurse, Or Circulating Morals*). But there were market pressures too. Just as many years later vigorous believers in the market undermined the Net Book Agreement, some publishers were keen to address the market directly with 6*s* novels. In 1890, new publisher Heinemann dutifully produced Hall Caine's *Manxman* in three volumes, but a bare eight months later produced a 3*s* 6*d* version, which was an immediate triumphant success.[37] Of course there were countervailing arguments from authors, publishers and booksellers, in effect fearing the winds of the open market, but their voices were swept aside. As so often in economic forecasting, the unquantifiable pent-up demand was underestimated. The prophets of doom were quickly silenced (just as happened with Penguin books in the 1930s). Demand quickly supplied enough low-price/high-volume sales; in fact the number of novels published continued to rise.

In May 1894, Edmund Downey of Ward & Downey in London published Somerville & Ross's *The Real Charlotte* in three volumes. As it happened, this was one of the last of the format, for the following month Mudie's and Smith's made an announcement that they would no longer buy books in that format. This quickly ended a publishing practice that had lasted for nearly three generations. From now on the comfortable intermediary of the circulating libraries would be removed and new novels would be sold directly to the customer, via the booksellers, at 6*s*. Like Soviet factory owners after 1989, publishers and authors had to adapt quickly to the new disciplines of an open market. Some, such as the leading fiction house of Richard Bentley or old Andrew Chatto of Chatto & Windus, never made the switch. Others, such as Heinemann, thrived.

Immediately, novels became shorter and new fiction suddenly came on to the shelves of ordinary bookshops, joining the other characteristic publishing technique of the period, the growing number of inexpensive series and 'libraries'. One scholar has identified more than 140 of these on the market, aided by the fact that the then current copyright law put books into the public domain seven years after the author's death (or forty-two years after publication, whichever was longer). The most sustained of these series were the World's Classics and the Everyman Library: itself a descendant of Dent's Temple Classics. Longman's had its Badminton Library and its Silver Library, Macmillan's its Colonial Library and its Globe Editions, Routledge its Universal Library and so on. Fisher Unwin's Pseudonym Library introduced Yeats' *John Sherman & Dhoya* and Somerset Maugham's first novel *Liza of Lambeth*. By 1917, Unwin had published no fewer than twenty-eight different series.[38] The Camelot series of Walter Scott (one of eighteen different series from this publisher) published Yeats' *Fairy and Folk Tales of the Irish Peasantry* (1888) and his *Tales from Carleton* (1889). The idea of a library of Irish classics, over which Yeats and Gavan Duffy were to quarrel, was therefore very much the standard book marketing ploy of the time. Both booksellers and book buyers kindled to the series, or better, a 'library', which carried the flattering hint of a carefully chosen array of books. In marketing terms, the series is almost a brand. By association, it helps persuade an individualistic and widespread book trade of the potential value of new publications. Any new title in a series by implication carries something of the known sales value of previous items.

Fixed Book Prices

The second major trade innovation in Britain in the 1890s was the introduction of fixed book prices. For most of the nineteenth century, British and Irish stockholding booksellers were vulnerable to competitive undercutting. This stems partly from the nature of the demand for books, whereby many people want the current bestseller, but only a few want anything else. When trade structures allow, it is easy for any retailer to 'free ride' the system by stocking only bestsellers, perhaps allowing purchasers a hefty discount to encourage sales. Stockholding bookshops which rely on the bestsellers to finance worthy but less popular titles lose out. In Ireland, department stores and cafés dabbled opportunistically in the book market using the current bestsellers as loss leaders, just as Tesco did in the early 2000s in Ireland by drastically undercutting the trade for *Harry Potter* titles, to the chagrin of the book trade.

The British trade had attempted to develop a fixed price agreement in the middle of the century but was rebuffed in 1852 by a combination of laissez-faire lawyers and front-rank authors (including Dickens) convinced that such an arrangement was against authors' interests. (The German Borsenverein had had fixed prices since the 1820s, followed by Denmark in 1837.) Following the free trade spirit of the day the arbitrator, Lord Campbell, deplored the booksellers' attempt to control aggressive price undercutting. The plan of booksellers to create artificial protection, especially given the element of coercion required to make the plan work, would, he declared patronisingly, 'lull them into habits of listlessness which may be detrimental to the community'.[39]

Twenty years later, the matter had got worse, with customers routinely demanding substantial discounts from booksellers or buying from opportunistic outlets. *The Bookseller* in 1871 counselled resignation: 'henceforth the pages of *The Bookseller* will not be open to complaints of underselling; for however much we may deplore it, free trade is the order of the day.'[40] By the 1880s, competitive price-cutting by booksellers had reached such an extent that there was a fear that ordinary stock-holding book retailing could not survive. The historian of the Associated Booksellers argued that:

> Far from increasing the circulation of books to the advantage of all concerned, unlimited competition had made the sales of new books completely unprofitable, and booksellers allowing 3*d* in the 1*s* discount [i.e. a customer's discount of 25 per cent off published price] survived, if at all, only through the gradual ruin of their rivals and by profit from the sale of stationery, fancy goods and bric-à-brac.[41]

In the book business at least, free trade and 'the market' had demonstrably not proved beneficial to consumers' interests.

The lack of thriving, stockholding bookshops was a serious impediment to the development of book publishing, especially in the exploitation of backlist. Acutely conscious of this, in 1890, Frederick Macmillan, in a letter to *The Bookseller*, proposed a system of fixed book prices which he called 'net' books (i.e. net of customer discount). Perhaps tactfully, he made no reference to the long-continued success of the German and Danish schemes, or the more recent French scheme, of which he must have known.

Macmillan published the first general trade 'net' book, Marshall's *Principles of Economics*, in July 1890. He chose this title because, as he wrote, it was 'a book of general interest intended for a wide sale' yet would not appeal to 'cheap-jack' booksellers. Perhaps, too, the idea of having a distinguished economist implicit in his new scheme appealed. The book's importance was immediately clear: as Keynes later put it, 'it ushered in a new age of economic thought'.[42] By the time of Marshall's death in 1924, the *Principles of Economics* had sold 37,000 copies and it was still in print (and in use as a UCD text-book) forty years later. Correspondence between Marshall and Macmillan make it clear, however, that the economist only partially understood what was afoot. He continually reverted to the idea that it was bad economics and indeed immoral that cash customers should pay the same price as those on credit. At one point he even proposed that they should abandon the whole scheme, an idea Macmillan tactfully kicked to touch. Marshall was annoyed that the proposed 25 per cent booksellers' discount was a multiple of what the author was to get and for very little input. For an economist specialising in trade and distribution he was curiously dismissive of the booksellers' contribution: 'I cannot discover,' he wrote, 'what booksellers do for the extension of knowledge.'[43]

Macmillan's rapidly escalated the number of 'net' titles over the next few years. Other publishers, conscious that the public were used to getting discounts, put their toes delicately into the water, thus my copy of Longmans' 1892 publication *Books and Bookmen* by Andrew Lang has a notice attached to the flyleaf declaring that 'Messrs Longmans intend this book to be sold to the Public at the advertised price, and supply it to the trade on terms which will not allow of discount.'

There was, however, no easy coronation for so radical an idea. Initial reaction was commonly negative, with aggressive comment from newspapers such as the *Pall Mall Gazette* and the London *Times*. The latter mounted a spirited attack on the net book idea in October 1894. Initially, both the authors and the publishers were unenthusiastic about an idea that seemed so obviously counter to the laissez-faire spirit and many booksellers regarded the idea as unworkable. 'Old booksellers' regularly wrote in to *The Bookseller* in the early 1890s deploring undercutting, but seeing no alternative, having no faith that the short-term opportunism of publishers could be legally restrained.

Nonetheless, a glimmer of the future lay in the development of trade associations. The first had been the Society of Authors in 1883; the Associated Booksellers (much later renamed the Booksellers Association) came in 1895 and the Publishers Association in 1896. Initially, the publishers, led by Charles Longman and John Murray, took the view that, as Longman put it:

> The doctrine which seemed reasonable and practical to Lord Campbell forty years ago does not seem less reasonable now … any ring or combination of booksellers and publishers originating for the purpose of regulating prices to the public and enforced by coercion or exclusive dealing, is altogether impracticable.[44]

Against the Longmans and the Murrays were more radically-minded publishers, notably William Heinemann, who pointed out that things had changed considerably since Lord Campbell's day. (The fundamental and crucial change he did not mention was a loosening of the grip of free trade ideology. By the end of the century, various Factory and Adulteration of Foods Acts had shown that Parliament was well capable of putting the general well-being above the theory of free trade. In 1895, a correspondent to *The Bookseller* noted that retail price maintenance had been adopted in other businesses: he instanced Wills' Tobacco, Vinolia Soap and Epps Cocoa.)

The following year the Associated Booksellers requested the Publishers Association to meet with them to discuss terms. The PA refused, stating that terms are 'a matter for arrangement by individual publishers', and referred to the old sticking-point, coercion. It declared that it could not 'entertain the adoption of any plan which would involve a system of coercion or "boycotting" on their part'.[45] *The Bookseller* commented acidly:

> The first time a question arises – and a very important question it is from the booksellers' point of view – the Publishers Association abdicates its functions. It is resolved into its constituent atoms, and the booksellers are referred to the individual units. In other words, the instant the first trade question comes up before it, the Association refuses to discuss it.[46]

Finally, after years of discussion, with the position of stockholding bookshops getting worse by the minute, and the Associated Booksellers pressing revised drafts on the authors and the publishers, in 1899, the organisations eventually achieved agreement. On 1 January 1900, the Net Book Agreement, cementing retail price maintenance in the British and Irish book trade, commenced its life. This agreement was to be the foundation of the retail trade until nearly the end of the century.

An important but unintended consequence of the net book system was the popular adoption of the royalty system of author payment based on list price, already in wide use in the United States. Previously there had been three common ways by which authors were paid:

Outright sale: The most common arrangement was an outright sale (or perhaps an edition- or time-limited lease) of the copyright. This was simple, and gave the author a lump sum, but both author and publisher were in effect gambling on the subsequent success of the book. If it flopped the author got paid anyway, but if it became a great success the publisher was not obliged to pay more than the original deal. Most three-deckers were published on this basis, which publishers were accustomed to. Only the most favoured authors were able to hold out for a royalty deal.[47]

Half-profits: In theory, sharing the profits of publication was the fairest system, but it was tainted with suspicion. Since the accounts were always drawn up by the publisher and too often included unverifiable lump sums – such as for 'establishment charges', 'office expenses' and perhaps dubious charges for advertising in the publisher's house journal, or overstated share of a joint advertisement – this method was vulnerable to the exploitation of unbusinesslike authors.

Publication on commission: This was the option recommended by the Society of Authors for those who could afford it. The authors paid all the expenses of publication and received all the income themselves, paying the publishers a commission for their work.

With attention focused on the net price of the book, the royalty system became (and remains) the typical way in which authors are paid, though nowadays, with the abolition of fixed prices and mounting bookseller discounts, the calculus is very often based on the publisher's net receipts rather than the list price.

Developing International Copyright

Copyright underpins publishing, because books have always been particularly vulnerable to piracy or freeloading. Commercial scale exploitation of copyrighted materials happened in the past in Ireland, the US, Austria and Belgium and is now happening in Latin America, India and notably Nigeria. It is estimated that at the beginning of the nineteenth century as much as 70 per cent of the American trade was in (unpaid) British authors and this was still 20 per cent of a much bigger market by 1860.[48] The Austrians did the same (encouraged, so it is said, by Empress Maria Theresa) and as for the Belgians: 'One out of three books published [in the early nineteenth century] were for export, most of them pirated ... at the height of the wave of Belgian literary piracy in the 1840s over 80 per cent of the titles published by two of the most prominent publishers in Belgium were illicit reproductions of French works.'[49]

The earliest copyright provisions were entirely national: a robust view was taken of the entitlements of foreigners. But as the book market developed internationally this was perceived as unsatisfactory and people began to envisage a universal copyright of authors and publishers, valid the world over. Tentative steps were made on a bilateral basis (such as the mutual recognition of copyright convention between Prussia and Britain in 1846).

Finally, and triumphantly, a multilateral treaty was signed: the Berne Convention of 1886. The fundamental statement of this convention was that henceforth each of the ten signatory countries should give foreign authors as many rights as its own nationals. The Convention was significantly revised in Berlin in 1908 with fifteen signatories, not including Russia, China, the US, or any Latin American country. Rights were made independent of any formalities (Article 4) and the copyright term of life plus fifty years was agreed, 'so far as such provisions are consistent with domestic law' (Article 7). This was thought more rational than the then current British terms of life plus seven years *or* forty-two years from the date of publication, whichever was longer. The British Copyright Act of 1911 enshrined the new Berne copyright period into English and Irish law.

The big absentee from the first Berne Convention was the United States. A long contest had raged there between the publishers and booksellers profiting from free use of texts and the authors and others who complained that such free use provided unfair competition to US authors and ideas. The dire fate of the early nineteenth-century Irish book trade after the introduction of copyright (described in Chapter 1) was used in the 1850s by those in the US publishing business to argue against the extension of copyright protection to non-American authors. Nonetheless, after numerous false starts throughout the post-Civil War period, another Bill (the thirteenth such proposal to come before Congress) was proposed by Senator Chace in 1886 and finally passed by both Houses of Congress in 1891. This offered reciprocal copyrights, but only for books and publications first printed in the United States. This manufacturing clause was the necessary sop to appease the trade lobby.[50]

Writers Flourish

The opening of the US market was only part of the raft of new opportunities for professional writers. The number of periodicals published in Britain rose from 250 in 1800 to 2,500 in 1900, a large proportion of which published stories, serials and freelance contributions. Domestic production of paper rose from 11,000 tons to more than 650,000 tons over the same period. Suddenly, it was possible to make money as a writer. As book historian Simon Eliot put it: 'The whole concept of the "man of letters" not as an inspired genius or a picturesque bohemian, but as a workaday professional, on a par in training, status and (with luck) income with a lawyer or doctor was the creation of this hopeful period.'[51]

'Half-a-dozen really popular novels,' thought Augustine Birrell, 'or a couple of successful, long-running plays will put their authors in possession of a sum of money more than equalling the slow accumulations of a laborious and successful professional life.'[52] Efficient storytellers made money feeding the appetite for amusing reading matter. Only the theatre and the music hall provided anything like such widespread popular entertainment.

Periodical publishing produced a sustained demand for short stories and writers of the 1890s turned happily to this new form. Almost everyone had a try. Joyce and Yeats wrote some, as did George Moore, Somerville & Ross and Oscar Wilde; only Bernard Shaw seems to have been exempt, though he did try fiction, writing four novels between 1879 and 1883. In England, there was a flowering: Henry James, Rudyard Kipling, Conan Doyle, J.M. Barrie, Edith Nesbit, R. L. Stevenson, Max Beerbohm, W. W. Jacobs, H.G. Wells and George Gissing were only the better known practitioners in an art which, as Wells himself put it, 'broke out everywhere'.

In May 1890, the newly formed Society of Authors began to publish its journal *The Author* with a constant stream of business advice to this newly affluent group. Like the egregious hero of Gissing's *New Grub Street*,

Jasper Milvain, 'the literary man of 1882', these writers increasingly thought 'literature nowadays is a trade'. As he explained:

> Putting aside men of genius, who may succeed by mere cosmic force, your successful man of letters is your skilful tradesman. He thinks first and foremost of the markets: when one kind of goods begins to go off slackly, he is ready with something new and appetising. He knows perfectly all the possible sources of income. Whatever he has to sell he'll get payment for it from all sorts of various quarters; none of your unpractical selling for a lump sum to a middleman.[53]

Of course, not all authors had the time or ability to identify and exploit the new opportunities. To meet their requirements a new breed of literary agents sprung up. Doyen of them (though not the very first) was A.P. Watt who set up his plate in the 1870s. In 1900, Yeats had joined his stable of authors. J.B. Pinker, starting in 1896, took over Somerville & Ross in 1897 and Joyce in 1915. The third important agent was the American, Curtis Brown, who had established his office by 1905 and represented Lady Gregory and Sean O'Casey.

Roy Foster's description of Yeats' circumstances before he placed his affairs in A.P. Watt's hands makes it clear how useful agents could be. After fifteen years of ducking and diving:

> [Yeats] never forgot that his professional status depended on the London marketplace. The shift from writing lyric poetry to plays and his abandonment of reviewing enforced careful consideration of his literary income. So did the increasingly inconvenient allocation of his various works between different publishers. Fisher Unwin still published his early poems, plays and novels. Lawrence & Bullen possessed his short stories, prose and the contract for *The Speckled Bird*. Elkin Mathews had published *The Wind Among the Reeds*, and Hodder and Stoughton had taken on *The Shadowy Waters*. WBY found Fisher Unwin too frugal (he paid an exceptionally low royalty) and Bullen erratic (he drank).[54]

Yeats remained with Watt for the rest of his life.

How Books Were Produced 1890–1960

The 1890s saw the final crucial development in mechanisation that established a system of book production that was to last until the 1960s. The introduction of case-binding in the 1820s, flatbed cylinder printing such as the widely used 'Wharfedale' from the 1860s, and machine section sewing in the 1870s, had left the mechanisation of typesetting as the inventor's target. Hand-typesetting was barely changed since Gutenburg's time and involved manually picking out letter by letter from a divided case in which they were stored in the conventional layout (capitals in the upper case and minuscules in the lower). This highly skilled work was time-consuming and expensive. As well as picking the letters quickly and correctly, the line had to be 'justified' with careful addition of spacing to avoid a ragged right-hand column. An experienced man working from clean simple copy could be expected to set perhaps 1,500 ens (characters) per hour. This represents fewer than 300 words, less than the conventional outcome of 400 or more words to a printed page. At the end of the process the letters had to be carefully cleaned and replaced in their correct compartments. Perhaps two thirds of the total production cost (i.e. including paper, printing and binding) of a short-run book could be consumed in setting.[55]

After various false starts (one of which swallowed the life savings of Mark Twain), finally, in the 1880s, the Linotype machine was patented, followed in the 1890s by the Monotype. Both used seated keyboards (a big change for the craftsmen of the day, used to standing to pick type from a case) and a system of moulds and molten lead mixture to create the letters. The Linotype produced a single line of type (called a 'slug') justified mechanically, creating the letters from moulds and setting them into a justified line in one action. *The Nation* described this invention as 'a revolution in printing' noting that, 'It is claimed that matter can be set from six to ten times more rapidly than the most expert compositor can set types in his composing stick and it is stated that the saving in cost is or should be about 40 per cent.'[56] (This is a stretch: Gaskell cites net rates of 6,000 ens (characters) per hour for Linotype, i.e. four times the hand-set rate.[57])

Linotype was launched in London in 1889 and from Ireland the principal initial interest came from the newspapers such as the *Freeman's Journal* and the *Evening Telegraph*.[58] Among printers, the first Linotype was installed in Ireland in the Dublin Steam Printing Company in 1893. This was a very large business in Abbey Street best known for producing Thom's *Directory*.[59]

Some years later the Monotype Corporation was launched on the London stock exchange and began marketing a more sophisticated machine.

The Monotype system was a two-stage process, with keyboards producing a punched tape which was then fed into a separate caster which moulded the type and produced a justified line of individual letters. Of the two systems, Linotype was undoubtedly quicker both in production and in making up the page on the stone, but it was clumsy in correction, for a single letter mistake meant resetting the whole line. Its type designs (notably the lack of a kerning facility) and the *force majeure* justification system were regarded by purists as suitable only for rough work such as newspapers. Importantly, both machines eliminated the time-consuming process of redistributing type into the cases. Used type, whether slugs or individual letters, was simply tipped back into the melting pot.

Until the advent of phototypesetting in the 1960s, most books were set hot metal by Monotype, though a comment in one of W.G. Lyon's letters (April 1916) where he refers to 'slugs' being misplaced, makes it likely that the Educational Company had plumped for Linotype. The more typographically sophisticated Dundalgan Press opted for Monotype, claiming to have installed the second such press in Ireland in 1903.[60] M.H. Gill was also a Monotype house. The contest between the two systems was like that more recently between PC/Microsoft and Apple for designers' approval. Monotype and Apple were dearer but more elegant. In the 1920s, Monotype consolidated its prime position in the book world by employing Stanley Morison (later famous for designing Times Roman) as typographical advisor. The result was a substantial series of elegant typefaces that were a joy to design with, which could not be said of Linotype faces. It is symptomatic that when Maunsel & Roberts went under the hammer in 1926, the firm had only Monotype and founder's type with which to set books. In 1937, Monotype issued the Irish typeface Columcille designed by Karl Uhlemann and Colm Ó Lochlainn of the Sign of the Three Candles.

The introduction of hot metal setting led to the abandonment of the picturesque old names for type sizes such as pica (12 pt), small pica (11 pt) and long primer (10 pt). Officially, the 1886 American system of points was generally adopted in Britain in 1898. In practice, it is easy to believe Irish printer Andrew Corrigan's report that in many houses machine- and hand-setting continued side by side for twenty years. He believed this was partly because the old founders' types were considered more elegant and partly because hand-setting gave jobbing houses a flexibility that the machines could not match.[61]

In this way, by the 1890s the production process that would last unchanged until the 1960s was in place. Type was set by hot metal, nearly always Monotype; printing was by flatbed letterpress machine capable of up to 2,000 perfected sheets an hour (though with lengthy make-ready etc. averaging much less), unless for very long runs when the rotary letterpress (as used in newspapers) became economic. One of a series of standard paper sizes such as demy or crown would be used (for history or biography, and fiction, respectively). For books that were expected to be reprinted without substantial corrections, or to meet the manufacturing clause in US copyright law, papier mâché moulds of the type could be made. These were light, robust and flexible, enabling them to be used as the source either of a conventional flatbed stereotype plate or of a curved plate for rotary letterpress printing. For books that were likely to be substantially changed it was possible to keep the original setting in galleys as 'standing metal', at the expense of locking away so much reusable lead. This was the system used by Thom's *Directory*.[62] Maunsel's liquidation list of 1926 records that most of the books were stored as moulds, some as moulds and plates, and a few as standing metal.

The sheer weight of metal and the awkwardness of the formes of made-up pages, effectively tied typesetting and printing into the same plant. So in most plants there was also facility for the next processes: folding into sections and gathering into books. Sewing and case-binding took place either on the printer's premises or at specialist bookbinders.

It was common to bind up only part of the run at first, leaving the balance of the run in printed sheets or folded sections for subsequent binding if the sales warranted. This practice can be clearly followed in Maunsel & Roberts' liquidation stock sheets, where we can see, for instance, Arthur Clery's *Dublin Essays* (originally published in 1919) held as 90 copies bound and 240 in sheets; Edward MacLysaght's *The Gael* was 175 volumes and 1,674 copies in sheets. (This looks suspiciously like an overprinting of a former director's book.) George O'Brien's *Economic History of the Seventeenth Century*, at 10*s* 6*d* one of the dearest books on the list, was held as 158 bound copies and 274 in sheets; Pearse's *Story of a Success* was available in two versions, at 3*s* 6*d* (219 bound copies, 2,500 in sheets – another overprinting) and 1*s* 6*d* (560 bound copies and 474 in sheets).[63]

The combination of these four restructurings and their unexpected consequences was to provide the technical structure within which the British and Irish book trade was to develop over the twentieth century.

3

Publishing During the Literary Revival

The Pull of the Metropolis

In every culture, bright, ambitious and talented people are drawn to the metropolis, whether it be Paris, London or New York. As Balzac put it in his 1840s novel about literary ambition: 'it's the same story, year after year, the same eager rush to Paris of ambitious youths from the provinces, who arrive – more and more each year – their heads erect, their hearts full of high hopes.'[1] Throughout the nineteenth century (as we have seen from Carleton) Irish men and women anxious for a literary career made their way to London, attracted by the bright lights lit by imperial wealth. Many, such as the brilliant Corkman, William Maginn (model for Thackeray's Captain Shandon in *Pendennis*), and a host of now obscure names, found themselves in the rackety Bohemia off Fleet Street and the Strand. The later generation of Katherine Tynan, Emily Lawless, W.B. Yeats, George Moore and Bernard Shaw were considerably less bibulous and, no doubt as a result, more productive.[2]

To an extent we now find difficult to credit, the British and Irish economies were steadily being drawn more and more tightly together, a process that was accelerated by the development of the railway system after the Famine. Mentalities too: English language and culture had sunk deeply into middle-class Ireland. English media (books, newspapers, periodicals, theatre, songs) coloured every life; English goods and brands filled the shops and jobs beckoned at every level from tattie-howking in Scotland to running the Empire. Dublin clearly was not in the position to provide either the rewards in stimulus or sales opportunities that London had so much of. And it only took about twelve hours to go by steam and rail from Dublin to London.

To add to the attraction for those wanting a political or literary career there was, at the end of the nineteenth century, a craze for all things Celtic (a publishing opportunity akin to the tide of Anglo-Irish studies that enthralled university literature departments from the 1970s). A 'wave of Celtic influence' swept fashionable London. The novelist and commentator Grant Allen wrote in 1891, that the fashion for Celtic culture:

> has brought with it many strange things, good, bad and indifferent. It has brought with it Home Rule, Land Nationalisation, Socialism, Radicalism, the Reverend Hugh Price Jones,[3] the Tithe War, the Crofter Question, the Plan of Campaign … The Celt in Britain, like Mr Burne-Jones' enchanted princess has lain silent for ages in an enforced long sleep; but the spirit of the century pushing aside the weeds and briars of privilege and caste, has set free the sleeper at last.[4]

The craze would, of course, wear off, until Anthony Powell was able to sneer at the Celtic Twilight as 'the mournful haunt of the third-rate', but that was not for some time to come.[5]

The Irish Literary Revival was both a cause and a consequence of this Celtic craze. Starting with the poetry of James Clarence Mangan (1803–49) and the heroic retellings of myths by Standish O'Grady in the mid-nineteenth century, the movement was a characteristic combination of poetry, antiquarian and country interests and a new national consciousness. In its most active phase, the Revival centred round W.B. Yeats, whose 1893 work *The Celtic Twilight* gave it its characteristic descriptor. But Yeats was by no means the only poet or playwright contributing to this outburst: there were John Millington Synge and Lady Gregory in the Abbey Theatre; there was Douglas Hyde, whose influential *Love Songs of Connacht* was published in the same year as *The Celtic Twilight*; other active participants included James Stephens, George Moore, Oliver St John Gogarty, Padraic Colum and Thomas MacDonagh.

The literary path from Ireland to London was so well-trodden that by the end of the century there was serious debate as to whether the hoped-for Irish literary revival should be based in London or Dublin. When the Southwark Literary Club transmuted itself into the Irish Literary Society in

December 1891, the London *Daily Telegraph* provocatively commented that it was eminently fitting that 'if an Irish Literary Society is to be formed, its seat should be London, not Dublin.' So long as English was the language of Ireland, the *Telegraph* declared, 'the literary and oratorical and characteristic genius of the country must of necessity gravitate towards the fountainhead and centre of intellectual life in England.' Yeats, however, had no such idea: in a letter to *United Ireland* he declared it 'absurd and impossible to make London "the intellectual centre of Ireland"'.[6]

A leading light of the new Society was the distinguished former Young Irelander Charles Gavan Duffy, now in his seventies. In his inaugural address to the Society in 1892, he proposed, just as he had done with success fifty years before, that a uniform library be established of the hundred best Irish books: the bones of a national literature. 'The youth of Ireland,' he declared, 'which used to be kindled and purified by … poetry and legends runs a serious risk of becoming debased, perhaps depraved … the books chiefly read by the young in Ireland are detective or other sensational stories from England and America, and vile translations from the French.'[7] As we have seen, exactly the kind of 'library' he was proposing was a characteristic vehicle of contemporary publishing. It was also, following Sir John Lubbock's 100 best books selection and its Irish counterpart 'Best Hundred Irish Books' (both published in 1886), a current craze.[8]

Providing technical advice to the venture was Edmund Downey, a highly-experienced London-based publisher, originally from Waterford. He had joined the fiction publishing firm Tinsleys in 1879 and had set up his own firm Ward & Downey (with a colleague from Tinsleys) in 1884. The bulk of its output was fiction, many in the three-decker format.[9] As well as fiction, Ward & Downey published translations from the French, journalistic memoirs, histories of the Restoration period and of early Georgian London. The firm published a biography of Gladstone and several travel and exploration titles, many of them by members of the Irish 'old Bohemia'. More specifically Irish titles included Lady Wilde's *Ancient Legends, Mystic Charms and Superstitions of Ireland*, William Daunt's *Eighty-five Years of Irish History 1800–85*, and a Waterford-based novel by Downey himself. In the early 1890s, Downey was a well-respected figure on the London publishing scene with extensive and friendly trade contacts. He was also a notable figure in the Irish literary scene in London. He was an early member of the Southwark Literary Club, and joined the Clapham branch of the Parnellite Irish National League in 1890, later becoming a vice-president of the branch.

His business unfortunately was not going well, for he had expanded too rapidly, resulting in a cash flow crisis in 1890. Accountants were called in and they proposed that some of the major creditors be formally asked for an extension of credit. Clearly, the writing was on the wall, and relations with his partner deteriorated. The company limped on, but the end, in 1893, was clearly foreseen. The idea lurking behind Gavan Duffy's plans, of his managing a well-capitalised Irish National Publishing Company, must have seemed extremely attractive.

Downey was not present at the initial meeting of the Irish Literary Society in December 1891 in Yeats' house in Bedford Park, but was invited to the first committee meeting in January 1892. With his intimate experience of the current publishing scene and his Irish background (including his Parnellite sympathies) he seemed the ideal man to steer Gavan Duffy's scheme to success.

Unfortunately, there were two obstacles. The first was a conviction by a group of younger men centred on W.B. Yeats that not only should Dublin, not London, be the intellectual capital of the revival, but that a quite different set of books than those envisaged by Gavan Duffy should be chosen. Yeats set up the Irish-based National Literary Society in 1892, one of whose objectives was the establishment of a network of reading rooms (a conspicuous success-point of the Young Ireland movement before the Famine), to overcome the well-known reluctance of the Irish to buy books. Yeats was busy preparing his own 'Library of Ireland' to be published by his current publisher, T. Fisher Unwin, with himself as general editor (Unwin insisted on this, apparently). Yeats was confident that he could deliver 500 Irish subscribers, in which case Unwin would publish the balance (possibly with an Irish co-publisher). The tantalising possibility beckoned of getting 800 subscribers, in which case they could do without Unwin.[10]

Meanwhile, Downey pressed on with preparing a publishing plan for Duffy. He envisaged a company operating from London ('it would', he thought, 'seriously damage the sales of any books in Great Britain to have an Irish publisher's imprint'). The core of the plan was to publish one book a month, priced at 1*s*, and it was hoped that US rights would also prove lucrative. The average print run would be 5,000 copies. It was clear to him, however, that though the Library of Ireland might be the jewel in the crown, by themselves twelve volumes a year (the titles of which he had not yet had sight of) were unlikely to generate enough income to sustain a publishing house. Thus was added another *casus belli* over and above the rumbling arguments between London and Dublin as the centre, between the old men and the young, between Gavan Duffy and Yeats. (The argument between Duffy and Yeats had nothing to do with what might appeal to the Irish people: both sides were only interested in what they thought of as 'sound national doctrine', to use Yeats' phrase.)[11]

With his experience, Downey knew that in the current conditions a publishing house needed a lot of titles: Ward & Downey published forty-seven new books in their first year of operation in 1885, rising to eighty in 1887. Heinemann published sixteen titles in his very first list in October 1890, and by 1893 had dozens in print; Mills & Boon, then publishing a general and educational list, signed 123 contracts in their first year of operation. In the following generation Gollancz's first list in 1928 had sixty-four titles.[12]

In a memorandum written at this time, Downey clearly had in mind a general publishing house (not unlike Ward & Downey, perhaps) based in London with an office in Dublin.[13] The company was to be called the College Green Publishing Company with a head office in London and a base also in Dublin; the capital requirement was estimated at £3,000. Gavan Duffy's particular interests would be met by the 'College Green Library' of books of his own selection. As Downey saw it, the company would thrive by:

> … publishing good and popular books by Irish authors and books and other publications dealing with subjects of special interest to Irish readers at home and abroad. While dealing with such publications it is intended that the majority of the books issued by the company shall be of general interest.

In a statement to prospective investors he wrote:

> We should be obliged to seek for profit out of books which, though they not be objectionable to Irish readers, would be of a less patriotic or ennobling character than the books which Sir Charles indicated in his address to the Irish Literary Society.

There were other proposals: a National Publishing Company with a capital of £10,000 was one and an Irish National Publishing Company was another. All fell before a combination of Gavan Duffy's non-commerciality (especially his deep reluctance to support his Library of Ireland with popular titles) and the intense literary politics of 1890s Dublin.[14] Yeats knew that the heavily academic flavour of some of Duffy's proposed titles would not do, but his priority was that both the London and Dublin Irish Literary Societies should reflect his views, which they had scant intention of doing. Gavan Duffy had no sense of what was likely to appeal to an Irish or any other reader, as was demonstrated by his choice of Thomas Davis's *Patriot Parliament* as his first title. Between a rock and a hard place, the 'College Green Publishing Company' proposal collapsed. Disappointed, Downey expressed his willingness to help with a reduced venture, but felt that it would be better 'if arrangements are made with a respectable London publishing firm.' Eventually, *Patriot Parliament* and eleven other titles were published by T. Fisher Unwin in London and co-published in Dublin by Sealy, Bryers & Walker.[15] In a crushing review, Yeats described Davis' work as suitable for 'the transactions of a learned society'. 'Pages upon pages of Acts of Parliament,' he continued, 'may be popular literature on the planet Neptune, or chillier Uranus, but our quick-blooded globe has altogether different needs.'[16]

Downey remained in London, continuing to publish on his own account throughout the 1890s. His best-known title was Somerville & Ross's great work *The Real Charlotte*. In 1902 he became the publishing manager for the phenomenally successful *T.P.'s Weekly*. This role ended with a bitter row in 1904 and so, after twenty-five years in London, Downey decided to come home.

There was a brief possibility that he would be able to buy a connection with the old publishing firm of James Duffy, where one of his sons was working. The plan was to buy out the existing directors, including one Thomas O'Carroll who, in a letter to Downey, described his fellow directors as 'no more fit to run a publishing house than run the British Empire'.[17] He and Downey planned to create 'a company that will be worthy of the title Catholic publisher', as O'Carroll put it. This ambition needed money and a lot of it: £3,000 to buy out the Duffy family, £1,600 to clear existing liabilities and some £6,400 for working capital.[18] By contrast, 'experienced men' had assured Gavan Duffy that the necessary capital for the publishing house he was proposing in the 1890s 'will not exceed £5,000', and this was the sum he proposed to raise among expatriates in the US and Britain, as well as in Ireland itself, to establish the Irish National Publishing Company.[19] For comparison, the initial investment for Heinemann in 1890 was £500, Mills & Boon in 1908 was £1,000, and Maunsel in 1905 was £2,000. There was no possibility that Downey's contacts would put up anything like the sum proposed for the new company, so the scheme collapsed. Indeed, so large were the sums that O'Carroll demanded that one wonders if he was altogether serious. He, after all, once wrote to Downey, 'I often think there is no good in publishing at best.' In 1906 Downey bought the *Waterford News* from an old school friend and settled down as a newspaper editor and proprietor in that city until his death in 1937, converting his Parnellite affections first to Sinn Féin and then to Fianna Fáil.

Irish Book Publishing in the 1890s

The dominant position of London as a publishing centre certainly depressed the opportunities for Irish-based publishing. This was, as we have seen, marked in the important category of fiction, where in the 1890s a mere twenty-eight novels were published in Ireland as opposed to over 600 Irish interest tales published in London. Nonetheless, Dublin was one of the four non-London centres of book production (the others were Edinburgh, Oxford and Cambridge) that with London contributed the vast majority of late Victorian book publishing.

A crucial difference between London and non-London publishing was whether the house had its own printing. One historian has written that from the nineteenth century, 'except for the two universities, no major [British] publisher was its own printer,'[20] a widely accepted generalisation which is undermined by such publisher-printers as Cassell, Collins, Dent, Eyre & Spottiswoode, Heinemann and Hutchinson. It was certainly not true of non-metropolitan British houses such as Walter Scott of Newcastle, publisher of two of Yeats' early works; Arrowsmith of Bristol, publishers of such famous titles as *The Diary of a Nobody*, *Three Men in a Boat*, *The Prisoner of Zenda* and *The Man who was Thursday*; Gale & Polden of Aldershot, specialist in books for the Army, and military matters generally; nor the educational publisher E.J. Arnold of Leeds, nor of A. H. Bullen, one of Yeats' publishers..[21] The generalisation was also not true of Dublin publishing houses of the 1890s, all of which had either a printing works or a bookshop, and sometimes both.

The combination of printing and publishing reflects the size of the non-metropolitan market. It is likely also that the scarcity of book production skills among Irish general printers (a direct consequence of the small number of books being produced) prompted Irish publishers to maintain their own facilities. However that may be, the possession of plant changes the economics of the house. A stand-alone publisher requires no more than an office, a manuscript and a pencil. A print shop requires machines with facilities for setting, printing, folding and probably binding. This requires a more or less considerable investment. Once up and running, the configurations run to a different yearly rhythm. A publishing house can survive happily on two bursts of activity (and cash income) in spring and autumn, but is dependent on successfully riding the vagaries of public taste. The costly machines of a print shop require to be fed with activity fifty-two weeks a year, but can survive on a stolid diet of jobbing print (posters, letterheads, visiting cards, invoice forms, circulars, forms, tickets, stock lists) as their predecessors had done since the beginning of printing. Moreover, anecdotal evidence confirms that the production tail tended to wag the publishing dog. Michael Gill well remembers how in his father's day the busyness or otherwise of M.H. Gill's print shop (which did virtually no outside work) dictated print runs, binding-up decisions and even whether a book should be published.

There were at least twelve regular book publishers in Dublin in the 1890–1910 period (see Table 2). There were also publishers in Belfast (typically specialising in evangelical religion), Cork and Waterford. Some of M.H. Gill's titles are described as coming from the latter city, where they had a bookshop on the Quay. According to the catalogue of the National Library of Ireland (which formally opened its doors in July 1890) twelve publishers produced just under 2,000 titles in the twenty years to 1909.

This is undoubtedly an underestimate of total activity. Then as now, anyone can have a book produced and (perhaps) taken up by commercial distribution systems. Many such books, of course, would never have been intended for more than private or local distribution, and, though a curious and interesting part of the book culture, would never have been seen by the National Library cataloguers. No doubt the same dynamics of enthusiasm, local piety and human vanity obtained in the 1890–1910 period as at present, so we assume that there were at least another thousand titles or so to add to those produced by professionals.[22]

The five-year totals from the twelve active publishers show a noticeable quickening of activity after the turn of the century. In every case except Eason's the output in the ten years after 1900 is markedly greater than in the ten years before. M.H. Gill, and Sealy, Bryers & Walker doubled their output, while Duffy, which had been quite dim, trebled theirs, from thirty-four titles before 1900 to ninety-four after. The growth was sustained up to the outbreak of the war.

The oldest of the Irish publishing houses of the 1890–1909 period was James Duffy, whose founding legend and heyday in the 1850s we have seen in an earlier chapter. By the 1890s James Duffy himself was long dead, and the firm was concentrating on printing, publishing no more than a few titles a year. The publishing gene had not descended from the founding father.

Nonetheless, Duffy's continued to publish, and at a quickening pace in the new century. In the 1890s, there were editions of the poetry of Mangan and Griffin, many Catholic religious items and lives of Fr Mathew, Kickham, Mitchel and Emmet. More politically, it published in 1900 Arthur Griffith's *The Sinn Féin Policy* (new edition 1906) and later D. P. Moran's *Philosophy of Irish Ireland* and Arthur Clery's *Idea of a Nation*.

Table 2. Books published by selected Irish publishers by subject 1890–1909

Publishers	*Subject*	*1890–94*	*1895–99*	*1900–04*	*1905–09*	*Total*
Duffy	General, Education, Catholic	19	15	42	52	128
Gill	General, Education, Catholic	92	89	147	210	538
Hodges Figgis	Academic	69	48	78	82	277
Thom	Law, Reference	44	29	31	61	165
Eason's	Law, Reference	13	10	10	5	38
Talbot	Literature	4	0	7	1	12
E. Ponsonby	Law	4	16	12	10	42
Maunsel	Literature	0	0	2	121	123
Sealy, Bryers & Walker	General	38	60	97	96	291
Browne & Nolan	General, Education, Catholic	31	48	74	58	211
Blackie	Education	9	30	39	29	107
Dun Emer/ Cuala	Literary	0	0	8	14	22
Total		323	345	547	739	1954

Source: National Library of Ireland Catalogue

Notes: Includes all items catalogued as 'books', which is sometimes a broad understanding of the term (e.g. Cuala's broadsheets, catalogues). Totals are taken from the simplest version of the name, which inevitably yields more items than full versions e.g. 'Gill' yields 794 items 1890–1919, 'M. H. Gill' only 521. The total for Maunsel includes 5 items for Maunsell (sic).

Browne & Nolan was a printing house based in Nassau Street which produced the occasional publication from the 1850s onwards. An early effort was a tourist guide to Cork, Queenstown and Blarney (the publication of a guide book was also the starting point for another of our publishers, Sealy, Bryers & Walker). It had good contacts with the hierarchy, acting as the printer/publisher of the *Irish Ecclesiastical Bulletin*. It was widely known for its series of diaries, a classic solution (adopted also, for instance, by Collins in Glasgow) to the desire to reconcile the rhythms of print and publishing. By 1890, it was publishing a rather miscellaneous uncoordinated list of economic commentaries, agricultural reports and items of a semi-official nature such as the Maynooth Centenary volumes; there were reprints of Creasey's *Decisive Battles* and Mitchel's *Jail Journal*, the librarian Thomas Lyster's *Poems*, the first edition of Stephen Brown's *Ireland in Fiction*, some titles by Canon Sheehan and local history books about Dublin and Armagh.

M.H. Gill was another house that traced its origins to the mid-nineteenth century. Chapter 1 has recorded its early history. The founder, Michael Henry, died in 1879 and his gifted son Henry Joseph took over. H.J. Gill was a linguist and an early member of the Society for the Preservation of the Irish Language; he was also a Dublin councillor and an MP. He did not neglect the business, however, as one historian of the firm wrote unctuously:

> During the closing decade of his exceptionally busy life, Henry J. Gill may be said to have concerned himself more especially with sustaining the high Christian tone of his firm's general publications, extending its already wide range of books of a religious nature – to which he added a special edition of the Roman breviary – and consolidating its business standing and connections not only in the provinces but all over England and Scotland and throughout the entire Catholic world indeed.[23]

Gill also published the Gaelic League's publications, including most of Douglas Hyde's output.[24] He was also the patentor of a widely used machine for drying and smoothing letterpress printed sheets.[25]

On H.J. Gill's death in 1903, his son Michael Joseph took over, expanding the firm's stock into devotional and ecclesiastical goods. The great nineteenth-century surge of Catholic and Protestant building, which had more than trebled the number of churches in the country, was now over, and the proud proprietors began to look to embellishing their new structures. In the early 1900s Gill established a brasswork factory (for candlesticks, lecterns, monstrances, etc.) and a carpentry shop (for cribs, confessionals and other church furnishings) to add to the basic portfolio of bookshop, publishing and printing, and ecclesiastical repository. His approach to book publishing can be judged from his little book *Public Libraries for Ireland*, in which he deplored, 'that great invasion of ephemeral English reading matter ... the chief attraction of which seems to be cheapness, joined to bulk, luridness and exaggerated romance'. *The Catholic Bulletin* was first published in 1911. It was originally designed to provide review information about books suitable for the Catholic sensibility; only later did it took on a rancorous Catholic nationalism. Michael Joseph Gill died unmarried in Rome in 1913, in his early 40s. He was succeeded by his brother Richard, who continued the devotional, educational and nationalist publishing traditions of the house but chose to devote his personal energies to introducing progressive methods and up-to-date machinery in the factory.[26]

Sealy, Bryers & Walker's exact trajectory is still to be thoroughly unravelled. The firm traced its origins to the establishment of a papermill in Jones's Road by James Walker and his partner John Sealy. According to his obituary in *The Irish Times* in 1915, Walker was a Presbyterian socialist Home Ruler with whom William Morris stayed when he came to Dublin.[27] The paper business failed, but the land was sold successfully to the Dublin Whiskey Distillery. Walker and Sealy established a colour printing business, and later acquired the Dublin Steam Printing Company, with George Bryers as its manager. By 1898, when the business was decimated by a fire, Alex Thom, the Dublin Steam Printing Company and Sealy, Bryers & Walker were all operating from conjoint premises in Middle Abbey Street.[28] In reports of the fire, which put over 100 people out of work, George Bryers was described as the senior partner in the concern. Walker retained an interest in his colour printers in Jones' Road, which was appointed colour printers to the Queen in 1900. There was also a papermill in Clonliffe Road specialising in papers for the grocery trade, which closed in 1893.

By the 1890s George Bryers was evidently the driving force behind Sealy, Bryers & Walker's publishing ambitions. It had started in the early 1870s with a tourist guide, *Walker's Handbook of Ireland*. In 1879, the Dublin Steam Printing company published an *Irish Agricultural Almanac* ('brought out in admirable style' thought *The Irish Times*),[29] and a centenary edition of *Moore's Melodies*. The following year it produced an *Irish Football Annual*. Publishing under the Sealy, Bryers & Walker imprint began in the early 1880s and by the 1890s it was publishing ten new books a year, many in a clear response to bookbuyers' growing interest in Irish affairs. Sales numbers are of course unavailable, so we cannot quantify this strength. Sealy, Bryers & Walker published on the land question, on Parnell and such books as Ferguson's *Story of Ireland before the Conquest*, and Hyde's *Story of Early Irish Celtic Literature*. It was the chosen local publisher of T. Fisher Unwin's New Irish Library. In 1890, the business was reconstructed under the general name of Alex Thom, taking in the educational publisher Sullivan Brothers and Sealy, Bryers & Walker. The capital of the new business was £150,000 which was three times, as we shall see, the sum required for the 1910 flotation of the Educational Company of Ireland. The prospectus announced that the three companies had a combined annual profit of £16,000.[30] George Bryers remained the chief executive. Later in the 1890s, Thom took over the law publisher and printer John Falconer (whose destruction of the sheets of Joyce's *Dubliners* has earned him some posthumous notoriety).

In his 1897 application for membership of the Royal Irish Academy, George Bryers described himself as a publisher, 'actively interested in the works of Irish archaeologists and historians', and 'conversant with Polite Literature'. Although these qualifications now seem weak, among his sponsors for membership were Canon O'Hanlon, the popular historian P.W. Joyce, John Healy, later Archbishop of Tuam, and the medical writer John Knott.[31] As well as a highly successful businessman and publisher, Bryers was clearly a convivial man, a leading light in the Companions of St Patrick and a founder of what became the Protestant Home Rule Association.[32]

In the 1890s, the firm published (under the Sealy, Bryers & Walker imprint) key Revival texts such as Standish O'Grady's *Flight of the Eagle*. The new century saw Sealy, Bryers & Walker adding to its publication list Yeats' first book *Mosada* (1886), Redmond's *Historical Addresses* (1898) and Gavan Duffy's *Life of Thomas Davis* (1895), multiple volumes of Eugene O'Growney's *Simple Lessons in Irish* (a title which was also published by other houses, as was Griffith's *Resurrection of Hungary*) and *An Macaomh* (edited by Patrick Pearse and written by the masters and pupils of St Enda's School). Although several of the Irish publishers had Irish language titles, the main concentration of writing in Irish was from the Gaelic League, which in 1899 set up a publication committee to oversee this activity. In 1908, the League established An Cló-Chumann (later Clódhanna Teoranta) to deal with the growing number of circulars, pamphlets and books of all kinds.[33]

Sealy, Bryers & Walker had a general list, with history, notably D'Alton's *History of Ireland*, but which included books on Japan, Elizabethan England, law (the Workman's Compensation Act, the Old Age Pensions Act and the Law of Labourers), poetry (Samuel Ferguson and T.D. Sullivan) and even some practical science (electricity and a laboratory handbook).

A key aspect of the empire was the mighty Thom's *Directory* which had been published in Dublin since 1844. The historian of Irish almanacs, Edward Evans, wrote in 1897 that Thom's was a 'truly wonderful and useful production ... the most comprehensive and most finished statesman's manual in the kingdom'.[34] The directory was not completely reset every year, but after printing the type was cleaned and stored in long galleys to await reuse the following year. This had the negative effect that without specific notification, no correction would be made and data in one part of the directory (for instance, the street listing) could contradict that in others (such as the classified trades directory). At one time, postmen were offered a bonus to report changes of occupancy. A consequence of the devastating fire caused by the 1916 Rising was that, as a history of Thom's put it, 'every scrap of the Directory's type, including the contents of formes left standing for years, was reduced to molten lead ... the entire volume was reset from cover to cover.'[35]

Blackie, a Scottish educational printer-publisher, bought the rights to the multi-bestselling Vere Foster copybook, subject to the condition that the printing remained in Ireland. True to the contract, a printing company was established in Dublin (at No. 89 Talbot Street) which concentrated for twenty years on the copybooks. By the 1890s, however, Blackie had begun to explore publishing in other aspects of the educational market, producing thirty titles a year. It established a vigorous educational publishing programme, but after the turn of the century began to find that the political climate made business increasingly difficult. Under the influence of the Gaelic League, buyers were actively seeking books from Irish publishers.

In 1910, Blackie responded to this pressure by setting up a separate company called the Educational Publishing Company of Ireland which took over its educational publishing in Ireland. The local manager since 1895, W.G. Lyon, became managing director. The independent firm Fallon & Co. (managed by C.J. Fallon) was added to the mix.[36] Among the early subscribers to the £50,000 capital was Professor William Magennis, who had been with Fallon & Co. and acted as reader/editor to the new firm. The very substantial capital sum (£42,000 of which related to the value of the two firms being taken over) was caused by the physical plant acquired (e.g. typesetting and printing machinery) more than copyrights. A prospectus issued in March 1910 announced the new company:

> The business of the company will be to supply all the books and school equipment required at each stage of the educational journey from kindergarten to college. The literary advisors of the company are well known

> scholars, each an expert in the theory and practice of education … to ensure continuity of the business methods to which the amalgamating firms owed their success the new company will be under the management of Mr W.G. Lyon (late manager of Messrs Blackie & Son Irish Business) as Director, Mr C.J. Fallon (late manager Fallon & Co.) and William Fitzsimmons Company Secretary.[37]

In 1919, the Educational Company bought out Blackie's shareholding altogether.[38] On his death in 1938, Fitzsimmons was described by *The Irish Times* as 'the guiding light' of the company[39], but from the archive it seems clear that, at least until the 1930s, Lyon was the editorial driver.

Over the years, Blackie had published the occasional general title under an imprint called Talbot Press.[40] Among these in the 1890s were some titles from Standish O'Grady and a book of translations from Irish by P.W. Joyce. In 1913, the new company formalised this and in 1917 incorporated a company of that name and plunged into a vigorous general publishing programme that, with Maunsel's similarly active engagement, became the key features of the pre-1922 publishing scene.

Hodges Figgis was Ireland's academic publisher. Its splendid letterhead proclaimed the firm 'Booksellers and Publishers to the University, the Royal Irish Academy, Royal Dublin Society, National Library of Ireland, Queen's Colleges, Law Society of Kings Inns, Royal College of Science and agents for the sale of Ordnance Survey maps' – a clean sweep. For the first two decades of the twentieth century, Hodges Figgis published some fifteen titles a year, mostly academic books, including classics, Celtic studies and mathematics and also, perhaps unexpectedly, the aggressively anti-Catholic barrister Michael McCarthy's *Five Years in Ireland*[41] and *Priests and People*. It had a strong line in natural history, including Colgan's *Flora of Co. Dublin*, Praeger's *Topographical Botany* and the remarkable series of sixty-seven reports from the Clare Island survey (1911–15).

Irish publishers of this period have typically been condemned as unenthusiastic about, if not actively hostile to, the Literary Revival, especially in the matter of publishing poetry. This is not quite accurate (though it is true that Yeats certainly managed to alienate the senior staff of M.H. Gill, not to mention senior members of the book trade). As we have seen, most Irish houses did publish poetry from time to time and very often titles indicating some degree of political involvement. But for commercial publishers with salaries, rents and machine costs to pay, modern poetry was/is rarely attractive, even if the (typically middle-aged) publishers' tastes had run in that direction.

Literary taste tends to lag a generation: thus when Tennyson began his publishing career in the 1830s his books sold in the low hundreds, while the older generation of Byron and Scott sold in thousands. By the 1890s, Tennyson, published by Macmillan since 1884, was selling between 15,000 and 20,000 copies a year.[42] By contrast, the two volumes of the *Book of the Rhymers Club* (one of which included the first airing in book form of 'The Lake Isle of Inisfree') sold 350 and 450 copies respectively. The bestselling new poets of the 1890s were not the Celtic Revivalists, but the manly pair of Rudyard Kipling (with *Barrackroom Ballads*) and Henry Newbolt (whose first book *Admirals All* sold 30,000 copies in twelve years).[43]

The numerous publishers Yeats dealt with before the agent A.P. Watt steered him in the direction of Macmillan in 1903 make it clear that even for a poet of Yeats' calibre and extensive London contacts getting published was difficult. The early pages of his bibliography include the names of Sealy, Bryers & Walker; Kegan Paul; T. Fisher Unwin; Lawrence & Bullen; Maunsel; Elkin Mathews; Quaritch; John Lane the Bodley Head; Warner Laurie; the Shakespeare Head Press; Walter Scott and even M.H. Gill (*Poems and Ballads of Young Ireland*), not to mention US publishers.[44]

One of the few publishers who managed to make poetry pay was Elkin Mathews of London, who in a long career produced books by Yeats, Joyce, Ezra Pound, Oscar Wilde and William Carlos Williams. He produced books in finely printed, handsomely bound and illustrated short-run or limited editions, or little books with few pages selling for 1*s* or 1*s* 6*d*. Mathews combined enthusiasm for literary publishing with the second desideratum for contemporary authors: a feeling for the book beautiful.

In Ireland two houses in the decade after 1900, Dun Emer (founded 1903 and renamed Cuala in 1908) and Maunsel (founded in 1905) set themselves to respond to the Literary Revival, in addition to Sealy, Bryers & Walker's not uncreditable efforts.

Dun Emer, later Cuala, was a private press run by W.B. Yeats' sister Elizabeth. Private presses, part of the Arts and Crafts movement, were a reaction to two forces. Firstly, there was a surge in the Western world in favour of individual craftsmanship as against 'soulless' mass production techniques. Secondly, in the book trade itself, the long hunt to provide ever cheaper books had driven down production standards. At the lower end of the market, books were printed in tiny cramped faces, often in two columns; setting, paper quality, machine work and binding were often poor. Between them these led to an alertness to the physical form of the book on the part of a few publishers and printers and some authors.

Leading the private press movement was William Morris with the Kelmscott Press, which flourished from 1891 to 1898 – though to an eye not besotted with medievalism he often produced pages as densely unreadable in their way as the worst shilling shocker. He was followed by names well-known to collectors such as Vine (1896) Doves (*c.* 1900) and Shakespeare Head (*c.* 1904).

Printing and book production was only one aspect of the Dun Emer mission 'to find work for Irish hands in the making of beautiful things'.[45] Like most private presses, Dun Emer/Cuala were not really original publishers, though they certainly published first editions of some of brother W.B.'s books. Their prime concern was with creating beautiful printed objects. 'Ours can never compete with cheap manufactured things,' wrote Elizabeth Yeats, 'they sell as exclusive and expressive things.'[46] As the *Freeman's Journal* put it, they 'aim less at unearthing new writers than at the artistic presentation of authors who like Mr W.B. Yeats have established their fame'.[47] This was typical of private presses, which were normally satisfied with exquisite reproductions of old favourites such as Chaucer, Dante and Shakespeare. In forty years of activity, writes one authority, 'the one and only event of literary significance in the history of the Ashendene Press' was its issue of some verses by the Poet Laureate Robert Bridges.[48]

Cuala did not advertise new books and did not send out many of the titles for review. The press was content to sell to an established band of collectors, principally based in the US and Britain: 'what is sold in Ireland,' wrote Elizabeth Yeats to P.S. O'Hegarty in 1939, 'would not pay one of my workers'.[49] Titles often sold out on the day of publication, but there was no thought of reprinting. Brochures announcing forthcoming titles were sent to the faithful, often containing long lists of previous publications, most of which were out of print.

In practice, commerciality was restricted by Cuala's hand printing equipment, a Demy Albion similar to one used in Kelmscott and subsequently by Dolmen. Clare Hutton writes: 'The combination of a complete lack of business sense on the part of Elizabeth Yeats with the imposition of some rather rigid controls by her brother [it was he who vetoed the despatch of review copies] resulted in continual problems with profit management at the press.'[50]

As a result, as Michael Yeats put it, 'my father was constantly expected to come to the rescue when financial difficulties arose.'[51] Clare Hutton continues:

> The fact that W.B. Yeats was prepared to invest so much capital in the venture suggests its profound importance to him. As editor to the press he had

> multiple motivations: controlling a literary principality, publishing [early versions] of his own work, creating a context of taste in which his works could be appreciated, and fulfilling an obligation to his family.[52]

Between 1903 and 1916 the press produced twenty-four titles, and a further thirty-eight up to Elizabeth Yeats' death in 1940. The great majority of these were either by or edited by W.B. Yeats.[53] This rate of production (three books every two years) was common to private presses: Doves Press produced forty-nine titles in seventeen years, and Ashendene forty-one books in forty years (a marked contrast to the rate of production thought commercially viable by knowledgeable insiders such as Edmund Downey). Only four of Cuala's titles contained more than 100 pages; runs were usually 250 or 350 copies, often, as we have seen, sold entirely to a coterie of collectors. With few exceptions the books were of a standard size and format, 210 x 145 mm (virtually the modern A5) and set in 14 pt Caslon and hand printed on substantial rag-based mould-made paper, with a weight in modern terms of 150 to 160 g/m^2 (i.e. notably heavier than the plate section in a modern book).[54] Each book took months to produce, so they were expensive, at 10*s* 6*d* (by contrast, two thirds of Maunsel's books were priced at 2*s* 6*d* or less).

Although strongly affected by the literary and artistic movements of the day, Maunsel set out from the beginning to be a commercial house. Because of its special position in respect of the Literary Revival, Maunsel has been written about more extensively than any other Irish publisher. It has been covered in three theses,[55] in Edward MacLysaght's memoirs (he was a director), and numerous articles, not least because of the abortive attempt to publish Joyce's *Dubliners* and the row over Synge's complete works.

Maunsel emerged from the Irish National Theatre of which George Roberts (who became managing director of the new company) was secretary. Initially under the name of Whaley & Co. the firm began to publish titles by Æ (George Russell), Seamus O'Sullivan (a member of the new company) and Standish O'Grady. Later it persuaded the young Joseph Maunsel Hone (who was to become Yeats' first biographer) to invest £2,000 and become chairman of the newly named Maunsel & Co. The literary advisor was the experienced Stephen Gwynn who was to retire when he became Redmondite MP for Galway in 1906. As Jane Mahony puts it: 'Maunsel made a promising start. It had energetic, well-connected directors, initial working capital, a publishing strategy reflecting the zeitgeist, a co-publishing partner in England and the support of Yeats and the other two members of the Abbey triumvirate, Lady Gregory and J.M. Synge.'[56]

The Abbey Plays continued to sell, and for the first few years Maunsel provided a new opportunity for an exciting range of writers from Yeats (*Poems 1899–1905*), Æ, Padraic Colum, Shan Bullock, Thomas Kettle, Susan Mitchell and even the viceroy's wife, Lady Aberdeen.

Roberts, however, was a difficult and disorganised man and frequently quarrelled with both authors and well-wishers. He argued with St John Greer Ervine (regarding the contents of his book on Carson), Lady Gregory (over the payment of royalties) Joyce (regarding the publication of *Dubliners*), Sean O'Casey (regarding payment for his book on the Citizen Army), Yeats and the executors of J.M. Synge (regarding the contents of the *Collected Works of J.M. Synge*). As Padraic Colum noted: 'there are people who study how to win friends and influence people; George Roberts knew how to lose friends and alienate people.'[57] On the other hand, the aesthetic quality of the books being published was a considerable improvement on the uninspired fare normally produced by Irish publishers. Indeed, from his memoir published years later in *The Irish Times*, one might surmise that he might have been happier dealing only with typesetting and print:

> I found a disused stable situated in a mews with slum surroundings that was within my meagre means. And there I saw my dream come true. I designed the layout of the books and watched every detail of the setting and machining and without any previous experience and with only the knowledge I had picked up from my dealings with other printers I set out gaily to produce a book that connoisseurs would welcome. And they did. I found a vacant stable that after some reconstruction would only just accommodate a Payne Double Royal Wharfedale but there was very little room to get round the machine. Had I known more about printing I doubt if I would have attempted it, but there it was, I plunged into it and being in I struggled hard to achieve success.[58]

By 1910, Hone had retreated from active involvement with the firm and Roberts had enraged Yeats by insisting on publishing articles by Synge in a *Collected Works*, that Yeats thought unworthy. 'With the loss of Yeats' advocacy,' writes Jane Mahony, 'Maunsel's position as the pre-eminent publishers of the Irish literary revival was fatally damaged.'[59] After long negotiations and much messing by Roberts, the American publishers, infuriated by Roberts' delays and procrastination, went ahead with the project for Synge's *Collected Works* on their own, thus depriving Maunsel of the financial return on which the project was costed.

The saga of Joyce's *Dubliners,* and what now seems exaggerated sensitivity to the *amour propre* of the dead King Edward VI and other scurrilities, is an oft-told tale. By the time *Dubliners* got to Maunsel it had gone the rounds: Grant Richards, John Lane, Heinemann, Constable, Elkin Mathews and others had read and rejected the stories. The manuscript was sent to Joseph Hone in 1908 and passed to Roberts a year later. Roberts issued a contract and seems to have typeset and even printed 1,000 sets of sheets, yet was still seeking certain cuts. Relations with Joyce became increasingly acerbic. Then, two years after they were printed, the sheets were destroyed, apparently by diktat from John Falconer, the head of the printing firm.[60]

In the years before the Rising, publishing emphasis moved to Nationalist titles from authors such as Pearse, Connolly, MacSwiney, Darrell Figgis and Joseph Mary Plunkett. Maunsel established a branch in London and a connection with Allen & Unwin. The firm published 132 titles between 1910 and 1916, hardly enough to sustain itself, even with the addition (from 1910) of typesetting and printing equipment. By 1916, the Great War was adding to the pressure: falling sales, paper shortages and inflated costs made the financial situation desperate, and liquidation loomed. And then, as we shall see in the next chapter, came the Rising, the destruction of the firm's offices and plant in Abbey Street and an extremely beneficent Compensation Committee.

Though not included in the figures above, the output of the Catholic Truth Society is in some ways the most characteristic publishing venture of the whole period up to 1960. The Society was initiated in June 1899 by Dr Michael O'Riordan, a priest from Limerick. Almost the only popular reading matter available in Ireland, he declared, was, 'the enormous quantity of literature of a questionably good and of an unquestionably bad character sent over from England week by week.' The only way out of this danger was, 'a supply of reading at once suitable and attractive'. The existing Catholic Truth Society of England was doing good work, it was thought, but its publications were not focused on Irish needs. (Publications from the British CTS discussing the English coronation oath or the status of the Church of England underlined the point.) O'Riordan's idea was quickly taken up; the Bishop of Waterford, backed by Cardinal Logue, proposed that a distinct Irish Society be established immediately, and this was done.[61]

The series was launched in June 1900 with a batch of twenty-five pamphlets, all between twenty-four and thirty-two pages, saddle stitched and priced at 1*d*. The breadth of the organisers' ambition was quickly revealed: the first twenty-five publications included fifteen books that were biographical and historical, five fiction and three social science. There was only one title described as 'devotional and doctrinal'. Distributed through 800 or more church boxes (grandly referred to as 'branches'), the pamphlets sold 650,000 in the first year. The success did not go unnoticed: by 1896 the educational publisher Fallon & Co. had launched its Catholic Home Library with lives of St Patrick and Oliver Plunkett at 1*d* each.

Despite the enormous sales, the Society's finances remained shaky and dependent on external donations, until an administrative wizard, Frank O'Reilly, left the Irish Post Office and became secretary in 1918. His first step was to double the price of the pamphlets, to 2*d*, which initially hit the sales badly, but they soon revived and the finances of the Society were established on firmer grounds. Sales continued to rise thereafter, reaching a peak of over two million copies in 1947.[62] Some years later, O'Reilly's administrative abilities were vigorously manifested by his organisation, firstly, of the 1929 celebrations of the centenary of Catholic Emancipation and then, in 1932, on a dramatic scale, in his running of the Eucharistic Conference.

Dublin Bookselling

The first meeting of a newly-formed Dublin Booksellers Association was held in Eason's in 1896. (The Dublin Booksellers Society of the 1840s, mentioned in Chapter 1, had long since run into the sand.) William McGee of No. 18 Nassau Street was the first chairman. McGee had been bookselling at No. 18 since 1859. The members present were Browne & Nolan, Christian Knowledge Association, Combridge, Dublin Tract Repository, J. Duffy, Eason's, Educational Depository, Fannin, M.H. Gill, John Greene, Hodges Figgis, Wm McGee, E. Ponsonby, Sibley, Robert Stewart. The key resolution (29 May) was, 'that the Dublin bookselling trade will not alter the present practice of allowing only 2*d* in the 1/- discount to the general public'.[63] No reference to the ongoing net book debate is recorded in the minutes.

After relapsing and being revived with the same membership in 1902 (perhaps under the stimulus of the formation in 1901 of a Belfast branch of the Associated Booksellers) the Association immediately embarked on a controversy with the department store Clerys which insisted on offering the public 3*d* in the 1*s* discount. The Association appealed to London to cease to supply 'price cutting drapers and others' and the current John Murray came over in an unsuccessful attempt to resolve the dispute. A year later, arbitration by W.H. Lecky persuaded his publisher Longmans to cease to supply Clerys and this was effectively the end of the long dispute. In 1904, Clerys finally accepted the restrictions of the Net Book Agreement.

The great talking point in the post-1900 trade, once the aftershocks of the Net Book Agreement had been sorted out, was the rapidly reducing price of books. As the last of the three-deckers came out, in 1895, new novels began to be published at 6*s*, but a quarter of new books were priced between 1*s* and 2*s*, and a further quarter between 2*s* and 3*s* 6*d*. Many reprint series were priced at 6*d* a volume and so many of these indeed were there that it was rather bitterly said, 'you may buy twenty books by dead men at the price of one work by a living man'.[64]

The next stage was for new novels to be priced at 2*s* or less. A wholesaler reported to the London magazine *The Bookman* in 1898 that 6*s* novels (the new norm) were being swamped by sixpenny reprints, some with runs of as many as 100,000 copies.[65] The trade looked on in dismay at this struggle between the new and the cheap, wondering how on earth it was going to be able to treble its sales to make the same revenue. In 1909, taking the authors' point of view, *The Irish Times* commented: 'it is generally established that 25 per cent on the published price is the maximum royalty that a 6*s* novel will stand.'[66] This royalty was hardly obtainable for the 'flood' of new novels published at 2*s* or less. In the end, the rising costs of the war period put a stop to this phenomenon, but it can well be understood how, when Allan Lane proposed his 6*d* paperback series in the mid 1930s, the older men in the trade remembered the pre-Great War controversies and looked at the venture askance.

It was clear from the statistics of books published that there were more titles in the market than ever before (though how many copies of each titles were being sold was unknown). In January 1911, *The Irish Times* published a patronising survey of the book scene:

> Last year was not a happy one for those who cater for the amusement of the public … in these degenerate days there are few things that people go without so readily as books, the public at large is little interested, for despite some improvement on recent years the public at large still does not buy books. [Yet] more books were printed in 1910 than in the preceding year. The most surprising tendency of last year in the book trade has been the decline in the production of fiction … the other feature of the year as far as fiction is concerned has been the production of new novels by well-known authors at extraordinarily cheap rates. These ventures have been largely experimental in their nature and we do not know how far they have

> been financially successful. The novel at a price varying from seven-pence to two shillings is certainly a great boon to the traveller and holiday maker ... the other surprising decrease on the year is that of the publication of history and biography ... The general reader is so densely ignorant that works which give him some knowledge of history are commendable even if the prescription has to include an excessive supply of jam to disguise the taste of the powder ... Religion and philosophy, law, social science and education works all show increase. On the other hand, the greatest growth of all is in the department of poetry and drama. It is easy to make the sarcastic comment that nothing great has been achieved in this department. We in Ireland do not treat our poets quite so badly as they do in England, but we are bad enough. We are still too apt to speak of a poet as a 'minor poet' in contemptuous terms ... a man who writes verse nowadays is labelled poet, and if he is not a great poet he is looked upon as a failure and something of a fraud. Under such circumstances the plucky authors of these four hundred new volumes of poetry and drama are much to be congratulated.[67]

Between 1891 and 1906, *The Bookman* asked local booksellers to list 'the volumes they have found most popular' during the previous month.[68] There was no attempt to quantify sales, and this does present an interpretive problem. Respondents (whose records were certainly not designed to yield such data) could too easily succumb to a combination of local patriotism and a desire to move stock.[69] Two (unidentified) bookshops from Dublin reported sales in this way and revealed a reading public that was notably different in tastes from the metropolis. Reports from Scottish booksellers indicate some differences between Scotland and London, but Dublin tastes were apparently more markedly different.

In Dublin, non-fiction loomed large, accounting for more than 60 per cent of reported titles. Of non-fiction the key areas were religion (Catholic topics and religious biography) and Irish history and politics. One of the shops, reporting in 1893, noted, 'Irish language and literary societies are awakening renewed interest in their subjects, but as usual cheap novels and religious works are most read.' The November 1893 'bestsellers' listing, remarkably, had *only* Irish-interest books – including Hyde's *Love Songs of Connacht*, P.W. Joyce's *History of Ireland*, Cardinal Newman's *Meditations* and Yeats' *Irish Fairy and Folktales* – despite the increase in interest in Irish matters, this was not a likely statistic.

Irish authors especially mentioned were Canon Sheehan, Jane Barlow, Standish O'Grady and Rosa Mulholland. Rosa Mulholland's novels were described by Stephen Brown as 'intensely Catholic, though without anti-Protestant feeling, and intensely national'. They were published in London. Jane Barlow wrote mostly 'little tragedies and comedies about the Western peasantry', of which Stephen Brown declared 'she knew the minutest details as far as an outsider could know them'.[70] Of English authors, Marie Corelli, Rudyard Kipling, Conan Doyle and Robert Louis Stevenson were prominent, but there was much less evidence of such London trends as New Woman fiction, or works of the Kailyard (Scottish) school.

The numbers of titles published in Britain and Ireland (as recorded in the trade journal *Publishers' Circular)* continued to surge upward in the new century. Having been just over 7,000 in 1900, they reached over 10,000 in 1910 and peaked at 12,379 in 1913. The Great War stopped the gallop, with total publications dropping to fewer than 8,000 in 1918.[71] By this time, as we shall see, Irish social and political rhythms had begun to diverge from those of 'the mainland'.

4

Into the New State: From the Rising to the Thirties

Clustered as it was around the centre of city, it is no surprise that the publishing industry suffered severely from the destruction caused by the 1916 Rising. The worst damage came to offices and factories on the north side of Middle Abbey Street, where Eason's, the *Freeman's Journal*, the *Irish Independent*, Alex Thom, Maunsel and various directories were based. The great complex housing Sealy, Bryers & Walker, Alex Thom, and Sullivan Brothers was utterly destroyed. Thousands of pages of typeset material in lead stored in galleys simply melted, running molten on to the floor. Maunsel, at No. 96, suffered severely according to George Roberts' subsequent claim for compensation, which even included the destruction of items stored by printers in Edinburgh (on the other hand, no claim was made for certain manuscripts, notably those of Pearse being prepared for the Collected Edition, presumably because it was feared they might prejudice the claim).[1] In Lower Abbey Street the offices of D.P. Moran's *The Leader*, *Ireland's Own* and the Percy Mecredy titles *Irish Cyclist* and *Motor News* were obliterated. Further up Sackville (O'Connell) Street M.H. Gill, at No. 50, was undamaged, as was the printer and law publisher John Falconer at No. 53. The Educational Company in Talbot Street, James Duffy in the Temple Bar area and Browne & Nolan in Nassau Street also suffered no damage.

Another firm that suffered no damage was the Talbot Press, which was incorporated just before the Great War broke out. We have seen how the old Scottish educational publisher Blackie, after expanding its list beyond the Vere Foster copybook series with which it started, felt in 1910 that the political climate forced it to change tack. It established the Educational Company with an all-Irish board (led by W.G. Lyon and William Fitzsimmons), retaining full control, at least until a management buyout in 1919. This buyout was not a small thing, the company's capital being £50,000. The Educational Company's motto was 'everything for schools', so it stocked and sold a wide variety of ancillary educational materials, not only in Ireland. It also had a number of schools reps, one of whom, briefly in the early 1920s, was Sean O'Faolain.

In 1913, Lyon and Fitzsimmons formally set up a trade publishing arm called Talbot Press, using an imprint that Blackie had published under intermittently since the 1890s. Talbot announced its policy was to 'publish books about Ireland and books written by Irish authors'.[2] The new imprint hit the ground running, with over 250 titles in the first decade. It was to be a dynamic presence in Irish publishing for decades. One of its first ventures was 'Every Irishman's Library': not an especially original idea, but a handsomely presented set of hardbacks, bound in green with elaborate 'Celtic' motifs blind-blocked on the covers. Titles included selections from Jonah Barrington, Maria Edgeworth, Gerald Griffin and Samuel Ferguson. The books were co-published with T. Fisher Unwin, at least until that firm was bought by Ernest Benn in 1923.

Undoubtedly, some members of the staffs of these firms participated in the Rising itself. Charles Eason recorded in a letter that 'several of the staff were mixed up in the rising, of whom some were taken to England for some months. Most of them were allowed to return to work.'[3] Thom's several hundred staff assuredly included similar individuals, the print industry being known for militancy. According to the unpublished manuscript of the strongly republican J.J. O'Kelly, the first historian of M.H. Gill, 'so closely was the house associated with the Republican movement many members of its extensive staff indeed being in arms and deported and at least two on the death roll. Already it was a Republican clearing-house.'[4] Michael Gill elaborates:

> Around the time of the Rising (1916) and later during the War of Independence, the Gill premises were used both as a training ground for the IRA and later as a post box for various members of Sinn Féin including Arthur Griffith and Eoin MacNeill, both of whom were Gill authors

so they were frequent visitors to the building. Several members of the Gill staff were arrested and interned in Frongoch in Wales. One of these was John King who served as manager of the bookshop for many years until his retirement in the early 1960s. He was a greatly respected member of the Dublin bookselling community.

There was a portable firing range in the basement set up by Dick McKee and colleagues with a picture of King George V as target. McKee worked in Gill's as a printer. He was close to Michael Collins and was a senior member of the Dublin Brigade of the IRA. On one occasion in 1920 when my father was visiting the bookshop on his way home from school at Belvedere, a search party of police and Auxiliaries surrounded Gill's looking for Dick McKee. My father was then twelve years old and was asked to slip through the cordon to meet McKee as he returned to work from his lunch break and warn him to go home. They met on O'Connell Street near the GPO and McKee escaped. However, he was arrested some days later, tortured and shot in Dublin Castle allegedly while trying to escape.

Messages for Sinn Féin and other republican groups were frequently left for collection in designated books in the shop. As a result, the premises was kept under regular surveillance. My father clearly remembered seeing men with long leather coats lingering about the bookshop, and being told who they were and how on occasion some held books upside down.[5]

The military demands of the Great War soon led to controls on the trade's basic raw material, paper. Since the beginning of the year, shipping experts had warned of the need to cut back the bulkier imported items to make space on scarce shipping for food and especially metals for armaments. Goods to be limited were fruit, tobacco, wood, slates and, critically for the print and publishing industry, pulp, other paper-making raw materials, paper and card. A Paper Commission was appointed in February 1916 to grant import licences, which were expected to allow only two thirds of the 1914 usage. In October 1916 and again in 1917, under pressure from the German submarine blockade, further restrictions were introduced.

Alarm at these restrictions was registered instantly: the Dublin Local Print and Kindred Trades Federation said that as many as 5,000 jobs could be put at risk,[6] the head of the Retail Newsagents Association said it would help his members to estimate usage less wastefully if people would only buy their morning and evening papers in the same place. The *Irish Independent* speculated that 'very few new books will be published, and the scientific author and the novelist will find their occupations gone.'[7] This was of course an exaggeration, but there is no doubt that the number of books published in Britain fell severely, to 7,700 in 1918, less than two thirds of the pre-war peak, a level last seen twenty years before.[8]

Table 3. Number of books published by leading Irish publishers 1910–24

Publisher	*1910–14*	*1915–19*	*1920–24*
James Duffy	31	32	6
M.H. Gill	156	75	79
Hodges Figgis	166	16	23
Thom	19	15	25
Eason	10	4	3
Maunsel	98	158	64
Sealy, Bryers & Walker	38	9	8
Browne & Nolan	49	27	49
Blackie	12	–	–
Cuala	19	12	12
Educational Company	17	14	40
Talbot	8	135	163
Martin Lester	–	5	15
Totals	623	502	487

Source: National Library of Ireland catalogue

In Ireland things were somewhat different. The table of books published by leading publishers between 1910 and 1925 (Table 3) shows how from 1914 to the end of the decade, the older houses such as Gill, Sealy, Bryers & Walker, Duffy and Browne & Nolan did cut back production, no doubt daunted by a combination of increased costs (even before the official restrictions on imports, shortages had driven paper prices up threefold by the end of 1915) and uncertain prospects. In Sealy, Bryers there had been a change of management, with the death of George Bryers (who, as we have seen, was the power behind the publishing programme) in 1908 and his replacement by William Robertson. There was also change at the top in M.H. Gill, when M.J. Gill died at the age of forty-two after only ten years as managing director. He was succeeded by his brother Richard who himself died ten years later in 1923.

The management of M.H. Gill was taken over by Sligo man Patrick Keohane, who had been company secretary since 1903, from 1923 until Keohane's death in 1939.

The Rising provided Maunsel with a new lease of financial life and a new editorial direction. A few months before it had been teetering on the brink of liquidation. Now the Property Losses (Ireland) Committee was responding generously to claims and its own insurance policy was paying up. Complimentary remarks in the press described the firm as 'a national institution'.

A new director, Edward MacLysaght, contributed an investment of £300 at this time. Not only that, but new editorial opportunities opened up. Clare Hutton notes:

> In response to the changing mood, Maunsel began to publish a greater number of titles relating to Irish politics and history. The Rising is a watershed in the firm's editorial development which signals the beginning of greater political engagement and a lessening of interest in cultural nationalism.[9]

Clare Hutton quotes Edward MacLysaght's unpublished memoir as confirming that times of national debate and contest are good for publishing. MacLysaght wrote:

> The Rising and the national spirit it engendered greatly encouraged the output of books about Ireland and so stimulated Irish publishing ... the altered conditions are reflected by a simple analysis of sales. In 1915 less than one-third of receipts for Maunsels came from Irish accounts, the balance being British and American. In 1918 more than two-thirds came from Ireland and less than one-third from exportation to England and elsewhere.[10]

The turmoil of ideas and possibilities encouraged publishing. Henry James wrote:

> Art lives upon discussion, upon experiment, upon curiosity, upon variety of attempt, upon the exchange of views and the comparison of standpoints; and there is a presumption that the times when no one has anything particular to say about it, and has no reason to give for practice or preference, though they may be times of genius, are not times of development, are times possibly even, a little, of dullness.[11]

Not everyone, of course, responded positively to the new atmosphere. The reaction of the Dublin professional class was negative; immediately after the Rising both the Law Society (for the solicitors) and the Institute of Chartered Accountants recorded formal condemnations.[12] W.G. Lyon the 3-year-old Talbot Press was shocked to learn that one of his would-be authors, Thomas MacDonagh, had played such a prominent part. He decided to postpone publication of *Literature in Ireland*.[13] His co-publisher in London, however, the veteran T. Fisher Unwin, would have nothing of such scruples and persuaded Lyon to publish immediately. In the event, the book was published in June and sold out the day after publication. Lyon however remained unhappy with what he referred to as 'such a thorny political issue'. Roberts in Maunsel took the opposite line, publishing no fewer than three separate accounts of the Rising – James Stephens' *The Insurrection in Dublin*, Joseph Hone's *History of the Irish Rebellion in 1916*, and Redmond-Howard's *Six Days of the Irish Republic* – not to mention a new edition of Connolly's *Labour in Irish History* and O'Casey's *History of the Irish Citizen Army*. 'They also', writes the firm's historian Frances-Jane French, published, 'a large number of pamphlets and tracts which advocated extreme republicanism. These were written in a highly inflammatory style, often the contents were semi-treasonable or seditious in nature.' Between 1916 and 1919 the firm published 117 new books and pamphlets, of which Roberts printed sixty-six himself. A further thirty books and pamphlets were suppressed by the authorities.[14]

The turmoil of ideas did not go unnoticed by the authorities, who in June 1916 established a Press Censor Office in Dublin. Its main focus was on newspapers and periodicals, and, compared for instance with the censorship regime initiated during the Emergency, was mild in the extreme. There appears to have been no obligation to submit material and, apart from Maunsel, few book publishers did. As Frances-Jane French puts it:

> The affairs of Maunsel and Company must have taken up a considerable amount of the Press Censor's time … the total submission to the Press Censor during the entire period [1916–19] by other publishers of books and pamphlets does not exceed two dozen. Maunsel it appears took a malicious pleasure in occupying so much of the Censor's time.[15]

The principals in the new firm of Martin Lester, which began publishing in 1919, were Bulmer Hobson, James MacNeill (brother to Eoin and later the second governor-general) and Colm Ó Lochlainn, who also published twenty or so titles under the Candle Press imprint between 1918 and 1920. The firm's

NORTHERN CIRCULATING LIBRARY,

Castle-Place, Belfast,

Book Societies and School Libraries supplied on Very Advantageous Terms.

Library Books forwarded to all parts of the Kingdom.

PUBLIC LIBRARY

JOHN HENDERSON
PRINTER PUBLISHER BOOKSELLER
WHOLESALE & RETAIL STATIONER

LONDON NEWSPAPER OFFICE

JOHN HENDERSON, PROPRIETOR.

Those who have not yet favoured this Establishment with a visit, are respectfully informed, that its distinguishing features are

LOW PRICES, GOOD ARTICLES, & PUNCTUALITY.

Northern Circulating Library: Henderson's of Belfast, newsagent/booksellers in the 1840s. Subscription libraries, especially Mudie's and Smith's, held great power in the era of three-decker novels. (Courtesy of Eason's)

Hand-setting in the Dun Emer Press 1903; Elizabeth Yeats (facing) is at the hand press, Beatrice Cassidy (standing, right) is rolling out ink, and Esther Ryan (seated) is correcting proofs. (Courtesy of Colin Smythe)

H.G. Tempest, printer and publisher, at the keyboard of the new Monotype typesetting and casting machine (the second in Ireland) 1903. The seated keyboard was a big change for the craftsmen of the day, who were used to standing. (Courtesy of Dundalgan Press)

The main composing room in Dundalgan Press 1900s; hand-typesetting had barely changed since Gutenburg's time and involved manually picking out letter by letter from a divided case. (Courtesy of Dundalgan Press)

The elegant interior staircase to Eason's lending library in the early 1900s. (Courtesy of Eason's)

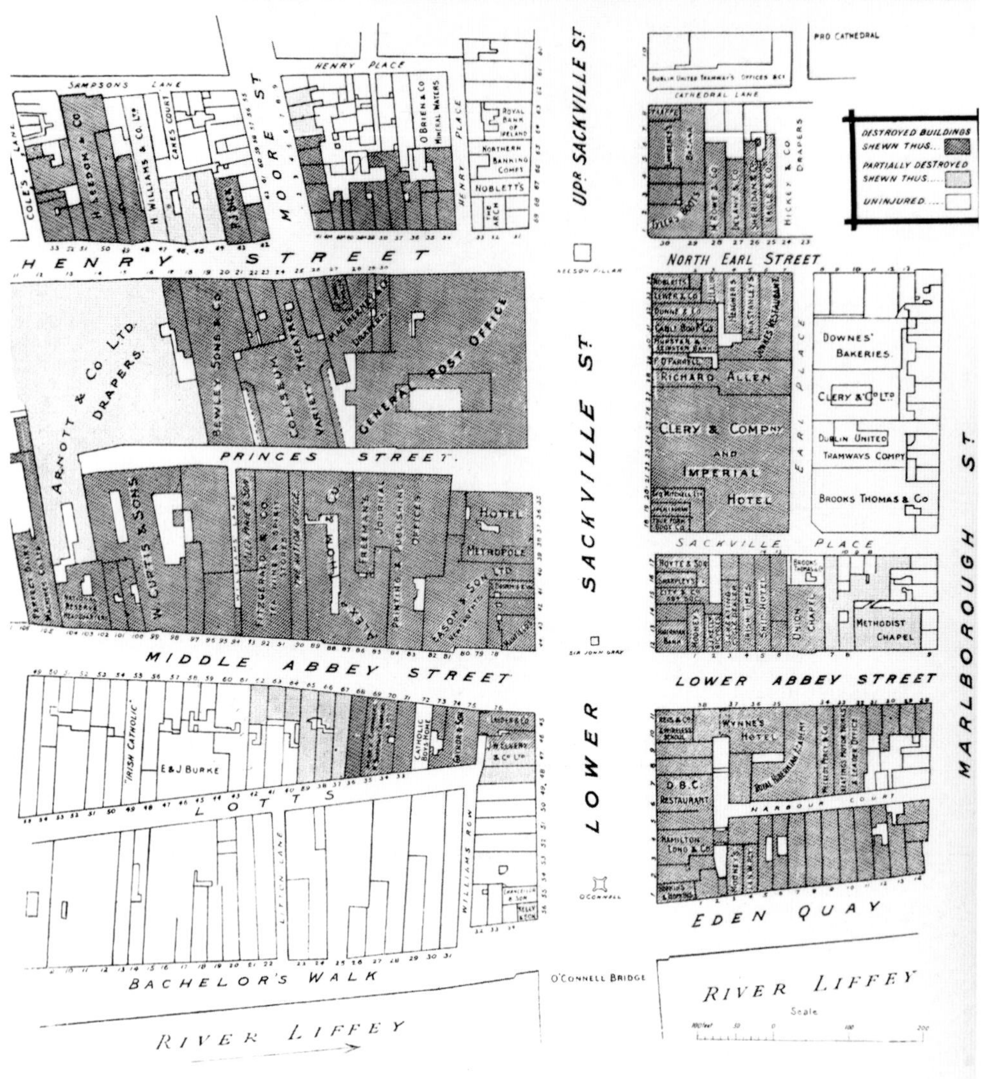

Messrs Longmans intend this book to be sold to the Public at the advertised price, and supply it to the Trade on terms which will not allow of discount.

Publishers' and printers' buildings destroyed in Dublin during the 1916 Rising; the plan was produced for the compensation board. In Middle Abbey Street the buildings housing Eason's, the *Freeman's Journal*, the *Irish Independent*, *The Nation*, Alex Thom, Maunsel, Sealy, Bryers & Walker and Sullivan Brothers, were all utterly destroyed.

The Net Book Agreement in action: a note tipped (pasted) into a Longman's title published in 1892.

Siopa na Leaḃar nGaeḋealaċ

THE IRISH BOOK SHOP

50 LOWER BAGGOT STREET, DUBLIN

SUPPLEMENTARY LIST

DECEMBER, 1917

Owing to the great difficulties in respect of paper, printing, etc., involved in issuing a complete Catalogue, revised up to date, we have not published a new list this Xmas, but have issued only this Supplementary List as an Appendix to our complete Catalogue of Xmas, 1916.

Owing to the fact that most publishers have increased the prices of a number of their books, many of those included in our Catalogue, issued Xmas, 1916, are now only obtainable at a somewhat higher rate than that indicated therein. Moreover, some of the books, especially the cheaper ones in that list, have since gone out of print.

POETRY.

BODKIN, THOMAS. May It Please Your Lordships. Reproduction of modern French Poems, with the originals. Printed on hand-made paper. Limited to 560 copies. **6/–.**

CAMPBELL, JOSEPH. Earth of Cualann. With 21 designs by Author. Limited to 500 copies for sale. Printed on hand-made paper. **5/–.**

CLARKE, AUSTIN. The Vengeance of Fionn. Cr. 8vo. **3/6.**

DOAK, H. L. Verdun and Other Poems. Wrappers **1/–.**

GRAVES, ALFRED PERCEVAL. Edited with an Introduction by. Poems of Sir Samuel Ferguson. Cr. 8vo. Cloth. **3/–.** Every Irishman's Library.

GREGORY, PADRIC. Ireland: A Song of Hope and Other Poems and Ballads. Cr. 8vo. Cloth. **2/6.**

GOODMAN, P. The Irish Minstrel. Complete. **8d.**

HUGGINS, H. C. Roadside Fancies. Paper cover. **1/–.**

MacENTEE, JOHN FRANCIS. The Poems of. Imp. 16mo. Cloth. **3/6.**

MULHOLLAND, CLARA. A Striking Contrast. Cloth. **3/6.**

O'BYRNE, CATHAL. The Grey Feet of the Wind. With portrait of the Author. **2/6.**

The book trade's problems during the First World War and following the Rising in 1916 can be seen in this Irish Book Shop supplementary list issued in 1917 in lieu of a catalogue 'owing to the great difficulties in respect of paper, printing etc'.

Interior of Gill's bookshop 1930s, with crucifix, statues and other church furnishings. (Courtesy of Gill)

Seán and Bríghid Uí Éigeartaigh, founders of Sáirséal & Dill (1947), on honeymoon in Inis Mór, 1943. (Courtesy of Cló Iar-Chonnacht)

CRÉ NA CILLE
MÁIRTÍN Ó CADHAIN

Jacket designed by Charles Lamb RHA for *Cré na Cille* by Máirtín Ó Cadhain, published by Sáirséal & Dill in 1949. The racy novel has been ranked as the most important prose work in modern Irish. (Courtesy of Cló Iar-Chonnacht)

Captain John (Seán) Feehan, founder of Mercier Press (1944), pictured in the mid-1980s; retired but still active as chairman of the firm. (Courtesy of *Books Ireland*)

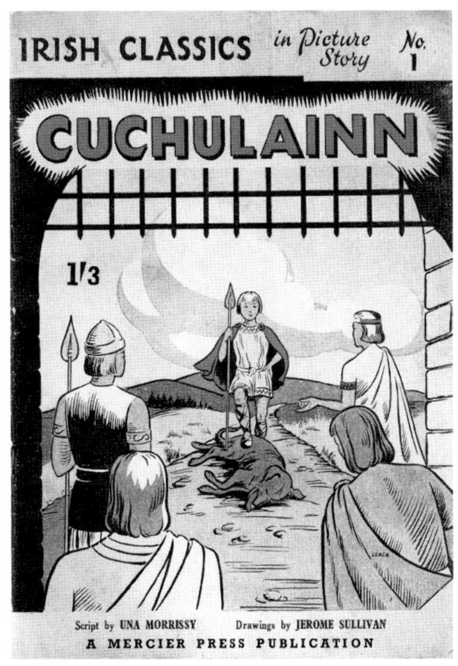

One of a comic book series published by Mercier in the 1950s based on the successful American series Classics Illustrated. (Courtesy of Mercier Press)

M.H. Gill bookshop, No. 50 O'Connell Street, 1950s. (Courtesy of Gill)

Eason's railway bookstall Cork No. 1, 1950s. (Courtesy of Eason's)

Liam Miller of Dolmen Press; etching by Jack Coughlin. (Courtesy of *Books Ireland*)

One of Clé's early promotions, 1971, with the logo designed by Liam Miller.

BOOKS FROM IRELAND
January-June 1971

DUBLIN
IRISH BOOK PUBLISHERS' ASSOCIATION
CUMANN LEABHARFHOILSITHEOÍRÍ ÉIREANN
1971

great author was Eimar O'Duffy. It published his 1916 novel *Wasted Island* and his cheerful skit *Printer's Errors* as well as others of his work. Hobson's republican contacts were no doubt responsible for acquiring Michael Collins' *Arguments for the Treaty* as well as the ill-fated government-commissioned memorial album paying homage to Griffith and Collins published in February 1923. Of the 25,000 copies printed, fewer than half had been sold six months later; by 1925 when the Talbot Press took over the title, there were still 7,800 in the warehouse.[16] Martin Lester published nothing after 1925.

Colm Ó Lochlainn, however, went on for many years, founding the Three Candles Press in 1926 and producing over 100 characteristically elegant book titles and a range of college annuals, journals and commemorative volumes.[17] From an office in Fleet Street the firm did jobbing printing as well as running a bookshop (among the staff was Paddy Hughes who later worked with Eason's and Mercier). Ó Lochlainn (born in 1892) who had been 'out' in 1916 – indeed had served as one of the abortive expedition to Kerry to establish a wireless station – first attracted attention with the *Dublin Civic Week Handbook* of 1927, of which Harry Tempest of Dundalgan Press wrote, 'it was evident at once that a new force had come into Irish printing … it was no small tribute to its excellence that the 10,000 copies issued on Friday were sold by Monday morning.'

The dash for growth represented by Maunsel's output had not improved its finances and by 1920 it was clearly in trouble again. Directors Joseph Hone and Edward MacLysaght approached W.G. Lyon of the Educational Company and Talbot to see if they would take over the firm. Lyon was positive about the idea (Maunsel had an enviable list of authors even without those Roberts had irrevocably offended), but while he would be happy to have Roberts as a technical print advisor, any kind of managerial post was not on.

Hone and MacLysaght put the idea to Roberts, who was not keen on the potential loss of status, but asked for time to consider. He used the time to devise a combination of Maunsel and his own printing company which would be called Maunsel & Roberts. Extraordinarily, he managed to persuade Lawrence Casey, the managing director of the Irish National Assurance Co., to underwrite the £20,000 flotation. Hone and MacLysaght were completely wrong-footed and despite their deep doubts, accepted the new configuration of Maunsel & Roberts.

The new company was launched in November 1920, and a prospectus was immediately issued inviting offers for the shares. It was perhaps the low point of the Troubles: the Black and Tans were first recruited in January and the Auxiliaries in July; Terence MacSwiney had starved himself to death in Brixton in October; Kevin Barry had been shot at the beginning of the month; in the North recruiting for the 'B' and 'C' Specials began and on 21 November the events of 'Bloody Sunday' unravelled. In the event, only £350 of shares were subscribed for, £250 of which came from the life savings of the old nanny of one of the directors. Lawrence Casey now found to his horror that Irish National Assurance had to stump up £14,465. His fellow-directors, who had not been consulted, were not pleased and eventually Casey, a ruined man, was sacked from his job, and obliged to sell his family estate in Co. Wicklow.

At this point Roberts appears to have completely lost his way. He became convinced that the way to develop the new company was by wholesale stationery for schools and general sale. In 1922, he went to a trade fair in Zurich and came back with £9,000 worth of pencils, penholders and various fancy goods which he told the board he would sell at a vast profit. Most of these items, including 44,640 boxes of crayons, 65,000 envelopes and 28,000 exercise book covers were still in the warehouse three years later, to be sold off by auction. Two of the directors, including Edward MacLysaght, resigned on the spot. For another two years Roberts did a good deal of ducking and diving, not publishing much, but mortgaging the company's property and assets. Ironically, while all this was happening, Roberts climaxed his printing career doing what he did best, producing a very fine piece of bookwork, the eight stately quarto volumes of *Ireland's Memorial Records 1914–1918*, an effort which rightly won a silver medal, the highest award, at the Tailteann Games in 1924. But the end could not be postponed indefinitely. In November 1925, a receiver was appointed and in April 1926 an auction of the firm's goods, book stocks, sheets, plates, stationery, printing machinery and equipment finally brought the saga to an end.[18]

In 1921, Talbot ran a competition for an Irish novel which was won by Annie M.P. Smithson who became one of its most regular and popular authors, publishing more than twenty novels with the firm. In November 1923, Talbot took over Martin Lester, which had overreached itself with the Griffith/Collins memorial volume, and in 1926 bought various items at the Maunsel & Roberts bankruptcy auction including the extravagantly produced *Collected Works of Patrick Pearse* later published under the Phoenix imprint, which specialised in door-to-door sales. According to his entry in the *Dictionary of Irish Biography* Roberts worked for Talbot for two years before going to England where he served as print advisor to Gollancz for a while.

A Digression: The Irish as Readers

A thriving publishing sector is dependent, above all, on an active community of readers with time, money, freedom and energy. Since the 1960s, Irish people have cherished ideas of themselves as great book readers. Unfortunately, statistics and knowledgeable opinion confirm that only a minority have ever been serious readers or buyers of books. The lovingly retailed legends of the ploughman whiling away his lunch break with a battered edition of Homer or Virgil, and the connected implication that hedge schools could on a good day rival the great Jesuit academies of France, remain just that – legend.

The gap between the aspiration and the reality can be traced a long way back. In the eighteenth century the first John Murray (on a visit to sell books) was dismayed to learn that, as a correspondent told him, Dublin 'was a drinking not a reading city'. When Walter Scott visited Ireland in 1825 he was 'gratified by a tremendous welcome, including reiterated calls to take a bow in the theatre and his carriage being pursued through the streets by crowds in every direction'.[19] But the book historian William St Clair noted:

> Of the initial huge editions of the Waverley novels at the height of their popularity, for example, about 6,000 copies were shipped to London for retail bookshops in London and the south, about 2,000 served Scotland and England north of York, but only 100 copies were sent to Dublin.[20]

An 1849 parliamentary committee observed that seventy-three of the larger towns in Ireland had no bookshop. By contrast, rich English provincial towns such as Bath, Canterbury, Manchester and Portsmouth mustered an average of one stationer/bookseller per thousand population.[21] Throughout Ireland wandering chapmen carried books of a sort (almanacs, chapbooks, ballads) into fairs and homes. On his travels in the West just before the Famine Thackeray records buying for 18*d* 'in a decent little library' six little yellow volumes full of legends and wonders, 'a thousand wild extravagant dangers' cunningly circumvented, verses on the Battle of Aughrim and the lives of highway robbers such as Captain Freney. Such titles were widely used as 'readers' in hedge schools, with the pupils bringing their own texts. But by the 1870s these were in decline, to be replaced by local newspapers and cheap books published in series such as Simms & McIntyre's Parlour Library, Cassell's National Library and Routledge's Railway Library.[22]

Those Irish towns that did have 'bookshops' generally had a few shelves of books squeezed in among a wild variety of other goods. In the following decade W.H. Smith (later Eason's) began to establish its nationwide network of railway bookstalls (so called from what were at least initially their primary wares); by the 1880s, however, these sold mainly magazines and newspapers, in competition with local independent retailers.

One of these was Thomas Kelly's combined stationers, printers and bookshop in Loughrea, Co. Galway. The firm printed a booklist in February 1882 listing over sixty titles. The first six titles on the list indicate the eclectic nature of the sales, though works relating to Ireland or Catholic piety and practice predominate. These six titles (indicating popularity?) were *Knocknagow*, *Modern Cookery*, *Works* of Cowper and Wordsworth, *Essays of Thomas Davis*, *History of Ireland*, and the domestic how-to manual *Enquire Within*. The most expensive books on the list, at 6*s* each, are three titles by the English hymn-writer and theologian Fr Faber, Newman's colleague and fellow convert. Cardinal Wiseman of Westminster (he was of Waterford descent) was represented by his *Recollections of the Last Four Popes* (5*s*) rather than his novel of the Catacombs *Fabiola*. Almost all of the other books are priced at less than 3*s*, including a *Douay Testament* at 1*s* 3*d* (probably New rather than Old: either refutes the old lie that Catholics were systematically forbidden to read the Bible). Novelists represented included Ouida, Dickens, Lover, Lever and, perhaps because of the publicity of his death the previous year, two 1830s titles from Disraeli.[23]

Contemporary evidence suggests that the tradition of book culture among the well-off and leisured Anglo-Irish (as represented by the Royal Dublin Society, the Royal Irish Academy, the Dublin Library and the professional libraries such as King's Inns) seems to have waned in the second half of the nineteenth century. In a scathing article about Irish landlords in 1882, J.P. Mahaffy of Trinity lamented the lack of enthusiasm for reading among his Anglo-Irish contemporaries:

> The splendid libraries so common before famine times are scattered, and it is now an exception to find a good library in a country house. They tell you it is not needed. Have they not their daily papers and can they not get books down from a library in Dublin?[24]

Molly Keane recounts that forty years later she had to conceal the fact that she wrote novels for fear of merciless teasing. Her contemporary, Geoffrey Taylor, recalls:

> Looking back, one remembers more of the hospitality of Irish country life than of its high-brow aspects. That intellect and learning had played their

> part was shown by the excellent libraries that all these houses contained – libraries however which had, of the most part, few books added to their calf-bound rows since the forties and fifties of the Victorian era.[25]

The sad story of the Dublin Library shows the same loss of vigour. The Dublin Library Society was founded in 1791 (long before the now-famous London Library of 1841), 'to procure those great and expensive books usually beyond the reach of private individuals'. It finally ended up in D'Olier Street. By 1825, there were 3,000 members, though this had fallen to 400 by the 1850s. In 1848, just as the London Library was getting under way, the Dublin Library was declared to be 'full' and a committee was established to sell some of the books, supposedly to finance new acquisitions. In 1854, Rev. MacDonnell, Provost of Trinity, was elected president of the society. The standard history of the society says, 'MacDonnell loved billiards. Under the guise of expanding both literature and amusements, he turned one of the first floor rooms into a billiard room. A second was quickly added. Dinners were provided.' The upper room became a billiard club.[26]

At this time an internal report revealed financial irregularities in the library's operations and noted that only sixty members had bothered to pay the 10*s* lending deposit. A new set of bylaws was written for the Society, firmly expunging the title 'librarian' for the senior employee and replacing it with 'secretary'. After 1870, there were no more 'literary evenings'. By 1880, the Society's entry in Thom's *Directory* read 'D'Olier Street Club, late Dublin Library Society'. The books were sold the following year.[27]

By the beginning of the twentieth century, there was a fixed opinion among the *bien pensant* that Irish people were reluctant to buy books. Partly this is to be accounted for by the universal tendency for the bookish to deplore the reading habits of their fellows. But in the Irish case there seems to be something substantial. Yeats once put the point thus:

> The people of Ireland respect letters and read nothing. They hold the words 'poet' and 'thinker' honourable, yet buy no books. They are proud of being a more imaginative people than the English, and yet compel their own imaginative writers to seek an audience across the sea.[28]

The historian Theodore Zeldin noted a similar phenomenon in France: 'The exceptional brilliance of French literature and the fame the country's great writers enjoyed have given the impression that literature mattered more in France … [than it did in fact].'[29]

In the *Irish Book Lover* Stephen Gwynn repeated the substance of a discourse he had given to a meeting of the (British and Irish) Associated Booksellers in Dublin in 1912:

> Irish people are very odd about books. They are, and every Irish writer knows it to his cost, the least book-buying of publics … Mr Yeats has done more than any man living, perhaps than any man living or dead, to raise the fame of Ireland in the craft of letters but heaven help Mr Yeats – heaven help any of us – if existence depended on the sale of books to the Irish public.[30]

Gwynn knew what he was talking about: he had been in his time a director of Maunsel and a literary advisor to Macmillan. We have seen how less than a third of the sales of this leading Irish Revival house sold in Ireland before Maunsel turned to more political matters after 1916.[31]

Writing in 1912, William Dawson, a member of the group of UCD intellectuals that included Tom Kettle and Arthur Clery, detected anti-local snobbery: 'Nobody in Dublin buys books – if we except text-books and seven-penny novels – but even the "intellectuals" will scarcely borrow from a library a book by a Dublin man published in Dublin.' He rather quaintly believed that 'a Parliament in Dublin would remedy at least this state of affairs'.[32]

Some years later, in 1930, the Minister for Finance, Ernest Blythe, attempted to cheer another meeting of the Associated Booksellers in Dublin with a vision of Irish reading in the Censorship era:

> I believe that the movements that are beginning to manifest themselves will before long change the people of this country from a people who do not read many books and do not buy books to a people who are book readers with the habits that might be expected from the descendants of those who a great many centuries ago undoubtedly spread the light of learning throughout the whole of Western Europe.[33]

He did not produce any evidence for this belief.

The reluctance to buy books was the subject of jokes: as for instance George Birmingham's Connacht dispensary doctor Lucius O'Grady, who bought a few books every year 'quite privately, for no one in the west would admit that he threw away his money wantonly'.[34] On the other hand, the appetite for 'seven-penny novels' among the Dublin intelligentsia startled Sean O'Casey. One day he spotted Lady Gregory 'her head lovingly close to a book'. Hearing him approach she snapped it shut, but not before he spotted it was *Peg O' My Heart*. On another occasion, Edgar Wallace novels embarrassingly tumbled out of Gogarty's suitcase. W.B. Yeats, on the other hand, 'made no bones about the disordered pile of books strewing the marble mantelpiece ... they were Wild Western Tales and Detective Stories'. Once, 'asking Æ for a Blood-and-Thunder novel', O'Casey writes, 'Æ fished one out without a search'.[35] Frank O'Connor recalled how 'in his days as editor [Æ] could glut himself on whodunits'.[36]

In theory there was a high level of literacy throughout the country. The 1901 Census reported that 95 per cent of the 15–24-year-old group claimed to be able to read and write. Many of these, however, so Canon Sheehan declared in a collection of essays, 'were barely able to spell laboriously through the columns of a newspaper'. Their education, he claimed, had left them effectively semi-literate. In both agricultural districts and manufacturing centres, 'a taste for reading anything beyond some light novel – or the weekly political newspaper – is absolutely unknown.' Discussing a 1910 American report on the Irish educational system Sheehan maintained that 'a taste for reading – I mean anything wholesome or elevating – is almost unknown in this country.'[37]

Quite soon after the publication of this book of essays by Maunsel, Canon Sheehan's clerical colleagues were to commence a thirty-year campaign to ensure that the Irish people read either what was, in their minds, 'wholesome or elevating' – or nothing at all. Many thought of reading as a mere distraction, and potentially worse. In a little book called *Christian Politeness and Counsels for Youth* (20th ed., 1934), the Christian Brothers acknowledged this point: 'parents and masters sometimes discourage reading under the pretext that it interferes with business'; on the contrary, say the Brothers, reading, especially in pursuit of useful knowledge, should be encouraged. Only 'if the love of books degenerates into a passion' should reading be discouraged.

Related to the educationalist viewpoint was that of the Catholic Church. The struggle against Modernism had begun with the French Revolution. Every priest knew the 1814 encyclical in which Pius VII drew the conclusion that:

> The licence of the press threatened the people with the greatest perils and with certain ruin ... this licence of the press has been the principal instrument which has first depraved the people's morals; then corrupted and destroyed their faith; and finally stirred up sedition, unrest and revolution.

In 1897, Leo XIII agreed: 'Most perilous of all,' he wrote, 'is the uncurbed freedom of writing and publishing noxious literature. Nothing can be conceived more perilous, and more apt to defile souls.' During their seminary training the school managers and curates and parish confessors of the future had their appetite – not perhaps strong to begin with – for any but the most severely scholastic reading crushed. As Canon Sheehan recorded of his time in Maynooth in the 1860s, despite the riches of the library, 'literature had to be read surreptitiously. It was a serious thing to be detected in such clandestine studies.'

Once in the parish few of these men were inclined to encourage so dangerous a pastime. For most of their parishioners, of course, there was little danger. As Patrick Kavanagh noted of the book-loving Tarry Flynn's house: 'The *Messenger of the Sacred Heart* was bought every month, and with *Old Moore's Almanac* and the local newspaper constituted the literature of Flynn's as of nearly every other country house.' Tarry's father:

> had bought several second-hand volumes in the market of the local town. His books were not very exciting, but they *were* books. A gazetteer for the year 1867, an antiquated treatise on Sound, Light and Heat and a medical book called *Thompson's Domestic Medicine*. The only one of the three which Tarry had ever known father read was the 'doctor's book'.[38]

As the old parish priest commented to his curate in Gerald O'Donovan's novel *Father Ralph*, 'I never knew much good to come out of books.' Norah Hoult's pious Catholic cattle-dealer Patrick O'Neill, who 'objected to book reading' on moral grounds, was not alone.[39]

Others resorted to a more violent rhetoric. Typical was Canon Peter O'Leary's (1908) fulmination against how in the English novel, 'the lowest and most degrading of human passions are searched for and exhibited to the mind of the reader'. The language in which these novels were written was, he declared, 'poisonous. It is rotten language, as rotten as anything which is corrupt. It is unwholesome. It ruins the mental health.' Some years later the Catholic librarian, Stephen Brown, thinking of Joyce, Lawrence and Proust, wrote of the 'lewdness, the worse than pagan vileness of certain writers on the moral side and on the intellectual side [the] grotesque absurdity of their theories'.[40]

In this context any but the most controlled reading matter was clearly a danger. In *The Mirror of True Womanhood*, first published in the US in 1877 but republished by M.H. Gill in the 1880s and reprinted in 1927, the reverend author warns mothers against those works which are:

> continually poured on the book market to entice the appetite of our boys and girls. Mothers cannot be too careful in protecting their dear ones against this impure deluge and in cautioning them when they are grown up against the dreadful effects of these literary poisons.

The author suggests that instead of 'the thousand-and-one "Cheap Novels", "Illustrated Weeklies" and "Fireside" or "Seaside Libraries"', girls especially should be encouraged to 'open the generous mind of youth' with Montalembert's multi-volume *Monks of the West*. The Christian Brothers, in Chapter 20 of their *Christian Politeness*, make it clear what they regard as desirable reading.

> The youthful reader should read slowly, attentively, with reflection and a little every day. He should take notes of those passages which strike him most; and should endeavour to fix well in his memory three leading points: names, dates and places ... the reading of light, frivolous and worthless publications should be discountenanced.

Even if there had been a widespread book-reading habit, the physical resources to feed it were poor. Although the Public Libraries (Ireland) Act 1851 had enabled local authorities to establish local libraries, by 1880 only Sligo and Dundalk had taken advantage of its terms. Four public libraries were established in Dublin between 1884 and 1905, but the stock was small and the borrowers few; when the system was temporarily closed for lack of funds in 1908 there were a mere 6,000 books on loan, in a population of 375,000 people. The Carnegie gifts ensured the erection of handsome buildings, but not books, so that when the new library in Great Brunswick (now Pearse) Street was completed in 1909 it remained empty for two and a half years 'like a canal without water'.[41] Eventually newspapers and magazines appeared, but no books for a further two years. The Irish public library system was to remain a poorly financed resource until the 1960s.

Many middle-class people in fact shunned public libraries as potential sources of disease. Lady Aberdeen's 'crusade against tuberculosis', initiated in 1907, had taught them to fear lurking bacilli in used clothes, books and crockery. The concurrent French campaign against TB made a particular point of the dangers in books from libraries. In December 1905, the medical columnist of *Le Matin*, 'Doctor Ox', claimed that an average book from a circulating collection or library could contain forty-three bacteria per square centimetre of printed surface. 'Who could know,' Doctor Ox mused, 'how many book borrowers or library readers were ill or convalescing and handled pages after coughing or sneezing on their hands?' 'Have you ever thought,' he asked his readers, 'about the number of volumes a consumptive can infect during the long months of his illness?'[42] The fear lingered.

In her autobiography the novelist Val Mulkerns recalled how, going to school in Eccles Street in the late 1930s the beautifully clean Junior Library 'finally broke my mother's taboo on borrowing books. How could you possibly associate noxious bugs and hideous infections with a school library that smelled sweetly of the convent?'[43] Commercial 'circulating libraries' such as those run by Eason's and Greene's, being patronised largely by the middle class, were seen as less dangerous. At a more popular level '2*d* a read' libraries of popular fiction flourished in small retailer outlets such as newsagents and dairies. This was the popular source for the readers described by Stephen Brown, 'who consume fiction at the rate of from four to ten novels per week'.[44]

Apart from the ninety-five railway bookstalls run by Eason's across the country, which mostly sold newspapers and magazines, the specialist provincial book trade, which had never been strong, had been further inhibited by the ability of the Post Office to deliver books direct to customers from London in forty-eight hours. Since all orders were 'firm' (i.e. non-returnable), booksellers were reluctant to take risks. E.M. Forster noted the result in 1919: 'the bookshops of Belfast are instructive. They are not only small, but incredibly provincial, and breathe Samuel Smiles when they are being responsible and "Aristotle" when they are not'.[45] ('Aristotle' is a reference to *Aristotle's Masterpiece*, a sex information guide first published in the seventeenth century, whose 'crooked botched print' and lurid illustrations attracted Leopold Bloom's attention as he perused a bookstall.) The *Freeman's Journal* wrote gloomily in 1920:

> The Irish book trade bears a striking and unpleasant resemblance to the uneconomic holdings of the West; and the parallel is strengthened by the similarity of our writers and artists to that of the migratory labourers of Connacht who have to seek abroad that pittance that enables them to keep a roof over their heads at home.[46]

Eason's and Hely's imported books on a wholesale basis, concentrating on popular titles that sold through local newsagent/general stores. Eason's *Monthly Bulletin of Trade News* showed these country retailers how to display and promote the stock of imported magazines such as *Titbits*, *Pearson's Weekly* and the *News of the World* to entice the reader in search of 'light reading'.

Romance, religion without theology and cowboy tales were the staples of this market, in which Talbot Press was the only significant Irish publisher.[47]

Specialist bookshops tended to be rather daunting, forbidding, places as Eimar O'Duffy's businessman hero found in a novel published in 1922:

> Books. Books in row upon row along the walls. Books stacked upon tables. Books everywhere ... There was an air of quiet sedateness too which completely differentiated it from any other kind of shop. There was no bustle of business, all was studious repose ... the shopmen remained unobtrusively in the background, or chatted urbanely to the customers. Mr Wolverhampton felt like an intruder.[48]

Irish-published books would have represented less than 3 per cent of the stock.

The Beginning of the Censorship Era

The period after the achievement of independence for the south was a troubled one for Irish publishers. From England came muffled echoes of battles between highbrows, middlebrows and lowbrows; between Modernists and traditionalists; between Bloomsbury and the adherents of robust and manly common sense; between strident Catholic apologetics and Fabian liberals. In Ireland quite a different note sounded above all.

The combatants in the 1916–22 period were idealists, who had sacrificed a great deal to create a new Ireland. They were almost all suspicious of 'England', harbouring what Roy Foster has recently called 'a robust Anglophobia'. The 'necessity to de-anglicise' was felt strongly. Although the generation is often characterised as conservative, in practice they were anything but. For these men and women, the freedom for the country to evolve peacefully, conservatively, was not enough. A radical cultural fracture and re-knitting was required.[49] They wanted a new Ireland that would be an example to the world. There was, as Professor John A. Murphy has described, 'an attitude akin to the stern Jacobins in revolutionary France'.[50] In his 1916 novel *The Wasted Island*, Eimar O'Duffy envisaged:

> a liberated and regenerated homeland [which] might hold up a banner which all men could see ... As once she had been the refuge of learning and religion in a Europe overrun by barbarism, so she might yet be the stronghold of the spirit in a world overwhelmed by materialism.[51]

De Valera had no less aspiration: in 1920 he declared in Mangan's words that the Irish mission was 'to show the world the might of moral beauty'.[52]

The head of M.H. Gill from 1923 until his death in 1939, Patrick Keohane, was completely committed to the new Catholic Ireland and a thorough break with England. A seven-page obituary by a distinguished Gaelic man of letters, published in the *Catholic Bulletin*, described the cast of mind of those who wanted to create a New Ireland. Keohane, declared the obituarist, 'embodied the ancient Ireland so perfectly [and] represented the new Ireland equally well – that Ireland of new Patricks, new Brigids, new Colums and Columbanus' in a new spiritual empire that is untainted by alien things.' For Keohane:

> It was Anglicisation which, while it drew the Gael away from his own heritage, robbed him of his second heritage, the full citizenship of Catholic Christendom … [His] mind stood where the mind of the Gael always stood. For him the schismatic island which lies between our island and the Continent might be said not to exist. He refused to let it either overshadow Irish culture, Irish rights, Irish claims, or yet cut him off from the Catholic Commonwealth that Ireland so largely built.[53]

Thus, after 1922, began a period in which much thought and effort was to go into protecting this moral beauty, especially from careless or malevolent outside forces. The first medium to be subject to censorship was film. Introducing the Censorship of Films Bill in May 1923, Kevin O'Higgins noted 'the insistent and increasing call for a National Censorship' to protect morality and social order (there already was an ineffective local film censorship).[54] The idea that traditional morality was under attack and must be defended had international weight. In 1923, thirty-five members of the League of Nations signed a treaty against the trade in obscene publications (obscenity was sensibly not defined). Those who thought, with Yeats, that the evil effect of films deemed to be morally dubious was 'greatly exaggerated' and that 'you can leave the arts, superior or inferior to the general conscience of mankind' were clearly in the minority.[55]

At that time, O'Higgins noted, there were some 150 cinemas throughout the country and thirty-one in Dublin, with an average attendance of 20,000; most of the audience, he believed, were under 18. Every one was a potential source of danger. 'We are risking', he said, 'something all sane and thoughtful men would hold to be a sacred thing and that is the clean-mindedness and decency of our citizens.'[56] Professor Magennis (whom we have previously seen as an investor in and editorial consultant to the Educational Company) unsurprisingly welcomed the Bill, deploring 'the vile lowering of values that belong to other races and other peoples' that 'were being forced upon our people through the popularity of the cinematograph … all reading, even novel reading, is being supplanted by those theatres.'

Some years later Professor Magennis made an unsuccessful attempt to change Irish copyright law in favour of local manufactures. During the 1926 debates on the Commercial and Industrial Property (Protection) Bill – a measure primarily concerned with patents – he proposed that Irish copyright should be dependent on the book being printed in Ireland, as was the case in the US and Canada.[57] Following advice, deputies assumed that no British publisher would bother to have books printed in Ireland in order to establish copyright unless the sale was likely to be at least 3,000 copies. In theory then any British-published book with a likely Irish sale of fewer copies (i.e. at least 95 per cent of British books) could be free of copyright in Ireland, exactly as they had been before 1801. A heady vista was briefly opened of an Irish book trade thriving, as its ancestors had done, on piracy. For the government Patrick McGilligan, Minister for Industry and Commerce, moved swiftly to close the curtain, declaring that if the amendment was passed Ireland would have to leave the Berne Convention. International copyright for Irish authors would become a thing of the past. The House soberly rejected the amendment by thirty-four votes to eight.

Among the clauses of the Bill that did get through was one adding the National Library and the constituent colleges of the National University to the legal deposit requirement for Irish publishers. It was proposed, by Professor Thrift among others, that the National Libraries of Wales and Scotland and the libraries of Cambridge and Oxford be removed from the list. Professor Magennis, on the losing side again, argued that the number of deposit copies produced an unfair burden on Irish publishers. Deputies were unsympathetic, one even claiming that the legal deposit scheme benefited publishers as a form of free advertising.[58]

As to censorship, films were only the start. For years a campaign had been brewing against so-called 'evil literature'. The specific focus of attack was English Sunday newspapers, notably the *News of the World*, a paper with a strong focus on sex, crime, deviancy and lengthy reports of divorce proceedings typically featuring servants' evidence of what they saw in the bedroom. In 1922, Æ's *New Statesman* noted that of the eighty or so columns in a typical issue, twenty-five dealt with 'matrimonial cases, sexual crime, and minor sexual misdemeanours, adultery, homosexuality, indecency, attempted rapes, improper or criminal treatment of girl children, venereal disease and so on'.[59] Boycotts and local bans were intermittently organised by active clergymen, but only tangentially impinged on the book trade. An exception was the growl from one vigilante, against whom Charles Eason attempted to defend himself, who commented 'the general feeling among priests is that [in publishing Catholic prayerbooks] you have got hold of a source of profit, legitimate of course, but outside the natural lines of a Protestant publisher'.[60] This bullying note was heard again some years later when Eason's support for censorship legislation was once again deemed tepid. Frank O'Reilly, secretary of the CTS, complained to the *Irish Independent* that 'as one of the largest distributors of Catholic prayer books in Ireland,' a role the CTS no doubt saw as more suitably its own, 'I should have expected [Charles Eason], consistently, to be one of the most emphatic in favour of banning printed matter advocating foul practices condemned by the Catholic Church.'[61] Similar intimidation of all sorts of Protestant businesses was to be heard even more loudly during the build-up to the Eucharistic Congress in 1932.

By this time, the 1929 Censorship of Publications Act was well established. The process was led by justice minister Kevin O'Higgins, under pressure of lobby groups, of a Committee on Evil Literature. This reported in 1927 and its unanimous report proposed the setting up of a board to advise the Minister as to the black-listing of certain publications. Literature advocating or explaining contraceptive methods was condemned not as intrinsically immoral (the standard Catholic view) but 'as opening the way to sensual indulgence for those who wish to avoid the responsibilities of the married state.' The spectre of 'race suicide', which had disastrously shrunk the French population relative to the Germans in the nineteenth century, brought Catholics and most Protestants together on this issue.[62]

A Censorship of Publications Bill was drafted and had its second reading in October 1928. The majority of speakers had no problem with the vigorous censorship of so-called 'fugitive literature'; indeed, many deputies felt that the scope proposed by the minister did not go far enough. Surely there were matters just as subversive of public morality as those 'calculated to excite sexual passion or to suggest or incite to sexual immorality', especially since, as one deputy put it, this 'is not the sin to which Irishmen are most prone'.[63] There was much discussion as to the operation of the proposed Censorship Board: how many members should it have? Who would they be – in particular, should clergy be excluded? How would the publications be identified (especially given the supposed Irish distaste for informers)? Would a list of banned publications not serve as a guide to the depraved?

But the most ticklish debate was on whether the Board should be asked to censor books. Opponents urged that the legal *maxim de minimis non curat lex* should apply: books were simply not significant. Some, such as the barrister Hugh Law (Cumann na nGaedheal) and Professor Thrift (Independent TD for TCD), felt that 'nine-tenths of the evil is got at if you can purify the Press'. Professor Thrift proposed that 'we are not, I think, a book reading people. We are very much a newspaper reading people' and, by implication, middle-class book-readers should be left alone. Professor Michael Tierney of UCD (Cumann na nGaedheal) presciently remarked, basing himself on a Canadian precedent, 'I am very much afraid that under the authority of this Dáil a list of prohibited books will be produced which will make a laughing-stock of this country.'[64] 'Go up and down the countryside,' declared Hugh Law, 'and in how many provincial towns, even of a considerable size, will you find books? There must be tens of thousands of houses in this country in which no book is to be found, unless it be a prayer-book, or possibly an old copy of *Knocknagow* or *Moore's Melodies*.'

On the other hand, deputies were defensively conscious that there had been vocal opposition to the Bill and specifically to this aspect. Yeats, trailing his Nobel Prize glory, had claimed (in the *Manchester Guardian* among other places) that 'every educated man in Ireland was against the Bill', and that it was being forced on the government by 'zealots'. He did not help the opposition cause by these and other patronising remarks (about the poor quality of Irish culture, that Irish primary schoolteachers never read books out of school and, somewhat gratuitously, that Catholics did not understand Aquinas).[65] The truth was that Yeats was quite out of touch with the fundamentalist nature of post-independence Ireland. As Deputy Peadar Doyle (Cumann na nGaedheal) put it, the great majority recognised that this kind of action was in line with regulations overseas, both in respect to pornography but also in respect of contraception. Doyle identified how:

> We have had the making of our political and economic destiny in our own hands for the past six years, but our ideas of life and morality are dominated from outside and are reflected in the literature that largely circulates in this country and largely shapes its opinions on matters of general interest. It is high time that this dominating influence should be examined critically, that it should be controlled by means of a censorship … [this] is but a step in the realisation of the intellectual autonomy which has already had its counterpart in other domains.[66]

Against those who argued that books should be excluded was Domhnall Ó Buachalla (Fianna Fáil, later de Valera's governor general) who urged that 'just as much harm is done by the cheap novels [as by doubtful periodicals] that are imported by the ton every week.' Knowing a bit more about country life than Professor Thrift, he went on vividly to describe this aspect of contemporary book culture:

> They are distributed to the shops throughout the country and they are sold in an underhand way. They are bought principally by young girls, I am sorry to say, and they go into almost every cabin in the country. A short time ago I had occasion to visit a poor woman in an out-of-the-way place in County Meath, about three miles from Maynooth. This woman lived in a two-roomed thatched cabin, and a storm took away half the roof one night. She asked me to go out to have a look at it to see if I could do anything for her. This poor woman and I were sitting by the fire in the kitchen – the roof had been taken off the bedroom – and we were chatting. I saw on a shelf inside the chimney breast a box with some books in it. 'Biddy,' said I to the woman. 'I see you have some books here. Perhaps there may be some valuable old Irish manuscripts among them. May I have a look at them?' She said that I might. I took down the box and examined the contents. There were about ten copies of the 'Irish Rosary' and just as many copies of these filthy novels, novels with attractively coloured covers, with their suggestive, immoral, filthy stories. I looked through one of them to see what they were like, and then I asked her where she got them. She said she got them to read from girls in the neighbourhood.[67]

Company director Seán Goulding (Fianna Fáil) confirmed that 'I have heard Catholic girls boasting of the fact that they could get a particular book. They get such books and lend them to their friends. These girls have been educated in Catholic schools, yet they take pleasure in circulating such books.'[68]

The books so deplored by Ó Buachalla and his colleagues were typically strong in lavish romance, exotic background, adventure, and ended with 'the whole world lit with the white flame of a pure passion', as one novelist put it.[69] They were by no means explicit or pornographic, but certainly affected a freedom in personal relations that Ó Buachalla and his contemporaries, who came of age in the 1880s, found disconcerting. This freedom was exhibited in different ways in the various levels of the fiction hierarchy and in various locations in the Irish book trade. All eventually came under the censors' scrutiny. In the high, thin air were Virginia Woolf, D.H. Lawrence, E.M. Forster and James Joyce, whose 'pagan vileness' had so upset Fr Stephen Brown; next came middle-brow 'literary novelists' such as Kate O'Brien, Norah Hoult, Rebecca West, Aldous Huxley, John Galsworthy, J.B. Priestley; then bestsellers such as Daphne du Maurier, Mary Webb, Georgette Heyer, and A.J. Cronin; and finally the unashamedly escapist romances with titles like *The Way of an Eagle*, *Zarah the Cruel* and *The Passionate Flame*. Straight pornography was quite uncontentious and was typically signalled with such titles as *Naked Truth about Nudism*, and *Lady Chatterley's Second Husband*, both banned in 1935. Bookshops and libraries at all levels did well with genres, such as crime, thrillers and westerns, which had their own, often male, niches.

Virtually all of these books were published in London. Reviewing three novels from Irish publishers in 1920 (two from Martin Lester and one from Talbot), the *Freeman's Journal* declared that 'at last a serious beginning has been made in the process of substituting Irish for English novels. Never before had Dublin publishers issued so many new works of fiction, with novels and short stories of a kind obviously designed to appeal to the taste of the average reader.' But although Talbot persevered, the market odds continued to be stacked against local fiction.

Arguments such as Ó Buachalla's overwhelmed the attempt to remove books as such from the scope of the Bill, which was passed with few contraries in 1929. The membership of the first Censorship Board was announced in early 1930. Forty-seven publications were banned in the Board's first year, including Aldous Huxley's *Point Counterpoint*, Somerset Maugham's *Cakes and Ale* and Ethel Mannin's *Confessions and Impressions*. None of these were published, of course, by Irish publishers, so as far as the Irish book trade was concerned, the burden fell entirely on importing booksellers for whom weeding out books ordered and subsequently banned became an administrative chore. In fact, during the whole period of censorship, only two books originally published in Ireland (as opposed to written in Ireland or by Irish authors) were banned. These were Frank O'Connor's translation of *The Midnight Court*, and Norah Hoult's *Selected Stories*, both published by Maurice Fridberg jointly in Dublin and London.[70] Law-abiding booksellers were certainly not going to risk prosecution for the sake of selling for instance Radclyffe Hall's *Well of Loneliness* (a saga of lesbian love, one of the earliest banned books), or any one of the numerous marriage manuals blacklisted. Their concern was to identify that their stock was purged of the offending titles.

The new Board was naturally a major topic for the Associated Booksellers of Great Britain and Ireland when they met in Dublin in July 1930 for the first time since 1912. Over fifty delegates came from Britain, including well-known names such as Alden, Blackwell, Wilson (a doyen of the trade, of the London bookshop Bumpus), Thornton, Bowes (Cambridge). The delegates from Ireland included W.R. Nolan (Browne & Nolan), Charles Eason (president of the local branch) W.G. Lyon (Talbot and Educational Company), Alfred Fannin (Fannin's), W.P. Figgis (Hodges Figgis), Colm Ó Lochlainn (Three Candles), H. Pembrey (Greene's), Frank O'Reilly (CTS). *The Irish Book Lover* reported that 'almost 97 per cent of the books available through the book trade in Ireland is the product of English publishing presses and printed in England and Scotland.' What if anything was to be done? 'Surely', it argued, 'it is time that a definitely Irish Publishing Syndicate be formed with the dual object of keeping in Ireland a fair proportion of the publishing and printing of books by Irish authors?' No reference was made to the similar dream dreamt by Edmund Downey, Gavan Duffy and Yeats thirty years before.

Welcoming the delegates, Ernest Blythe (vice-president and minister for finance), disingenuously claimed that:

> None of the books condemned by the new Censorship Act was of any appreciable literary value, and nobody would lose by being unable to get a copy of any of them. The bookseller also would lose nothing by being unable to deal in them because none of them was a book likely to have a very wide circulation ... Nobody could say that the censorship interfered with the trade of any good class bookseller or with the rights of the intelligent and right minded citizen (Applause)'.[71]

Two books by Aldous Huxley had already been banned when he delivered this speech.

5

The Censorship Years: 1929 to 1959

The 1929 Censorship of Publications Act initiated the period of the 'seven censorships' which were to inhibit the book trade for a generation. As identified by the Irish Association of Civil Liberties these were: censorship by fear; by the Censorship Board; by the booksellers; by librarians; by library users; by library committees; by the public (especially clergymen and would-be clergymen). In concert, these generated an uncomfortable atmosphere of doubting self-censorship.[1] As is always the case, the non-official censorships were more rigorous and intrusive than the official. Michael Gill recalled 'objections being voiced to books on the shelves [of Gill's shop in O'Connell Street] even though they had not fallen foul of the Censorship Board.' Before showing the stock to her library buyer customers, Gill's Miss Fox had carefully to check that the latest banned titles were eliminated. As late as the early 1960s, Michael Gill was involved with a UCD publication called *St Stephen's* which ran into trouble with an article on the Rosary. He was asked by the Eblana Bookshop (by no means a 'religious' shop) to take away all copies of the magazine, as they had had complaints.[2] Brendan Behan told the story of how he once looked for a copy of Plato's *Symposium* and was told:

> We saw a slight run on it, and the same sort of people looking for it, so we just took it out of circulation ourselves. After all, we don't have to be made decent minded by Act of Dáil. We have our own way of detecting smut, however ancient.[3]

For a civil libertarian, of course this was Bad. For others, such as Senator Patrick Keohane, managing director of M.H. Gill from 1923 to his death in 1939, it was, as his fulsome obituary declared, nothing less than a fight against 'the forces of evil … the arrogant, the subversive and the vile'. The obituarist described how:

> if it was proposed to include in a schoolbook, selections from certain noted figures, he said no and meant no … I have heard one of his decisions in this sphere questioned: 'Oh, but Mr Keohane, this writer is well known in the world.' 'He has no place in our world.' 'But the actual piece, Mr Keohane, is quite inoffensive.' 'It may be, but it is not fitting that this man's name be put before Irish Catholic children as the name of a writer they are to look up to.'

With 'heroic intolerance' the Senator made it clear that no tainted authors (by which he meant Yeats and his associates most notably, but a long list of others) need look for publication by M.H. Gill as long as he was in charge.[4]

In the Educational Company and Talbot Press, the latter by now the predominant publisher of literary materials, a less root-and-branch line was adopted, but they quickly sensed that the censorship grip was steadily growing tighter. Not that they had been insensitive before the Act was passed. In November 1925, W.G. Lyon, signing as managing director of the Educational Publishing Company, wrote to Oxford University Press to suggest a royalty of 12.5 per cent for D.H. Lawrence's potboiler *Movements in European History*. Although, as he told Stephen Gwynn, Lyon thought the book 'most delightful and charming', for Irish use, he admitted, 'it requires revisions on every page'. He claimed to OUP that:

> We shall have considerable editorial expense to add to the new edition, as after the book has passed through our own editors it will require to be read finally by a Censor, because there would be no use bringing it out unless it had Episcopal approval (though of course this approval will not appear on the printed book).[5]

In July 1932, writing as the manager of Talbot, Lyon wrote to Allen & Unwin, 'as you may know, the Censorship Act is becoming more rigid in its operation and no Irish Publishing House could afford to run the slightest risk of having a book placed on the banned list.' A suspect reputation could affect not only Talbot's ordinary publishing programme, but also, potentially disastrously, the Educational Company's schools list. Clerical and other vigilantes were quick to denounce an entire list as tainted. This double jeopardy inhibited other trade/educational publishers too. In 1932, Lyon wrote to Allen & Unwin, 'we thank you for sending a copy of [Austin Clarke's first novel] *The Bright Temptation* but we imagine that sooner or later the incidents in Chapter III will catch the Censor's eye.'[6] As indeed they did, for *The Bright Temptation*, as published by Allen & Unwin later that year, was very quickly banned.

Nonetheless, Lyon was not closing doors and indeed was quickly alert to a new possibility presented by Fianna Fáil's 1932 policy of protecting and stimulating local industry: by building, as in Bishop Berkeley's query, 'a wall a thousand cubits high round this kingdom'.[7] 'If you have any other books in preparation by Irish authors or about Ireland,' he wrote, 'we would welcome the opportunity of reading advance proofs, with a view to the possibility of joint-publication to avoid Import Duty.' This last was a reference to the tariff of 10 per cent on imported books imposed in the Budget of May 1932. As Lyon explained to Blackie's in Glasgow, with whom they still did considerable business:

> You will have seen from the newspaper that our Free State Government have adopted a very drastic tariff policy ... on the Budget Day 43 new tariffs were imposed, including a tariff of 10% on 'bound books' but excluding 'printed books unbound'. This of course means that we shall have to add 10% to the retail price of all books we sell and which are not produced in Ireland ... if we were optimistic enough (which we certainly are not) that a new trade revival as a consequence of the tariffs would bring an era of prosperity, matters might turn out better than we anticipate.[8]

There was no doubt, however, that the change in tariff would help a trend that *The Irish Times* had already noted in 1932, that 'one of the most notable developments in the printing industry in the Free State within the last few years has been the production of cheap novels for London publishing houses.'[9]

Places to Meet

Literary culture requires meeting places. In Paris or Vienna it was the cafés, in Dublin it became the pubs. In the 1920s there had also been the 'at homes' held in various drawing rooms around the centre of the city. 'In those days', wrote Frank O'Connor, 'Sunday was Russell's night, Monday Yeats', Tuesday afternoon Sarah Purser, Sunday afternoon Seamus O'Sullivan's'.[10] At Russell's the guests ate cherry cake and drank tea, while their host boomed away; at one such gathering Olivia Roberston noticed a sudden hush, while Lennox Robinson and Walter Starkie began 'a duel of wit … they cut and thrust verbally at each other, they backed they feinted, they parried, attacked, and all the time the audience listened as connoisseurs … it was not the meaning that mattered, it was the technique.'[11]

By the 1930s, these gatherings had come to seem effete and writers sought the stronger drink provided in the Arts Club or in the pubs. There was the Bailey, where Gogarty and Liam O'Flaherty drank; the Palace Bar in Fleet Street where journalists from *The Irish Times* assembled, with Brinsley MacNamara and Austin Clarke as well; the Duke in Duke Street and Davy Byrne's across the road, where Brendan Behan and Kavanagh might be found.[12] Eager young editors from contemporary Irish publishers are not mentioned as part of these gatherings, though Honor Tracy of *The Bell* noted 'the belief [in England] that in Ireland a rich vein of talent was very persistent and publishers and agents were in the habit of coming over in relays to scout for themselves.'[13] Later commentators were to call this trawling of Irish talent the 'Dublin Raid'.

As a counterweight to the censorship era, Yeats, who liked nothing better than organising people, created the Irish Academy of Letters, no doubt with the French model in mind, but perhaps mindful also of the Academic Committee of English Letters created by Edmund Gosse in 1910, of which he was an early member.[14] This was only one of several formal gatherings of writers founded then: the Women Writers Club was established in 1933, the Irish branch of PEN (originally Poets, Essayists, Novelists) in 1935 and, in 1941, the Writers, Actors, Artists and Musicians Association: WAAMA. Other groups founded at this time, not specifically for writers, included the Library Association of Ireland in 1929 and the Book Association of Ireland around 1943.

WAAMA was established in September of 1941 with Sean O'Faolain as its president. It held a fair in the Mansion House in November 1942 and published at least two issues of an anthology called *Puck Fare*. Its main impact appears to have been as a precursor to Irish Actors' Equity. Myles na gCopaleen ensured the survival of the name by his sardonic comment on contemporary book culture in his 'Cruiskeen Lawn' column in *The Irish Times*. He fantasised that WAAMA could provide a book handling service for those who bought books but had neither the time nor inclination to read them.[15] It would come at various levels, from Popular (dog-eared, with tram tickets as bookmarks) up to Superb, in which every volume was to be thoroughly handled, forged letters from famous literati inserted as bookmarks, and passages underlined with comments such as 'I remember poor Joyce saying the very same thing' added at appropriate places.[16]

As to the Irish Academy of Letters, 'the idea,' wrote Frank O'Connor, 'was sound enough – a solid body of informed opinion that might encourage young writers and discourage the Catholic Church from suppressing them; but for both purposes it suffered from the fact that apart from Yeats its most important members lived in England and had no notion of what conditions in Ireland were like.'[17] In practice, its main function, for the fifty years or so it survived, was to award prizes and to operate as what the *Irish Press* once called 'the most exclusive club in Ireland' with only thirty-five members.[18] The most prestigious award was the Gregory Medal, given every three years for a substantial body of meritorious work. The first awards were in 1937 to G. Bernard Shaw, W.B. Yeats, Æ and Douglas Hyde; the first three being respectively president, vice-president and secretary of the Academy. Apart from these, eleven Gregory Medals were awarded at three-year intervals, for instance to Mary Lavin, Padraic Colum, Austin Clarke and Edith Somerville. There were also two funded prizes, the Casement Prize for the best work in poetry and drama and the Harmsworth Award for the best original work of prose by an Irish author. But as an anti-censorship group its impact was negligible and as early as 1936 members of the Academy such as Frank O'Connor and Stephen Gwynn were complaining that it was 'a moribund institution'.

Nevertheless, the Academy kept going, with the Friends of the Irish Academy of Letters (founded in 1940 to promote the Academy) organising two lively book fairs in 1941 and 1942. By 1956, the Casement and Harmsworth awards had become defunct, and the Gregory Medal was 'the only one the Academy was in a position to bestow'. Some years later the newly founded Allied Irish Bank asked the Academy to advise on its literary awards, and this became the main annual activity. Its accounts in 1978 showed that although there was £506 in the bank, the Academy had rather feebly spent just £54 that year, £40 of which was on the annual audit, and the balance being for stationery, postage and hire of the room for the AGM. The Academy was still extant in the 1980s, though by this time Aosdána (established in 1981 and financed by the Arts Council) looked about to steal its limelight. As late as 1984, however, Anthony Cronin, Jennifer Johnston and John Banville were proposed as members. The sad last item in the archive is a copy of a 1987 letter from the then secretary Seán White to the bibliographer Alan Eager apologising that 'due to death, illness and absence of various members' no Council meeting had been held since the previous year.[19]

Publishing in Irish

Apart from occasional titles, the substantial history of book publishing in the Irish language began with the vigorous operations of the Gaelic League, founded in 1893. 'As far as Irish letters were concerned,' wrote Leon Ó Broin, 'the Irish people of the 18th century had become illiterate.'[20] Books printed in Irish were a rarity: Ó Broin (writing in 1938) said that more books in Irish had been published 'in the preceding eight years than probably in the whole of the preceding three centuries.' Consequently, as the historian of Gaelic prose Philip O'Leary puts it, 'many of the leading writers of the Gaelic Revival never read a book in the Irish language in their formative years. Some had not even imagined that such a thing was possible.'[21]

In 1897, the League founded an annual cultural festival offering prizes for literary work, and in the same year began to publish original creative work as well as educational booklets. 'By 1899,' writes Philip O'Leary, 'the organisation felt it necessary to coordinate these activities under the aegis of a Publications Committee and by 1908 it had established its own press An Cló-Chumann (later Clódhanna Teoranta) to deal with the growing number of circulars, pamphlets and books of all kinds.'[22]

Of course, getting into print was only the first step; selling was the next, and this often proved difficult as M.H. Gill's figures for some Irish language books sold on behalf of the League showed:

> The first and most basic of O'Growney's instructional series sold 5,645 copies, the more difficult fifth book sold but ninety. Little pamphlets containing single simple folktales could sell as many as 4,206 copies while a more scholarly anthology of folk material was bought by only forty-four people. An original comic story set in the country attracted 3,106 buyers while of four plays the best-seller was bought by 145 and the worst by thirteen.[23]

It is no wonder then that by 1915, Clódhanna's financial difficulties were such that a temporary halt had to be called to operations. The destruction of original plates during the Rising and in the War of Independence, combined with poor storage facilities, further contributed to losses.[24] By the 1920s, the League was publishing very little.

The difficulties of 'bootstrapping' a great national literary culture were daunting. As P.S. O'Hegarty (father of the founder of Sáirséal & Dill) pointed out in 1925, Irish had:

> practically no modern literature save school text books, it has practically no translations, its vocabulary is centuries out of date, it is not habitually used anywhere in Ireland for official, church, business or professional purposes, nor is it possible so to use it. It has no international value outside philology.[25]

There was also no market for books in Irish: people in the Gaeltacht did not buy Irish books partly because they were so few, and partly for the same reason as people elsewhere did not buy books in English, with the added constraint, as Ó Broin put it, that 'the routine of agricultural life permits neither the comfort nor the leisure in which people can become fond of reading.'[26]

How was it to be done? With passionate intensity some Gaeilgeoirí argued that it was necessary to lead Irish readers down the nursery slopes of literature first – others, equally intensely, believed that such milk-and-water stuff would never sustain adult interest. Some said the spelling should be simplified and modernised – others deplored such a loss of cultural and etymological history and saw any such simplification as back-door Anglicisation (often noting at the same time that these changes to the national heritage were proposed by a central Dublin government whose legitimacy was doubtful). Equally bitter arguments pitched proponents of the old Gaelic type, first used in 1571, against modern roman faces. As Philip O'Leary puts it, 'in the first two decades of the independent state the related questions of orthography and typeface were argued with a ferocity that could divide families and friends, and drive would-be sympathisers away from the revival in amazed disgust'.[27] At one of its very first meetings, in March 1932, the incoming Fianna Fáil cabinet resolved to commit to the old Gaelic typeface and the traditional spelling for official documents.

Behind these causes of contention was the deep split between the three ways of speaking and spelling the language: the so-called dialect wars. Was the Irish of Munster, Connacht or Ulster the true, authentic, note? Munster Irish was favoured in the centres of power, but proponents of the Ulster 'dialect' resisted vehemently; some were even found to say that they would rather

Irish died altogether than that Munster Irish should prevail.[28] The bitterness of these debates, that so repelled outsiders, stemmed from an acute feeling that this, now, was the only chance to redress hundreds of years of neglect and recreate a Gaelic culture. This was combined too often with a relish for rhetoric: like Hotspur, they preferred oaths to be mouth-filling.

'To meet the situation created by the State assuming the leadership in the language revival', wrote Leon Ó Broin, 'it was inevitable that the State should become itself a publisher.'[29] This had been recognised by the first Dáil which had drafted a programme of textbook publications. The Ministry for Irish, 'decided to support Cumann na hÚdair' (the Authors Club) a collection of writers formed in 1920 whose aim was to work together in getting help with the publication of books, and the issue was considered 'a Matter of Urgency'.[30] With the encouragement of minister for finance Ernest Blythe, An Gúm ('the scheme') began to evolve. Initially the object was to produce books for secondary schools. A committee (Coiste na Leabhar) began to meet in May 1926 to advise the Department of Education primarily on books suitable for secondary schools, but also for other beginners. Gearóidín Uí Laighléis writes:

> The primary business of Coiste na Leabhar was to examine the manuscripts put before the Department and advise the Department as to a) should they be accepted, as they were, b) should they be accepted on condition they are changed, or c) should they be rejected? They were also responsible for the binding, cover, and appearance of the books, and of the price to be paid to the writers.[31]

A second committee (An Coiste Foilsiúcháin) with a brief to address the wider public was formed in September 1927. In July 1928, these two committees were merged under the title Coiste na Leabhar.

Once An Gúm was up and running it employed proofreaders and editors, but there seems to have been no clear plan as to how the actual physical business of publishing should be carried out. At first it was thought that the printing would be arranged through the Stationery Office and the actual publishing done by existing commercial firms. After experimenting with selling through Eason's, it was decided that all selling would be through the Stationery Office, not a body noted for its vigorous sales energy.

The *Annual Report* of 1930/31 showed that the agency had published 102 titles, and twelve years later several hundred titles had been published, at a rate substantially greater than Gill or Talbot or Browne & Nolan in the same period. By this time, the original policy of commissioning translations from well-known English books was being revised. The idea that people in the Gaeltacht would now be happy to read *Three Men in a Boat*, *Kidnapped* or *War of the Worlds* in Irish (all translated for An Gúm by Ó Broin himself) did not quite stack up with the understanding that 'native Irish speakers are still largely illiterate in the Irish language – when they read a book it is usually an English one.' But accepting more original Irish books gave rise to quality problems: it was reported that perhaps half of the books submitted were eventually published, a ratio (when compared to the 1 in 1,000 or fewer accepted by English language publishers) that does not inspire confidence. A more substantial objection was that the reasonably well-paid translation scheme was deflecting the attention of Irish writers from original work. 'As a young writer,' reported Ó Broin, 'I found the terms for both original work and translations very attractive;' they 'kept the wolf from the door'.[32]

An Gúm was, of course, the subject of constant attack (the very word Gúm was held to be doubtfully Irish). Some of the major Irish literary figures argued, in the vehement ways they had, that it was itself one of the biggest obstacles facing the language revival. And certainly some of its choices were questionable, as Roibeárd Ó Faracháin (later controller of programmes, Radio Éireann 1947–74) pointed out, complaining that there was little poetry (accounted by most the glory of Gaelic) and asking why translate *Three Men in a Boat* and none of the Christian spiritual classics? Séamus Ó Grianna (who had worked at the agency as a translator) was particularly vehement: 'The Gúm must go,' he wrote in *An Phoblact*, 'with its committee of doubtful credentials, and its swarm of ordinary civil servants. It is underselling the other Irish publishers. It is wasting the taxpayer's money to the extent of £20,000 a year … Bury the Gúm. Then go on to something honest, impartial, creative and Gaelic.'[33]

A substantial cause of complaint was the time that books took to go through the system, which could be six or seven years and sometimes even more. An article by Ernest Blythe in the *Irish Independent* in 1936 addressed the issue of delay in An Gúm. He described how An Gúm, the Stationery Office and the authors all blamed each other, in a very 'civil service' way:

> The writers would blame the proof-readers; the editors would blame the writers: When, five years ago, I was investigating the cause of the terrible delays which occur in publishing accepted manuscripts, I found that the system that still exists baffled all attempts to fix responsibility. The author dealt with the Publication Section of the Department of Education, which dealt with the Stationery Office, a sub-department of the Department

> of Finance, which dealt with the printers. The author laid the blame for delays on the Gúm, the Stationery Office or the printer, but naturally held himself faultless.
>
> The Education Office blamed the writers, or some of them, whose erratic spelling and careless work, including, in the case of certain translators, a tendency to skip difficult passages, caused the task of editorial revision to be unduly prolonged and laborious: it also blamed the Stationery Office for delaying copy and proofs on their way to and from the printer, and for failing to adopt any firm attitude towards printers, no matter how dilatory they were.[34]

The compulsory use of Gaelic type after 1932 was cited as a further cause of delay.

An Gúm was of course not to be buried. By 1938, the agency had produced over 500 subsidised titles, some original, most translated. But the sales make it clear why ordinary publishers had not ventured far into Irish language publishing. Ó Broin wrote:

> The Gúm publications fall under two heads, those that are described as Secondary School texts, and works of general literature. Up to the present there are 64 books in the first category with an average sale of 1,600 copies each, and 358 in the second category with an average sale of 480 copies each.

As a result of this sales pattern, while thirteen of the sixty-four textbooks had repaid their expenses, only five of the 358 other works had managed to cover their costs.[35] New publishers often over-print, but there was an awkward moment for An Gúm in the 1950s when it was discovered that 97,000 books had been pulped, some having sold in twenty years one third or less than their print run.[36]

By the 1940s the indictment against An Gúm was clear.[37] Despite its effective monopoly it had by no means inspired any revival of writing in Irish: the civil servants had none of the breadth of mind, creative focus or vision that the independent publisher Sáirséal & Dill was later to provide. The production process was often heartbreakingly slow and once printed the books were never advertised or promoted, so the sight of an Irish book in a bookshop window was a rarity. And, finally, the texts were insipid. A combination of its focus on the schools market and the natural civil service disinclination to disturb anyone in authority, resulted in inoffensive publications that would not upset the juveniles or their moral guardians. One writer, quoted by O'Leary, noted that 'it is not permitted to put a bad person [in a book]. It is not permitted to do a bad deed.'[38] In disappointment, Ernest Blythe (the founding Minister) wrote in 1950 that An Gúm had by then produced more than 800 titles, but he would be hard-pressed to find even a dozen of those he would read if they had been published in English. As with the Soviet regime in the same era, the experiment of state-driven publishing was not a triumph.

Extraordinarily, dark as the Irish language scene looked at the beginning of the 1940s, by the end of the decade, as we shall see, there was quite a new impetus.

Educational Publishing

In the free world, educational publishing is a key component of the business mix and so it was in Ireland. Typically, as in Gill, Browne & Nolan and the Educational Company/Talbot combination, the same house published both trade and educational books. This was obviously efficient in that the same skills and working practices were deployed over both sets of books and the educational books provided a stable leg to the financial stool. In the censorship years, however, the combination made the house vulnerable. Objectors to a trade title could, it was feared, easily turn their ire to persuading the clerical managers of primary and secondary schools not to purchase titles from the offending publisher.

The administration of education was inherited by the new State from nineteenth-century arrangements going back to the 1830s. There had been a significant shift around 1900 in the primary programme from the 'murder machine' so vividly (though anachronistically) described by Pearse. Following European and American models, the syllabus had become markedly more child-centred in the new century, with science, nature study, drawing, physical education and singing as compulsory elements.[39] With the new State things changed radically: now, as John Coolahan put it, 'the most important function of the school programme was the promotion of a knowledge of Irish'.[40] Impressed by the speed and facility with which children in other countries learned languages virtually in the playground, enthusiasts hoped to see the language becoming universal in a generation.

To achieve this, a new syllabus, concentrating on Irish, English and arithmetic, with additional history, geography and singing was devised. Ideally, all would be taught through the medium of Irish. The grace notes of the 1900 syllabus were abandoned for the one great object. There was equally no attempt to centralise management of the schools or monitor the quality of the buildings.

From 1924, control of the curriculum of National Schools was vested in the new Department of Education. This included the right to refuse admission to the so-called 'sanctioned' list of any books that did not pass a very detailed scrutiny. National School teachers were required to choose their books for Irish, English, history and maths from such lists. For secondary schools the department merely laid down a syllabus, and left it up to the teacher to be satisfied that the publisher's offering did in fact properly cover the syllabus.

In 1940, however, de Valera as Minister for Education proposed that the State compile and edit an Irish Reader for Standards V and VI to be ready for the school year 1941/2. Speaking to a deputation of Irish publishers, 'he recognised that the measure would interfere with the ordinary course of publishing of books for these Standards but in the National interests that could not be helped.' His plan was that in subsequent years the state would produce an arithmetic for Standard IV and upwards, a history, a geography and possibly a grammar.[41] Perhaps because of the war, or perhaps in response to second, better, thoughts, this did not happen, but clearly the publishing industry was regarded as completely dispensable.[42]

The department, of course, had been given a clear agenda. As the chief inspector put it in 1926, 'they were going to make Irish the language of the country and he did not care what hog, dog or devil stood in the way, they were going to smite them.'[43] From the point of view of the publishing industry this meant close examination of the proposed schoolbooks. Publishers were required to submit all text and illustrations to the Department, latterly in page proof form.

The Department subjected each text to intense scrutiny and the tone of the letters does not suggest an equal relationship: 'A Chara,' writes W.G. Lyon, 2 April 1932, 'the minor revisions which you so kindly suggested have received our close attention and are embodied in the manuscript we send herewith. We are substituting fresh lessons for those whose deletion you recommended.'[44] 'A Chara' was only the start. The Educational Company acquired a typewriter fitted with the old Gaelic alphabet, on which many letters were written to the department's officials. These letters were usually identified as from 'An S', or An Seabhac – aka Pádraig Ó Siochfhradha, author of the famous text *Jimín Máire Thaidhg* – who had joined the company as an editor in 1932.

Little attention was paid to the commercial interests of the publishers. In 1933, a revised list of sanctioned books for primary schools was issued, leaving very little time for publishers 'to provide sufficient and varied supplies of new books in substitution for those that your Department desires to have withdrawn'. The revision, of course, left publishers holding unsaleable stock.[45]

In 1938, the Educational Company wrote stoically to the Office of National Education: 'we thank you for the criticism of the Senior Clonard reader'. Eight stories from the reader (with titles such as 'a Roman dinner', 'a French duel', 'Among the Eskimoes') were to be deleted from the proof and replaced with 'Wicklow in Autumn', 'Parnell defends his policy', 'The West's asleep', 'Life in Aran', etc. Later that year the company proposed using 18 pt type for the introductory and beginner's texts of a new series, 14 pt for the preparatory and 12 pt for the junior etc.: 'you will do us a great favour if you can let me know as soon as possible – a phone message would do – whether these types will meet your wishes.'

In the absence of detailed guidelines, there was a suspicion of arbitrariness. In 1932, the company complained that a 'Rural Outlook Reader' had been rejected (which was of course the kiss of death) 'as it contained few of the features this Department would expect to find in a rural reader for Irish schools'. How could we know what was required? wrote the company, 'the Department's expectations must to any publisher be largely a matter of intelligent surmise.' On another occasion a literary reader was rejected because it contained poems the advisor described as 'hackneyed' and which were already contained in sanctioned books – which, considering over 300 titles had been sanctioned, was neither surprising nor avoidable.[46]

Even at the cost of so much trouble, the prize remained worth seeking. A schoolbook would normally be printed for a three-year run of several thousand copies and if teachers liked it could look forward to multiple reprintings. Trade books rarely aspired to such longevity.

What Ireland was Reading

The introduction of a duty on bound novels in the 1932 national budget meant that it was now possible to identify just how much fiction was coming in from England. Fr R.S. Devane (the author of the original *Evil Literature* pamphlet of 1926) identified that just over one novel per household per year was being imported (see Table 4). The import figures show also that there was a steadily diminishing impact of British daily papers during the period 1933–49, a phenomenon particularly marked after the isolation of the Emergency period. Periodicals, on the other hand, seemed if anything to have increased in popularity.

Table 4. Imported publications *1933–49*

Year	*Books*	*Dailies*	*Periodicals liable to duty*	*Books per house-hold*	*Dailies per house-hold*	*Periodicals per house-hold*
1933	756,353	2,631,121	870,375	1.20	50	17
1935	710,037	1,345,349	1,075,069	1.13	26	20
1937	653,982	1,232,587	1,165,268	1.04	23	22
1938	560,901	1,166,696	1,241,576	0.89	22	24
No data during the Emergency						
1947	450,800	380,963	1,544,255	0.68	7	28
1948	567,973	343,786	1,625,225	0.86	6	29
1949	742,678	444,585	1,909,040	1.12	8	35

Source: based on Rev. R.S. Devane *The Imported Press* (Dublin, 1950) pp. 14, 22, 23

Most of the imported novels would have been for use in commercial circulating libraries, for the low priority given to public libraries by the new State meant that, as Máirín O'Byrne of Dublin City Library put it, 'little progress was achieved during the period 1930–47 and the spirit of Irish librarianship was at its lowest ebb at that time.' A report of the Library Council in 1958 noted that only a small proportion of the population used the service, no doubt partly because of 'serious deficiencies in relation to stock, premises and staff,'[47] a situation that was not remedied until the 1970s. Other limiting factors were the fear of contagion (referred to in Chapter 4), the fact that only ratepayers could get library cards, an elitist view that popular novels were inferior, and the professional idea that the ideal library had a stock suitable for scholars (hence only one copy of any title) not for ordinary leisure book readers. Even where there were books, moral vigilantes kept up a close scrutiny of stockholdings. A tight control was kept on the content of books: in 1928, the county librarian of Donegal reported that in 1921 'an agreed list of authors whose works were not to be admitted was drawn up and has always been adhered to.' During restocking after a fire, 'all books of which there were any doubts were set aside and not allowed into circulation until they had been examined and reported on.'[48] In 1938, it was alleged by *The Irish Times*' diarist that, following complaints, books on Spain, Mexico, Russia and 'certain philosophical and sociological issues' were being quietly withdrawn from the Dublin Public Library stock, unless they were published by one of two approved firms. An anonymous official effectively confirmed the story, stating that there was an 'inquiry into the opinions expressed by the authors whose works have been temporarily withdrawn.'[49]

The weakness of the public library system stimulated a network of commercial circulating libraries such as that described by Bryan MacMahon in an article in *The Bell*. As well as educational books and a wide range of stationery (pencils, Mass cards, rosary beads, inks, cake-cups, chalks, confetti, Christmas cards, betting books etc.) his Listowel shop contained a circulating library supplied by Argosy & Sundial from Liverpool. Starting with 500 titles, the service provided fresh titles every week, so that the whole stock more or less turned over in a year. Charges for new publications were 3*d* for four days, and older publications 2*d* for seven days. Popular Irish authors were Maurice Walsh (a local man), Frank O'Connor, Sean O'Faolain and Peadar O'Donnell; but the stock in light romantic fiction, such as Anne Duffield, Mary Burchell and Kathleen Norris were 'the real money-spinners'. The Western novel also had 'an amazing grip' on the rural reading public. MacMahon was scathing about actual book-buying: 'people scarcely buy books now except the outstanding best sellers to be given as presents.' (Perhaps surprisingly, MacMahon found that 'the venture pays sufficiently well to be interesting ... I am thoroughly well satisfied with the undertaking.' [50])

Among the companies servicing these libraries was Argosy, whose founder John McCourt had been agent to the Liverpool company Argosy and Sundial Libraries before they pulled out of Ireland in the early 1940s. McCourt soon had three vans on the road, fitted with internal shelves so they could double as mobile libraries.[51] The customers were post offices, sweetshops, chemists and other shops running little libraries (perhaps only a shelf or two at the back of the shop). By the late 1940s, Argosy had four libraries of their own in the Dublin area, including the one in their headquarters in Ranelagh. Here, women were employed to prepare the books for circulation: as well as colour coding the spines (yellow for Westerns, pink for romance, green for crime), and inserting a borrowings page, they were, crucially, responsible for protecting the jackets from adverse comment from clerical and other busybodies. This involved covering up short skirts or décolletage, and separating embracing or even touching couples. The jacket would be taken off, modesty patches applied and perhaps an innocuous object (a dog or a plant snipped from a now-disused cover) pasted between the separated pair before laminating.

This process, as McCourt's granddaughter, Mary Stanley remembered, was conducted by three 'highly moral, even uptight' women (with the enthusiastic help of Mary, her sister Lucy and her brother, Fergal, who became skilled at this). For most of the books, as it happened, suggestiveness was more in the mind of the jacket artist than in the text. There were exceptions. In 1938, a Mills & Boon title was banned for mentioning contraception and so, as the company's historian writes, 'in later years the fear of offending the Irish – and jeopardising the lucrative Irish market – would become a cornerstone of editorial policy.'[52]

Between 1934 and 1941, *The Irish Times* ran a weekly survey in various formats called 'What Dublin is reading', which gave a snapshot of the tastes of the upmarket city-centre customers. The table, printed on the Saturday book page, was initiated in November 1934 with reports from bookshops Browne & Nolan, Combridge, James Duffy, Eason's, Hanna's, Hodges Figgis, Gill, and Three Candles, and the libraries run by Greene's, and the Times Book Club. Each outlet reported its bestselling/borrowed fiction and non-fiction titles. In the first survey Francis Brett Young and P. G. Wodehouse each had two titles in the list; but in non-fiction Queen Marie of Romania's *Story of My Life* was the only title mentioned by two outlets. Irish authors Joseph O'Neill, Kate O'Brien, 'Máire' and Canon Sheehan each had one title.[53]

Around the time of Edward VIII's abdication in December 1936, *Gone with the Wind* was doing well in fiction and H.V. Morton's *In the Steps of St Paul* in non-fiction. Irish-interest titles, including lives of Tom Clarke and Michael Ó Cléirigh, and T.H. Mason's *Islands of Ireland*, represented four out of eight titles mentioned. In September 1938, the time of the Munich crisis, Maurice Walsh's *Sons of the Swordmaker* nearly swept the board, being identified as their top fiction title by seven out of ten shops reporting. In non-fiction, Chesterton and Belloc both appeared and the controversial General Crozier's *The Men I Killed* in two outlets, Hanna's and Humphries of Trinity Street. The survey was discontinued in the early 1940s, though revived twenty years later in the mid 1960s. The last outing was an interview with J.T. Dowling of the Dublin County Libraries Committee who 'disclosed to our reporter' that fiction was popular, followed by travel and biography. He recorded a sustained demand for books about the war, and among (male) juveniles books about air and sea adventure had replaced school stories. Girls were still keen on school stories, however.[54]

The Publishing Scene in the 1940s and 1950s

A listing published in 1944 by the Book Association of Ireland identified 390 books published in Ireland between 1938 and 1943 and still in print. This represents no more than sixty-five titles a year. Although only 20 per cent of the titles are explicitly categorised as 'Religious', in practice, at least a third of the 'Biography, History' category – with titles such as *Pius XII: Priest and Statesmen* and *Irish Saints in Ten Countries* – would today be so categorised, as would at least half of the 'Philosophy, Sociology' category. Altogether, at least a third of titles had explicit Catholic religious content. Fiction would have scored much less well if Talbot had not taken advantage of wartime conditions to issue a complete reprint of Annie M.P. Smithson's twelve novels. (In 1946, *The Irish Times* gave an elitist sneer at such popular publishing: 'a good deal of trash managed to use paper which would have been employed to better advantage on the reprints of "classics" and larger editions of more reputable and useful literature'.) [55]

Table 5. Irish-published books 1938–44 by assigned class

Subject	*Books*	*Per cent*
Religious	77	20
Philosophy, sociology	26	6.5
Biography & history	75	19
Poetry & belles-lettres	59	15
Fiction	53	13.5
Plays	46	12
Children	6	1.5
Travel	6	1.5
Miscellaneous	42	11
Total	390	100

Source: Book Association of Ireland, 1944.

Note: 'Miscellaneous' is a wide-ranging set including *Irish Without Worry*, *Acts and Orders Relating to Death Duties*, *The Practical Bee Guide* and the *Irish Ecclesiastical Record*, which was of course a periodical. The 'Fiction' total includes 19 reprints of Annie M.P. Smithson titles and 'Plays' includes 13 by Sinéad de Valera.

Books from twenty-four publishers were listed, with outputs falling into three divisions. With thirty or more titles in the period M.H. Gill, Duffy, Browne & Nolan and Talbot represent over half the total. In the second division, with ten to thirty titles, come Hodges Figgis, Quota, Dundalgan, the Stationery Office, CTS, the Irish Tourist Authority, Three Candles. Publishing only a few titles are occasional publishers such as the Waterford News, Cork University Press, printers Guy and O'Gorman and the Assisi Press.

The state of Irish publishing was certainly depressed in the late 1940s and early 1950s. Sean O'Faolain complained in *The Bell* in 1943, 'an Irish publisher will print a book, if you take it to him under your arm and if it is 100 per cent safe. These two provisos are rigid' (i.e. no advances for unwritten books, and no risks).[56] It was not, he claimed, that books of Irish interest did not sell reasonably well: O'Faolain instanced a recent novel by an unnamed young Irishman which sold 2,000 copies and a history title with sales of over 15,000. (He did not mention that his own *A Nest of Simple Folk*, published ten years before, had been feted by the *New York Times*, but sold a mere twenty-six copies in Ireland in its first week.)[57] A post-war British ban on imported books and magazines did not help. The British Board of Trade claimed that this action, which also affected the Netherlands, Australia and other Commonwealth countries, was required by the terms of an American loan which prohibited preferential rates. The ban effectively prevented the sale in Britain or Northern Ireland of books or periodicals published in the Republic from 1946.[58] The ban came in just before David Marcus secured a big order from a British distributor for the first edition of his new periodical *Irish Writing*. His excitement at receiving the order was quickly dashed when he was told it required a licence from the British Board of Trade. This proved impossible to get, so sales were restricted to Ireland, with devastating effects on his overdraft.[59] The ban was finally lifted in October 1949.

Being restricted to sales in Ireland was not comfortable. In 1948, the manager of Browne & Nolan commented: 'our home market is at present too small to absorb editions of an economic size … with the present cost of printing it is hardly worth a publisher's while producing a book of any kind for which a sale of 2,500 copies is not reasonably expected.'[60]

Ireland, wrote Ivan Morris, printer and journal publisher, 'is not a book-buying country. Considering the population of the twenty-six counties, remarkably few books are bought, and a light novel of which 5,000 would be sold in England, will realise sales of about 200 after a vigorous sales campaign.'[61]

Around this time Cork University Press, publishing serious hardback non-fiction, sold 1,200 copies of *Modern Democracy* by James Hogan between 1938 and 1943, 1,000 copies of Alfred O'Rahilly's *Money* in 1941 (a 700-copy reprint in 1942 was reduced to fewer than 100 by 1943), and 1,650 copies of *Moral Principles* by the same author between 1948 and 1953.[62] If Browne & Nolan's figures were not exaggerated, these, their 'bestsellers', were all loss-makers.

Cork University Press was the creation of the ever-active Alfred O'Rahilly, long-time registrar and then president of University College Cork.[63] According to its historian John A. Murphy, 'The Press was founded to stimulate and serve the publishing needs of UCC academics and to flaunt the Cork flag in Dublin's face.' It was a visionary enterprise, long before the success of US academic houses showed what could be done with a fair wind from library budgets. The press started bravely with four titles in 1925, two in 1926 and another four in 1928. That year saw the handing over of the press to the University which set up an annual grant of £128 for its running. This recognised the perennial problem of academic presses: how to maintain at the same time cash flow and academic standards. Memorable titles (though none likely to provide a lasting income) published in the early days included Corkery's *Synge and Anglo-Irish Literature*, the Irish poetry anthology of T.F. O'Rahilly, Hogan's *Election and Representation* and MacLysaght's *Irish Life in the Seventeenth Century*. But, as Alfred O'Rahilly pointed out in the 1950s, 'the market for our books is limited by their nature: no amount of advertising will convince the average creamery manager that he should read *The Psychology of Sartre* or the psychologist that he should buy *Commercial Methods of Testing Milk*.'[64]

Experiments to bridge the gap were several: publishing the UCC *Record* for the governing body was one, publishing texts for students (frowned on by members of the board) was another. As is often the case, the technical problems of book production, marketing, storage and dispatch were continual headaches. O'Rahilly's friendship with Basil Blackwell of Oxford provided some assistance and then 'two ill-fated experiments to promote sales by employment of an outside manager' were tried. One in 1942–45, whose grandiose schemes nearly led to the collapse of the Press, and another more short-lived with Mercier Press in 1954. O'Rahilly's influence waned in the mid-1950s and Denis Gwynn, professor of modern history at UCC, became general editor. 'The Press,' comments its historian severely, 'did not experience any significant growth during his editorship,' which lasted until 1963. The later history of the press, with the employment of a professional manager trained at Longmans, will be dealt with in a subsequent chapter.

Another venture, in the Cuala Press style, began publishing in 1937 with its founder Blánaid Salkeld's *the engine is left running*. This was Gayfield Press, based in Morehampton Road, Dublin. Its most distinguished author was the poet Ewart Milne, whose first book *Forty North Fifty West* it published in 1938. The physical press on which Gayfield's small number of publications was printed was taken over by Liam Miller's Dolmen in the early 1950s.[65] More conventional in aspiration was the Belfast-based Quota Press, run by Dora Kennedy, who published over 100 titles between 1927 and 1954, printing very often in the Channel Isles.[66]

A survey of the titles published by the main Dublin firms in 1950, after twenty years of the censorship regime, reveals a scene that was actually less lively than that previously described for the Dublin of 1750. In a 1951 pamphlet Waterford librarian Fergus Murphy (president of the Library Association 1959) noted that Irish publishers had produced 555 books in the eleven years to 1948. Although these were generally years of severe paper shortage, by way of contrast he noted that Norway produced 2,384 books in just one of those years and Switzerland, with three competing contiguous languages, 2,162. He urged Irish publishers to employ joint marketing strategies.[67]

Perhaps the reason that Irish people were such poor book buyers (as the commentators so frequently lamented) was simple poverty. This no doubt may have been true for many, for the Irish economy did not do well under de Valera. The first Household Budget Survey (1951, covering urban households only), however, reported that the average household spent more than four times as much on going to the cinema as on books and three times as much on newspapers and magazines as on books. These figures, which include purchases of school books, demonstrate a clear relegation of books to second or third choice. Furthermore, since two thirds of book expenditure was in the second half of the year, it is probable that school books and Christmas gifts, rather than personal reading, made up the bulk of book purchases.

Religion had always been important to Irish publishers, such as in 1750, as we have seen, but in 1950 it was of claustrophobic impact. It was of course a Holy Year, in which the Pope urged the Faithful to pilgrimage and prayer. Of the ninety-eight titles recorded by the National Library catalogue from the twelve top publishers, from the Catholic Truth Society to Three Candles, one third were explicitly religious.[68] (This echoes the one third religion of the titles in the Book Association's listing.) Despite mounting fears that the international situation would soon result in a catastrophic East–West war there was no reflection of this in publishers' lists. The year 1949 had been full of ominous happenings: the Western alliance, NATO, had been established in April; the Russians had tested their first atomic bomb in August; in the same month the

Communist Party took over China, so that now virtually the whole Eurasian land mass was under Communist control; in December, Mao Tse Tung went to Moscow and signed a friendship pact with Stalin. The Korean War broke out in June 1950. In the Dáil, de Valera spoke gloomily of 'the prospect of a conflict far more terrible than that through which we have just passed'.[69] Irish publishing, presumably reflecting the readers, made no comment. Only one Irish-published title addressed current international affairs (from Browne & Nolan on the Council of Europe). M.H. Gill published a book on the Six Counties, Dundalgan one on Highland dress in Ireland and the Isle of Man (and two valuable county floras), Clonmore & Reynolds gave us *The Pope and the Vatican City*, *Ireland and Italy* and *God, Satan and Man*, but the general focus was deeply inward-looking, exemplified perhaps by *Courtesy in the Convent* from Mercier.

Unexpectedly, the most lively part of the Irish publishing scene in the 1940s was that in the Irish language. After the vitriolic and debilitating internal debates of the 1920s and 1930s, described by Philip O'Leary, 'the war years in fact witnessed an unexpected upsurge in Gaelic creative writing ... there emerged a handful of authors whose work ranks with the best of the century's writing in Irish.'[70] Philip O'Leary identified four elements in what he called 'a remarkable synergy that transformed Gaelic literary energy in the late 1940s'. The four elements were (in chronological order): the foundation in 1942 of the journal *Comhar* which served as an innovatory literary centre, drawing into its ambit many who would later become prominent in Irish language circles such as Seán Ó hÉigeartaigh, Dónal Ó Móráin and Tomás de Bhaldraithe; the publication in 1943 of the newspaper *Inniú* (edited by Ciarán Ó Nualláin, Myles' brother), with its move to weekly publication in 1945 and the establishment of the printing press Foilseacháin Náisiúnta Teo (FNT) in Westport by taking over the *Mayo News* plant and paper;[71] the launching of an independent book publisher called Sáirséal & Dill, which broke the effective monopoly of An Gúm and provided an outlet for a new generation of Irish writers; and finally the creation of an Irish language book club, An Club Leabhar, in 1948.[72]

Sáirséal & Dill was established with a bequest from an aunt by a young Department of Finance official Seán Ó hÉigeartaigh and his wife Bríghid, who rapidly became an effective and sensitive editor. The first publication was *Tonn Tuile* by Séamus Ó Néill published in November 1947, with an ambitious 3,500 copies, selling 1,300 in the first year at 7*s* 6*d*. Something went wrong with the finances, however, so Seán reckoned that even if the 3,500 copies sold out (which they did not until 1964) there would still be a loss of £100.

Nonetheless, Seán and Bríghid persevered, greatly aided by the establishment of the book club An Club Leabhar. By 1960 they had published some fifty books and various smaller printed materials. The most famous book Sáirséal & Dill published was the racy novel *Cré na Cille* by Máirtín Ó Cadhain, often ranked as the most important prose work in modern Irish. It was, of course, far too racy for An Gúm.[73]

Cré na Cille was actually published in March 1950, not 1949 as the title pages (and so various catalogues and reference books) state. It had been intended as a Christmas 1949 publication, but production problems with the printer FNT, caused ultimately by lack of experience of book printing and poor equipment, resulted in delays (these problems continued for years to plague Irish publishers that did not have their own printing equipment). FNT's inexperience can be seen in, for instance, the miscounting of the preliminary pages, the lack of signature or collation marks, the grey inking and the fact that the boards on the case are 2mm wider at the bottom. The typesetting was done on an ill-maintained Linotype, with broken letters (e.g. the lower-case 'o') and characters lifting from the baseline. No wonder Ó hÉigeartaigh later did his own setting, on a Varityper.

An Club Leabhar was sponsored by Comhdháil Náisiúnta na Gaeilge (the now defunct steering body for voluntary Irish language bodies) and commenced operations in 1948.[74] It started with 850 Charter members, and the number of subscribers quickly rose to over 2,000 by the autumn of 1950. Members paid £1 a year and were promised four titles of the most suitable books published in Irish that year. Books were chosen from a range of publishers. The selections in 1948–51 included five from the new entrant Sáirséal & Dill, three from An Gúm, two from the printer/publisher FNT and one each from Three Candles, Browne & Nolan and Talbot.

The quick success of the Club, which certainly transformed Irish language publishing, was heady, with the Club organiser rather absurdly declaring that 'there is as wide a market in this country for books in Irish as there is for books in English as a result of the Club Leabhar scheme'.[75] In 1950, Frank Aiken stated that there was no reason why the membership should not rise to 10,000. 'But will they come when you do call them?', murmured the sceptics. As it happened, they did not, and membership never rose much above the 1950 level.

The Cooling of the Censorship Pressure

In the 1950s the pace of book-banning hotted up. As Michael Adams put it, in this period 'the volume of bannings increased phenomenally; the mounting figures of 500, 600, 700 and 1,000 bannings per year rendered all pre-1946 bannings pale by comparison.'[76]

A remarkable record of how the censoring was actually done has emerged since Michael Adams' book was published in 1968. Christopher O'Reilly taught Irish at St Patrick's College, Drumcondra; he was a leading member of the Knights of St Columbanus. O'Reilly was appointed to the Censorship Board in 1951 and resigned five years later in protest at a more liberal policy being adopted by other members of the Board. According to his notebooks, O'Reilly examined just under 1,300 books in his time on the Board. In 1951, he examined 305 books, in 1952 267, and in 1953 481.[77] The great majority of referrals came from the customs authorities opening parcels and crates (perhaps as many as 600 in a day). Typically, these were initially identified as coming from known publishers and addressed to booksellers. The initial judgement was therefore in the hands of completely unqualified tevenue officials working in haste. Individual copies of banned books sent to private addresses were rarely held up.[78] More than three quarters of the titles examined by O'Reilly were banned by the Board, nodded down on his word.

At an average of a book a day for three years, it is clear that O'Reilly would have had no time to consider the 'general tenor' of a book despite the importance this was given during the debates. Further, his regular comment that a book was 'vulgar' indicates how strong a factor were his austere personal tastes. His main target was 'indecency', very widely interpreted. Descriptions of nudity were out, as were homosexuality, adultery and, in fact, sexual intercourse in general; also illegitimacy, prostitution and any consequences arising from sex, such as pregnancy or childbirth. O'Reilly's notebooks also confirm how he was prepared, as James Kelly puts it, 'to proscribe any work critical of the Church or slighting of its clergy and [ready] to prohibit any work that could be judged blasphemous'.[79] This presumably could be justified as preventing works 'injurious or detrimental to, or subversive of public morality' (section 7 subsection 3).

By the late 1950s, the number of books being banned was over 400 a year. This was fewer than the heroic peaks of 1952 (640 banned), 1953 (766) and 1954 (1,034), but as Michael Adams put it: 'As the lists grew, so too did public opposition to the Censorship: not simply because the public was perturbed at the scale of bannings, but because the Board seemed to make no distinction between books by established authors and the rest; Hemingway and Mickey Spillane appeared side by side on the lists.'[80]

Perhaps also there was a growing feeling that one could be patriotic without being so intensely moral. Was it really true in Catholic Ireland in 1951 (539 books banned), as the well-known Fr Aloysius argued, 'that parental control has weakened, that Christian discipline has relaxed, that home life and family ties are breaking down, and that religious and moral standards are deteriorating'?[81] Or could it be that this continual over-selling opened a gap of doubt, which reflected on the censorship process and perhaps on the approach of the Church itself? The Church's intervention into the Mother and Child Scheme of 1950 no doubt added to this feeling.

Eventually there was a row. Two appointees to the Board started to take a very different approach to the existing members (the fact that these appointments had been applauded by the Civil Liberties Association was noted as ominous by conservatives). The issue came to a head with the consideration of certain 'omnibus editions'. These, a favourite way of reworking a novelist's oeuvre, might contain four or more novels bound together, one of which perhaps had already been banned. For the chairman, Professor Pigott, and Christopher O'Reilly this was an open and shut case deserving immediate banning, and their opinion was backed by the Attorney General. The two new appointees (A.F. Comyn, a Co. Cork solicitor, and R.R. Figgis, a TCD graduate and company director well known in arts circles) refused to accept the AG's ruling and, by the rules, one dissentient vote was enough to prevent a ban. A six-month stalemate occurred as Professor Piggott refused to summon meetings of the Board. Finally, urged by the minister, Pigott and his supporters resigned and a new, more liberal, board was appointed. As Michael Adams described the change, 'the motto of the old school was "when in doubt, ban"; that of the new "when in doubt, release".' It would take a long time, however, before the mental habits inculcated during the censorship years lost their potency.[82]

6

Tide on the Turn: The 1960s and 1970s

The relaxation of the censorship was only one way in which southern Ireland began to open out in the 1960s. Policy changes radically improved the economy and very soon newly established companies were bringing money and, importantly, confidence surging through the country. This followed the economic policy shifts associated with Seán Lemass and T.K. Whitaker's famous *Economic Development*: published in November 1958 with the very reasonable print run, for a government document, of 2,500 copies.

It used to be supposed that economic booms and busts left the book trade more or less unscathed. Book reading was a habit and a lifestyle, went the argument, and since books represented a very small proportion of household expenditure, an increase or decrease in personal wealth hardly altered the amount spent. Technically, the demand for books was described as inelastic, as it was for addictive substances such as tobacco and alcohol. This was perhaps true for a core of readers, 'those who buy', as Diana Athill put it, 'because they love books and what they can get from them', but there were also those 'for whom books are one form of entertainment among many'.[1] This seemed to be new. The optimistic Captain Feehan of Mercier, writing in 1959, believed that, in Ireland, 'a large proportion of the population has decided that reading is worthwhile.' Enabled by increased leisure, he wrote, 'all manner of people now read for pleasure and information … this is largely due to mass media like radio and television and to what has been called the Paperback Revolution.'[2]

As the market expanded in the 1960s and afterwards the new leisure readers became more significant and the market's response to economic cycles more volatile. The sales collapse in the 1980s and the dire experience of the post-2008 period in Ireland (discussed in Chapter 10) confirm this. In these two periods, it appeared that demand for books was not *immediately* affected by economic downturn, for a while all carried on normally. But eventually households did modify their book buying behaviour and the recession began to affect the book trade. Certainly the surge of economic enthusiasm of the early 1960s was only rather slowly associated with a revived publishing industry.

In other areas, however, there was a quick and remarkable response to these policy initiatives. By 1960, *The Irish Times*' annual news round-up, the *Irish Review and Annual* was able to list thirty-nine foreign companies that had established themselves in Ireland since January 1959 and a further twenty in the pipeline. Among those already in operation were firms with American, Belgian, British, Dutch, German, Japanese and Swedish backgrounds. Products included everything from cranes (Liebherr) to greeting cards (Hallmark) and radios (Sony).

There was a boost in industrial production, up 35 per cent in five years, which meant that there was more to spend in the wages packets, and, crucially, the confidence to spend it. In January 1961, the *Irish Review and Annual* reported that hire purchase for cars, household equipment, furniture and clothing had risen by 35 per cent in twelve months. By 1963, all sorts of economic indicators were cheerfully breaking bounds: motor car sales were up 11 per cent on the previous year; electricity usage was up 50 per cent on the 1958 baseline; over the same period the stock exchange had shot from an index figure of 94 to a high of 252. Even the population, which, apart from during war times, had been declining steadily since the Famine, showed a momentary increase, caused by a one third drop in emigration.[3]

In Dublin's upmarket woman's magazine *Creation*, under the headline 'Super Living in the Super Sixties', journalist Caroline Mitchell enthused: 'This country is on the way up. We are going up financially, industrially and artistically … the first whiffs of outside air have been stimulating, enabling us to see ourselves more clearly as other see us, and in many cases for the first time.'[4] Others noticed the same. In *The Irish Times*, Michael Viney commented on 'the sweet tang of optimism … like an aura of aftershave applied freshly each morning.'[5]

Despite a growing body of opinion (exemplified in the reaction to the Mother and Child row, and the easing of the censorship practices) that the Catholic hegemony had gone too far, the Church retained a great deal of its traditional high esteem. In research done in 1963–64, over 90 per cent of people agreed with the statement that 'the Church is the greatest force for good in Ireland today.' One priestly respondent told the researcher, an American Jesuit called Fr Bruce Biever: 'no one questions our authority. How can they? We have more education, thank God, and with that education comes responsibility to lead.'[6]

The old attitudes were, however, in the process of revision, particularly as the new medium of television applied its levelling acid (Telefís Éireann began broadcasting at the very end of 1961). *The Late Late Show* in particular gave people a new sense of how the world worked and of what mattered and after watching, people would never feel quite the same about politicians, about the rich, about the clergy, about themselves. You might for instance see a real live communist (who turned out not to have horns, despite what the parish priest had implied); you might hear a woman describing what she wore on her honeymoon night (very little, by all accounts); or even a Trinity student calling a bishop a 'moron'! In his study of the 1960s, historian and book publisher Fergal Tobin wrote:

> The television service was the most obvious example of a pattern that ran through the decade. Before the 1960s a great many of the country's bright and enterprising people had emigrated, in the absence of any future for them at home. Now there was a future for them at home, with an expanding economy and a genuine sense of optimism about the future. The vigour of Irish social and intellectual life in the 1960s owed much to their staying. Busy, restless, ambitious people … they were unlikely to be satisfied with the complacent certainties that had passed for social thought in Ireland for two generations.[7]

The Second Vatican Council (1962–65) added to the heady sense of change in what had seemed immemorial patterns. It was to energise clergy and lay people alike and incidentally create havoc in the backlists of traditional Catholic publishers. For some, the new excitement around interest in religion, if not long-lasting, did provide opportunities. M.H. Gill (from 1968, as we shall see, Gill & Macmillan) was able to respond to the undoubted new demand with its bestselling author the French priest Michel Quoist. On the other hand, Burns & Oates, Clonmore & Reynolds and Eason's prayer book divisions closed around this time.

According to the 1965/6 Household Budget Survey the national average weekly expenditure on books was 1*s* 6*d* per household, which was about a quarter of what was spent on newspapers and magazines. It was, however, nearly double the previous survey figure. As in the 1950s, two thirds of expenditure was in the second half of the year, with the third quarter (schoolbooks) the heaviest. Gradually the old prejudices noted in Chapter 4 against any but 'useful' reading were lifting, and people began to grumble about Irish children having little choice but to read about an English, Home-Counties, middle-class world of red post-boxes and 'bobbies' with pointed hats. (On the other hand, Patricia Craig, a Catholic bookworm from Belfast, writing of the 1950s, notes that 'we Falls Road eleven-year-olds lapped up the doings of a range of characters from William Brown to Captain W.E. Johns' Worrals … [however] once out of our reading trance we reserved the right to revert to a statutory verbal defiance of England and English ways.'[8] Anne Tannahill of Blackstaff, also from Belfast, remembers much preferring *Just William* to Enid Blyton.) The Dublin City Librarian Máirín O'Byrne complained that 'with the exception of Dolmen and Three Candles, the standard is low … generally speaking publishing in Ireland is not in a flourishing condition. The standard of children's books – particularly in regard to illustration – is very bad indeed.'[9]

At this point in the history of Irish book publishing it was low tide, slack water. Despite the patriotic boosting of local publications by booksellers in their reports of 'What Dublin is Reading', it is unlikely that Irish books accounted for much more than one book in forty sold in Irish bookshops. The very long-established publishers such as James Duffy, Browne & Nolan, Hodges Figgis, Talbot and M.H. Gill were not particularly active, producing a total of twenty-five titles between them in 1965. At least in the original incarnations, the leading companies were working out an endgame.

Typical of the older houses was Browne & Nolan, which traced its history to the 1850s. It was one of the landmark businesses in Dublin, with shops and a large printing facility as well as educational and general book publishing. In the intimate Dublin of the 1930s no one was surprised when Patrick Kavanagh regularly turned up in the office to meet his sometime lover Peggy Gough, an editor with the firm. She gave him lunch in the canteen and sometimes went out with him. But as usual he pushed too far and, as his biographer put it, 'he haunted her office in Browne and Nolan to such an extent that the firm politely asked her to keep him off the premises.'[10] In 1960, R. Allen Nolan, the ex Downside head of the firm recruited Jeremy Addis, who left behind a letterpress printing company in Cornwall to manage the general book publishing.[11] The recruitment ad was, characteristically, placed in the *Catholic Herald*. Addis (a recent convert) quickly settled in, fortified by his knowledge of print technology. He soon found that his bosses Allen Nolan and Dan McGee were markedly risk-averse. Thus his proposal to publish Tom McCaughren's *Run with the Wind* (later successfully published by Wolfhound) was turned down on the grounds that there was no sale for Irish children's books. Too often, publishing opportunities, as Addis put it, 'melted in my hand'. In 1967, Longman Browne & Nolan was set up, ostensibly to create the kind of agency, particularly for educational books, common in Canada, Australia and New Zealand. In this model local houses depended for a significant part of their revenue on the sales of books published by the partner overseas (usually British). The original impulse for the establishment of Gill & Macmillan in 1968 was very similar but the outcome significantly different. Very soon after Longman Browne & Nolan was established Addis was headhunted by Irish University Press.

Newer houses such as Clonmore & Reynolds and Burns & Oates produced twenty-nine titles in 1965, but as we have seen were about to have their comfortable Tridentine publishing styles mortally disrupted by the Vatican Council. The newest houses, Mercier (founded 1944), Dolmen (founded 1951) and Allen Figgis (founded 1960) were moderately more productive, with forty-seven titles between them. They would survive to become the elder statesmen of the surge of publishing that began in the middle 1970s.

Digression: The Growth of Editing

The detailed editing of every book, for form and content as well as technical conformity with the rules of grammar, spelling and punctuation, is a relatively new phenomenon in book publishing.

For much of the nineteenth century it was common for a publisher to accept an outside reader's judgement and the author's bona fides and send the manuscripts more or less untouched to a printer for setting, layout and printing. Mark-up (assigning typographic styles such as heading levels, long quotations, special sorts, indented text and so on) and minimal copy-editing were done by the printer's staff. In Heinemann in the 1950s, as the trainee Nicholas Hudson found, there were 'two people called editors, but they were bright young literary gentlemen whose job was more or less that of today's commissioning editors … in the Educational Department even these creatures didn't exist.'[12] As late as 1968, the 'Notes for Suppliers' produced by the Macmillan Group announced that copy could be supplied to the typesetter in one of three modes: 'A, fully prepared; B, part prepared; C unprepared'.

C copy, the author explained, 'should be marked up by the printer in accordance with our House Style'.[13] In Ireland, a 1970 report on the publishing and printing industry recommended that 'there is a case to be made for printers rejecting manuscripts which are not explicitly marked up.'[14]

The developing practice was a consequence of the changing role of the publisher, as identified for instance by Douglas Jerrold (chair of Eyre & Spottiswood and Burns & Oates). When he started in publishing, as a colleague of Victor Gollancz in Ernest Benn, he 'was under the impression that it was the author's business to write books, the publisher's to publish them and the bookseller's to sell them'. But alas, Jerrold writes, 'this division of labour no longer has any basis in reality. Only those publishers who themselves are manufacturers of books or sell direct to the public can make a living with any comfort.'[15] By 'manufacturing' he meant the active seeking and commissioning of books, not printing and binding. This was the future. Writing in *Hibernia* in 1971 Michael Gill estimated that 'more than half [of books published] were originated from publishers' suggestions, and that half again originated from manuscripts which were radically transformed as a result of a publisher's editorial intervention'.[16] This left a mere quarter of published books in which the manuscript arrived at the printer without major intervention by the publisher. Many of the new authors lacked traditional bookish skills, so they needed in-house editors.

How much actual editing was done varied from house to house. Some publishers routinely went into detail: typically fiction houses dependent on storytellers who could spin a bestselling yarn but could not spell or remember whether the heroine's pet was a dog or a cat and often got facts oddly wrong, (famous literary examples being Shakespeare's Bohemian coastline or Joyce putting debit and credit on the wrong sides in the Ithaca episode of *Ulysses*). Others did much less: it is clear from Stanley Unwin's *The Truth About Publishing* and from his autobiography that routine close editing was not part of Allen & Unwin's practice.[17] In July 1932, the Talbot Press wrote to a Mrs Powell of Yorkshire:

> The Autumn publishing season commences in September, but to be in time for the Christmas sale a book could be delayed until October. I do not think that your mother's volume is very large and if we had the manuscript about the middle of August we would put it through in good time for the Christmas season.[18]

This does not suggest a very elaborate editorial routine.

Many authors (typically the less experienced) resisted detailed 'interference'. In his memoir published in *The Irish Times* in 1955, George Roberts of Maunsel talked bluntly of the editorial process as he practised it:

> Let me pay a hearty tribute to George Moore. I found him, almost alone among authors, quite ready to consider suggestions even from his publisher and to accept them if he thought fit. This was quite contrary to my experience of some nonentities I had published for (they paying for the publication of course) who would not have a comma altered.[19]

In Ireland the vigilante scrutiny of both trade and educational books after independence no doubt made editorial reading mandatory. In December 1925, W.G. Lyon of Talbot Press wrote to Katherine Tynan about an Irish girls' school story she was planning. Since she could not avoid the 'convent atmosphere', she was advised to make it as unobtrusive as possible and 'not ruffle the susceptibilities of anyone in the country'.[20] A few years later, one of Talbot's editors wrote to an author with clear confidence in her craft. For his attention she has made 'lightly pencilled marks on pages 52, 62, 66, 79, 115, 197'. The novel was in fact rejected, but 'had the novel suited us in its general theme, the strong language here and there might have raised some difficulty. So might a couple of allusions on pages 24 and 43, which would offend certain susceptibilities if passed by an Irish publisher.'[21] Incidentally, this editor was by no means always so polite – to another author she wrote bluntly: 'We regret that your novel ... is not suited to our requirements. Even if it were a more competent work than it is, it has no distinctively Irish interest and such an interest is almost essential in a Talbot Press book.'[22]

Writing in 1959 Captain Feehan of Mercier Press clearly envisaged a considerable involvement in the writing process by the publisher. He recommended 'the closest liaison ... between author and publisher at every stage of a book's growth; from the time when it is still an idea tossed back and forth across a table to the moment when it has assumed the tangible form of galley proofs.' By the 1960s, authors such as Iris Murdoch, who would not allow a comma to be changed, were the exception. [23] The Irish University Press's house style (*c.* 1970) assumed that texts would be exposed to both 'mechanical' editing (checking capitalisation, spellings etc.) and 'substantive' editing. This 'involves rewriting, reorganising or suggesting other ways to present material'. Perhaps not all authors would have been wholly reassured by the statement that 'no substantive changes are made in a manuscript without the author's permission.'[24]

Too often the first an author saw of the editor's changes was the proofs, by which time any reinstatement was difficult. Hot metal setting technology made corrections expensive, out of proportion to the original setting charge, so much so that it was worthwhile elaborately to colour code the sources of alterations (green for printer's own marks, red for author/publisher corrections of typesetting errors, blue and black for changes chargeable to author or publisher). Authors were usually allowed a small proportion of the original setting charge for alterations, but anything beyond that was charged against royalty.

Texts were routinely normalised in-house to match the firm's house style, described by Captain Feehan as 'certain uniform standards of spelling and typography that are followed in all his books'.[25] The purpose of the house style was to make it easier for the copy-editor to achieve consistency of usage, without having to spend time puzzling over each author's personal practices (or it might be, lack of them). Feehan continued, 'these standards are a matter of individual preference and tradition'. So, though the details were more or less arbitrary, and consistency the only object, many happy hours could be spent by copyediting nerds debating the finer details. Anne Tannahill of Blackstaff remembers her partner Michael Burns turning to her in amazement: 'Have I just heard the two editors discussing the placing of a comma – for twenty minutes?'[26] (The use, or not, of the Oxford comma was always a fruitful topic.) The editors of Irish University Press clearly enjoyed assembling their house style, which ran to multiple drafts of over 100 folio pages, dense with detailed instruction, for example: 'in most cases, in forming the possessive', the editors write, 'add 's (e.g. Charles's house), except in multi-syllable words of Greek origin (e.g. Rameses' pyramid, Moses' laws)'.[27] Irish houses such as Gill and Arlen (heavy on sexist writing) also produced their own house styles. For those content with printed sources there was the Oxford *Hart's Rules*, (by 1967 in its 37th edition, but still for print professionals, i.e. *For Compositors and Readers*, not *For Writers and Editors* as it was to become) Rees' *Rules of Printed English* (1970) Judith Butcher's Cambridge University Press-based *Copy-editing* (1975) or perhaps the *Manual of Style* from Chicago (sixth edition 1965).

Editors generally had little or no formal training in the job. They saw themselves as the first really attentive reader and as such privileged to propose amendments beyond spellings, references, headings, consistency etc. Amendments such as 'could you expand on so-and-so's motivation here: it seems a bit thin', or, 'can you develop the consequences of this a bit?'[28] By the beginning of the twenty-first century a degree of editing which would have astonished Stanley Unwin had become normal across the English-speaking world. It had also largely abandoned the 'pencil and corner of a table' approach to become technical, software-driven, on-screen, to an unprecedented degree: not least in using Google and the Wiki sites rather than battered reference books to check facts.

Nowadays, as London agent Carole Blake put it, talking of the competitive and specialised commercial fiction market, 'very few books reach the shops without some – often very extensive editing. I firmly believe that the more pairs of eyes that scrutinize material before publication the better that novel or story will read.'[29] A 2010 account of practice in large New York publishing corporations well described the ideal of current practice:

> An editor will typically invest a good deal of time and effort in the 8–12 books they will be putting into production each year. How much time they will put into a book depends entirely on the book – some will need a lot of work, others may need relatively little. Most books go through at least one revise, at many imprints. It is not uncommon for an editor to read a manuscript once very carefully and write a letter to the author with comments – this can vary from two pages to 30 or 40 pages.[30]

The Irish University Press Adventure

The most impressive single feat of publishing in Ireland in the twentieth century was the 1,000 volume set of *British Parliamentary Papers* issued by Irish University Press between 1968 and 1974. For good measure, IUP produced some 500 other titles as well. Among these was a wide range of reprints covering fields from africana to typography.[31] There were also original publications from current authors. Apart from what it published, the IUP is important in the history of Irish publishing because after its collapse so many of its alumni went on to found publishing or publishing-related enterprises. Like a dandelion seed head, once blown apart IUP was the source of a multitude of successors.

The adventure began with the 1962 purchase, for £1.75 million, of the Scottish publishing and printing house Thomas Nelson by the Thomson Organisation. (Thomson owned by this time over 160 newspapers and magazines across the world including the *Sunday Times*, *The Scotsman* and the *Belfast Telegraph*.[32]) After the purchase, the heir, Ronnie Nelson, set up an investment company called Trinity Holdings with an ex Thomson divisional manager called James MacMahon. Among numerous investments in printing, binding, bookshops and publishing Trinity Holdings acquired the printer Cahill's (including the publishing imprints Fallon's, Parkside and Mellifont) in 1966. MacMahon became CEO of Cahill's, leaving the previous owner, the well-known Dublin businessman J.J. O'Leary, as chairman.[33]

It soon became obvious that MacMahon was not planning to rest on his laurels as the major government printer in the country. The creation of many well-endowed new universities in the United State and Japan had opened up a voracious market for reprints of out-of-print books: as Michael Adams, later sales director of IUP, put it, 'seemingly every printed book since Caxton was at risk'.[34] Not only was there a market to be met, but if the printing was based in the Shannon Free Trade Zone (established in 1959) exports to the key markets of Japan and the United States would attract favourable tax treatment. All that was needed for the business model was a stream of books. T.P. O'Neill, later professor of history at UCG, proposed the enormous cache of reports of select committees of the British parliament in the nineteenth century. With the aid of Professor Peter Ford of Southampton University and his wife Grace, specialists in the parliamentary papers, a dazzling potential range was identified, the result of the fact-obsessed nineteenth-century parliaments wrestling with issues from 'Able-bodied paupers' to 'Zealand, New'. Most of these were available to IUP from the National Library. Seamus Cashman remembered many cramped hours spent in the stacks, passing in and out by the staff entrance.

Following closely the advice given by the Fords (who were delighted to see their life's work brought thus out into the open[35]), the meaty reports could be conveniently sold in eighty multi-volume sets for specialists. One set dealt with the slave trade, another with banking, another with the Irish Famine. There were sets dealing with ore mining, with industry and commerce, transport, the colonies, America and so on. As it happened, IUP was not the only firm with its eye on this goldmine. The UK reprint publisher Frank Cass even managed to get eight volumes into the market, but, daunted by the size and vigour of IUP's ambitions, was no doubt happy to be bought off for the promise of £13,900.

From the beginning, the volumes were large and handsomely bound and sold at very stiff prices. Thus, the *British Parliamentary Papers* reprint of 1889–90 reports on infectious diseases sold at £52.50 for 728 pages, and a reprint of an 1867 report on religion at £45 for 900 pages. A full set of 1,000 volumes was nominally priced at $60,000. By comparison, the most expensive book Gill & Macmillan published in 1970 was John Whyte's *Church and State* which retailed at £4.25 for 466 pages; Thom's *Dublin Street Directory* cost £6.50 for 928 pages. Internally, IUP calculated a per copy production cost of £5.70 for its accounts, giving a very comfortable gross profit on sales.

The original scale of the project was mind-blowing. It was estimated by the Fords that there were some 7,000 volumes of these papers, some of which were trivial, but many of great potential interest to historians and librarians. The published volumes could contain one whole report by itself or a multiple of reports on the same subject from, for instance, the 1840s, the 1850s and so on. Initially it was thought that 700 volumes would meet the market needs. This early estimate was quickly expanded.

The vaunting ambition of the project is revealed in the maths. Seven hundred copies, multiplied by the average income per volume of £20–23 (all sold direct to libraries, so no retail discounts and of course no returns), multiplied by the original print run of 2,000 copies per volume, gave a projected income of £32 million: at a time when Penguin's worldwide turnover in 1970 was just over £7 million, and Gill & Macmillan's annual sales were of the order of £200,000. As time went on it became clear that the print run of 2,000 copies of each volume (insisted on from the start by MacMahon) was wildly over-ambitious and the run was cut first in July 1969 to 1,000 copies and then, in mid 1971, to 400.

In September 1967, the public was first told of the plans to build a £1 million printing and publishing concern based in Shannon, to employ over 200 people. The publishing division, based in Dublin, was to be headed up by an ex army officer, Captain Tadhg MacGlinchey, a well-known book collector. He was to be responsible for the extensive non-Parliamentary Papers list. Since the reports were reproduced in facsimile, it was convenient that this was the time of general industry change from letterpress to offset litho printing. M.H. Gill had, the previous year, moved out of printing, having decided not to invest in the new equipment. Fuelled by Nelson money, Cahill's itself completely re-equipped, so that by 1969, MacMahon could boast that none of the equipment was more than three years old. This was quite a statement for Irish printing where fifty-year-old bits of equipment commonly lurked in dusty silence in the corners of machine rooms.

Early in the planning phase J.J. O'Leary approached M.H. Gill to provide the editorial skill base for the venture, but was turned down,[36] so Tadhg MacGlinchey and Tom Turley set about recruiting. Gradually they drew into the net numerous people who later made names for themselves in Irish publishing including Turley himself, Michael Adams, Seán Browne, Seamus Cashman and many others.

At first things went extremely well, driven by the buoyancy of the US market. In 1969, MacMahon financed further expansion by announcing the sale of 20 per cent of its shares to a subsidiary of First National City Bank. (In the event, the share purchase did not take place, but First National provided some £650,000 by way of debenture.) Making the announcement, MacMahon declared that the 1,000 volume set of Parliamentary Papers was nearly complete: it was actually finished in 1972. In his grandiloquent way he stated that the company had publishing projects already fully researched and known to be viable sufficient to last IUP at its present production level 'for the next thirty years'. In addition to existing offices in Shannon, Dublin, London and New York plans were advanced for openings in Rome and Sydney.[37]

This was, of course, a bit too good to last. By 1970 the financial recession and US university budget cutbacks (stimulated, some thought, by a resentment in the political and donor class of years of student protests) meant that sales were running at half what they should have been. Other publishers were also suffering: McGraw-Hill had made 300 staff redundant and McCall had axed a newly established book division. Very soon the retreating tide exposed a gross structural imbalance in the firm. There was an exemplary team of editors and indexers, an enormous, state-of-the-art printing and binding facility, but an exiguous sales team. To drum up sales, senior editors such as Marilyn Nordstedt,[38] Seamus Cashman and Gerry O'Flaherty were sent to the US to call on potential library purchasers. Robert Hogg, manager of the Shannon printing division, was instructed to look for outside work. A much more realistic sales estimate of 200 sets from the US and as many from the rest of the world was now accepted.

At the same time the money from the Nelsons and from First National had run out. According to *The Irish Times* the Nelson investment in Cahill's and IUP amounted to £1.7 million by this time and Elizabeth Nelson, Ronnie's new wife (from a racing family based in Mallow, and master of the local hunt), was starting to ask questions.[39]

In March 1971, a series of redundancies began which eventually reduced the printing staff in Shannon to a mere sixty. In Dublin, senior staff, citing the 'financial and control crisis' in which the company found itself, issued a round robin memorandum to the executive committee deploring the 'authority vacuum' and 'ill-judged decisions'. Rumours buzzed. MacMahon resigned from the board of IUP at the end of March and the Nelsons installed temporary managers. The situation seemed to be resolved by the sale in November 1971 of the entire Cahill's/IUP operation to a London property company called Stern Family Holdings, a deal in which the Nelsons barely got back their initial investment. It was hoped that the new owner, William Stern, would inject capital into the operation.[40]

A new managing director, Mark Matthews, was installed by Stern, and he began a series of elegantly written reports to the board. His first described the 'intense traumatic experiences' of 1971 and he stressed how the imminent completion of the *Parliamentary Papers* project left the organisation 'unprepared for the more normal flow of projects'. But knowing little about publishing, he did not have much to offer as to what might be done. His typically witty comment, intended to inculcate a forward- rather than backward-looking approach, that 'there is no future in history' was perhaps more smart than appropriate in a firm devoted to reprinting nineteenth-century materials. He was replaced in 1973 by a much tougher proposition, accountant Paul Caffrey, but despite the final closure of the Shannon plant in April, the loss for the six months to December 1973 was £39,195.

Michael Adams has dismissed the short-lived Stern regime as 'making no lasting improvement to IUP's fortunes'[41] and certainly, apart from completing the 1,000 volume set of the *Parliamentary Papers*, the books actually published showed an unfocused variety. In 1973, for instance, there were books on Plotinus, Goethe, heroin addiction and Irish surnames; in 1974, books on the influence of the sea on the political history of Japan 1862–1948, industrial relations and Douglas Hyde.

As the financial position worsened, various schemes were tried to rescue the company. Drastically lowering the price of the *Parliamentary Papers* was floated, as was extending the credit period beyond the existing three years. Another was a microform business, which actually survived the end. Another was a new imprint called Millington (an IUP imprint already in the US) which was launched to publish twenty titles a year with more popular, non-academic appeal. Tom Turley was the manager responsible. As the crisis worsened, in November 1973, Turley devoted two whole pages of his report to the board to his own ideas on morality and publishing policy. He bizarrely proposed that one book already accepted – *The Corruption of Harold Hoskins* – be printed in only 2,000 copies. *Kirkus Review* described the book as 'a breezy, light-hearted romp ... too good-natured to be offensive'.[42] But Turley seems to have found it so. He did not consider it pornographic, he said, just not funny: it was not to be sold in Ireland, not advertised and the paperback rights were not to be sold. What the author thought of this 'privishing' is not recorded.

The end came more suddenly than could have been expected. It was hoped at first that Cahill's and its wholly owned subsidiaries IUP and Fallon's would be unaffected when the Stern property group succumbed to the 1974 slump in the British property market. Unfortunately, that collapse exposed First National City Bank's claims on IUP as having no guarantee and the bank put in Lawrence Crowley as receiver on 15 June 1974. This was the end. It was now Crowley's task to make as much of the assets as he could.

These consisted in unsold stock (bound and unbound), materials, contracts and leases, worth perhaps £50,000 as pulp, but potentially considerably more as part of a going concern. The receiver invited bids in excess of £1 million, but got no takers. The staff were fired. Michael Adams, the sales director, put together various possibilities (including an unlikely partnership with Albert Folens which got as far as a draft contract) and eventually came up with a successful consortium of Frank Cass, some outside interests and himself. This was the group that in November 1974 became the Irish Academic Press.

The Smurfit Shake-Up

In the meantime, a brash newcomer from the least glamorous end of the paper business, brown paper for boxes, was about to shake up the entire Irish printing (and thus publishing) business. The 30-year-old Michael Smurfit had become joint managing director (with his brother Jefferson) of the family brown paper and box company in 1966 and immediately began an aggressive programme of acquisitions. In 1968, he doubled the size of the company with the purchase of the prestigious Temple Press. The following year he bought the family-dominated Browne & Nolan for 7.6 times their annual profits. This included a printing plant in Clonskeagh, 50 per cent of the publishing company now called Longman Browne & Nolan and shops in Dublin and Cork. Robert Allen Nolan, the Browne & Nolan managing director, became a Smurfit main-board director but did not stay long. It is difficult to imagine he found the boardroom atmosphere congenial. He died in 1974.

In the meantime, the Hely Group had also been expanding by acquisition from its original involvement in stationery and printing. By 1970, it had become the fifth largest company in Ireland, with 2,800 employees. Among a range of acquisitions, it had bought Alex Thom (including the long silent Sealy, Bryers & Walker) in 1960 and the Educational Company and Talbot in 1965. By the late 1960s, however, Hely's was a strategic mess, with a bewildering number of subsidiaries. It was the country's largest printer, but also had interests in air conditioners, bicycles, dog requisites, musical instruments, publishing, toys, radios and televisions. It even owned a hire purchase company, to help customers finance their home entertainment.

Very soon after buying Browne & Nolan, Smurfit bid £2.9 million for the Hely Group. The Hely board (reeling from a disastrous investment in a greeting card company called Avon) recommended the purchase, but since Smurfit only owned 7 per cent of the shares it became a battle for the assent of the shareholders. Rumours that the Clondalkin Group, or possibly a UK company, was going to counter-bid, confused the market, but by the middle of March the Smurfit contingent had closed the deal and attended the first board meeting as the new owners. The former joint managing director, George Hetherington, a published poet, a skilled watercolourist and director of The Irish Times Ltd, resigned immediately.[43]

Michael Smurfit, controlling Alex Thom, Browne & Nolan, Talbot and the Educational Company, was now the most extensive book publisher in Ireland, not that he cared. Buying these companies was one thing: running them was another. Smurfit moved into a small training office in the main Hely-Thom building. He said: 'I let [the existing managers] stay in their offices. The only thing was that I took all the power. Copies of all letters going into the building had to come to me … there were lots of problems. It took nearly two years to sort things out.'[44] He introduced a much tougher, numerate, results-oriented style of management. It was the difference between the 1950s and the 1970s. One old Hely's hand described the difference as 'like changing from a ride in a pleasure steamer to a journey in a destroyer. We could feel the vibrations in the soles of our feet.'[45]

For Michael Smurfit, Browne & Nolan was printing and retailing; its publishing fell silent. Initially, for instance in the 1971 Annual Report, the importance of Talbot, 'the prima donna amongst Irish publishers in the 1920s', was recognised. The imprint was stated 'to have been revived and export markets expanded.' For a few months the idea of Talbot buying Sáirséal & Dill was discussed, with Kevin Etchingham of the Educational Company leading the negotiations on the Smurfit side. Discussions went on for several months, with sums of money such as £25,000 being on the table, but they came to nothing.[46] Although several books were subsequently published, especially up to 1975, the impetus was not sustained, and Talbot concentrated on the profitable liturgical publishing, a market that had been thoroughly stirred-up by the Vatican Council. Thom's *Directory* came out just as a street directory but never again as the in-depth reference book it had been, and eventually went online. The Educational Company, on the other hand continues to this day (as the annual report anticipated: 'your Group is very mindful of the part it has to play in the years to come').[47] Alex Tarbett, an ex seminarian who had been instrumental in creating a profitable

Missal for Geoffrey Chapman, was appointed first managing director of the education and publishing division.[48]

A New Irish Book Publishers' Association

As Irish University Press was getting into its stride, and Michael Smurfit was starting his remodelling of the Hely-Thom organisation, a new straw in the wind showed how Irish publishing was going to develop. In 1969, a group of Irish publishers was sponsored by the state export agency Córas Tráchtála to visit the Frankfurt Book Fair for the first time. This annual gathering of book publishers from across the world traced its lineage to the earliest years of print, when booksellers/printers/publishers used to gather to swap their books, helped by the fact that a large proportion of them were in Latin. The Frankfurt Fair was revived after the Second World War and has gone from strength to strength since, as the number of publishers in the world sky-rocketed. Its key function, as it had been 500 years before, is to facilitate the sale of books from one country to another. These days it is less often physical books that are exchanged than publication rights (i.e. the right under copyright to translate or reprint books, or sometimes to bind sheets).

For Irish publishers, especially on their first visit to Frankfurt, selling rights remained an uphill business. But regardless of specific success, for those used to Ireland's small pond, the dazzling variety and extent of the world book trade could be enlightening – though it might also be, as Bernard Share thought in 1967, then with a mere 1,500 stands with 30,000 books, a daunting, even depressing vista, perhaps particularly for a writer.[49] For most, however, it was stimulating to meet New Zealand or Canadian publishers with much the same problems; to see how British publishers, though big, were dwarfed by the Americans; to see hundreds of religious or scientific and medical publishers in their special halls; to be stimulated by the range of childrens' books; to admire crisp French typography (as copied for instance by Sáirséal & Dill) and austerely beautiful German-designed books; to see the book packagers, the agents, the printers and fine paper suppliers and, of course, the brazen pornographers (in-lodge jokes told of one venerable Irish publisher who found the frequent wine stalls and the half-naked models equally irresistible). Recognition of this encouraged some publishers to send more people than strict economic criteria might have justified. In 1972, for instance five representatives came from IUP and three each from Talbot and Gill & Macmillan. It was not, incidentally, in the luxury of the Frankfurter Hof they stayed; a shared room in a seedy hotel near the railway station was more likely.

It was the general understanding that the future for the Irish publishing industry lay in reaching beyond Ireland and Britain and mastering the intricate web of foreign rights sales. A set of deals made by Gill & Macmillan for a straightforward trade title such as Theodora FitzGibbon's *Irish Traditional Food* (first published in 1983) exemplifies how such sales could, with an appropriate title, enable Irish publishers to overcome the handicap of the small local market. The publisher initially estimated that sales in Ireland would amount to no more than 1,500 copies in hardback at £9.95. By selling international rights Gill & Macmillan succeeded in increasing the net revenue from a prospective £3,936 to nearly £7,000 and increasing the author's receipts nearly fourfold. The extra earnings were made up of 750 copies to a UK publisher, 250 to an Australian and 1,500 to a US publisher which also took the US paperback rights. There was also the publisher's share of the non-US paperback rights (British Commonwealth including Canada) sold to Pan.[50]

Such an elaborate package as this could not be put in hand overnight; it required multiple presentations to potential contacts in Frankfurt (showing the mock-up, samples of writing and pictures, discussing terms), followed up over months with numerous potential partners. After his visit in 1967, assisting Allen Figgis, Bernard Share commented that given the number of Irish-interest books published by British publishers the great difficulty he experienced was to persuade German, French and US publishers that the British had not taken the cream and what was being offered was not mere leftovers, or too Irish to be of general interest.[51]

All this took time and added to overhead costs. The days when such titles could be received inhouse in the summer for Christmas publication, with the main delays caused by the technology of typesetting and printing, were long gone. The original contract for *Irish Traditional Food* with a £2,000 advance on royalties (payable as was normal one third on signature, one third on delivery and the balance on publication), was signed in November 1979 and the book was finally published in September 1983. The paperback edition was published eighteen months later. The relatively high investment in the advance was more than covered by the rights sales.

Mercier and M.H. Gill had been regular attenders at the fair (both in the Religious Hall), but in 1969 fourteen publishers exhibited 363 books at the Fair. Representatives included the British-owned Geoffrey Chapman; Dolmen; Allen Figgis; Irish University Press; Scepter; Talbot and Gill & Macmillan. Mercier, wrote John Horgan, 'in an elder-statesman-like way kept its own counsel'.[52] Three Irish language publishers, An Clóchomhar, Sáirséal & Dill and Cló Móráin, had books on display. Although there was some talk of rights sales (Bernard Share's cartoon books for Allen Figgis had attracted attention, as had Fr James Mackey for Michael Gill) the amount of actual business done was probably small.

John Horgan finished his 1969 report on Frankfurt for *The Irish Times* by remarking that, 'one of the most concrete results of the Fair for the Irish book world, however, may be the formation of a genuinely representative Irish Publishers Association'.[53] There had been a similar organisation in the 1940s and 1950s whose main function had been liaison with the Department of Education, though occasionally other issues arose. By the early 1960s however this group was described as 'moribund'.[54]

Following discussions with the Federation of Irish Industries and the Export Board Córas Tráchtála, the new Irish Book Publishers' Association was formally founded on 9 September 1970.[55] Eleven people attended the inaugural meeting presided over by Michael Gill, including Maurice Ledwidge representing the Irish Educational Publishers Association and two Irish language publishers, Bríghid Bean Uí Éigearthaigh from Saírseál & Dill and L. Ó Dulacann from An Clóchomhar. Denis Devlin of Córas Tráchtála attended, and spoke of the importance of exports, apparently thinking of physical books rather than rights. Liam Miller of Dolmen was elected president and Michael Gill of Gill & Macmillan treasurer. Bernard Share was named secretary, for which he received a stipend. The new Association was, unexpectedly, welcomed by a leader in *The Irish Times*. The paper pointed out how authors (by which they meant novelists and poets) 'have a far better chance of selling [their] book if it is published in London or New York', and declared that 'the new association has a tough battle on its hands … [it] deserves support, and will get it from authors, but it must be able to do for them what London publishers are able to do.'[56] A reference to 'London editors' who assumed that a novel published in Ireland had been rejected in Britain no doubt applied also to *The Irish Times*. A constitution based on the Australian Publishers Association was adopted on 30 November 1970.[57]

By the third meeting, in May 1971, the acronym 'Clé', proposed by Bríghid Bean Uí Éigearthaigh from the initials of its daunting Irish name Cumann Leabharfhoilsitheoirí Éireann, began to be used, its usage greatly enhanced by the elegant logo designed by Liam Miller. The acronym was long the common way of referring to the new association. The Irish term however lacked that easy recognisability that was felt to be important and, in 2010, the name was changed to the pretentious 'Publishing Ireland' (members did not publish either magazines or newspapers, nor even the whole book publishing field, there being a separate association catering for educational publishers).

One early activity was the publication of *Books from Ireland*, subtitled (with Frankfurt in mind) *Bücher aus Irland 1969/70*. This handsome twenty-four-page booklet listed fourteen publishers and 350 titles. The newness and volatility of the book publishing scene is demonstrated by the fact that of those fourteen, only Mercier is still going under the same name (though from Gill & Macmillan to Gill is not much of a jump). Anvil, Dolmen, James Duffy, Allen Figgis, New Writers Press, IUP, Sáirséal & Dill, Talbot, names once to conjure with, are all gone.

In 1970, however these names were all current. A government-sponsored report on the print and publishing business at this time reported that 680 separate titles had been produced by 155 publishers in 1968. The vast majority of these were not in the publishing business at all: 108 produced one title each. Only eleven firms (all in the Republic) produced more than ten titles and a further nine firms produced between six and ten titles each. Eight or nine firms were actively engaged in exporting. Sixteen firms produced Irish language titles. The report (one of a series designed to explore Ireland's readiness for the Common Marker) saw a 'bright future' for educational publishing, as a result of major syllabus changes. It was less positive about general publishing, stating that 'there may, however, be further tendencies for book publishing to move to "paper-backs"' a trend it evidently regarded as a mixed blessing, presumably fearing that lower prices meant less revenue.[58] We have seen before how booksellers pessimistically failed to see the potential in change, when the three-decker era collapsed, and again in 1935 with the introduction of Penguin paperbacks. The extraordinary and continuing growth in book sales the world trade had experienced since the 1950s was simply not to be believed: in 1962, for instance, *The Irish Times* readers were solemnly told that 'sales of paperbacks in Britain have virtually reached saturation point', whatever that might mean. Luckily, this was not the case in Ireland, 'the spokesman for a Dublin firm of distributors' said, where sales were running at a million copies a year and rising.[59]

Also in 1970, journalist John Armstrong picked five leading trade publishers for a series of features to help him explore what he described as 'something of a boom in the Irish publishing industry'. With some exaggeration, he identified 'no fewer than 48 publishers listed in the Dublin area alone'.[60] The publishers he chose as leading the revival of publishing were (with number of titles published in 1970, based on the NLI catalogue): Dolmen (14), Allen Figgis (15), Sáirséal & Dill (8), Mercier (28) and Gill & Macmillan (35).

First featured was Liam Miller of Dolmen Press, who was, Armstrong wrote, 'regarded by many as the father of the [publishing] revival'. Miller and his wife began Dolmen in 1951 as a kind of hobby, in the private press tradition. It was no coincidence that he was the historian of the Cuala Press. In the early years the press produced sixteen small books of sixteen pages or so and runs of 500 copies.[61] There was an Albion press in the basement and a font of Caslon 12 pt type for hand-setting. Friends and authors were expected to help: 'poets setting up their own work, slitting large sheets of paper with a kitchen knife, folding inky sheets and distributing type back into the cases so that another couple of pages could be set up'.[62] Perhaps the poets were insufficiently generous with the ink, for 'the thinness of the inking', and poor quality of presswork were regular complaints.[63]

Miller, by profession an architect, gave up the day job in 1955, but quickly found that his elegant publications could not earn enough, so he turned to jobbing printing. His first 'professional' publication was Thomas Kinsella's *Another September* which was chosen by the British Poetry Book Society (the first book published outside England to be so honoured). Other poets Miller published to great acclaim included Richard Murphy, Padraic Colum, Austin Clarke, John Montague and David Marcus (notably his translation of *The Midnight Court*). But Miller's range was limited, as Peter Fallon has pointed out. He did not publish Patrick Kavanagh ('Ireland's most important poet since Yeats') or Philip Larkin (an approach from Larkin was supposed to have gone nowhere) or younger men such as Seamus Heaney, Richard Murphy, Michael Longley and Paul Muldoon.[64]

Becoming friendly with many of his writers, Miller liked nothing better than convivial sessions in Phil Ryan's pub in Baggot Street, where older writers such as Kate O'Brien and Patrick Kavanagh could be found, as well as younger poets straying from McDaid's. 'More than most publishers,' wrote John Montague, 'Liam liked to be part of the action, and meet his writers socially.' His devotion to the text and to the design was deeply attractive to these writers. 'To work on a text with Liam was fascinating,' wrote Montague, 'a kind of intellectual dance. He experimented with various typefaces, lengths of page and quality of paper, always inviting comment, seeking an ideal blend or marriage of the visual and the verbal.' No wonder writers loved this attention, this sanctifying of their texts.[65]

Miller was helped by a sales arrangement with Oxford University Press from 1960 and by the publication of the bestselling *Táin* in 1969. This 'lovely man', that Kathleen Raine fondly remembered, was also extremely generous with advice and help to nascent publishers such as Blackstaff Press (the Graceys, Anne Tannahill, Michael Burns and designer Wendy Dunbar all benefited hugely from his contribution). For all Miller's talk of overseas sales, however, the Dolmen Press met financial disaster more than once and finally collapsed on his death.

The second publisher featured by Armstrong was Allen Figgis. Figgis, the 35-year-old bachelor director of the Hodges Figgis bookshop (ex St Columba's, trained as an accountant), launched his first list in 1960. He lacked the quick charm of many successful publishers, but he was a professional, as befitted one with so long a pedigree in the book world. Figgis' first list, published for Christmas 1960, was a mixed bag of biography, memoirs, a book about Christmas and a thriller. His advent was marked by an enthusiastic but not very knowledgeable profile in *The Irish Times*, in which readers were told (no doubt to their relief) that 'Allen Figgis is not aiming to publish every book that is written by every Irishman'. He had apparently been to the Frankfurt Fair recently seeking to sell film and serialisation rights for his titles. The anonymous journalist's statement that a publisher's return on sales of 3,000 copies (described as 'the average edition') produced a profit of a mere £300 'after all the many expenses involved' is therefore interesting, but may not carry much weight.[66] In a more serious interview, ten years later, Figgis explained how his elegant Riverrun imprint for paperbacks (fiction and non-fiction) had been launched in late 1969 and already reprints of Maurice James Craig's *Dublin*, Robert Lloyd Praeger's *The Way that I Went* and Brendan Kennelly's *Selected Poems* had sold extremely well. His most successful book to date had been an *Encyclopaedia of Ireland*, co-published with a US publisher, of which 16,000 copies had been sold.

Sáirséal & Dill was the subject of the third of John Armstong's interviews. Its founding influence, Seán Ó hÉigheartaigh, had died in 1967, worn out by the struggle to hold down a demanding job in the department of finance as well as running the firm. The critic Alan Titley believes that the 1960s saw some of the very best Irish prose produced. These were the books that Sáirséal & Dill had been founded a generation before to publish.[67] Sadly, just at this time, as one critic put it, due to exhaustion and financial factors 'publishing in Irish had sunk to an abysmal depth.'[68] Nonetheless, by 1966, Seán Ó hÉigheartaigh and his wife Bríghid had published ninety titles since 1948, to high editorial and production standards.

Sales, however, remained a problem, as Bríghid Bean Uí Éigearthaigh explained: 'the great difficulty is that you are publishing for such a limited market … [in which] 4,000 copies would be an extremely big sale'. They were constantly tempted by the educational market where, for instance, their bestseller

Bullaí Mhártain, which was on the intermediate course, was expected to sell 35,000 copies.[69] They saw that market, however tempting, as a reneging on their primary goal, which was to publish literature which An Gúm and other official bodies would not risk. By 1966, despite grants and family money Sáirséal & Dill was £11,000 in debt (i.e. three or four times Seán's civil service salary) and would have closed down had not a public protest prodded the Minister for Education George Colley to clear the company's debts and provide a monthly grant.

By the mid 1970s however, Bríghid had been running the company on her own for nearly ten years and was beginning to feel disillusioned. Her natural market, the Gaeltacht, was just not responding. 'The man-in-the-field,' she told a correspondent, 'has not yet acquired the habit of buying books … Seán used to say that our function was to cater for the writers – give them a decent publication service, and the readers would follow. I'm beginning to doubt that.' As we have seen, there was briefly a possibility in the early 1970s that Smurfit might buy the company, and a few years later, after three years of negotiations, Caoimhín Ó Marcaigh, then a director of Mercier Press, actually did.[70]

In 1944, Cork-based Captain Seán (John) Feehan, a serving officer with the Irish army, founded the Mercier Press and published his first title – *The Music of Life* by Professor O'Mahony of UCC. This was not a well-financed operation but Feehan would eventually establish a press warranting fourth place in Armstrong's list. Like Maunsel, Feehan started with just £90 and some credit from a local printer. Distribution was by a local bookseller, Liam Ruiséal. Within two months, however, with the aid of several thousand fliers, he had sold out the first edition of 2,000 copies, and four reprints were sold within nine months. Continuing his shrewd choices, he next published Ben Kiely's first book, *Counties of Contention*, a study of partition, and then *Pictures in the National Gallery*. By his second year he had staff, his own office, a small warehouse and had attracted new capital. In 1946, he published his sustaining bestseller Dom Eugene Boylan's *This Tremendous Lover* (a book whose title, he facetiously declared, left many a disappointed reader).[71]

By 1949, Mercier was publishing some twelve books a year, which, with backlist sales, was enough in those days of low wages to support six office and warehouse staff. His accountant, Jack O'Connor, had contacts with the McGraths (of the Hospital Sweepstakes) and they took a 25 per cent share and a seat on the board. Board meetings were regularly held in the Sweep's offices in Dublin. Captain Feehan (unlike many of his colleagues) was an assiduous reader of books about the book trade, paying detailed attention to the 1948 US edition of O.H. Cheney's *Economic Survey of the Book Industry 1930–31*. In his copy, which is in my possession, he has marked the sections dealing with publishing management. Feehan's own book, *An Irish Publisher and his World*, highlighted the importance of the new concept of the 'list': a unified set of books appealing to a particular audience. This is more than just trade books or education books, but not quite so tightly focused as the earlier approach, the series or library. Feehan evidently thought of the 'list' as a single entity, whereas later publishers would have more than one list: chess, poetry, agriculture, etc., as for instance Faber had done. Feehan decided to specialise in Catholic publishing – not least to cater for the 3,300 clerical students in the country, by far the biggest block of third-level students.

Realising the riches of continental theological publishing, in the 1950s Feehan set out on a great tour of the foreign publishing capitals. He returned with an options book bursting with over 100 potential titles. In those days the economics of religious publishing were favourable. 'Catholic publishing,' as he wrote about those years, 'was a serene and ordered garden.' The right titles were not price sensitive and reprinted regularly, providing a backlist income to cushion future investments. The international focus fed through to overseas sales, for, as he noted, foreign booksellers might find no sale for Irish interest books but every major city in every country had a bookshop specialising in Catholic literature.

And then the bombshell of the Second Vatican Council (1962–65) exploded, rewriting the whole Catholic religious outlook. The carefully accumulated backlist of titles representing the Tridentine theological outlook became, almost overnight, quite unsaleable: and with its loss went the economic security of the publishing houses. Cutting his own output from forty titles a year to six, Feehan noted that 'the warehouses of many religious publishers [were] crammed full of hundreds of thousands of pounds worth of unsaleable titles. I know of one firm who had recently to destroy a quarter of a million books.'[72] Many old and famous names in Catholic publishing – notably Burns & Oates in London – simply went to the wall. In an interview in 1970, in his vehement way, Feehan told *The Irish Times*, 'the entire theological market is smashed, broken, finished.'[73] John Spillane (later managing director) recalled that one of his first jobs in Mercier Press was to:

> dump thousands and thousands of religious books. Textbooks which Mercier had issued and reissued for years all became virtually useless overnight. But almost as quickly as our books became obsolete, the Captain changed course and reversed our publishing priorities. Where we had been publishing 90 per cent religious books and 10 per cent Irish-interest, we turned that around completely in the aftermath of Vatican II.[74]

This did not, however, totally deter Mercier: its 'Theology Today' series continued throughout the 1970s.

Captain Feehan was a stocky man, and both active and enterprising. He was as well known as any publisher in the country for his TV appearances and his strongly expressed opinions. As well as the publishing house, he owned a bookshop, a recording studio and a factory with five staff making small souvenir statues for tourists. In the late 1940s, he set up a small publishing house in Liverpool to get round the current import restrictions. He experimented in the 1950s with a comic book series based on the successful American Classics Illustrated series (four were published). Among the directors of the company set up to publish these comics was Allen Lane of Penguin.[75] Also in the 1950s, Feehan and his wife Mary set up a Cork branch of the Disabled Artists organisation. In the 1960s, he was producing vinyl records of his authors and cassettes of religious content for seminaries (these latter got into trouble with Archbishop John Charles McQuaid who complained that they had not been passed by his censors.) By 1970, Feehan's reading of trade publications had convinced him that the book as such was not going to survive. As he put it: 'I visualise that in about four or five years you won't go into a shop to buy a book. You'll go in to buy a cassette. This is,' he added, 'going to play hell with the book market … the number of books which we will publish will be considerably reduced and the number of cassettes will go up accordingly.'[76] This conviction waned in due time, for in 1972 he recruited Caoimhín Ó Marcaigh from the Educational Company with the idea of going into the education market; around this time he offered his staff a share participation scheme.

The largest publishing house and the one that most matched the traditional UK model, was Gill & Macmillan, which had been formed in 1968 by a joint venture of London Macmillan (founded 1843) and M.H. Gill (founded 1856) with the Gill family retaining a slight majority of shares. In the old style it operated in the educational, trade and academic markets (this spread was later to become uncommon in Ireland) and had a printing department and a bookshop. Michael Gill closed the printing business in 1966 and in 1979 finally closed the bookshop in O'Connell Street after the disastrous fire of that year during Pope John Paul II's visit. The total turnover from publishing in 1970 was £205,000 (though this had doubled by 1975). Of this, 62 per cent came from educational books and the balance from trade and academic. There were 142 titles in the stockroom, with fifty-seven being reprints.[77] In the old-fashioned manner Gill & Macmillan relied on backlist (books published in previous years, on which no money need be spent) for over 60 per cent of the firm's income and the education list was especially strong in backlist.

The list did not include Francis Stuart's new book, *Black List Section H*, which Gill & Macmillan had recently decided not to publish. Stuart wrote a spiteful letter to *The Irish Times* complaining how 'a publisher' had encouraged him to send the book in, but 'after considerable delay, I got it back'. He wrote as 'a word of warning to young and adventurous writers ... this experience of mine does not bode well for a happy relationship between serious Irish writers and at least one of our new publishers.' This attempt to damage the revival in Irish publishing, quoting no names so all were tarred, was published in *The Irish Times*, 12 June 1970, in the context of John Armstrong's interviews, for which Gill & Macmillan provided the fifth subject. In 1911, James Joyce, sore at the way he was being treated by Maunsel and Grant Richards over *Dubliners* wrote a similar letter to the press to 'throw some light on the present conditions of authorship in England and Ireland'.[78]

Sales of educational books were almost totally in the Republic and the North, while trade and academic titles managed a wider spread, selling to Australia, the USA and Africa, though mostly in small quantities, 82 per cent of sales being in Ireland and the UK.

As to the financial side of publishing, Michael Gill circulated to his staff a *Bookseller* double article at this time, which he described as 'very useful information' from which we can infer that it represented his broad experience.[79] In the article, the author assumes a 10 per cent of list price royalty, a 33.33 per cent discount off list price to the book trade (on which the retailer, all going well, was likely to make a net profit of 8.5 per cent of turnover) and a mark-up of 4.8 per cent (more generally between 4.5 and 5) from unit (average) production cost to list price. This widely-used rule of thumb expressed the industry's view that production costs should be between 20 and 25 per cent of list price, a considerable drop from the 50 per cent that was common in the 1890s.[80] But the publisher still had to sell nearly three quarters of the run to cover external costs and only started to make a profit as the last 13 per cent of the run was sold. The author also points out the weakness of the formula approach which is that it takes no account of time. (Clearly, a book that reprints often ties up less cash and is less risky than one that takes five years to sell out, even if the numbers are the same.) The main change over the next twenty years was that the proportion of the consumer pound going to the distribution system (wholesale and retail) was to expand considerably, and so publisher margins tightened and the multiplier of unit production cost to price went up accordingly.

This was the world of Irish book publishing up to the mid 1970s. Very soon it was to move up a gear, with the foundation of the successor houses to IUP and many other new firms.

7

The First Phase of the Publishing Resurgence: From 1975 to the Mid 1980s

The 1970s were a decade of shifts in Irish society and with them growth in the publishing industry. For both there was a kind of 'coming of age'.[1]

In international affairs: Ireland had opened out to the world since the 1960s. The number of countries with which we had diplomatic relations tripled, notably through membership of the EEC from 1972, but also as a result of greater involvement with the UN. Relations with Britain over the North reached a new intensity. The fear of communism subsided and TASS opened an office in Dublin.

In the population: The long post-Famine decline in the population began to be reversed after 1961. Emigration began to fall and some emigrants even returned to Ireland. The median age of marriage dropped and the marriage rate increased; at the same time the number of children per marriage dropped. Employment in agriculture fell below that in industry or services. Secondary education was now available to all.

In the economy: The boom years of the 1960s were consolidated when Ireland joined the EEC, with its regional funds and Common Agricultural Policy benefiting the 25 per cent of the population who still worked on the land. The EEC quickly rejected the Government's request for a derogation on the equal pay rules for men and women and in 1973 the Civil Service was forced to lift the 'marriage ban'. In 1976, Córas Tráchtála announced that for the first time at least half of Irish exports were of manufactured goods and non-UK sales represented half of their value. Ireland's dependence on imported oil, however, meant that the country was badly hit when the Arab 'oil weapon' was in play; the Republic's rate of inflation was the highest in Europe in 1976.

In law: 1974 saw the Supreme Court's decision in *McGee v Attorney-General*, in which the court agreed that Mrs McGee had the right to import contraceptives for her private family use. More importantly, the decision affirmed that there were natural rights above the statute law. The Constitution suddenly became a source and a battleground for social change. This was, said a recent writer, 'arguably the most significant decision the Supreme Court has ever taken.'[2] It led directly to the Eighth Amendment of the Constitution.

In communications: The rising number of telephone lines forced the Department of Posts and Telegraphs to split its national telephone directory into two volumes for the first time. Nobody had a mobile phone. Television, radio, newspapers, magazines seemed to be thriving. The number of books being published throughout the world, said UNESCO, had climbed to 557,000 in 1975, up from 360,000 in 1960. Irish publishers were probably producing 400 new titles a year, up from fewer than fifty in 1960.

In the Church: A referendum had removed the 'special position' of the Catholic Church from the Constitution. As an index of waning influence, in 1974 the Archbishop of Dublin gave up the long-cherished ambition to build a cathedral in Merrion Square, a building planned to loom over the national legislature across the road.

Behind all this were the relentless Troubles in the North, which became crueller and apparently more hopeless by the year. Violence spilled into the south, with bombings, kidnap threats, bank robberies and a general sense of vulnerability. In July 1972, the managing director of Irish University Press prefaced his report to the board by declaring quite seriously that 'the Company operates from a country which may well be on the brink of Civil War' – though few would have gone so far. Despite the burning of the British Embassy in Dublin following Bloody Sunday (January 1972), there was no question that the continuing series of horrors and the exposure of so much hatred, forced people to think and to write in new ways. It was one thing to accept the traditional aspiration to a united Ireland, or to deplore the sectarian governance of the North, but was the murderous activity of the IRA an acceptable price? Thomas Kinsella's creation of his own imprint, the Peppercanister Press, in 1973, to publish his protest against the Widgery Report on Bloody Sunday, was only a single instance of how the crisis drove new publishing initiatives. Another, a bit later, was Dermot Bolger's Raven Arts Press, which, as he said, began in 1977 as 'a loose movement for change. It grew out of a void, out of a need.'[3]

The Wider Publishing World in 1975

Since the 1920s the British publishing world (still the source of nine out of ten books sold in Ireland) had been dominated by independent, often family-run, publishing houses. Sometimes, as in the case of Allen & Unwin, Collins, Hodder & Stoughton, Macmillan or Thames & Hudson, they were large, publishing hundreds of titles every year; often they were smaller, such as Chatto & Windus, John Murray, Faber, Gollancz and Jonathan Cape. Although all of these were independent in the early 1970s, they were over the next decades to be the subject of a continuous series of mergers and acquisitions which was to transform the top end of the British publishing world. At the same time, there was a huge worldwide increase in the number of small publishers, driven probably by the concurrent surge in third-level education. In 2006, Laura Miller described this in America: 'there has been a tremendous increase in small presses in the last four decades. From a total US publisher population of 2,350 in 1958, the number jumped to 6,113 in 1972 to 10,803 in 1978, to about 22,500 in 1987.'[4] Similar increases occurred in Germany, Italy and France. As we shall see, Ireland was part of this trend.

Initially, the amalgamations were driven, both in the UK and the US, by an idea that somehow synergies could be found between television, IT and education companies and what were beginning to be called 'content providers'. This turned out to be a dead end. As the world book market expanded, however, the demand for capital, so difficult for a small firm, became paramount. Another key factor was the growing strength of the paperback reprint, described by one commentator as 'the cuckoo in the independent publisher's nest'. Initially perceived as a nice little earner on the side, by the 1960s paperback rights had become the key to financial soundness. Over 100 million paperbacks were being sold in Britain alone. It was no longer enough to rely on the traditional hardback, mid-list, market. Pressure from authors and others forced small independent hardback houses to combine.[5]

Some of this pressure came from authors, who were understandably keen to strike an inclusive hardback/paperback deal instead of having to go to a separate paperback firm. The new paperbacks were larger and sold at higher prices, so they could be economically produced in runs of 10,000 to 15,000, many fewer than the typical mass paperback run.[6]

The effect of the drastic structural changes can be seen in the statistics: in 1981 with 43,000 titles published in Britain and Ireland (down somewhat on the previous year), the top three firms had an estimated 5 per cent of the market and the top 100 titles sold 16 million copies; by 2005 there were 115,000 titles published and the greatly enlarged top three firms had 40 per cent of a greatly enlarged market, in which the top 100 titles sold 32 million copies.[7] This constant increase in the numbers of books published and, we must suppose, read is the engine throbbing in the background of these decades of publishing history.

From the point of view of Irish publishers and most writers, this movement was, at least until recently, merely noises off in the distance. By 1975, the foreign houses that had come to Ireland in the 1960s, such as Burns & Oates, Geoffrey Chapman, Herder and Longman had virtually all left. Only Macmillan remained. British publishers continued to expect Irish authors to come to them, perhaps with a little lordly encouragement, as Macmillan had done in the twenties and Hutchinson and Faber in the fifties. They continued to expect some 5 per cent of their sales to come from Ireland, which they treated for administrative purposes as part of the home market.[8] (This was good for booksellers, since carriage from the publisher's warehouse to the bookshop was usually paid by the publisher on 'home' orders, but not on orders defined as export.) Some used local agents such as Philip MacDermott – who carried Faber, Hutchinson and several paperback lists – or the Eason's-owned Irish Representation, but many, including at this time Oxford University Press, sent reps here twice a year, adding Ireland to the journeys covering Wales or Scotland.

The great majority of the books sold (with the crucial exception of primary and secondary education texts) were published in London and the traditional hardback bindings still held pride of place, supported by book review pages which rarely mentioned paperbacks. Paperbacks were stocked and there were two Dublin shops that specialised in them alone. 'Maybe even 90 per cent of the books we sell come from the UK,' Robin Montgomery of the Paperback Shop in Stillorgan told *Books Ireland*. The Paperback Shop was the first bookshop in Ireland to be located – American style – in a shopping mall.[9]

The economic position of Irish bookshops was still underpinned by the British publishers' fixed book price cartel called the Net Book Agreement, which, as we have seen, originated in the 1890s. In this, members of the Publishers Association combined to refuse to supply any bookseller who sold books at less than the declared or 'net' price. The agreement ensured that booksellers could not and did not compete on price, the retailer's favourite weapon. Booksellers in Ireland, as members of the British-based Booksellers' Association (Irish or Northern branches), firmly supported the agreement. A key result was that, just as the Latin Mass was the same whether you heard it in Rome or Edinburgh or Berlin, the English book was the same price in Cork or Bath or London. Irish publishers, not being members of the British Publishers Association, were never asked what they thought, though booksellers always treated Irish-published books as if they were net. One implication of the agreement was that publishers were not supposed to sell their own books, even at launches and the book trade keenly defended this exclusion, as Róisín Conroy of Attic (not of course a signatory of the agreement) found when she tried to sell direct to generate some cash.[10]

A stiff and successful defence of the agreement had been fought in the British courts in 1962 and for the moment it was unassailable, especially since the European Commission's Directorate-General for Competition gave a favourable verdict to the principle of fixed book prices in February 1978.

In March 1979, the Irish pound ceased to be par with sterling, for the first time since 1826, as a consequence of joining the European Monetary System. Exchange differentials and surcharges now meant that a book could be priced differently in neighbouring shops, thus breaking one of the treasured effects of the Net Book Agreement. Michael Gill wondered out loud in the December 1978 edition of *Books Ireland* whether the agreement could survive (and was scolded in *The Bookseller* for his temerity) but others such as Harold Clarke of Eason's were sure that it was too valuable to lose: '[it] brings order to the trade … it makes economic sense,' he argued. John Davey of Hodges Figgis agreed: 'If the Net Book Agreement went, the whole tradition of bookselling would suffer … we would never be able to carry as wide a stock as we do now.'[11]

Not that such faithful support delivered profits. The Charter Group of stockholding bookshops (an elite subset of the Booksellers Association which got an extra discount) reported in 1976/77 that the fifteen most substantial bookshops in Ireland made a wafer-thin 1.1 per cent profit, down from 1.8 per cent the previous year. In a paper delivered to the Irish Booksellers Conference in Kilkenny in February 1982, Frank O'Mahony (of the Limerick shop) reported an average gross profit of 30 per cent for three stockholding bookshops.[12] Staff costs hovered between 15 and 20 per cent of sales and some 85 per cent of sales came from the UK and so were exposed to exchange risk. The idea of buying sterling forward was complicated by the extreme seasonality of sales, with 41 per cent occurring in October–December (26 per cent in December alone).

A contributory cause of the booksellers' plight was the ungenerous terms of trade offered by publishers to independent booksellers (still by far the majority). Those laid down by Gill & Macmillan in 1982, were an absolutely typical set:

G+M's terms of trade (1982)

- *General net*: Single copy single line: 25%. Two or more single copies 35%. Two books or more 35%. Subscription stock and special orders: 35%.
- *Academic net*: Single copy single line: 25%. Two books or more 30%. Subscription, stick and special orders: 25% or 30%.
- *Non-net*: Subscription, stick and special orders: 20% Single copy single line: 20%. Two books or more 20%.
- *Other terms*: carriage only on export orders. Service 30p on orders valued at less than £6.00.

The trade reference book from which these terms are taken listed a labyrinth of trade terms in which each publisher was slightly different to all the others.[13] Gill & Macmillan offered booksellers a discount off the list or 'net' price of 35 per cent, equivalent to a 54 per cent mark-up (though this term was never used). The discount for academic or educational titles (described as 'non-net') was notably lower and the retailer was penalised for attempting to fulfil a customer's order for one book at a time, especially if it was priced at less than £6. Mercier stuck to the traditional 33.3 per cent discount (not yet rounded up to 35 for the convenience of the house computer), as did Penguin and Eason's (for their Irish Heritage series). Mercier's terms were less elaborate than G&M's, not distinguishing special discounts for non-net or academic books, but they too penalised single-copy single-line orders (i.e. one copy of one title) and whereas G&M charged carriage only on export orders, Mercier charged the retailer carriage for orders under £10.

The restrictive impact of these terms made bookselling difficult. The gross margin (i.e. the discount) was of course diminished by 'shrinkage' which might amount to 6 per cent. This left the balance, at 29 per cent of sales, perilously near to an ever-increasing overhead, especially rents and wages. Several traditional bookshops closed in the late 1970s and early 1980s, notably Gill's, Browne & Nolan, Combridge's, Willis, and the Eblana. Hodges Figgis closed one of its two city-centre shops (on Stephen's Green) citing the VAT rate and problems with the sterling differential.[14] The general imposition of such fiddling and penal discount rules shows how publishers (as a bloc) had achieved a dominance over booksellers (as a bloc) since the 1890s. The next twenty years would see a dramatic change in this relationship.

Bootstrapping a Publishing Industry[15]

In the 1970s, British editors and publishers were not much interested in Ireland's cultural challenges and re-positionings, nor in the soul-searching demanded by the Northern problem. Yet there were, as Dermot Bolger reported, things that needed to be said and a new generation eager to let them be said. The allure of publishing, a business at the same time complex and doubtfully lucrative, is elusive but strong (and, paradoxically, not exclusively for the bookish – as Jonathan Cape and Allen Lane demonstrated). As Jason Epstein, the founder of Anchor Books, the Library of America and the *New York Review of Books*, wrote:

> Book publishing is not a conventional business … it more resembles a vocation or amateur sport in which the primary goal is the activity itself rather than its financial outcome. For owners and editors willing to work for the joy of the task, book publishing in my time has been immensely rewarding. For investors looking for conventional returns it has been disappointing.[16]

A remarkable generation of new Irish publishers felt that allure in the 1970s. The treefall of Irish University Press had thrown up numerous seedlings, not least the successor, Irish Academic Press, run by Michael Adams, which was for many years not much more than a sales office for the remaining stock, though he began to publish with his other imprint Four Courts as early as 1977. New foundations around this time included Seamus Cashman's Wolfhound (first title 1974), Seán Browne's Academy Press (1976), Tom Turley's Blackwater (1976), Jeremy Addis' *Books Ireland* (1976); these jostled with the previously founded Gifford & Craven (1972).

Outside of the IUP alumni, Appletree (first title 1974) joined Blackstaff (1971) as new non-sectarian voices in the North; in the south O'Brien Press (1974), Arlen House (1975), Poolbeg (1976), the Irish Writers Co-operative (1976) and Villa Books (1978) joined Gallery (1970) and the older firms Gill &

Macmillan, Mercier and Dolmen. Allen Figgis had largely ceased publishing in 1973 and was to sell the Hodges Figgis bookshop to Pentos in 1978. On the educational side, the Educational Company continued in Smurfit ownership. There was a management buyout of C.J. Fallon. Folens' sixteen-volume Irish language encyclopaedia project (on foot of which it had taken a substantial factory in Tallaght) collapsed when the Department of Education withdrew its order. Folens subsequently sued for costs and loss of £500,000 profits – it was awarded £57,600.[17]

We have seen that there was a great surge in the number of small presses in the western world from the 1960s. Seamus Cashman remembers his disappointment when he realised that his own firm and his contemporaries in Ireland were not part of a uniquely Irish response to Irish conditions (though they were of course that) but part of a larger world movement, which he ascribed to the much greater access to third-level education.[18] Irish booksellers were conscious, as Eric Pembrey of Greene's put it in 1980, that 'the increase in reading in the last ten to fifteen years is incredible. Possibly it could be free education or television, I don't know.'[19]

The new publishing houses of the 1970s initiated a period of local innovation, drive and (occasionally) aggression that was quickly noticed by the media. 'Publishing revival under way,' wrote Brian Rothery in 1972, adding optimistically, 'Irish writers may be coming home at last.'[20] The occasion of the Sense of Ireland (a London festival of Irish Arts organised by the Arts Council and the Department of Foreign Affairs) gave journalists a chance to marvel at the recent growth in Irish publishing. 'They're producing real books,' said the *Guardian*, 'not just reprints.'[21] In 1980 *The Bookseller* published an eight-page article about the new houses, complete with a mini-directory; and a year later the US trade magazine *Publishers' Weekly* devoted a supplement to a very kind overview of Irish publishing. The supplement ran to a full forty pages on what it described as 'a new flowering … a burgeoning publishing community that, though still in its infancy is growing in vigor and confidence'. Writers and their agents began to sit up and take notice of this new phenomenon.[22]

That is not to say that these new houses did not face formidable problems. As we have seen in Chapter 1, publishing a book calls on a range of skills. The critical starting point, of course, is to identify a book to publish: everything stems from that. Afterwards, from a standing start, you need some capital to keep you going before the hoped-for sales kick in; you need editing skill and book assembly knowledge; you need to know enough about the arcane arts of specifying design, typesetting, paper, printing and binding to ensure that the final book stands up reasonably against the polished products of the British industry; you need to curb your natural optimism and not print too many copies; you need the drive and chutzpah to persuade unenthusiastic booksellers to stock the book and ideally to recommend it to their customers; you need (or did until reliable distribution services were established) the practical skills to store, invoice, pack and despatch them against orders; you need the financial controls to co-ordinate cash flow and to calculate and pay royalties and overhead expenses. And then, if you want to be 'a publisher', you have to do it all over again, and again.

Painfully, book by book, the new Irish publishers learned their business, spurred, if they were lucky, by a success or two. The immediate success of Appletree's first book *Faces of the Past* convinced publisher John Murphy that publishing was 'easy'. Just as he took it to the bookshops on 10 December 1974 ('I didn't know you were supposed to sell in advance') it was featured on a BBC NI news magazine. He sold twelve copies to Erskine Mayne and by the time he got back home they had ordered another fifty, and there were none left by the close of business. Appletree reprinted and got the books into the shops on 18 December and sold that run by Christmas. John Murphy, was, he puts it, 'hooked' on this marvellous business. By coincidence, a similar success with their first book, cartoons by Rowel Friers, confirmed Blackstaff's founders Diane and Jim Gracey in their activity. Since each book paid for the previous one, it was essential for sales to be quick and you could not afford to get much wrong. Starting out, unless you followed Stanley Unwin's prescription to buy and revive a moribund list (which Michael Adams effectively did, but was rarely possible in Ireland), you had no comfortable backlist as a cushion.[23] Fatalities were therefore common. As a result, of the twenty-eight members of Clé listed in the first edition of *Books Ireland* in March 1976, as many as nine produced only one or no books in 1980.[24]

New publishers quickly discover that there are always plenty of manuscripts, but at first it seems that any author you know about is either no good or published by someone else, often in London. Various strategies have been adopted. One is to start with a local interest book, as Sealy, Bryers & Walker (and later Collins Press) did; a guide to evening classes taken over from IUP did the job for Seamus Cashman of Wolfhound. Or there is self-publishing, as Michael O'Brien did with his *Dublin Changing* which he published after Gill & Macmillan had turned it down and Catherine Rose of Arlen in 1975 after Mercier refused her book *The Female Experience: The Story of the Woman Movement in Ireland*. Savage and ungenerous reviews in *The Irish Times* deterred Catherine Rose from further authorial efforts, but she published over fifty titles in the next ten years.[25]

In editing and assembling the book there are no rules, but a great number of conventions. Thus it was a symptom of inexperience (instantly to be spotted as such by unfriendly booksellers) to start, as Poolbeg did, Bryan MacMahon's 1976 collection of short stories with no half-title and two copyright pages. (David Marcus was a fine editor, and Philip MacDermott hopped with ideas and was a good marketeer, but neither then knew much about the conventions for assembling a book.) None of the new publishers had their own printing or binding, so they were obliged to depend on the general print industry. In England it was famously possible to go to a printer with a manuscript in one hand and a Jonathan Cape book in the other with the instruction: 'make this look like this'.[26] In Ireland this was not an option, because outside of the tied houses such as Browne & Nolan and the Educational Company the skills and knowledge were either not there or in immense demand. This was why Sáirséal & Dill set up its own printing unit.

Once the books were produced it was then necessary to promote and sell them. On the whole, Irish newspapers were keen to give the new publishers publicity, dutifully attending launches and publishing periodic 'New from Irish Publishers' columns. As Philip MacDermott found, the public was keen to support that relative rarity, an Irish-published book that was neither religious nor educational: the Graceys in Belfast found a similar, if anything more intense, local support.[27] Except in the specialised journal *Books Ireland* advertising was not an option, so the relationships with Eason's (with its dominant position as wholesale book distributor) and key independent bookshops was critical.

In the context of the burgeoning new Ireland it might have been expected that Dublin booksellers would welcome the new publishers on the scene. But the predominantly Protestant heads of houses such as Combridge's, Eason's, Hanna's and Hodges Figgis (the major Dublin outlets) enjoyed their established relationships with the London publishers and were often dismissive of the iconoclastic newcomers. A director of Eason's was once heard to refer to Michael O'Brien as 'our peasant publisher', and the same man initially declined to stock O'Brien's totally apolitical early title *Me Jewel and Darlin' Dublin* because of the IRA background of the author (who was in Mountjoy Jail at the time of the launch for offences connected with his editorship of *An Phoblact*).[28] Eason's market position (estimated at perhaps half of the Irish book trade) was such that when it refused for fear of libel to stock Poolbeg's *The Boss*, the publishers believed that if Eason's had stocked the book, sales might have been doubled.[29]

Combridge's refused to stock Irish-published books at all and at a heated Clé meeting in 1983 the president Seán O'Boyle, then of Veritas, was obliged to admit that (in his experience) 'one member of the Irish Books Marketing Group was not sympathetic to Irish publishers: this was Fred Hanna.'[30] It is fair to say, however, that when a ginger group of Irish publishers thought that it would be good to combine booksellers and publishers into one Book House Ireland on the Dutch or German model, rather than continuing the traditional British model of separate trade associations, there was a tolerant acquiescence. This radical experiment, however, lasted only ten years.

There was some practical excuse for this stand-offishness. Existing UK publishers were members of an Accounts Clearing House, which Irish publishers were not. The Clearing House combined all member-publishers' invoices each month so the bookseller merely paid a single cheque and cleared them all. Setting up an account which had to be handled outside of this system was obviously unattractive. An incidental effect of the Clearing House system was that payment of its account every month was top priority and if there was a cash flow shortage, accounts outside of it were at the back of the queue. Irish publishers were made to know their place.

Nonetheless, however unenthusiastically, the books were stocked, though often rather unintelligently in 'Irish Interest' ghettos so that, as Attic Press complained, Irish books on feminist issues would not find themselves with comparable British or American feminist titles, but along the shelf from those well-known feminists Patrick Kavanagh, James Joyce and Oscar Wilde.

Getting the Books from the Publishers' Warehouses

The most pressing difficulty that the new Irish publishers faced was that of distribution. (At this time the poor quality of British publishers' distribution was proverbial. This persisted at least until the widespread use of computers. In Sligo, John Keohane found it could take three to six weeks to get a book from London, and that generally when a sales rep called, the order he had taken on the previous visit had not yet been delivered. [31])

Most Irish publishers started by distributing themselves, wrapping books on the kitchen table, carrying their own car stock, delivering personally to the shops, as Seán and Bríghid Uí Éigearthaigh had done, and others after them. *Publishers Weekly* was told, 'too many good editors are spending time overseeing production and packing books for shipment … if a bookseller in Dublin calls and asks for three books, I get in my car and drop them off myself.'[32] This was clearly a short-term solution, being time-consuming and inefficient, and such informal amateurism did not always appeal to booksellers. What was badly needed was an Irish sales and distribution house and it took a few years before a solution was found.

In 1978, manager Paddy Willis took over the declining Association for the Propagation of Christian Knowledge (always known as APCK), which traced its history to 1792. In the previous generation, Arthur Gray, who had become manager of the Dawson Street branch in 1942, had transformed APCK into a profitable bookselling chain. Under Willis the chain was given a stylish makeover and renamed Willis Books. At the same time, he established a distribution arm called Andrews. Although immediately successful, by 1981, struggling with an adverse sales climate, Willis and Andrews went into liquidation, with debts of over half a million pounds. Forty staff lost their jobs. The closing of the shops in Cork, Limerick, Coleraine and Derry was bad news for the Irish publishing industry, but the losses specifically from the collapse were not severe (though the liquidator's selling off unpaid-for stock at remainder prices was regarded as adding insult to injury). This did not apply, as it happened, to O'Brien Press's stock in the Dawson Street shop, which Michael O'Brien personally 'liberated', overawing an attempted protest from one of the staff.[33] Gill & Macmillan lost £1,519 from Willis and £317 from Andrews; Mercier lost £1,470. The big losers were the British paperback houses Pan, Granada and Penguin which lost nearly £60,000 between them. Macmillan and Longman together lost £10,000.[34]

Another attempt to create a distribution company was initiated a year later, in November 1982, by the newspaper distributor Dermot McDermott. It was initially successful, achieving some éclat with its work on Poolbeg's *The Boss*, the bestselling description of C.J. Haughey in government. In the sixteen months to May 1985 Dermot McDermott had a turnover of £1.3 million. By then, however, it had a deficit of over £200,000 and a liquidator was appointed. Once again, the main portion of liabilities fell to British publishers (£322,000 out of a total debt of £516,000), but two Irish publishers in particular, Tom Turleys's Glendale (£17,000) and Gill & Macmillan (£14,500), were hit.[35] A judicious piece of insider knowledge enabled Philip MacDermott to remove his Poolbeg stock before the liquidator closed the place.

In the meantime, Clé had commissioned a study of the problem from the UCD Faculty of Commerce and was steadily progressing towards a distribution scheme. While work on this was in progress, however, to general surprise, in 1979, O'Brien Press, Dolmen and Wolfhound announced their own scheme, in which a new organisation called Irish Bookhandling (IBh; the German echo was deliberate) was set up in the building off South Richmond

Street that had previously been used by Dolmen as a print factory. After some tight-lipped discussion, and with a contribution from the Arts Council, the IBh three agreed that Clé members could participate. A representative from Clé (first Seán O'Boyle then the author) joined the IBh board.

'Participation' meant moving some if not all of a publisher's stock to South Richmond Street and delegating to the new firm not only the selling of the books to the trade but crucially taking in all the money owed by booksellers. Trust took some time to develop and in the meantime IBh was racking up costs without the planned-for throughput to pay them. The costs were met by reducing the amounts that should have been paid to the three founding publishers from the sales of their books, leaving an increasing debt owed to them. Eventually, Clé members did join and their books began to generate revenue. Unfortunately, a board decision laid down that each publisher be paid not according to the previous month's sales, but a proportion of the whole amount outstanding, including the debt generated in the fallow months before the Clé members joined. Not surprisingly, the new participants complained bitterly about being asked to participate in the payment of a debt of which they knew nothing. Most left, so that by 1986 only a rump was still involved, including Rena Dardis' Anvil, the first Lilliput titles and Caoimhín Ó Marcaigh's Sáirséal Ó Marcaigh.

From 1984, the Dolmen representative, Liam Miller's daughter Máire Block, who had been a director since 1983, became the day-to-day manager of IBh. In the early months of 1986 she travelled the country in an intensive 'pay your debts to IBh' campaign. This resulted in a large cash balance in the company's AIB Baggot Street account. In March 1986, Máire Block resigned as manager, announcing her intention to set up a book sales business to be called Cover to Cover. As a parting gesture she charged IBh with her costs and expenses to the April London Book Fair where she looked for clients for her new business. On her return, she arranged for the Dolmen stock to be surreptitiously removed from the warehouse to a purpose-built store in the family home in Mountrath; such was the overnight haste of this move that stocks of the expensive limited editions were overlooked. This was a breach of Dolmen's agreement with the firm.[36]

Worse was to come. From cheque books and other documents it emerged that she had illegitimately paid Dolmen and its associated company Pilgrim some £26,400 more than they were entitled to. O'Brien Press, Wolfhound and the other publishers were left high and dry. This fraud was reported to the Gardaí, including the telling counter-signature of some of the cheques by Liam Miller, but the case was not pursued.

Despite a record sales year in 1985, with a net turnover of £425,000 (including the high of 17 per cent returns, partly attributed to the Dermot McDermott collapse), this fraud effectively killed IBh. Over 80 per cent of income was from sales for the three principals: O'Brien Press (accounting for 37 per cent), Wolfhound (32 per cent) and Dolmen (15 per cent). By May 1986, however, there was a substantial excess of liabilities over assets, represented in large degree by money owed to O'Brien Press and Wolfhound. The loss of these sums nearly saw the end of both of those houses, since the debts supporting their balance sheets were now worthless.

By happy coincidence, at this time Gill & Macmillan had recently moved to a new office and warehouse facility in Goldenbridge. This had become its resting place after the devastating fire in No. 50 O'Connell Street during the Pope's visit in September 1979. Though the company had offices also in Eden Quay, O'Connell Street had operated as offices, shop and warehouse, with the stock stored in a rat-infested basement stretching under the street, the same basement that had, in the Troubles, housed a republican shooting gallery with target pictures of the British king. House gossip told of how one manager, interrupted in the basement Gents by a rat 'the size of a cat', burst out of the door, pants and trousers round his ankles, right into the arms of a reverend mother who was collecting a consignment of school books.[37]

The fire destroyed Christmas titles, backlist and education books – the lot, except for some palleted books due for pulping. Luckily, financial records were off-site with a computer bureau, but ordinary files, film, art and paperwork had gone up in flames, not to mention Gill's substantial historic archives. Although there was initial speculation that this was some kind of extreme Protestant backlash during the Pope's visit against an obviously Catholic publishing house, it is likely it was caused by children breaking in and starting a fire which got out of control. A fire caused in this way had destroyed £50,000 worth of books in the APCK in Dawson Street a few years before.

Before the IBh collapse, Gill & Macmillan had been planning to use the new space to extend its distribution service (currently handling just its own books and Brandon). In June 1986, all the stocks of O'Brien Press and Wolfhound were moved from the North Richmond Street warehouse to Goldenbridge and a new regime began. Between 23 and 27 June some 135,000 books, representing over 100 titles, were moved from North Richmond Street. The exercise underlined some physical and practical details about book publishing. To build a secure income you need to publish a lot, since generally each title contributes only a certain amount, and perhaps that for only a relatively short time. In a publisher's warehouse, as in a maternity ward, one baby is of course the author/parent's special joy, but you need more than that to sustain a continuing operation.

Despite some initial suspicions (what was to stop the Gill & Macmillan sales director Peter Thew keeping an eye on his rivals' sales figures?), the efficiency and reliability of this service from the start was a revelation. It is a telling measure of the time-consuming and unsatisfactory nature of previous distribution arrangements that Michael O'Brien later commented, as a wonder, 'they never missed a monthly payment, not once'.[38] As other publishers joined the Gill & Macmillan service, it became a crucial hub of the Irish trade.

It was no coincidence that the need for adequate distribution was also felt by the Irish language publishers, despite a bizarre finding in the *Irish Statistical Bulletin* that Irish language books represented 28 per cent of books sold.[39] In 1980, Bord na Gaeilge set up its own sales and distribution operation called ÁIS (in full Áisínteacht Dáiliúchan Leabhar) in Fenian Street, Dublin, and installed Diarmuid Ó Cathasaigh as manager. With the decline of An Club Leabhar, the outlets for Irish books were few, one of the reasons that decided Bríghid Uí Éigearthaigh to sell. Four big-selling titles, *Anois is Arís*, *An Biblio*, *An Duanaire* and *Learning Irish*, came in 1981, giving ÁIS a flying start, with a first year turnover of £190,000. The next year, 1982, was not so good, with sales of £158,000. By 1985, sales had climbed back to £209,000 with 1,800 titles from 90 suppliers.[40]

Digression on Print-Buying

The second major distraction faced by the new publishers of the 1970s and 1980s was a significant change in the way books were manufactured. The comfortable technical conjunction established in the 1890s, with hot metal typesetting combined with flatbed letterpress printing and sewn cased books, typically with all functions in the same factory, held good until the late 1960s, or just before the new Irish publishers came on the scene. By then improvements in the design of offset litho printing led printers in both Ireland and England to invest in these simpler, faster and more economical machines, and the inevitable counterpart, some form of non-hot-metal typesetting. All this change involved publishers wrestling with new technologies that they would much have preferred to be invisible.

The *Clé Manual of Book Publishing*, which was published in 1981, described the situation as it seemed then. The new technologies forced publishers into an unwelcome immersion into new areas of manufacturing, which were awkward to find out about and a mistake in any of which could materially worsen the appearance of the book. The first choice the neophyte publisher had to make was in typesetting, a time-consuming and troublesome process which was still usually bought from an outside supplier. 'The days when your printer was also your typesetter have almost disappeared,' the *Manual* states. 'It is now common to have the copy set by a trade-setter and supplied to a printer.'[41] A directory published in 1983 listed thirty-four different typesetters in the Dublin area.[42] Rapid recent developments had meant that very few Irish printers retained hot metal setting. For most people the choice was between direct-impression and film setting, both of which being keyed from marked-up hard copy in the traditional way.

Direct impression (also 'cold type') was basically glorified typewriting, on sophisticated machines such as the Varityper (as owned by Sáirséal & Dill) and, after 1972, the IBM Selectric and Electronic Composer machines with the golfball heads capable of producing camera-ready justified professional-looking type. To avoid the expense and difficulty associated with typesetting, some publishers brought these inhouse. The O'Brien Press was an early user of these machines, Michael O'Brien having seen its use in his father's printing company E. & T. O'Brien. The range of faces was not great and the image quality was often weak. It did not do the system's reputation any good that the most used face was the weak Press Roman, a kind of bastardised Times. Nonetheless, the Composer could produce a perfectly adequate page and was widely used for straight text setting, especially academic.[43] The letter-by-letter transfer system Letraset was widely used for display type.

More expensively, by 1981 most printers had installed one of the bewildering variety of film-output systems. Capturing the keystrokes (a favourite jargon phrase) digitally or on paper tape, typically a laser flash was triggered through a negative film or glass plate, creating the letters on sensitive film. The hyphenation and justification systems were part of this machine's operation.

In whatever manner the pages were created, they inevitably had to be proofed and corrected. At the final stages this involved manually stripping in replacement lines of paper text or film with Cow Gum, a messy process that can occasionally be seen in print as the compositor has accidentally stripped the correction over the wrong line. It was to be a decade before publishers were released from the troublesome and expensive routines of cold or film setting by desktop publishing.

There was more to learn, for printers as well as their customers. The corrected pages were then planned or laid out by hand on to a large sheet, perhaps sixteen to view so that when printed and folded the pages fell into the correct sequence and ideally the text areas and the page numbers (folios) fell neatly and exactly one under the first. Printing was inevitably by offset litho, which brought with it its own technical problems and an unfamiliar vocabulary of defects: such as scum (a grey wash effect caused by failure of the ink–water balance), hickeys (a dot with a nonprinting halo), doubling (plate/blanket misalignment) and dot gain (midtones printing too dark). Gone were the creamy antique woves, which bulked well, and on which one could feel the indentation of the letterpress with the tip of a finger; the faster and more chemically sensitive litho process required a smoother sheet, so the whiter, less bulky cartridge was typically used.

Binding was usually by a single shot of hot-melt adhesive on to a book block of single pages with the folds trimmed away – the quaintly named 'perfect' binding system. Though conceptually simple, this technique was difficult to get consistently right. Small maladjustments of the equipment might cause the glue to be so thick that the pages would not open, or so thin or brittle that the spines cracked and pages fell out. Common problems included faulty gathering (section omitted or repeated), or the cover paper grain being wrong, which caused the cover to rise up like a bird's wing.[44]

One of the new publishers, Rena Dardis of Anvil, complained bitterly in *Books Ireland* of the effects of the print trade's lack of bookwork experience. Part of the problem was the size of the market, which inhibited specialisation: as John Spillane of Mercier put it 'they were doing cigarette cartons one minute, raffle tickets the next.'[45] Rena Dardis reported problems printers were having with setting (the need to learn the new technology not helping), in which the hyphenation and justification routine 'produced proofs with more than half the lines on a page hyphenated. Not even four letter words were safe. "King" was cut into k-ing.' There were also problems with planning (before platemaking), where a colour illustration supposed to start 8mm from the top actually started 12mm, so the bottom was cut off. Or a reprint where the bottom margin of the left-hand page could come out at half that of the right-hand page; Rena Dardis also cited a book which 'by a miracle of technology' had been cut on the slant and on some copies had badly chawed edges due to a blunt guillotine knife. Furthermore, the influence of the variation clause allowing a binder to deliver 10 per cent too few jackets, necessitating an expensive reprint. Then there was paper: one printer used a variety of newsprints, 'giving a layered effect like a Battenberg cake'; another silently substituted a bulkier paper for that specified and ignored the fact that the preprinted cover did not then fit, so the spine extended into the blurb.[46] 'Almost everyone,' reported the *Publishers Weekly* Irish supplement, 'had a horror story to tell of books that were bound with pages missing or upside-down.'

Rena Dardis freely admitted her own and her colleagues' inexperience, since 'very few small publishers have fulltime production staff.' This was a key point, because it meant that heads of companies had to grapple with these uncongenial technical problems themselves. There was no doubt that 'some excellent books are produced by Irish printers,' continued Rena Dardis, 'but why should it be on a two-times-out-of-three basis?' As Gill & Macmillan's print buyer, ex printer Eamon O'Rourke complained in 1980, not only were many of the industry's machines old and out of date, but they were habitually run at slower rates than in Britain. As a result, the charge for hardback binding a 224-page book in Britain might be £450, as against £750 in Ireland; printing 500 copies of thirty-two pages in Britain would cost £44, in Ireland £130.[47]

What the New Publishers Published

By 1980, there were over sixty paying members of the Irish Book Publishers Association (commonly referred to as Clé). This was the association for publishers of trade books, normally in English. There was also a separate association for educational publishers, with six members. Its main function was to liaise with the Department of Education. And finally there was the Cumann na bhFoilsitheoirí Gaeilge, with twenty or so Irish language publishers, whose main focus was relating to the various grant bodies for the language. Contact, let alone liaison, between these three trade associations was rare. Communication between Irish booksellers and the trade publishers was closer, with the 1981 establishment of the Book House Ireland joint secretariat.

The *Irish Publishing Record* 1980 records 745 new books and pamphlets published in 1980, coming from 288 publishers, three quarters of them Dublin-based. The great majority of the publishers were, as usual, one-book wonders, with only Appletree, Blackstaff, Four Courts, Gill & Macmillan, Mercier, O'Brien Press and Poolbeg publishing more than ten titles.[48] The new publishers were on the whole eclectic in output, typically making no austere attempt to publish a dedicated 'list' limited to a single subject. As *Publishers Weekly* put it:

> The Irish trade is still a cottage industry in the most literal sense; many of its fledging smaller publishers work out of their homes – from Dublin apartments to a sheep farm in the Irish countryside. These often-youthful publishers are each year collectively turning out between 500 and 600 mostly Irish-accented books on social and political history, biography,

> crafts, literary criticism and cooking. In addition, they are providing unprecedented opportunities for new Irish fiction writing. What these newcomers lack in experience, expertise and capital they are trying to counter with energy and commitment.[49]

Classified under broad Dewey numbers, by far the largest category of books published, nearly 30 per cent of titles, was 'social sciences, government and education', although a number of these titles might more properly have been classified as history. Of these, fifty-eight were new school textbooks, but the rest show a quizzing of the new society that had not been encouraged before.

Some of these books were published by state agencies such as the Institute of Public Administration, the Economic and Social Research Institute and the National Economic and Social Council. There were several books on the working of the Constitution, on Ireland and Europe, on law and consumer rights and public administration and on social problems and policy. There were now twice as many books published in this category as in the previously dominant category of religion. Not that religion was neglected: indeed one of the new publishers, Anthony Dwyer of Villa Books, had come all the way from his father's firm in Australia to specialise in religious books. In that capacity, he had appalling luck with popes: first he produced a 'quickie' biography of the newly installed Pope John Paul I, which reached the market (incidentally beating Collins in the race) two days before John Paul's death. Then, in 1979, Villa had stored film and artwork and other materials in the Gill offices above the bookshop in O'Connell Street. It was impossible to move anything during John Paul II's visit to Dublin so Anthony Dwyer took a risk and ran on for a few days without insurance. The big fire in the Gill building, over the crucial weekend, destroyed everything in the old house, including the Gill archive and Villa's artwork, film-setting and preparatory work.

The next two largest categories were 'literature and criticism' and 'history, biography and geography'; these were the areas that the new publishers were strongest in. The largest trade house was Gill & Macmillan, with a publishing turnover of £1.1 million of which 60 per cent was from educational sales. (It was the only house to straddle the trade and educational markets. Apart from the occasional foray from Folens, educational publishers tended to stick to the knitting.) The bulk of the rest came from its strong history list and a deliberate decision not to publish fiction or poetry. Michael Gill told *Publishers Weekly*:

> If you look at publishing throughout the English-speaking world, you'll see that the major fiction publishers are still in the centers of London and

> New York ... Dublin has to be seen as a fairly provincial center. It would be a bad place to publish *Princess Daisy*, just as Philadelphia would.[50]

Captain Feehan agreed, saying he would only begin to publish fiction if he could dine once a week with the literary editor of the *Sunday Times* (John B. Keane was obviously an exception to this rule). In July 1976, Eason's buyer Maura Hastings told *Books Ireland* 'on the whole the Irish do not read novels': well, not the novels she cared to stock, for, as she said, 'we have no violence, no pro-hard drugs books. It's not Eason's policy to encourage that element in the shops.' She described Irish readers as 'dead practical ... they buy books on management, natural foods, and poetry, yes, mostly Irish.'[51]

Luckily there were others interested in fiction. Most notably perhaps David Marcus and Philip MacDermott's Poolbeg. Marcus had been running a short story page in the *Irish Press* since 1968 and some of his contributors had, as he put it, 'the nucleus of an excellent collection with little or no chance of finding a publisher in Ireland or Britain'. He met Philip MacDermott in a pub near the *Irish Press* office, where he was promoting some of the authors he repped (from Faber, Hutchinson and Hodder among others) to *Irish Press* executives and they hatched the idea of a publishing house with the special aim of promoting Irish short stories.[52] The first collections came out in 1976 and over the years they became increasingly professional in appearance, helped by the employment of Robert Ballagh to do cover art. Among the authors Poolbeg published were Michael McLaverty, Julia O'Faolain, Tom Murphy, Ita Daly, Val Mulkerns and Bryan MacMahon.

Marcus ceased to act as editor in 1983, but Philip MacDermott carried on, sparkling with creativity as usual – which was just as well since his senior salesman, Gill Hess, had established his own sales agency business in 1982, taking with him several of the best agencies, including Faber and Hutchinson. This had been MacDermott's equivalent to a backlist, providing cashflow protection. So when ideas such as a Louis le Brocquy art book, or the Robert Ballagh photographs, proved too expensive for the market, Poolbeg was caught in a storm. And to cap it all the firm was hit by a back-tax demand. Managing director Kieran Devlin remembers how he became at that time 'on familiar terms with the sheriff'.[53]

By 1985, Poolbeg had published over sixty titles, mostly short stories, but also some non-fiction, with 50,000 sales from Tim Pat Coogan's *On the Blanket* (1980) and more from Joe Joyce and Peter Murtagh's *The Boss* (1983). They were published under the short-lived Ward River imprint. The first of these contained an expensive libel of Kevin Boland, and indemnifying Eason's cost the company dear, added to which an expensive print deal from Cahill's meant the books were sold at a loss. The company somehow continued, gradually gaining control over its costs (deciding to print in Guernsey rather than at Cahill's was a step forward) until the 1990s when it blossomed with a powerful new list of commercial fiction starting with Patricia Scanlan's *City Girl* (1992). This venture really did, at least for a while, look like the breakout from the purely Irish-interest publishing that commentators interviewed by *Publishers Weekly* saw as a limitation.

A more specialised house was Peter Fallon's Gallery Press which began its long career of poetry and drama publishing in 1970. Like many similar enterprises this was born out of a feeling that 'there wasn't a particularly receptive book publishing presence at that time.'[54] New Writers Press, he believed, was too fixed on Modernism and Dolmen (like Cuala) on sumptuous, expensive editions that precluded the possibility of a wide readership. His first title was *Answers* by Des O'Mahony, and he quickly built up a distinguished list, widening out into plays in 1974 (happily including the ever-popular Brian Friel). By 1985, with the significant help of the Arts Council and a coolly professional approach to contracts, advances, royalty payments etc., he had published over eighty titles. Such professionalism he aptly described as 'a pioneering notion in Irish poetry publishing'. Among his authors were Derek Mahon and Medbh McGuckian who had been published in England, but also those published by Dolmen such as Pearse Hutchinson, Desmond O'Grady and Aidan Carl Mathews. By the turn of the century the list had reached 300 titles (half of which were still in print), from Brendan Kennelly and Paul Durcan to Eiléan Ní Chuilleanáin. Cavillers complained his authors were mostly white, Christian, and (apparently) heterosexual, who tended to write a relatively formal poetry. But that, as Peter Fallon retorted, reflected the Irish tradition in which they wrote. (The accusation that they were overwhelmingly male was more difficult, but Fallon maintained that 'I don't believe that there *was* a woman poet who was being excluded.')[55]

The View from 1986

There had been rough times for the book trade in the early 1980s, with Eric Pembrey of Greene's complaining of a 25 per cent drop in business in 1980 alone, a plaint echoed by Harold Clarke of Eason's and Fred Hanna. Paddy Willis spoke gloomily of 'publishers publishing less and less' and booksellers having to sell cards and magazines. 'Maybe,' he speculated, 'the days of the traditional bookseller are numbered'.[56] Some of this was evidenced in the closing of several of the traditional Dublin bookshops, though the sudden and unexpected abolition of VAT on books in 1982 had given sales a great boost. One bookseller commented: 'the day before VAT came off, we sold £57 worth of books; on the day £1,000's worth.'[57] VAT had been at 15 per cent, in marked contrast with the zero rating in Britain. This had been an added aggravation to the sterling differential as suspicious book buyers lifted the price labels to see what was the 'real price' i.e. in sterling and without VAT. As it happened, a report in 1982 by the English academic Francis Fishwick found that only 13 per cent of buyers had made any attempt to shop around for better prices.[58]

Once again, as in 1969 with the artists' tax relief scheme, the trade gave total credit for the VAT coup to Charles Haughey, for they were as taken by surprise as anyone.[59] A tense meeting of the heads of Clé companies about whether a militant campaign for removal of the tax was desirable, called – as it happened – on the day of the Budget, was dramatically interrupted by a message that the Minister for Finance had just announced in the Dáil his intention to do precisely that.[60] Luckily, money had been collected to support such a campaign, from British and from the educational publishers. This financed the quickly founded Irish Books Marketing Group's campaign to hammer home the slogan 'books are cheaper now'. Finance Minister Ray MacSharry incidentally estimated the cost to the public purse of the removal of VAT to be £4.5 million, which, grossed-up, implies an estimate of £27 million to book sales as a whole.

An increasing number of those sales were being made in stockholding bookshops around the country. As recently as 1976 Eason's buyer Maura Hastings had commented on 'the dearth of bookshops' in the country. Ten years later, however, there had been, as Harold Clarke (then chairman of Eason's) put it, with a touch of exaggeration, 'the establishment of good stock-holding bookshops in virtually every town in the country'.[61] The key influence in shifting Eason's focus towards books, Clarke was inclined to large, cheerfully positive statements. For instance, he told *Business and Finance* that sales 'rose by 40 per cent almost immediately' after the removal of VAT.[62] He was also an assiduous promoter of the Irish reader myth: 'we are a highly literate market', he told the same reporter. In 1985, he made the unlikely claim that 'book-buying in Ireland is a classless activity', arguing that this unique attribute was the result of Irish children conquering their timidity about bookshops because they bought their schoolbooks there.[63]

Where before there had been newsagents with a shelf or two of paperbacks, a new evolution took place. For example: in Cork, there was the Mercier

Bookshop in Bishop Street, the venerable Liam Ruiséal and Collins in Carey's Lane; in Galway, Kenny's; in Kilkenny, Don and Mary Roberts; in Sligo, Keohane's (originally opened in 1947) and its branch in Ballina; there was O'Mahony's in Limerick, which expanded to Tralee in 1986; in Belfast, Anna Crane and William Mullan, though the much-loved Erskine Mayne closed in 1982; there was the Book Centre chain in Waterford, Wexford and Kilkenny; Josie Corcoran in Dundrum; Helen Clear's bookshop in Bray; Books Upstairs in Dublin's South King Street and Alan Hanna's in Rathmines; Day's Bazaar in Mullingar and the innovative Café Liteartha in Dingle; in Derry, there was the Bookworm and there were small but interesting shops in Schull and Nenagh. These are in addition to the sixteen Eason's stores north and south which were increasingly oriented to books following a symbolic moment in 1983 when the Eason's headquarters branch in O'Connell Street had moved magazines and newspapers, the previous staple, to the back and side to make room for a more effective book display. Despite the universal power of television, there was in Ireland, as in other Western countries, a growing appetite for books and, particularly in non-fiction, for Irish published books.

Among the stranger manifestations of the publishing business in these years was Tycooly International (named after an ancestral townland in Galway). This company was established in 1981 in Dún Laoghaire with the imaginative idea of producing publications for UN agencies. The core idea was that once a year each of the seventy or more agencies had to justify their existence to a body of international diplomats and a subsidised book was a perfect way for the agency to explain its work in progress. The scheme's initiator was Count Francis O'Kelly (whose uncle had been caught up in the Irish University Press affair). He successfully sold the idea to these agencies – in competition with the British company Pergamon – that Ireland would operate on their behalf as 'a freeport of information'. There was also a subsidised magazine published on behalf of the United Nations Environment Programme.

O'Kelly, a great wearer of his old-Downside tie, managed to impress the IDA with his international connections, and secured £55,000 of grants from them. Unfortunately, though his core idea was promising, the persuasive Count knew little about publishing and less about company management. So, despite regular inputs from UN agencies (peaking at $105,000 for one particular title) the company ran into difficulties within three years of foundation. The fundamental problem was the complete failure to top up the subsidies by selling even a few copies of the highly specialised titles. As the financial pressures worsened, the Count found it necessary to take frequent and lengthy scouting trips abroad, adding to the cost burdens symbolised by the company's account in the upmarket department store Brown Thomas. By 1984, Tycooly was in liquidation, with debts of £313,000. An earlier venture in Nairobi, Africa Science Publications, run by O'Kelly's wife, had been closed down in 1983.[64]

The 1986 edition of *Irish Publishing Record* identified 976 new titles, up from 905 in 1985. These came from 387 publishers, of which two thirds were Dublin-based. As it happened, two of the most important beginnings around this time – Brandon and Lilliput – were not Dublin-based (and by coincidence led by products of the English public-school system). Steve MacDonogh's Brandon (first titles 1982) emerged from the Irish Writers Co-operative, set up by Neil Jordan and Des Hogan in 1976. This was an outcome of that positive feeling we have seen already, described by MacDonogh in his autobiography as 'a mood, particularly in the media but also in the book trade and amongst a broad readership that was overwhelmingly positive towards new Irish writing from Irish publishers.'[65] Although there were a dozen members by 1978, many of them now distinguished names, somehow 'rarely if ever was there a really collective feeling about the Co-op'. It was too loosely structured and weakly capitalised to endure. One constant difficulty was that although British publishers had initially been cool, once writers like Neil Jordan and Des Hogan had been launched, British publishers 'happily picked them up'. For the Co-op and for others 'while we were able to launch new writers, we were not able to hold them, and thus we were confined to an area of publishing which was inherently uneconomic.'[66] This was/is a perennial grievance of non-metropolitan publishers, whether the metropolis is New York, London or Paris.

The Co-op ceased publishing in 1983 in circumstances of confusion and acrimony. By this time MacDonogh had, with a local partner Bernie Goggin, established Brandon Books of Dingle, Co. Kerry, intending to publish, as he put it 'innovative fiction and challenging non-fiction'. Through Anthony Cronin, who was advisor to both, the offices – with a view of the harbour – were opened on 22 August 1982 by Taoiseach Charles Haughey, then in the middle of the GUBU affair.[67] As well as fiction, notably Neil Jordan, Leland Bardwell, Dermot Healy, Philip Davison and Aidan Higgins, MacDonogh set about teasing the British lion with such titles as *Falls Memories* by Gerry Adams (and his more overtly political *Politics of Irish Freedom*) and *British Intelligence and Covert Action*, the first Irish-published book to be subject to a D-Notice. His 1985 publication *One Girl's War* further annoyed British officialdom.

The non-applicability of the D-Notice system in Ireland infuriated the London political establishment and MacDonogh only compounded their rage and suspicion by attending the Moscow Book Fair, in his capacity as president of Clé. Here he discussed translation rights with the Soviet publishers Progress House and Politizdat.[68] Was British intelligence aware, one wonders, of Steve's involvement in the Fourth International in the 1970s?[69] Although it was not mentioned in his autobiography, his Stalinist adherence was not a secret. MacDonogh's comments in 1999 on the fall of the Soviet Union and the Warsaw Pact suggest, however, that his opinions had not softened over time:

> The collapse of the Soviet Union and specifically its Communist Party control is almost universally regarded in the west as simply a good thing for freedom … [yet] we have to consider the new freedom now extended to millions who never experienced it before – the freedom to be unemployed; there is also the freedom to be a prostitute; the freedom to build organised crime syndicates; and the freedom to have one's pension rendered worthless by inflation.[70]

In 1985, MacDonogh had a go at the Irish establishment with Joanne Hayes' *My Story* about the then-notorious Kerry Babies case. This sold well, but ended disastrously years later with a £72,000 settlement to the senior Gardaí who claimed to have been libelled.

Antony Farrell's Lilliput (incorporated 1981, first title 1984) was also to build a substantial fiction list.[71] His background was unusual in that his father was a soldier with a Catholic Ascendancy background and his mother Church of Ireland, centrally involved in establishing St Michael's House. Educated at Harrow and Trinity (where he represented the university as a flyweight boxer, losing teeth in the process), Farrell learned his craft at various British firms before coming to Dublin. There, for a while, he split his time between making a famous cheese in his mother's farm in Gigginstown, Co. Westmeath and reading and editing for O'Brien Press, Wolfhound and Irish Academic Press. But, as he put it, 'I did not want to be an editor, I wanted to be a publisher'. Friends made at Trinity were to prove invaluable when he set up for himself, first at Gigginstown in 1984 (the company's name comes from a local townland, appropriated by Swift) and from 1989 in offices in Arbour Hill, Dublin.

At weekends, as he put it, 'as a labour of love' he had begun assembling Hubert Butler's essays which he published in May 1985 under the title *Escape from the Anthill*; five other titles appeared in that year. A year before, he had published the first of his Tim Robinson titles, a pamphlet called *Setting Foot on the Shores of Connemara.* This was to lead to the publication in 1986 of the first volume of Robinson's magisterial *Stones of Aran*.

By 1986, those of the new publishers that had survived (actually most of them, as a mini-directory published in *Books Ireland* in October made clear) had discovered at least the basic secrets of keeping alive as a publishing house and some were doing better. Several houses, such as Appletree, Blackstaff, O'Brien and Wolfhound, now had over 100 titles in print, others such as Mercier, Gill & Macmillan and Veritas had many more. Although the country was about to endure severe government spending cuts under the new Fianna Fáil government, the book trade was prospering. We have seen the increase in non-Dublin shops and soon Waterstones was added to the mix in Dublin, Cork and Belfast.

Of the two key obstacles identified earlier in this chapter, the first, the distribution problem, was effectively solved; the second, the production problem, was coming to solution. The key to this would be (but not yet) the personal computer, which began to appear on to people's desks in the mid 1980s. A 1981 study of the use of word processing in British publishing houses stressed the new devices' usefulness in producing updated production schedules, bulletins, newsletters and journal abstracts; digital texts were assumed to come on magnetic tape.[72] The Amstrad PCW 8256 was launched in 1985; being priced at £750, it was regarded as relatively cheap and became the first widely used word processor for writers.[73] Early adopters include *The Irish Times* journalists Maeve Binchy, Marion FitzGerald and Michael Viney. It was only later that the incompatibility of its disks with any other systems (for editing or typesetting) began to cause problems. On the horizon also was desktop publishing, which a print-industry sympathiser described as 'the latest typesetting bombshell to hit the trade', although at £10,000 for a full Apple system they ended up mainly in design bureaux rather than publishers.[74]

In theory it was now possible for the author to 'capture the keystrokes', so saving a time-consuming labour. In practice the technology threw up endless incompatibilities: from one program to another, from one platform to another and from one physical system to another. According to Ray Hammond there were over 400 different word processing programs in the market, of which 100 were specifically for the IBM PC. Hammond's entertaining book is full of interviews with pioneer users such as Len Deighton and their stories of whole chapters irrevocably lost at a single errant keystroke, comically unexpected effects of the search and replace function, disk and program failure, etc. It vividly illustrates how far things have come. See for instance his recommendation that 'word processing of the type required by writers isn't really possible with a machine with less than 48k RAM and I think 64k is a far safer minimum size.'[75]

One Irish typesetting house claimed to be able to read over 500 different disk/program combinations. Digitally-aware authors commonly used PCs (if not the completely unfriendly Amstrad or some dedicated word processor) and repro houses used Apples; the publisher, by no means necessarily a technical wizard, was caught in between. Entirely sensible was the response of one production manager to the offer of texts on disk: 'We smile sweetly, make sure we have a manuscript, and leave the disks carefully in a drawer'.[76]

8

Change in the Village: Into the 1990s

We have seen in earlier chapters how the world of publishing was turned on its head in the 1890s. Something of the sort happened again in the 1980s and 1990s, though on this occasion Irish publishing houses, being small, were only peripherally exposed. The key changes experienced by the great names in English language publishing were the consolidation of medium sized publishing companies into a few large corporations, the establishment of powerful retail chains and a new power and prominence for authors' agents.[1]

A series of mergers and acquisitions transformed the industry from the comfortable world pictured in 1984 by the chairman of Collins, Ian Chapman. 'Until the middle of this century,' he remembered nostalgically, 'publishers were individuals who carried on their businesses with relatively meagre financial resources at their own risk. The publisher was the proprietor, the shareholders were likely to be composed of members of his family, and broadly speaking he could publish whatever he liked as long as he remained solvent.'[2]

Real life was of course never that simple. We can be sure, however, that the legendary proprietors he had in mind – such as André Deutsch, Victor Gollancz, Jonathan Cape and Stanley Unwin – did not find themselves much hampered by corporate disciplines, or feel much need to consult their sales managers or accountants before making a publishing decision. Indeed, Unwin specifically deplored what he called the 'conference method' of list-building. 'The best publishing businesses,' he wrote, 'will usually be found to be the creation of one man.'[3]

To the dismay of book lovers, one by one respected names were snapped up into conglomerates. By 1985, the industry's 'seven sisters' (HarperCollins, Hodder Headline, Macmillan, Penguin, Random House, Reed and Transworld) accounted for more than half of sales in Britain and Ireland. A few more or less eccentric houses maintained an uneasy independence, notably Faber, Fourth Estate and Profile. Most interesting to the Irish as a model was the Scottish house of Canongate. Founded in 1973 by the charismatic Stephanie Wolfe Murray and her husband Angus, in due course it had the luck to take over a small established imprint called Southside, founded by the first chair of the Scottish Publishers Association, Robin Lorimer. This gave the house some ballast, and a valuable connection to Calder & Boyars in London. Nonetheless, Stephanie Wolfe Murray's appetites and ambitions (poetry, novels, current affairs, over 100 classic Scottish authors, a children's book imprint) meant that Canongate tumbled from one near-bankruptcy episode to another until it was taken over by Jamie Byng in 1994.[4] Byng widened its interests to books from the West Indies, an early autobiography of Barack Obama, a series of single volumes of books of the Bible with introductions from a range of personalities including Bono and the Dalai Lama, and even a Man Booker Prize winner – *The Life of Pi*.

Despite these valiant players, however, it had become increasingly clear that there were basically two comfortable sizes a publishing house could be: huge or tiny. The bestsellers and the well-publicised advances came from the cash-rich conglomerates, which were in a position to exploit world rights, but some of the most interesting publishing came from the tens of thousands of houses with annual sales of £10 million or (often) much less. All Irish trade houses fitted into this category and as such retained much of the editorially-driven approach of the publishers Ian Chapman remembered so fondly. They also faced similar challenges, most notably chronic cashflow difficulties, a shortage of capital and problems retaining authors.

Jeremy Lewis, for ten years a director of Chatto & Windus in the 1980s, takes up the story:

> In the late 1980s something very curious happened. The big publishing groups were becoming ever larger and more musclebound, swallowing up firms to left and right; and yet, in what seemed like an act of self-immolation, they and their fellow-publishers wilfully abdicated their

> position as ringmasters of the literary circus. Far from ruling the roost, they became in effect supplicants, seemingly at the mercy of people whom in days gone by they had regarded as inherently inferior, namely booksellers and literary agents.[5]

Irish publishing was clearly on the side of the small battalions, but nonetheless had come a long way by 1987. *Books Ireland* claimed that Irish-published books made up 22 per cent of bestsellers in 1986 and a whopping 57 per cent of non-fiction paperbacks.[6] Two titles stood out. The bestseller of all was Noel Browne's mendacious autobiography *Against the Tide*, published as its Christmas lead by Gill & Macmillan. This had subscribed slowly. As sales director Peter Thew explained, 'most of the young buyers had never heard of him', so the company cautiously printed a mere 3,000 copies. The response to an *Irish Independent* extract justified a reprint of 8,000, and a triumphant appearance on the *Late Late Show* triggered a further 7,500. By now it was clear Gill & Macmillan had a hit on its hands. Another reprint, of 12,000, was quickly consumed, as was a fifth and a sixth. (The fact that these reprints had to be ordered from Clay's in East Anglia complicated matters, as did a strike at Holyhead.) By the close of Christmas, Gill & Macmillan estimated that the company had pushed £400,000 worth of books through the shops in six weeks.[7]

Remarkable for another reason was the Brandon offering *One Girl's War* with its big revelation that the head of MI5's wartime counter-espionage section had been gay. The revelations otherwise were anodyne, but this did not stop the British Attorney General from attempting to stop publication. The habitually overcautious Eason's quickly withdrew the book from display, which of course would have killed its sales. Judge Mella Carroll, however, decided that the proposed injunction could not be sustained, and immediately the book was back on sale, in Eason's as well as elsewhere. 'At the front of [Eason's] a large crowd was gathered around a pile of copies of the book,' wrote publisher Steve MacDonogh with satisfaction, 'and at the back harassed staff were preparing to put more on the shelves.' Within hours the stock was gone, and a reprint of 8,000 copies ordered. The British courts, by contrast, upheld the injunction for as long as they could, so sales there were impossible. In the event, 'the book was successful beyond my wildest dreams.'[8]

According to the 1987 Fishwick report *The Market for Books in the Republic of Ireland* the total market for books was £56 million, of which three quarters was household expenditure (the rest purchases by libraries, tourists and corporations).[9] Fully 29 per cent of the total was spent on schoolbooks, which seemed a lot when compared with below 10 per cent in the UK and

16 per cent in the USA. As we shall see, this represents not so much large expenditure on schoolbooks as relatively low expenditure on general books. The educational market (primary and secondary), was effectively a local monopoly with 90 per cent supplied by local publishers. Conversely, the trade market was 86 per cent supplied by British publishers.

The Irish educational market was serviced by five intensely competitive large houses – the Educational Company, Fallon's, Folens, Gill & Macmillan and School & College – and five smaller players – with a total turnover of £11.8 million. This was controlled, focused, publishing, with no space for *jeux d'esprit*. Apart from Gill & Macmillan, these publishers kept clear of other sectors such as the tertiary educational market. Gill & Macmillan had a substantial trade list, and it was a market that Folens also dabbled in.

The sector had enjoyed good times in the 1970s, with the introduction of free secondary education and a high birth rate swelling school populations; by the 1980s things were not so rosy. Birth rates were down and syllabus developments meant that publishers had to produce more texts and more colour for a shrinking market. The cosy days of a five- to seven-year life for a text and plenty of backlist sales were gone; the average life was now three to five years. Folens' managing director Dirk Folens estimated that employment in the sector had nearly halved since the beginning of the decade, and guessed that at least two of the current publishers would soon be gone (as indeed happened).[10] The economic difference between schoolbook and general publishing was underlined when Fishwick compared the £8,062 annual sales generated by the average schoolbook and the much smaller £1,021 generated by trade titles. Schoolbook runs were longer and average spend for schoolbooks was £13.30 per primary pupil and twice that per secondary pupil.

Despite *Books Ireland*'s boosterish estimates, in cold numbers Irish-published books had clawed their way up to 12 per cent of the trade market and had a turnover of some £4.5 million. (A survey of retailers suggested that local Irish publishers represented 15 per cent of the general book market, but Fishwick thought this an over-estimate.)[11] Fishwick commented positively on the success the new wave of publishers had had in explaining Ireland to itself: 'the major successes of Irish publishers have been in the areas of non-fiction and children's books. Titles published in Ireland are well represented in bestsellers lists of non-fiction titles, especially in paperback.' He confirmed, however, that, especially in fiction, the overmighty neighbour continued to be a factor: 'Irish authors of novels likely to have wider international appeal tend to have these published by larger companies based in Britain, with large-scale marketing resources.'[12] Ireland's very first book agent, Jonathan Williams, found that three quarters of his work was in non-fiction. This was of less interest to the metropolitan publishers, and also gave a much easier handle to local media. As it happened, one of his early successes was with Alan Shatter's racy novel *Laura* sold to Poolbeg.[13]

A particular focus of Fishwick's research was the behaviour of Irish book-buyers and readers, and especially the self-serving legend that the Irish were prodigious readers and buyers of books. This of course turned out to be nonsense (as the trade had known all along). Only 19 per cent of those interviewed in October/November 1985 had bought any new books at all in the previous month, compared with 32 per cent answering a similar question in Britain. Fishwick declared: 'Our estimates suggest that household expenditure on books other than schoolbooks in Ireland is lower as a proportion of total expenditure than is the case in the USA, France or the United Kingdom.' In general, Fishwick confirmed that women bought significantly more books than men, and older people and people in rural areas fewer than younger, better educated and urban readers. The typical book purchase (four times out of five) was a paperback: hardbacks were generally bought as presents. For themselves, people generally spent less than £4 a year, the price of three or four pints of Guinness.[14]

The second edition of *The Irish Book World*, published in 1985, recorded sixty-five members of Clé under its president, Michael Adams of Four Courts and Irish Academic Press.[15] The directory listed nearly 100 members of the Irish branch of the Booksellers Association, and seventy members of the characteristically separate Northern Ireland branch. As well as these there were other listings indicating an increasingly dense market for the editing, design, production and marketing of books. There were pages devoted to freelance editors (the Association of Freelance Editors, Proofreaders and Indexers was set up in 1985), production services and book designers. Numerous other bookish organisations were also listed, from the venerable Irish Academy of Letters (on its last legs) and PEN to more recent foundations such as the Irish Books Marketing Group and Book House Ireland. This last was a brave attempt to match the German book trade in having an umbrella body uniting booksellers and publishers. Under its first administrator, the super-efficient Clara Clark, it prospered, but afterwards the problems of combining the two sets of demanding and opinionated masters overwhelmed her successor and it was folded in 1992.

The political and financial backgrounds were not comfortable. Although the country was much richer than a generation before, a certain disillusion had set in compared to the heady euphoria of the 1960s. After the election in

February 1987 Charles Haughey became Taoiseach for the third time, at the head of a minority government. Crucially, he appointed Ray MacSharry to the Department of Finance and a long-needed corrective to excessive borrowing (largely to support the inflated public service) was put in train. MacSharry later characterised the scale of the problem he faced by recording that £4 out of £5 of income tax was used to pay debt interest. He was greatly helped by Fine Gael's so-called 'Tallaght Strategy' by which it committed not to oppose reforms. The actions taken at this time included suppression or merger of state bodies, voluntary redundancies in the civil service, cuts to developing countries' aid, and – what pricked an otherwise compliant public – slashing health expenditure leading to hospital closures. Though painful, these actions have subsequently been seen as the essential foundation for the prosperous years of the Celtic Tiger.

From a larger perspective it was clear that in some ways Ireland had changed radically since the 1960s. Manufacturing had increased fourfold since then and had replaced agriculture as the dominant source of exports. Ireland's vulnerable position as a small open economy was increasingly clear. On the other hand, membership of the European Monetary System protected the punt from the difficulties sterling was suffering, and by 1988 shares and business confidence were rising.[16] The publishing industry was not the only one that recognised that exports were the means of escaping the limitations of a small home market. For Irish publishers that meant exploiting the language advantage by selling into Britain, the US and the Commonwealth countries; sales to non-English-speaking countries were to be achieved through translation rights deals typically initiated at the Frankfurt Book Fair held every October. Not that any of this was easy. The story was told of one Irish publisher earnestly explaining his wares to a British publisher. At the end of the conversation her colleague came over: 'Who was that?' he asked. 'I don't know,' she replied, 'some Irish nut.'[17] And there was undoubtedly some prejudice to overcome. The agent George Greenfield described Irish publishers as 'relying on a mixture of blarney and verbose broguery', lacking third level education and being 'unsuited to the rigours of publishing'.[18]

Over the years there had been a spectacular growth in the public sector, especially the state-sponsored bodies, of which by the 1980s there were over 100. Bizarrely for a country that so feared communism, Ireland had become one of the most socialised countries outside the Soviet bloc. As much as a quarter of economic output was generated by these bodies. The publishing activities of certain of them, notably the ESRI, NESC and An Foras Forbartha, made a constant and valuable contribution to the public understanding of key social and economic issues. The Institute of Public Administration produced its widely used *Administration Yearbook and Diary*, which sold 9,000 copies a year (one for every 140 working men and women, as it boasted) and valuably described hundreds of active organisations from government departments, commercial and arts organisations, to specialised pressure groups. A regular publishing programme run from its Lansdowne Road office produced several hundred dull but critically informative books on governmental and legal issues, beginning in 1959.

There were, of course, other ways in which Ireland had barely changed: there were, for instance, still at least 1,000 participant members of the Provisional IRA and they were cruelly active as the Enniskillen bombing in November 1987 showed. Relations between Britain and Ireland over combating the IRA could scarcely have been worse, and were not eased by Mrs Thatcher's intemperate outbursts. Catholicism was still strong. In 1986, a majority had voted in the Tenth Amendment to the Constitution to deny access to divorce. During this campaign the heavy hand of the hierarchy was felt by media and politicians alike. The sensibilities and attitudes of town and country were still far apart, as the divorce referendum clearly showed. Irish publishers did their best to keep up with the persistent agonised enquiries about Irish identity.

The Last Symbol of the 1950s

In May 1987, less than a year after the collapse of Irish Bookhandling, Liam Miller died in Our Lady's Hospice, aged 63. His publications, which he once described as 'a couple of shelves of mainly slim volumes', had made him famous, and not only in Ireland. He had been perceived almost from 1951 as the only 'real' publisher in Ireland, the doyen of Irish publishing, a multi-talented Renaissance man with interests in poetry, typography, theatre and postage stamps. He was seen as a man who had developed and embellished the private press tradition and yet also published commercially. (Quite how commercially was unclear: his bestseller was Thomas Kinsella's translation of *The Táin*; but did he sell 90,000 copies, as he told the *Irish Press* in 1982, or 'more than 60,000 copies', as he told the same paper in 1983?) Miller's public reputation was of a typographer and designer of world reputation, and for most people, as John Montague put it 'his creative generosity outweighed his financial uncertainties.'[19] The rumours that he had rejected both Philip Larkin and Seamus Heaney at different times added, if anything, to the legend.

In May 2017, Thomas Kinsella wrote in *The Irish Times* that there had been no formal rejection of Heaney by Dolmen: 'In the amateur, unbusinesslike nature of the early Dolmen Press, offers were not made; it was assumed that in giving your work to the press you were eager for its publication. There was no question of payment. Timing was not a consideration: your book took its turn.' While waiting for a response from Dolmen, Heaney received a formal offer from Faber and went with them. Kinsella also stated that Larkin's connection with Dolmen came via Donald Davie, who was friendly with both sides: 'I don't think [Larkin] was interested in publication by Dolmen.'[20]

As recently as 1985, Liam Miller had been described in *The Irish Times* as 'one of the most respected men in Irish publishing'.[21] A suggestion that he might be offered an honorary doctorate by Trinity was dropped after vigorous protests from Michael O'Brien and Seamus Cashman.

It came as quite a shock, then, that when his company was wound up in August 1987 it admitted to unsecured creditors of £169,000 (it was afterwards alleged that this list was woefully undercounted). Accounts were published showing that his turnover, for instance in the year to October 1983, had been a mere £75,000, less than half of what O'Brien Press was selling, and a fraction of Gill & Macmillan's turnover. No wonder Miller constantly accepted jobs on the side such as his work as typographic advisor to IUP, An Post's Philatelic Advisory Committee or designing the Roman Missal. Miller's director's salary was put down at £12,780: roughly what an assistant principal in the civil service got.[22] This may not of course have been the whole story. There were other companies Miller was involved with, including one called Capricorn and another called Pilgrim (the recipient of some of Máire Block's fraudulent cheques). Lady Bracknell thought that three addresses inspired confidence: in business multiple addresses generally suggest something to hide.

At a stormy meeting of the creditors in August 1987, coloured by rumours of bomb threats and lurking Special Branch officers, Máire Block attempted to intimidate potential creditors. It was soon revealed, however, that Dolmen directors had known that it was insolvent for more than a year and had been engaged in attempts to restructure by transferring all the author contracts (without permission), debtors and book stocks to Capricorn, which they hoped to sell as a going concern. This was why, to their annoyance, certain authors found that they were not listed among Dolmen's creditors. This also meant that the same authors were refused permission to vote at the meeting. The meeting lasted three hours, eventually ending with the appointment of a liquidator. The media reported 'Publisher folds amid fury' (*Sunday Independent*), 'Irate creditors' (*Sunday Tribune*) and, a few months later, 'Writers

Union protest at sale of Dolmen assets' (*Sunday Tribune*). Questions remained as to the ownership of the archive of letters to Dolmen from Irish writers such as Thomas Kinsella, John Montague and Austin Clarke.

John Montague has argued that single-mindedness such as Liam Miller's 'obsessive passion to corral and organise a number of writers … at best fosters talent and creates lovely books'. Obsession there was: Liam Miller once declared that he had completely reset the prize-winning *Holinshed's Chronicles* four times before he was happy. 'But it had its dark side as well', continued Montague, 'as when Dolmen felt no urgency to pay royalties, or absorbed authors' cheques into their own coffers; sometimes the imprint is seen as greater than the authors it serves.'[23] Others have been harsher, pointing out how Miller would in public say how he 'genuflected to the genius of Thomas Kinsella' and in private pay him no royalties.[24] Miller's treatment of Austin Clarke, latterly an old man who badly needed the money, was callous. In 1970, the veteran Canadian academic publisher Marsh Jeanneret took a hard line on the non-payment of royalties, which is of course a constant temptation to cash-strapped publishers. 'Royalties,' he wrote, 'are … covered by moneys already received by the publisher and held in trust by him for transmittal to his authors. Publishers who do not have the money to pay royalties that have been earned are guilty of conversion.'[25]

For Seamus Cashman and Michael O'Brien, to whom as young publishers Miller had been a greatly-respected mentor, the personal betrayal and indeed the near capsizing of the two houses at the ending of Irish Bookhandling, was unforgivable. Although the fraudulent deeds were Máire Block's, the countersigned cheques make it clear that her father, though sick, was closely involved. He and she demonstrated a gross self-centredness, as a result of which, as Maurice Harmon put it, 'Miller did not seem to appreciate how humiliating this was [to authors], and it has not been a good legacy for publishers.'[26] In the 1990s, one of the weapons British publishers used when trying to tempt Poolbeg authors to publish in London was the continuing accusation that Irish publishers could not be trusted to pay royalties.

Another Report in 1987

A year later another report (*Developing Publishing in Ireland*), this time by the veteran UK publisher Charles Pick (managing director, then chairman, of Heinemann 1961–84) focused on five 'growth-oriented' publishers in an attempt to prepare Irish publishing for the threat believed to loom in the 1992

European Single Market. The report, tastefully produced in thick paper and two colours, was sponsored by the Arts Council with three other state industries: the IDA (industrial development); CTT (exports) and Bord na Gaeilge (Irish language). This last body was no doubt responsible for the inclusion of the Irish language house Coiscéim, which demonstrated its lack of concern with the market by refusing for ideological reasons to assign ISBNs to its titles. The Pick Report was not a success. Its sole radical suggestion was that Irish books were underpriced, perhaps by as much as 25 per cent, though it was also instrumental in persuading the Arts Council to support book publishers more vigorously.

Otherwise, trade observers felt that the contribution of Mr Pick's accountant colleague, stressing the necessity for accurate stock valuations, full costing of titles and elaborate budgets, rather over-flavoured the pudding. Irish journalists such as Ciaran Carty of the *Sunday Tribune* took the concern with discipline in accountancy matters (to the exclusion of more serious matters such as list-building techniques or capital sources) as an indictment, unaware that Pick was simply repeating the recipe that seemed to have worked for so long in the Heinemann Group.[27] The aspiration that the State agencies involved should cooperate in developing publishing was honoured in the breach. For readers thirty years later, however, there is an interest in the evident dread with which the 1992 European Single Market was viewed. Ivor Kenny, the IMI director, was quoted in *Books Ireland* as declaring at the report's launch, 'the breezes of competition that we have felt will turn to gale force'. To his credit *Books Ireland* editor Jeremy Addis (who knew something about the book trade, as Kenny did not, despite his family connection with the great Galway bookshop) poured scorn on this fear, asking 'just who are the great English language publishing bogeymen who are going to leap on us from out of Greater Europe?'[28]

In an article intended to coincide with the publication of the Pick Report, Kathy Sheridan of *The Irish Times* described a kind of public disillusion with the publishing industry after the high hopes of previous decades. (Ironically, in light of criticisms of the operative inefficiency of the publishing industry, the Report was subject to 'inexplicable delay' in the Arts Council, so she was unable to comment specifically on it.) There was, as she put it, 'a disappointment following hard on the heels of great expectations'.[29] There were, it was true, now sixty-five members of Clé, though perhaps only fifteen of these made up the industry's commercial core. These sixty-five (and 350 others) produced some 935 titles in 1988, comfortably more than the 679 of ten years before.[30]

'Booksellers and authors are the industry's greatest critics,' we were told. A so-called 'well-wisher' was extensively quoted: '[Irish publishers] are not sufficiently business-like … they are too dedicated to the idea of quality and politics and literature and "messages" and "believing" in writers. All that this idealism has done is to leave them at the cottage industry stage.'[31] The idea evidently did not occur to the writer that readers might *want* publishers who are 'dedicated to the idea of quality', who do believe in writers and are supportive of them because of such belief. (Unfortunately these attributes turn publishing into a 'lifestyle business', a phenomenon hard-nosed would-be investors run a mile from.)

Behind this comment was an outdated image of publishing in which resolute and businesslike proprietors such as Jonathan Cape and Stanley Unwin, by canny title-picking and nurturing their backlists, grew steadily from small to medium to large. It was a complete misunderstanding of the way publishing was going, into the dichotomy of very large and small. This outcome was in fact exactly what contemporary modelling of business organisation under conditions of competition expected.

As it happened, there have been two instances in which Irish houses soared, Icarus-like, to the empyrean. In the 1970s it was possible for Irish University Press, fuelled by Thomson money, to dream of a turnover greater than Penguin and produce the extraordinary 1,000-volume series of *British Parliamentary Papers*. A generation later, in 2006, Irish investment banker Barry Callaghan paid $4 billion for Houghton Mifflin, becoming for a while the largest educational publisher in the US. Both of these ventures ended in tears.

A contributing factor to the industry's problems, thought Kathy Sheridan, was that some Irish publishers would 'spurn the idea of being judged by commercial criteria alone'. As a result, 'bad financial management' had prevented the Irish industry 'meet[ing] the challenge' of the British industry. There had been 'little real commercial growth in the past five years', we were told. (In fact there was a 28 per cent increase in the number of titles recorded by the *Irish Publishing Record* in that time.) Ms Sheridan did notice a few positive aspects, such as the professionalism of the Gill & Macmillan distribution system, the sales initiative in the UK and other overseas markets such as Germany.[32]

The Publishers of 1988

With a little benefit of hindsight, we can see that Appletree and Blackstaff, in Belfast; Brandon in Co. Kerry; Columba, Four Courts/IAP/Round

Hall, Gill & Macmillan, O'Brien Press, Poolbeg/Ward River, Town House/ Country House and Wolfhound, all in Dublin; Mercier in Cork; Lilliput in Co. Westmeath (it moved to Dublin in 1989); and Gallery in Co. Meath were the Irish trade publishers of interest in 1988. They were those whom Kathy Sheridan referred to as 'the commercial core'. These publishers accounted for about 20 per cent of the 935 titles published that year (including 85 in Irish), from 421 separate publishers. Of these, 235 were based in Dublin and 37 in Northern Ireland.[33] This imbalance (aided by the low cost of entry to the market) between the output of professional commercial publishers and others, typically one-offs, is normal; members of the British Publishers Association produced an even smaller proportion of books published there and the phenomenon is evident in the US also.

Appletree Press, founded in 1974, had survived three bombings during the Troubles (as collateral damage: the bombs were not aimed at publisher John Murphy), and had published over 150 titles, including several in the trademark 'Little Cooking' series. Blackstaff's Anne Tannahill became managing director of the firm in 1980 and was to become one of Ireland's most distinguished publishers, winning the *Sunday Times* Small Publisher of the Year Award in 1992.

Steve MacDonogh's great triumph of 1988 was the publication of Brandon's *To School Through the Fields*, a sentimental look back on rural life in North Cork in the 1950s. This unlikely emanation from a publisher previously better known for Gerry Adams and annoying the British with books about their secret service, was an enormous success, selling over 142,000 copies.

After running Veritas (the Catholic Church's publishing arm, renamed from the Catholic Truth Society in 1969) and a bookshop in Stillorgan, both in Dublin, Seán O'Boyle set up Columba Press, a Catholic publishing house, in 1985, with the assistance of the invaluable Cecilia West.

Four Courts/IAP/Round Hall were Michael Adams' three imprints. The newest, Round Hall, a law publishing specialist was in 1988 threatened by the advent of Butterworths to Dublin and would soon be bought by Sweet & Maxwell.

Gill & Macmillan was celebrating its twentieth year of partnership. If Michael Gill had been an aggressive, Napoleonic type, he might perhaps have dominated Irish publishing even more than he did.

In Cork, Mercier's founder, Captain Feehan, had retired in 1985, leaving the accountant John Spillane and the editor, Feehan's daughter Mary, in charge.

Michael O'Brien's outspoken and vehemently expressed comments at Clé meetings did not always make him friends, but he was undoubtedly one of the leading personalities of the publishing industry. He and Seamus Cashman of Wolfhound, a more literary and cerebral publisher than O'Brien, established a close and lasting comradeship, and at one point they even shared editorial. Between them they initiated Irish Bookhandling.

Poolbeg/Ward River was founded by Philip MacDermott. The non-fiction imprint Ward River published some sixty books between 1979 and 1985 (it was revived as a fiction imprint in 2015).

Town House/Country House publisher Treasa Coady came into publishing as a result of the connection with the Irish wildlife broadcaster and writer Éamon de Butléir. A stylish and innovative operator, she initially put all her publishing through Eason's.

Remarkably, all but two of these businesses were still active twenty years later. The exceptions were Wolfhound and Town House/Country House. In 2001, Seamus Cashman sold his company as a going concern to Merlin, which was still trading in 2008. Town House's last titles were published in 2006.[34] It seems that the much-criticised financial management was not quite as bad as it was painted.

The New Style of Bookselling

Traditionally, Irish bookshops, like their British counterparts, had been single-proprietor and generally single-outlet operations. Their economic weakness was such that they really valued the protection provided by the Net Book Agreement. Matters were about to change, however, starting with the steady increase in the number of titles published, going from 50,000 in the UK in 1980 to 104,000 in 1995. In the US, the annual number of titles published went from 40,000 in 1980 to 275,000 (new ISBNs) in 2008. (It is daunting to think that the books actually published represent a tiny fraction of those written. Publishers and agents regularly referred to accepting perhaps 1 in 1,000 of the slush pile of proposals.) This relentless increase in titles was driven by the simple fact that no one could say in advance which title was going to do well: the well-meant accountant's advice 'why don't you just publish best-sellers?' completely misses this point. Of every ten titles published, Fergal Tobin, editorial director of Gill & Macmillan, found, two would struggle to meet their direct costs, six would make a small contribution and a blessed two would pay for the rest.[35] The problem was: which two? So, the more you published (given that the direct costs for any one title were not large) the better the chance of a success.

This remorseless logic drove the number of books being published higher and higher. The available book trade shelf space, though increasing, could not handle this avalanche. As a result, the time any one book was held in the shop before either being sold or returned dropped to weeks rather than months. The comfortable old category of 'stock item', meaning a book that would be reordered more-or-less automatically became a thing of the past. Returns of unsold books went up, not in Ireland to the levels of 50 per cent or more experienced in the US, but to 20 per cent and higher for certain titles.

In the 1960s and 1970s, news seeped across the Atlantic of an extraordinary development in US bookselling, whereby two chains of mall-based bookshops, B. Dalton and Waldenbooks, began to count their numbers of branches in hundreds. By 1980, there were 450 B. Dalton stores and 750 Waldenbooks sites. This growth was admittedly from a low base: in 1962 there were actually fewer bookshops in the US than in Britain, with nearly four times the population.[36] The next development was of superstores, with three times as many titles as, for instance, Fred Hanna's would have stocked, notably Barnes & Noble and Borders. In Britain, these developments were echoed by the Waterstones chain (set up in 1982 after Tim Waterstone had failed to establish the W.H. Smith brand in the US). Waterstones expanded rapidly and profitably, coming to Dublin in 1987.

The new bookshop style made an immediate impression, with its highly literate graduate staff, its US-influenced large stocks and 'open-all-hours' policies. In Dublin from 1987, and Cork and Belfast the following year, Waterstones at once made a big impact on bookselling in Ireland. Fred Hanna complained that they were promising as innovations all sorts of things, such as qualified staff and book ordering, that serious shops had provided for years. Hanna employed graduates also, though it was some time before he opened on Saturday afternoons and, as a sound Church of Ireland man, there was no question of Sundays. Hanna was still cross with Waterstones when he retired a few years later. 'The very mention of Waterstone's is enough to raise my hackles' he told *Books Ireland* (Summer 1999).

Within a year of the arrival of Waterstones, the Paperback Bookshop in Dublin's Suffolk Street had closed, as had Crane's in Belfast, and Collins of Cork had decided to diversify into publishing. Waterstones pioneered a new form of customer-oriented bookselling. As one American author noted, 'making the customer feel pampered and well-liked was not something that regular booksellers typically tried to do' until the 1980s.[37] Irish book buyers loved the new approach and Waterstones in Dublin became one of the UK firm's stellar performers.

There was at the same time a redefinition of the relationship between the book buyer and the retailer. Gone were the days when the booksellers saw themselves as having a quasi-educational role, as dispensers of a Very Special Product: 'books are different' went the favourite mantra. Maura Hastings, as we have seen, had declined to stock certain thrillers, declaring that Eason's 'did not cater for that element' and May O'Flaherty in Parsons bookshop drove her customers towards books she liked, while carefully wrapping the more expensive items in unyielding plastic. In Brendan Behan's sketch 'Overheard in a Bookshop', Ida, the assistant, 'gently but firmly removed the volume from my lifeless fingers and smiled but shook her head: "sorry, but no free reads. I may be only here for a week, but I don't want the shop robbed barefaced!"'[38]

A special service expected from the Charter Group of stockholding booksellers was the bibliography function. Robert Towers, then of Hanna's, described how he:

> used to scour the catalogues for books on Mongolia for one customer and mountaineering for another. There was a farmer in Wexford who collected language dictionaries – any language into English and vice-versa – he must have had hundreds by the time I left off. We were regularly visited by authors – mainly UK and US researching books – and I would keep them informed of books that would interest them ... we would get [library] orders of £1,000 for new books on music or chess.[39]

The Charter Group was also supposed to provide training programmes for staff, but, as Robert Towers put it: 'Training in Hanna's was to watch the Master at work. I never heard of any Irish bookseller doing the BA's Diploma in Bookselling.'[40]

The new approach, as in America, posited that 'only the individual can really know what book is most suitable for her needs; for the book professional to presume otherwise is paternalistic and an imposition of his arbitrary values.'[41] In bookselling, as elsewhere in Western culture, automatic deference to professionals, politicians and men in soutanes was draining from the public mind.

At the same time, there was a new interest in display, prompted partly by influential market research published in the early 1980s. This identified that two thirds of people entering bookshops left without buying anything and 11 per cent failed to buy a book they had come in to the shop specifically to purchase. A quarter of these latter were unidentifiable ('the one the girl on TV talked about last week' etc.); a third were simply not in stock. These groups were in fact the starting point of the research. As the report put it, 'the most startling factor to emerge from the survey is the scale of the impulse market: 45 per cent of book buyers, 47 per cent of books sales by unit and 42 per cent of book sales by value.'[42] In other words, nearly half of the books actually bought were bought on impulse stimulated by in-store display. This turned out to be a stable insight. Research in the US in 2007 confirmed the general conclusion. There it was found that some 57 per cent of books were bought by purchasers who had had no prior intent to buy that specific book. This figure dropped to 31 per cent for Amazon, and rose to as much as 70 per cent for supermarkets.[43]

This surprise discovery focused the attention of both retailers and publishers on the instore encounter and how the design and presentation of books might convert some of the non-buyers into buyers. Michael O'Brien especially remembers being influenced by this research. Retailers began to make more conscious use of 'directed buying' techniques such as bestseller lists and carefully balanced windows and in-store displays (some of which publishers were later, in what the American bookstore chains called 'co-op', asked to pay for.)[44]

From the late 1980s, this series of developments drastically changed the relationship of publishers and booksellers. Publishers (as a bloc) had had the upper hand from the time of the final introduction of the Net Book Agreement in 1900. This did not mean, for instance, that a small new publisher could insist that Hanna's or Erskine Mayne stock, or restock, a particular title (a great source of friction and embarrassment, as indignant authors passed on their relatives' comments that his or her book was simply not available in the local bookshop). It did mean, though, that new publishers benefited from the general terms of trade negotiated by much larger players. As in other industries, this power was to shift in the 1980s from the producers (authors and publishers) to the consumers (as represented by retailers).

Bookseller chains (which as far as Ireland was concerned basically meant Eason's, Waterstones and Pentos) began to exercise muscles that the predominantly single-shop independent booksellers of the past never had. Just as the Irish publishers had quietly benefited from terms originally set by Collins, Macmillan and Cape, now they suffered as those terms worsened. Discounts began to rise: in 1991, for instance, Hodges Figgis (then owned by UK retailer group HMV/Pentos, which also owned Waterstones) announced that 'to bring its terms in line with the UK' it was insisting on discounts of 42.5 per cent off list prices rather than 35 per cent. There was little or nothing Irish publishers could do about this unilateral 20 per cent worsening of their terms of trade.

Discount was only one factor in the power shift. The hard numbers produced by computer-based EPOS (Electronic Point of Sale) technology undermined the traditional booksellers' rule of thumb division between 'sellers', 'stayers' (stock items) and 'stickers' ('mostly poetry and philosophy').[45] Booksellers could now quickly and accurately track what had and had not sold and ruthlessly return what was failing to contribute to sales per shelf metre. Titles published in previous years ('backlist') struggled to justify their presence on the shelf, which in turn meant that the comfortable cushion that backlist sales had provided for publishers in previous years was rapidly reduced from perhaps 30 per cent of sales to little or nothing. Now, everything depended on sales of newly published books, which were given less and less time to prove themselves.

Computers had contributed to the solution of the distribution problems of the trade, so it was now feasible to think of a bookseller's order taking a day or two instead of so many weeks, as in the past. Combined with EPOS control, this meant that booksellers could cut back their subscription (pre-publication) orders, confident that if copies were needed they could be supplied rapidly. Peter Thew, sales manager of Gill & Macmillan, vividly remembered that Fred Hanna initially took only ten copies of Noel Browne's autobiography, and when urged to take more, simply declared, 'I have got enough.' In the end some 49,000 books were sold in a few weeks.[46] In the old regime publishers had reckoned to sell perhaps one third of the eventual two-year sales as subscription orders. In the old dispensation, the level of the subscription was a key factor in deciding the final print run: subscription 1,500 copies, print 4,500, or if feeling bullish, 5,000. EPOS and efficient distribution enabled booksellers to work on a little-and-often basis, even for new publications, especially since the carriage costs for home orders were borne by the publishers. Publishers were of course keen to have as many books as possible in the bookshops, stimulating the impulse buy.

This opened a fruitful space inside which booksellers could bargain (You want 'sale or return'? No problem![47] Extra 'promotion discount'? Of course! Co-operative promotion contribution to encourage the bookseller to display the book in windows and specially attractive positions? Definitely! Payment to be included in bestseller lists and staff picks? Not proven.)[48] Sensibly, the booksellers generally sought these benefits from deep-pocketed British publishers, aware that Irish publishers did not allocate so much to promotion. Naturally the people paying for favours got them, to the disadvantage of the local industry.

The End of the Net Book Agreement

The Net Book Agreement (i.e. resale price maintenance) had been a key article of faith in the British and Irish book trade since its establishment in 1900. The legal core of the Net Book Agreement was an agreement among British publishers not to supply any outlet found to have sold books below the recommended (so-called 'net') price. Neither Irish nor British booksellers were specifically involved, though of course they were intimately affected. Irish publishers were not privy to the agreement, but Irish booksellers always treated their books as if they were 'net'. Education books were typically non-net and so potentially subject to price competition. Being sold at 'net' price meant that books were available at the same price in Dublin, Guildford or Dundee.

Initially the Net Book Agreement was an initiative by the British publishers of the day to protect stockholding booksellers from attack by cherry-picking undersellers. As such, it did a good job and the British book trade was undoubtedly healthier in the first half of the twentieth century than it had been in the second half of the nineteenth. Over time the Net Book Agreement became an article of faith in the trade. Dire warnings were repeated by senior trade figures as to how the trade would collapse if the Agreement were dismantled.

Historically, most countries with a substantial book trade have had some form of fixed price agreement. Some, such as the US, Sweden and Finland, have given it up. The Australian 'statement of terms' was declared illegal in 1972, a move the veteran bookseller Michael Zifcak deplored, claiming twenty years later that it benefited mainly remainder merchants and frontlist publishers. 'Bookselling in Australia has not suffered from the abolition of retail price maintenance,' he wrote, 'the public interest has.'[49] Many countries, including Germany, the Netherlands, Spain and Italy, still have such an arrangement. In France, there was a wobble in 1979 when it was abolished. *The Bookseller* reported how large bookshops were happy with the new freedom, while for smaller ones it was a nightmare. Looking at the retail prices for a recent Prix Goncourt winner, the reporter found a supermarket charging 51 francs and a small bookshop charging 68 francs and variations in between.[50] Fixed book pricing was reinstated in 1981. Tellingly, the abolition was initiated by the Minister for Finance, the reinstatement by the Minister for Culture.

The US version of fixed book prices was established by the American Publishers and the American Booksellers Associations in 1901. It was challenged by Macy's department store and struck down on anti-trust grounds by the Supreme Court as early as 1913.[51] The court specifically rejected the

American publishers' argument that the special status of copyright books meant they were exempt from normal anti-trust law. Perhaps the lack of such an arrangement contributed to the fact that in the 1960s, the US had one quarter the number of bookshops per head as Britain.

For the first fifty years of operation, there had been very little challenge, even to its most aggressive feature, the element of coercion as publishers collectively enforced their will on recalcitrant retailers. After the Second World War, however, the public mood began to turn against such arrangements. In 1953, the Oireachtas established a Fair Trade Commission, but of course this had no jurisdiction over the British Net Book Agreement, so things went on as before. Then, in 1956, the British passed the Restrictive Trade Practices Act by which a variety of boycotts, deprivations of supply, blacklists and private trade courts were made illegal. A Restrictive Practices Court was established to enforce the law and, in June 1962, this court met to consider the legality of the Net Book Agreement. A massive effort was launched to defend the Agreement, keenly supported by the Irish book trade. In the event, the judge accepted the trade's arguments that if the Net Book Agreement were abolished, there would be fewer stockholding bookshops, more expensive books and fewer published titles. None of which has occurred.

By the 1980s, however, the ecology of the British trade had changed. Just 100 years after Mudie's and W.H. Smith had decided not to support three-deckers, W.H. Smith, Random House and HarperCollins gave the *coup de grace* to the Net Book Agreement: the two publishers 'announced that they would de-net their books from the 1st of October 1962. Two hours after that, W.H. Smith announced a major de-netted promotion with Random House and HarperCollins. That was the beginning of the colossal shift of power from publishers to retailers'.[52]

In the end, of course, the sky did not fall in. Despite the dire predictions, the book trade continued merrily after the collapse of the Net Book Agreement. Although many wise heads believed, and still do, that (as with France and other EU countries) the price of new books as cultural commodities should be protected, in the short term at least statistics were against them. There was no collapse, the numbers of books published soared. Indeed, Antony Farrell of Lilliput in his specialist market, claimed he hardly noticed the change.[53] In truth, the abolition of the cornerstone of the older type of trading merely underlined the fact that the book trade, where the balance of power had been with the suppliers (the publishers), had been overtaken by history.[54]

There are still many people in both Ireland and Britain who look with envy at the fixed price arrangements in other EU countries. They argue that the book trade and therefore publishing would be more author-friendly with a reintroduction of fixed book prices. The logic of their argument is that the brief of the abolitionists is to consider only the consumer and to ignore and even disrespect the producers – the writers. For instance, BOGOF ('buy one get one free') in a bookshop merely reinforces the idea that one book is the same as another: not a doctrine most authors would subscribe to.

The last of the series of reports on the Irish publishing industry (the industry leaders of the day were great believers in reports) came out in 1995.[55] Commissioned by the Arts Council, the report brought together Clé, the Irish Educational Publishers Association (founded in the 1960s), Bord na Leabhar Gaeilge and Forbairt (the industrial development agency). It was assembled by the Corporate Finance Service of Coopers & Lybrand and weighed in with eight hefty chapters. Despite the best advice of John Spillane of Mercier, Seamus Cashman of Wolfhound and Henry McNicholas of Fallon's, its authors were not quite comfortable with the industry, expressing from time to time some odd ideas: a hankering after title-by-title market research, for instance, or worrying about the succession to existing owners and, at one point, confusing new titles with books in print. There was also a rather simple-minded adherence to the arithmetic mean as the only possible way of summarising data. Nonetheless, it was a substantial achievement.

9

Overview of the Irish Book Market: 1995–2010

As all of us who study the book trade know, its statistics are notoriously problematic. To arrive at an accurate analysis we need to look behind sales figures and bestseller lists. In theory, the ISBN system which allocates a special number to each book, might be expected to yield hard information: in practice it always overstates numbers. Thus the sixth *Harry Potter* book was available in hardback and paperback, in adult and juvenile versions and in various display packs, yielding perhaps as many as ten ISBNs for a single title. The multiple possibilities of eBook versions and print-on-demand copies for the same basic text further undermine the utility of the ISBN system for estimating title output. In short, just because there were 125,000 separate ISBNs issued in any one year, that by no means implies that there were 125,000 separate titles published. Nonetheless, as an indicator of business done, the number of ISBNs traded at the till is perfectly adequate.

If the number of titles issued is problematic, the situation with sales has been even more cloudy. Publishers have traditionally exaggerated sales, sometimes, as in Gollancz' case, stopping the press in the middle of the initial run to insert '2nd, 3rd, 4th enormous printing etc.' on to the jacket and inside of the book. These customary exaggerations naturally hurt no one but the statistically minded historian.

So until recently it has been very difficult to get a clear and fully documented view of book trade activity in Ireland. Publishing Ireland (previously called Clé) has produced a survey of Irish publishers' activity every two years since 1994, but this perforce ignores the elephant in the room, i.e. the activity of British-owned publishers in this market. The useful *Irish Publishing Record* has been discontinued by the National Library and replaced by a bald listing of acquisitions under the Copyright Act, without Dewey classifications. *Books Ireland* produces a valuable rating of books of Irish interest, but makes no attempt to be comprehensive, or to assign useful search classifications to the titles it lists. However, pulling together the listings for the 'First Flush' feature in *Books Ireland* for 1995 (Table 6) gives a snapshot of the subject areas favoured that year by Irish-based publishers.

Table 6. Irish-published trade books, 1995, by class

Class	*Total Titles (no.)*	*Per cent. %*	*Av. extent No. of pages*	*Av. price £*
Children and young adults	86	13	118	4.46
Poetry and drama	67	10	95	6.87
History	59	9	238	14.17
Mind-body-spirit	56	9	194	9.97
Fiction	55	8.5	237	7.56
Biography	54	8	219	10.44
Professional	42	6.5	296	22.95
Art	35	5.5	133	15.59
Literature	30	5	221	15.24
Miscellaneous	30	5	170	11.09
Irish	29	4.5	146	5.29
Social and political	29	4.5	208	9.76
Local history	21	3	222	12.05
Travel, guides, natural history	20	3	286	15.79
Fiction revivals	15	2	338	6.65
Food, wine, cooking	12	2	133	7.66
Hobbies, interests	7	1	209	9.70
Scientific, technical, medical	3	0.5	154	9.67
	650	100	(av.) 191	(av.) 10.39

Source: *Books Ireland* 'First Flush' 1995

In 2002, coincidentally the same year that the British publishers Penguin and Hodder Headline arrived in Ireland, the Nielsen BookScan company set up an Irish Consumer Panel (expanded in 2004 and again in 2010) and this began to provide detailed and believable information about the Irish market. The data is based on an accumulation of the till sales of a selection of Irish bookshops and outlets, including supermarkets. The Irish service is the counterpart to similar operations in the UK and in the US, South Africa, Italy, Spain and other countries. This exciting new service has one major drawback. Because the data is based on information recorded on Electronic Point of Sale (EPOS) tills, small independent bookshops – which do have an interestingly different sales pattern, but do not run such tills – are excluded. A problem that is likely to become more significant is that direct sales through the web are also not covered. Nielsen estimates that the coverage is about 70 per cent of the market, while independent work using actual data from Gill & Macmillan and others suggests the real coverage is probably between 62 and 65 per cent. This is, however, better than has been achieved in the US, where cover is claimed of no more than half the market. The UK coverage is believed to be much higher, but short of 100 per cent.

In 2010, Nielsen identified a total market in the Republic of Ireland of €147.7 million sales and 13.7 million books, at an average till price (including three-for-twos and other discounts) of €10.78. These figures were a few per cent down on the previous year's results. This total is made up of sales from 293,000 separate ISBNs, some of which sold very few copies (and of course many sold none at all and therefore did not appear in the records).

Table 7. Overview of the Irish bookselling market 2007–10

Total market (by Nielsen)	*2007*	*2008*	*2009*	*2010*
Value (€m)	152.2	164.9	156.5	147.7
Volume (m)	12.1	13.9	14.6	13.7
No. of ISBNs traded	250,307	278,630	306,461	293,971
Average till receipts per ISBN	€593	€511	€504	€609

Source: Nielsen BookScan

The value of the market in 2010 was down 10 per cent since its peak in 2008 when the economy crashed, though interestingly the number of ISBNs traded continued to rise in 2009 (a recession year) and only began to come down in 2010. The steady fall in the average receipts per ISBN figure reveals that in order to keep the volume up bookshops were discounting from 2007 onwards. If we gross up the sales that Nielsen identified from electronic tills by the amount we believe that they understate the market, we get an estimate for the local book trade sales of some €227 million in 2010 rather than €147.7 million. As usual with book trade statistics there is a twist. In normal calculations publishers prefer to distinguish between books aimed at ordinary consumers (what they call 'trade books') and educational textbooks. Retailers are less interested in making this distinction, so Nielsen's figures include a proportion of educational books sold over the counter. If we estimate this as 10 per cent or so of the total, we get a value for the trade book market in the bookshops of the order of €200 million. This is more or less the value of the jewellery market in Ireland and less than half the value of the footware retail trade. It is considerably more substantial a trade than the sports and camping sector or the stationery, office and schools supplies business.

We can see the number of ISBNs traded as peaking at 306,000 in 2009. However, virtually all of these (304,000 to be precise) sold fewer than 1,000 copies. This illustrates the fundamental fact about the book trade, no doubt shared with other fashion- and fancy-led businesses: *a very small number of titles sell hugely, while a very large number of titles sell little or nothing*. Almost every important fact about the book business stems from the reality that the trade rests on a very large number of supports, only a few of which are actually bearing any weight. Market research in the US in 2004 reported that sales there were even more skewed than they are here. Some 93 per cent of titles in print sold fewer than 1,000 copies a year and, by contrast, 87 per cent of sales were accounted for by just 7 per cent of titles.

Awareness of the disproportionate contribution of the bestsellers of course adds force to the temptation that regularly assails accountancy-minded booksellers: to stock only those high sellers. What stops them is a belief that two thirds of books are bought by 'heavy-users' i.e. those who buy once a month or more. Outside of the November/December Christmas season, these buyers are even more important. Unlike in an off-licence or a pharmacy, where the retailer can reasonably expect the customer to keep buying the same favourite claret or skin cream, repeat purchases of books are not likely. So breadth of stock is important to retain the interest of these crucial buyers.

In 2010, a mere seventy-five titles sold 10,000 copies or more each. Virtually all of these were new publications. They represented some 10 per cent of the bookshops' trade. A further 780 (i.e. 0.26 per cent of books sold) carried the next 20 per cent of the business: the remaining

292,000 titles carried the rest. Of course the trick is to identify the seventy-five and that is not easy: who, for instance, would have predicted the phenomenal sales of a book about punctuation called *Eats, Shoots and Leaves*? So, even if the commercial logic allowed a retailer to pick just a few titles, the acute problem of selecting those titles would remain.

Table 8. The pattern of volume sales 2007-10: number of titles in each category

Copies per title (000s)	*2007*	*2008*	*2009*	*2010*
50,000 or more	2	1	6	2
40–49,999	3	1	2	2
30–39,999	3	7	2	4
20–29,999	16	18	18	12
10–19,999	45	47	48	55
5–9,999	156	164	156	216
4–4,999	78	84	95	87
3–3,999	143	147	142	155
2–2,999	255	315	347	285

Source: Nielsen BookScan

Nielsen believes that in this period in an average week some 250,000 books were sold in the Republic, coming from 42,000 titles. On the face of it, this seems a lot of purchases, apparently suggesting that one in thirteen of the population buy a book every week. In fact, multiple copy purchases mean that many fewer buy a book every week.

For the purpose of analysis, this chapter is limited to the Nielsen so-called Irish Consumer Market Top 1,000 report. As we have seen, the reports include the sale of educational books bought by parents through bookshops; in order to comply with the normal book trade categories these educational titles are stripped out. That done, we find that the top 850 titles remaining deliver around €50 million a year in cash sales, from sales of about 4.4 million volumes. Sales of this group range from tens of thousands to a mere 1,500 copies. These strong performers number fewer than half a per cent of actual titles available and yet deliver a quarter of cash sales and at least one third in volume.

In line with the market as a whole, value for this elite group was down 6 per cent between 2007 and 2008, 5 per cent between 2008 and 2009 and a further 2 per cent in 2010.

Table 9. Summary of top 850 published titles 2007–10 (i.e. top 1,000 less educational titles)

Year	*2007*	*2008*	*2009*	*2010*
Value (€m)	53.5	50	46	45.3
Volume (m)	4.3	4.3	4.5	4.1
Irish-published in top 850				
Value (€m)	12.2	11.8	10	8.9
Volume (m)	0.9	0.9	0.9	0.7
Irish-published share of top 850*				
	22%	23%	21%	20%

Source: Nielsen BookScan

* Irish-published includes titles published by British-owned firms based in the country.

It could have been worse, though the drop in the Irish-published market value and volume is interesting. Before the modern high-advance celebrity memoir publishing, it used to be said that the book market was relatively immune to economic cycles, since nobody attempted to read more books just because they were rich, nor did book-buying constitute so large a part of the family budget as to attract much more than token cuts if money was tight (unlike, say, foreign holidays). This no longer seems to be true.

The average till price for these bestsellers, at €11.60, was higher than that for the market as a whole. This probably reflects the fact that books still in print are not generally repriced, so would retain the older price despite inflation. Not that titles from previous years represented many of the bestsellers. In 2009, for instance, 72 per cent of the top titles by value were published in that year, 15 per cent in 2008 and 13 per cent in 2007 and earlier. This means that backlist (defined as books published in previous years) contributes 28 per cent of the bestseller revenue. This is quite healthy considering that little or no new money needs to be spent on these books, so the revenue is in that sense cost-free.

For the market as a whole (i.e. not just the bestsellers) it is likely that the contribution of backlist is higher. In 2009 not quite £900,000 of sales were recorded of books originally published before 2000: and these are only the ones that sold as many as 1,500 copies or more in the year.

One striking fact that emerges from this research is that the Irish-published share of the market is around 22 per cent. By way of comparison, in 2008 Publishing Ireland's bi-annual survey reported a trade publishers' turnover of €31.58 million. To translate that into sales at the bookshop till, which is what Nielsen measures, we can assume an average discount of 50 per cent. This gives a trade turnover of €63 million. If this is correct, Irish publishers would claim 30 per cent of the trade book market. This seems very high, suggesting that either Nielsen's figures are too low or Publishing Ireland's are too high.

As we shall see, a significant proportion of Irish-published sales is ascribable to the vigorous and well-financed activities of the Irish-based subsidiaries of British firms. Nonetheless, this share of the local market is a considerably stronger performance than, for instance Austria, which suffers from the same problem of a powerful, same-language publishing neighbour and no real barriers to access. Austria claims no more than 15 per cent of the market for locally based publishers.

In recent years the British-owned firms based in Ireland have made a striking impact on the market. Available data shows the steady growth of these firms in the top-selling 850 titles, evidently at the expense of local publishers. British-owned, Ireland-based firms increased their market share from 7 per cent in 2007 to 11 per cent in 2009, with a corresponding decline in the share of Irish-owned firms. (Rounding somewhat exaggerates the effect. In fact, the Irish-owned share in 2009 was 10.48 per cent and the British-owned firms achieved 10.90 per cent.) Unfortunately for the Irish-owned group, not only was the share of the market down from 15 per cent to 10 per cent, but the market itself fell. A reduced share of a falling market is not a happy place. It is salutary to realise how far these shares are dependent on the happenstance of particular books and their authors. For instance, if Paul Howard/Ross O'Carroll-Kelly had achieved the sales he did for an Irish-owned company, the British-owned share would have been 9 per cent of the market and the Irish-owned 12 per cent.

Author Origin

Irish authors have long looked to Britain for publication, just as Scottish authors tend to look to London, and Francophile Belgians to Paris. This is, of course, a major problem for Irish publishers, since it drains away significant talent. The Nielsen bestsellers data suggest, however, that Irish readers are far from being slavish followers of British taste. They have a marked preference for authors of Irish origin, no matter where they are actually published.

Even at the very top of the bestsellers, where we see a heterogeneous cavalcade of the international fancy of the day (Rhonda Byrne and Hosseini Khaled one year, Stieg Larsson and Stephenie Meyer the next), we also see Irish-origin authors very strongly holding their own. In 2009, for instance, 57 per cent of the top 50 selling titles by value were from authors of Irish origin. In 2008, the figure was 59 per cent.

This is all the more remarkable when compared to the figures for UK-origin authors, who achieved a mere 7 per cent of the value in 2009 and 16 per cent in 2008. Evidently the strong UK media presence is less effective in selling books than had previously been supposed. It seems that Irish readers have a strong preference for Irish-origin authors, but no particular feeling about where these authors are published. It is probable, however, that outside the top sellers the sheer depth of the backlist would enable UK authors to more than hold their own.

Sales by Product Class

Exploring a bit more deeply, we can identify the top-selling categories in the bestseller lists. The overwhelming categories are fiction (standard, crime and children's), which together amount to virtually half the market. The next significant category is autobiography, which barely makes 10 per cent of the market. The Irish are not, by northern European standards, particularly avid book readers. But these figures make it clear that when they read, they read fiction, and specifically general and literary fiction. This is a wide category, including for instance Sebastian Barry, Ross O'Carroll-Kelly and Cecelia Aherne.

Depending on specific titles, certain categories do better in some years than others. The category, 'current affairs', for instance, was big in 2009, but negligible in 2008. (The categories are allocated from the Book Industry Classification listings by the individual publisher, and this sometimes gives rise to vagaries. Thus, one of the best-known 'what went wrong?' titles, Fintan O'Toole's *Ship of Fools*, was classified as economics rather than current affairs. Even if we add his sales into the current affairs category, the total sales of these titles do not overtake sports autobiographies.)

We have seen that Irish publishing achieved a fairly consistent 22 per cent or so of the overall bestseller market between 2007 and 2009. But this proportion is by no means uniform across categories. For instance, Irish publishers claim 24 per cent of the original fiction category (thanks largely to Poolbeg's speciality in this area), but a mere 2 per cent of the crime and thrillers category. This is not fastidiousness: Irish publishers have a robust 63 per cent of the true crime category. Other areas where Irish publishing is strong include current affairs, sport and humour, where the local advantage is obvious.

The preponderance of fiction in the bestseller lists would not come as a surprise to anyone who has scrutinised the Nielsen (all-Ireland) figures reported in *The Irish Times* every week. Though listing no more than the top five titles in a very restricted range of categories, it is clear that fiction is king. In March 2009, for instance, sales of 84,000 volumes were recorded, 58,000 of those were fiction. In October 98,000 volumes were sold (coming up to Christmas) of which 62,000 were fiction. Outside of the Christmas season, it appears that Irish enthusiasm for new and original fiction (as opposed to paperback reprints) is markedly stronger than Britain's.

In a search for patterns it is easy to get carried away. The broad patterns (the Irish share, the proportion of fiction etc.) are clear; but the statistics can easily be shifted by the success of a particular book. For instance: in 2007, the top-selling title was *Harry Potter and the Deathly Hallows* with sales of 116,000 copies, an Irish record; in 2008, the top seller was Marian Keyes with *This Charming Man* at only 52,000 copies and in 2009, Sebastian Barry's *The Secret Scripture*, helped by Man Booker Prize nomination and winning the Costa Book of the Year 2008, just triumphed over Dan Brown with 74,000 sales. Despite these fluctuations, in each of these three years the top ten selling titles by value represented a remarkably steady 10 per cent of the market.

Irish Publishers

The success of the British-owned firms in the Irish market is obvious. In fact in 2009, exceptionally, they represented just over half of Irish-published sales. The top three Irish-owned firms achieved just 20 per cent of the sales, leaving 30 per cent of sales to be divided among forty or more Irish publishers.

In 2008, Penguin was also head of the list, but this time with just under 20 per cent of the Irish-published market, followed by Gill & Macmillan, Transworld and Poolbeg. In 2009, the top ten Irish-based firms contributed 84 per cent of Irish published sales, with other well-known names such as Lilliput, Liberties and Mercier in the following pack. This is broadly in line with the results from Publishing Ireland, which reported that in 2008 the top ten firms (including educational establishments) recorded 91 per cent of sales.

Penguin's success in 2009 was a function of the fact that they won the 'what went wrong and who is to blame?' battle hands down, with the market leaders Shane Ross and Matt Cooper. Gill & Macmillan's entry to that race was the latest David McWilliams book, which did not do so well, though its sales are not to be despised. Despite what might be deduced from the airwaves, Irish book buyers are evidently by no means obsessed with current affairs. Barely one in five of the books sold of the top ten are in that category, being out-sold by Paul Howard (Ross O'Carroll-Kelly) on his own. His four titles sold a comfortable 60,000 copies between them. He has earned the substantial advance that Penguin were willing and able to pay, and O'Brien and Gill & Macmillan were not.

We can draw some broad conclusions from this blizzard of figures. The first is that the Irish trade book market is something over €200 million in retail sales and that Irish publishers account for about 22 per cent of that. Depending on the year, the foreign-owned publishing houses contribute 40–50 per cent of the Irish-published sales.

As is usual in the book world, the market is extremely skewed, in that a small number of titles represent an overwhelming majority of sales. In my analysis the top 850 titles, that is less than 0.3 per cent, took at least a quarter of all sales. Only a few books (and sometimes only one) achieve more than 50,000 sales in a year and not many more manage above 30,000. Between 150 and 200 titles achieve a solid 5,000–10,000 sales, but the majority of books, more than double the rest combined, sell between 2,000 and 4,000 copies.

There is, as it is called, a long tail – in fact a very long tail. So long that the economics of the trade depends on it. In an average week some 42,000 titles are sold, at an average of six copies per title. Very few sell multiple copies; very many sell one only. The many pay the rent.

The typical sales graph of a non-educational book shows that perhaps three quarters of its lifetime's sales occur within six months of publication. This is not a new phenomenon: in George Paston's *A Writer of Books* (1898) the publisher explains to the first-time author that 'the average life of the average novel was three months at most. After that it was as dead as the romances of Madamoiselle Scuddery or Sarah Fielding.'

At least 70 per cent of the top sellers are published in the current year. This makes the trade volatile, and difficult to predict. Thus in 2007, the top-selling title sold 116,000 copies, the following year the number 1 sold only 54,000 copies and in 2009, the top seller sold 74,000 copies. Curiously, though, in each of these years, together the top ten titles sold between 2 and 3 per cent of the market. There is no sign here of the feared 'bestsellerisation' in which a small number of titles were supposed increasingly to take over the market.

Even in 2007, the last of the 'Harry Potter years', J.K. Rowling's *Harry Potter and the Deathly Hallows* sold fewer copies and made less money than the next three titles. One of these was the *Official Driver Theory Test*, benefiting no doubt from the change in the regulations in 2007 relating to holders of provisional driving licences. This success by a non-mainstream publisher was not a fluke. It is a striking characteristic of the book market that the cost of entry is low. The number of professional publishers is small, but thousands of organisations publish books, more or less successfully. So, in both the 2008 and 2009 yop 10 Irish-published lists, there are prominent titles by organisations whose core business is not publishing: the Irish Hospice Foundation and the Professional Photographers.

10

Meeting the Challenges of the Twenty-First Century

By Conor Kostick

The Arrival of the Multinationals

In 2002, a new phase began in the world of Irish publishing, with the appearance of the British-owned Penguin Ireland and Hodder Headline Ireland (now Hachette). These were publishers who were aiming to win the battle for the top spots. Indeed, due to their business model, they were not interested in the majority 2,000–4,000 range. With their arrival, a whole new level of competition began, along with a new set of challenges for existing Irish publishers: to match Penguin and Hodder not only in attracting and retaining top-selling authors but in every aspect of book production, from marketing, to cover design, to editorial, etc.

Of course, UK publishers had always been able to access the Irish market and had experienced considerable success in sales.[1] What was new about the establishment of Penguin Ireland and Hodder Headline Ireland was that these were local operations, run by people with experience of Irish culture and Irish publishing. Up until 2002, the UK publishers had tended to miss 'the next big thing' in Ireland and to pitch their marketing in a fashion that wasn't nuanced for Ireland. They had generally failed to build one-to-one relationships with the bookshops and the media. Now these two companies arrived with Irish staff who were highly networked locally.

A key figure behind this development was Michael McLoughlin. McLoughin had a strong background in Irish publishing, having started with Poolbeg in 1991 and, in 1995, having moved to becoming a publisher's PR agent, representing authors from Random House, Simon & Schuster and other major multinationals. By 1998, his clients included Penguin, and this introduced him to key figures interested in improving Penguin's performance in the country and who were aware they 'didn't get Ireland'.[2]

In spring 2002, McLoughlin pitched an idea to senior executives in London: that there should be a Penguin Ireland, just as there was a Penguin New Zealand. The pitch was well received, but to get the go-ahead McLoughlin had to take it before Anthony Forbes Watson. The mute chief executive of Penguin gave no indication at the time as to whether he was convinced or not, but a week later the project got the green light. Penguin Ireland was under way, with Michael McLoughlin as managing director.[3]

The official announcement of this new development was made by press release on 13 August 2002. The following day – not entirely by coincidence – journalists were surprised to be given a similar announcement from Hodder Headline. Managing director Breda Purdue told *The Irish Times*, 'we had been talking about it for a long time. Hodder had such a big programme of Irish writers anyway, but they were being looked after from London. We had set up the Lir imprint four years ago, which was looked after through London. We had an editor there, but when she left we had the choice of either letting it go or taking it a step further, so we decided to take a step further.'[4]

The two new publishers had somewhat different business models. Penguin Ireland has automatic distribution in the UK, 'without any negotiation' and avails itself of all the resources that the powerful UK sales team can bring to bear for a title. This obvious strength, especially in the eyes of authors, does come at a price. Penguin Ireland takes an overhead charge for its books that is the same as that in Penguin General and – given that Penguin General is in London, in the Strand, with large offices and 1,200 staff in London, these are significant.

This, along with a commitment to having a high-profile presence in central Dublin, is the main reason why Penguin Ireland has a focus on the top end of the market and frontlist sales. 'We need to have the book that sells twenty to thirty thousand copies,' said McLoughlin, 'and they are not easy to get.'[5]

Hodder Headline Ireland titles are not automatically accepted for distribution in the UK and other Hodder Headline territories. The editors therefore have to make a case for a title and, if partnership with other regions cannot be established, make the decision as to whether to go it alone.[6] Although not having to face the same level of overheads as Penguin Ireland, Hodder Headline was also established with the intention of competing for the best-selling title spot and of concentrating on frontlist.[7]

Naturally, Tony Farmar, then president of Clé brought a historical perspective to these developments. 'The "Dublin raid" – for want of a better word – is a perennial strategy by British publishers when they can't think of anything else,' he told the *Sunday Independent*. For example, in the 1920s, Macmillan came and signed up Synge, O'Casey and Yeats.[8]

Fergal Tobin, then publishing director at Gill & Macmillan, was sanguine about the arrival of Penguin Ireland and Hodder Headline Ireland; there was no need for existing Irish publishers to be alarmed: 'new players coming into the marketplace have clearly changed the assumptions that publishers have to make when considering major books. But we wouldn't want to exaggerate that change.'[9] And Tobin was even more upbeat in an interview with *The Irish Times*: 'I think it's a good thing. It injects a degree of vitality into the trade. I know that companies always say that they welcome competition when they don't, but in this case we really do.'

Tobin's explanation for this positive assessment of the increased competition in Irish publishing was prophetic:

> There's always some sort of danger of publishers either being bought out or being squeezed out of the market, but I'm struck by how many have survived in the UK and the US. Publishing does lend itself to the small. Even large houses tend to be broken down into smaller units through their imprints. To be honest, I would feel that it is small bookshops which face a greater danger than small publishers.[10]

These two ideas – that there was room for both large and small publishers in the Irish market and that there was more likelihood of small bookshops going under – were borne out over the subsequent period.

Again, Antony Farrell, publisher of Lilliput Press, refused to be alarmed:

> A lot of what we do is not necessarily market driven. But it will put us on our toes, even if we don't see them as a massive commercial threat. I'm in the market long enough not to be particularly worried, although we can't match the advances.[11]

It was certainly the case that those publishing titles whose expected performance was in the order of 2,000 to 6,000 copies had nothing to fear from the

Jonathan Williams, Ireland's first literary agent from 1986, pictured in 1973 shortly after he joined the IPA as an editor. (Courtesy of *Books Ireland*)

Ireland's first feminist publisher, Catherine Rose, founder in 1975 of Arlen House. (Courtesy of *Books Ireland*)

Philip MacDermott, founder in 1976 with David Marcus of Poolbeg, the highly successful fiction imprint. (Courtesy of *Books Ireland*)

Anne Tannahill and Michael Burns; 1978 they took over Blackstaff Press from the founders, Jim and Diane Gracey. (Courtesy of *Books Ireland*)

Liam Miller (Dolmen Press), Michael O'Brien (O'Brien Press) and Hilary Kennedy (Clé administrator) at the Frankfurt Book Fair, 1979. (Courtesy of *Books Ireland*)

Steve MacDonogh speaking at the opening of Brandon's offices in Dingle, Co. Kerry, August 1982. Taoiseach Charles J. Haughey is waiting to speak. (Courtesy of O'Brien Press)

Tony and Anna Farmar; founders in 1992 of A. & A. Farmar in Ranelagh.

Celebrating the removal of VAT from books in 1982, at the launch of the *IPA Yearbook and Diary*. Front, left to right: Michael Gill (Gill & Macmillan), Frank O'Mahony (O'Mahony's bookshop), Ray MacSharry TD, Charles Haughey TD, Jim O'Donnell (IPA). Back, left to right: Harold Clarke (Eason's), Seán O'Boyle (Veritas), Jim Walsh (Gill & Macmillan), Pádraig Ó Snodaigh (Coiscéim).

Rena Dardis, of Anvil Books and the Children's Press. (Courtesy of *Books Ireland*)

Taoiseach Garret FitzGerald launching the Irish Book Marketing Group's 'Top of the Irish' campaign (1983). Left to right: Fred Hanna, Taoiseach Garret FitzGerald, Michael Gill, Harold Clarke, Sean O'Boyle. (Courtesy of *Books Ireland*)

Boland, late of O'Brien Press and Tony Farmar of the Institute of Public Administration at the Irish Book Design Awards party 1983. Both had just joined the short-lived Tycooly International, which went into liquidation in 1984. (Courtesy of *Books Ireland*)

Kenny's Bookshop, Galway, in the 1980s, with Maureen Kenny in the foreground. (Courtesy of *Books Ireland*)

Irish Book Design Awards 1987 reception at the Linen Hall Library in Belfast: Antony Farrell (Lilliput Press), Tom McCaughren (author), Dermot Bolger (Raven Arts Press), Garret FitzGerald TD, Tim Robinson (author of *The Stones of Aran*), Fergal Tobin (Gill & Macmillan), Peter Fallon (Gallery Press). (Courtesy of *Books Ireland*)

AIB Irish Book Awards medallists, September 1990: Michael Adams (Four Courts and IAP), Pat Donlon (National Library of Ireland) Anne Tannahill (Blackstaff) (behind) Michael O'Brien (O'Brien Press), Lady Lucy Faulkner, Gay Byrne (RTE), Seamus Cashman (Wolfhound). (Courtesy of *Books Ireland*)

John Murphy of Appletree Press in Moscow: he travelled 40,000 miles in 1990 negotiating distribution of the *Little Cookbook* series. (Courtesy of *Books Ireland*)

TownHouse and CountryHouse publisher Treasa Coady (left) and author Deirdre Purcell (right) celebrating the publication of Deirdre's first novel in 1991. (Courtesy of *Books Ireland*)

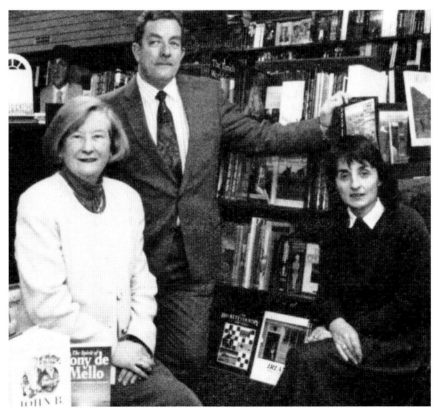

Mercier Bookshop manager Loretto McNamara with Mercier publishers John Spillane and Mary Feehan, Cork 1994. (Courtesy of *Books Ireland*)

Siobhán Parkinson, founder in 2010 of the children's books publisher Little Island; first Laureate na nÓg in 2010. (Courtesy of *Books Ireland*)

Reception on 16 April 2016 at the Irish Embassy in London to celebrate forty years of *Books Ireland*: Conor Graham (Irish Academic Press), Jeremy Addis (*Books Ireland*) and Ivan O'Brien (O'Brien Press). (Courtesy of *Books Ireland*)

Ruth Gill, from 2017 the sixth generation from the Gill family to run the firm. (Courtesy of *The Bookseller*)

Michael McLoughlin, head of Penguin Ireland from 2002. (Courtesy of *The Bookseller*)

ambitions of Penguin Ireland and Hodder Headline Ireland. But for Tivoli, the new imprint established by Gill & Macmillian in 2001 to publish top-spot fiction, there was a battle on. It must have been a shock to face competitors with the ability to offer significant advances even before Tivoli's first publication. Under commissioning editor Alison Walsh, formerly editor at Orion and Harper Collins in the UK, Tivoli published twenty-four titles between 2003 and 2006, when the imprint was ended.

An important turning point in the establishment of Penguin Ireland was the signing of Mícheál Ó Muircheartaigh and the publication of his 2004 autobiography, *From Dún Sion to Croke Park*. That title was the bestselling hardback of the year and it 'really woke people up', explained Michael McLoughlin:

> After that, other authors could see that we could be successful ... We got lucky following on from Mícheál. Brian O'Driscoll came out in the depths of the recession, selling 75,000 copies in Ireland and another 75,000 outside of Ireland. It is those extra sales that sustain the business.[12]

Two other UK publishers followed the Penguin Ireland model during this period and one of those was Nonsuch Ireland, founded in 2004. This was set up as the Irish imprint of the UK-based NPI Media Group. The first editors of Nonsuch Ireland were Eoin Purcell (now head of Amazon Publishing UK), Noelle Moran (now executive editor of UCD Press) and Sarah O'Connor. Nonsuch Ireland began as a local history publisher, introducing the long-running *Images of Ireland* series, which has published over 300 titles since its inception. In 2006, Ronan Colgan succeeded Purcell as publisher of Nonsuch Ireland as it expanded into general history, current affairs and non-fiction.

Over the course of the next two years, NPI Media Group, then led by Alan Sutton, began to grow rapidly through acquisitions. This expansion created difficulties, however, and in 2007 the group was taken over by The History Press and Sutton left his role as CEO. [13]The new CEO, Tony Morris, worked to restore relations with authors, which had become strained. Nonsuch Ireland left the group in 2007 to begin life as an independent under Ronan Colgan, alongside Maeve Convery and Stephanie Boner. In 2008 Nonsuch Ireland joined The History Press fold, rebranding as The History Press Ireland. By the time of the rebranding, the company had published eighty titles.[14]

Transworld Ireland, a subsidiary of Random House, was set up in 2007, with publisher Eoin McHugh. McHugh had started in Fred Hanna, gaining his job by strolling into Hanna's on Nassau Street and asked what it was like to work in a bookshop, and then had worked his way to becoming head book buyer at Eason's after Hanna's was taken over in 1999. Transworld transferred its Irish commercial women's fiction authors to the new company, successful writers such as Patricia Scanlan and Marita Conlon McKenna. This unusual step, not generally replicated by the other UK publishers, gave Transworld Ireland a solid start but the gift was accompanied by a challenge: how could the company avoid being identified solely with women's commercial fiction? One solution for the publisher was to source and commission non-fiction for the Irish market (that might also sell in the UK market). Ronan O'Gara's autobiography provided the ideal opportunity to both set a new tone and also prove the value of the Irish operation to the founders. As Eoin McHugh told the website www.writing.ie, *Ronan O'Gara – My Autobiography* 'was a great way to start in terms of announcing our arrival as a publishing imprint'.[15]

Given that the publisher also wanted to attract literary authors and compete in the market for literary fiction a second solution to the image challenge was proposed by Brian Langan (who had joined Transworld as editor in 2010) and McHugh: the establishment of Doubleday Ireland in 2012. Langan recalls, 'we created that imprint as a vehicle for literary fiction and we were very lucky our first publication was *The Spinning Heart*; we couldn't have gotten a better start than that.'[16] Donal Ryan's novel was initially a joint publication with Lilliput Press, as was *The Thing About December*, published in 2013 though actually written first. *The Spinning Heart* was longlisted for the Man Booker Prize and was awarded the EU Prize for Literature in 2015.

The timing of the Transworld Ireland/Doubleday Ireland project was unfortunate, however, with the official announcement of the company's formation in May 2008 coming just as the boom years for the Irish economy turned to bust.

Publishing in a Cold Climate

In 2008, the Irish economy fell off a cliff. Businesses closed and people lost their jobs on an astonishing scale, a scale that was unanticipated even by those who had been warning that the boom years of the 'Celtic Tiger' were unsustainable. The number of unemployed persons in Ireland rose from 99,000 in 2006 to 323,000 in 2012. And that figure would have been higher still but for a similar upsurge in emigration. In the five years 2008–12, there were 358,000 emigrants. In 2012, 2 per cent of the Irish population emigrated.[17]

Of the types of business that suffered the most, it was construction that was hardest hit. House prices collapsed and, as hundreds of thousands of mortgage holders went into arrears (and negative equity), property developers found they were unable to pay back bank loans. The effect of this double whammy on the Irish financial system was catastrophic and – compounded by international banking turmoil – all the major Irish banks faced collapse.

No industry is entirely recession-proof and this kind of economic turbulence accompanied by the slashing of government expenditure was bound to drastically reduce disposable income and wreak havoc in every sector. As we have seen in Chapter 6, the international publishing market's response to economic cycles, which had traditionally been relatively stable, became much more volatile after the 1960s. Although there was a lag between the onset of recession and the effect on publishing, in the early 1970s and again in the 1980s book sales collapsed in the aftermath of recession. The same pattern was evident in Ireland and (although unevenly) across the world after 2008.

According to the Central Statistics Office, sales of books, stationery and magazines in Ireland fell by 9.3 per cent from December 2009 to March 2011.[18] Writing in *The Bookseller*, Eoin Purcell analysed the 2009 figures from Nielsen. The overall fall in book sales that year was 5 per cent. Within that figure, however, was a sharper decline in the performance of Irish publishers. Gill & Macmillan was down almost 10 per cent, Mercier (having reached a new turnover high of €1.2 million in 2006 and having acquired Anvil in 2008) 12 per cent, O'Brien Press 20 per cent and Maverick and Merlin even more.[19]

Several major bookshop chains retreated or collapsed. In 2009, Borders closed its Irish shops; in February 2010, Hughes & Hughes collapsed (just as O'Brien Press was about to announce an innovative voucher reward scheme established between Kellogg's cereals and the chain) and Waterstones closed two Dublin shops in February 2011 with 52 job losses.[20]

Despite their limitations, it is the Nielsen figures that provide the best overview of the continuing difficulties faced by Irish publishers after 2008.

Table 10. Overview of the Irish bookselling market 2007–14

Total market (by Nielsen)	*2007*	*2008*	*2009*	*2010*	*2011*	*2012*	*2013*	*2014*
Value (€m)	152	165	156	148	134	123	103	106
Volume (m)	12.1	13.9	14.6	13.7	12.6	11.5	9.4	9.6
No. of new Irish ISBNs traded	1,822	2,018	2,109	2,277	2,412	2,345	2,269	2,063

Source: Nielsen BookScan[21]

The fact that the number of new Irish ISBNs traded remained fairly robust throughout the recession (in part attributable to a new curriculum coming on stream in 2010–12, requiring new educational titles) is far less significant than the severe decline in the value of the book trade, which fell from a high of €165 million in 2008 to a low of €103 million in 2012. A similar number of titles competing for a share of a market that declined by nearly a third in four years means, of course, a significantly diminishing average receipt per title. There are difficulties extracting a measure for this, but, as we have seen, average till receipts per ISBNs traded fell from €609 to €504 in 2010. This decline in receipts per ISBN of around 17 per cent is not only a reflection of the diminution of the value of the market, it also reflects efforts by retailers, especially the large supermarkets entering the market, to insist on increased discounts from publishers.

These figures demonstrate how challenging was the publishing environment in the five-year period from 2008. As Ivan O'Brien (managing director of the O'Brien Press from 2006) experienced it:

> Our sales fell by 40 per cent overnight from August 2008 and the completely sale-or-return nature of the business meant that we took huge hits from returns through 2009 in particular. We had to make very hard decisions, including letting valued staff go and reducing pay across the board. We had to drop publishing projects and save money wherever we could. It was extremely challenging, but as a result of those very difficult decisions we managed to get back to (bare) profitability after only one year. Thankfully, our previous strategic decision to ensure that we had revenue throughout the year and reduce the emphasis on publishing for the Christmas season, meant that we had created a solid programme of books for visitors to

> Ireland. During the crisis, tourists kept buying when Irish people did not: in both 2009 and 2010, July was our best month of the year for sales.[22]

Merlin Publishing did not survive. In the harsh circumstances of 2009 and 2010, any mistake was liable to become a catastrophe and a mistake was made when, in 2008, the state took action against Merlin over information published in a true crime book by Paul Williams. In his book, *Crime Wars*, Williams revealed details of an 'in camera' court hearing involving information from the Criminal Assets Bureau. This resulted in a €5,000 fine for contempt of court for Merlin and an obligation for them to withdraw the 10,000 books they had printed and distributed ready for the Christmas market. Subsequently, the High Court awarded legal costs against the company.

By August 2010, Merlin could not continue. It announced a fire sale of some forty titles as a part of a process of liquidation, citing a 'devastating collapse in book sales, at the same time that returns have skyrocketed'.[23] Explaining the decision to Eoin Purcell's Irish Publishing News blog, publisher Chenile Keogh said:

> Due to the very significant downturn in the book trade which has seriously affected the level of sales of books, the Directors of Merlin Books Limited (trading as Merlin Publishing under the Merlin imprint), have made the decision to cease its current publishing activities. As a consequence, Merlin Publishing will not be releasing any new titles for the foreseeable future.[24]

In 2001, Merlin had acquired Seamus Cashman's Wolfhound Publishing for an undisclosed sum. The imprint survived and continued to market its backlist.

The History Press Ireland also experienced difficulties, leading to staff losses. Despite success with *Strangest Genius*, a full-colour hardback biography of stained-glass window artist Harry Clarke, in August 2010 the company announced that in order to 'make sure it will have a future' restructuring had taken place. Two editorial staff were no longer permanent, but working freelance, while the sales rep left and was not replaced. Gill & Macmillan took over the sales operation.[25]

In October 2010, New Island announced staff cuts. One-full time staff member and two part-time staff were laid off. 'All contracted titles will be published,' the company said, which was a better situation for the authors than those signed up to Mercier when that company announced significant curtailment in publishing plans, especially in regard to children's books, caused largely by the loss of Arts Council funding.[26]

Another long-established publisher to cease trading at this time was Anvil and its imprint, the Children's Press. Anvil had its roots as the book publishing arm of *The Kerryman*, which mainly published memoirs by nationalist combatants in the War of Independence. Anvil proper was set up by Rena Dardis, Seamus McConville and Dan Nolan. The Children's Press was set up in 1981. In 2009, Rena Dardis sold Anvil and the Children's Press to Mercier. Naturally, Mercier kept the most successful titles in print and gave some a rebrand, such as Tom McCaughren's classic children's books: *The Legend of the Golden Key*; *The Legend of the Phantom Highwayman* and *The Legend of the Corrib King*.[27]

Brandon Books had become an imprint of Mount Eagle in 1997 when Steve MacDonogh founded the new company and bought out his partner after an acrimonius dispute. It had ceased operating with Steve's sudden death on 17 November 2010, aged 62. Brandon, as described in Chapter 7, having initially brought out provocative non-fiction had also begun to publish literary fiction. When, a year later, O'Brien Press acquired Brandon Books, the acquisition gave O'Brien a new dimension to its publishing, with a backlist and an imprint for the kinds of works it had not previously published.[28]

A further much regretted casualty to the sector more broadly, was Ireland's largest dedicated book printer, Colour Books, which went into receivership in March 2011, having posted losses of €238,812 in 2009 and accumulated losses at year end 2009 of over €1.8 million. Combined with an overdraft of €888,745, its net debts were over €3 million.[29]

Throughout the recession, Gill & Macmillan Distribution gained new clients such as The History Press. Particular impetus for these gains came with the closure of rival CMD Booksource, which ceased trading in September 2010 due to losses in the Irish market. Amongst others, A. & A. Farmar and Liberties Press made the transition from CMD to Gill & Macmillan. Argosy, which, as noted in Chapter 5, began life as three vans servicing libraries, launched Irish Books Distribution with Mercier – which had been with CMD – as its first client.

Although able to generate some additional revenue by operating the main distribution service for independent Irish trade publishers, Gill & Macmillan was not immune to the impacts of these developments and the company came out of the recession years with a very different structure from before. In 2010, Macmillan had indicated a strategic move to exit curriculum education publishing internationally and all distribution activities outside the UK and USA. A year later, Macmillan's owners, G. von Holtzbrinck announced a radical overhaul of the group structure. G&M management felt that they would have difficulty in accepting the new strategic direction and that the Irish publisher would be lost in the new group structure, with half the company (education) reporting to London and the other half (trade and distribution) to New York. The G&M shareholders agreement provided a structure for shares to be bought out by either partner as well as a formula for valuation. Negotiations were completed in 2013 and in 2016 the company was formally renamed M.H. Gill & Co. in 2016 with three distinct operating divisions: Gill Education, Gill Books and Gill Distribution.

In the middle of this international restructuring, Gill & Co. had to cope with its own particular challenges. Ruth Gill (chief executive officer of Gill from 2017, the sixth generation of the Gill family to run the business) explained:

> Our revenues declined with our markets and we were forced to revisit and cut our overhead base. The recession alongside the arrival of Penguin, Hachette and Transworld encouraged us to sharpen our offering within the Trade side of our business and focus on our strengths … Retail retrenchment leading to heavy returns were problems particular to trade publishers. Educational publishers also saw decline in market with renewed emphasis on second hand books, rental schemes, charities blaming publishers for excessive cost of school books and unnecessary new editions, etc.[30]

The figures from the directors' report 2008 quantify the economic challenge for the company. Total sales for Gill & Macmillan decreased by 12.5 per cent in 2008 compared to 2007, with trade sales down 18.4 per cent and educational sales 9.6 per cent. Distribution income, however, rose 5.6 per cent due to the addition of new client publishers. The company was still able to declare 2008 profitable, although after tax, the retention was €64,166, compared to €735,277 in 2007.[31]

Gill's statement about the decline for educational publishers is borne out by figures from Prim-Ed, which saw turnover drop from a peak of €7 million in 2007 to €4 million in 2011. The company had to retrench and, along with redundancies that reduced staff numbers from thirty-six to twenty-two, staff pay was cut by 10 per cent. Founder and owner Seamus McGuinness was interviewed by the *Sunday Times* in 2011: 'We sat down two years ago and tidied up our costs to make everything as tight as possible. Everybody we have is now working harder than ever and gradually we have fought our way through the downturn and brought things back up.'[32] Prim-Ed fought back: it had forty-six staff in 2016 and that year bought out its partner RIC Publications for €15 million.[33]

One strategy for coping with the particularly sharp form of the recession in Ireland and the drying up of domestic disposable income, was to focus on international sales to other markets. The sale of secondary rights generates income with almost no cost and where it can be achieved – typically via efforts made to attend international book fairs and through hiring agents – Irish publishers have provided themselves with crucial revenue streams from abroad. O'Brien Press has been particularly vigorous in this regard, 'Children's books travel well,' Ivan O'Brien told the *Sunday Independent*. 'Children are very open to great stories, no matter where they come from, and this is definitely a growth area for us.'[34]

The same global trend was observed (three years later) by Markus Dohle, global CEO of Penguin Random House:

> Our addressable global market and readership – especially for English language content – is growing substantially ever year and demographic change gives us additional tailwind. What's really heartening is that children's books have been the fastest growing segment of our business over the past decade.[35]

Irish language Publishing in the Recession

The impact of the recession on Irish language publishing was delayed but severe when it took hold. Foras na Gaeilge, of which An Gúm is a part, suffered deep cuts during the recession (the funding for Irish language writing and publishing available through Foras na Gaeilge fell by 44 per cent) and – apart from extra funding allocated to individually sanctioned projects – those cuts remained substantially in place in 2018. This meant a considerably reduced annual output for Irish language publishing since 2007.[36]

During the recession there was a consolidation of the Irish language publishing sector, largely because availabity of funding from Foras na Gaeilge made the difference as to whether a company was viable or not. Móinín, run by writer–publisher Ré Ó Laighléis, based in Co. Clare, ceased trading, as did Cló Mhaigh Eo, a children's publisher, run by Colmán Ó Raghallaigh, which had some success with the picture book *Drochlá Ruairí* selling over 14,000 copies. Sáirséal Ó Marcaigh, which was founded by Seán and Bríghid Uí Éigeartaigh as Sáirséal & Dill in 1947 (and which for a twenty-year period had Anne Yeats as a cover designer), was taken over by Cló Iar-Chonnacht in

2009 and with no new publications under that imprint, essentially became just a backlist; a similar fate befell An Clóchomhar, an academic press, run by the late Stiofán Ó hAnnracháin.[37]

The unfortunate loss of these publishers meant that there was more funding available from Foras na Gaeilge for the surviving Irish language publishers. Moreover, Foras na Gaeilge took the decision to let the axe fall on support for the annual Gradam Uí Shúilleabháin and Réics Carló Book of the Year Awards rather than on the publishers directly.

Tadhg Mac Dhonnagáin of Futa Fata found the post-2007 period a real challenge:

> As the recession bit deeper, trading became extremely difficult: schools' budgets for buying books were slashed, as were libraries'. Sales through bookshops dipped alarmingly and booksellers, struggling to trade through the crisis, came under pressure to fill their precious shelf-space with titles more likely to sell than books in Irish. Print runs contracted: our typical picture book run, 2,000 copies, which compares respectably with language communities who have millions of native speakers, fell to 1,500 and on for a year or two, 1,000 copies.[38]

A crucial development for Irish language publishing was a change in funding policy that made it possible for established publishers to create Irish editions of well-known children's series from English. Seizing the opportunity, Futa Fata began publishing David Walliams and also Jeff Kinney's *Diary of a Wimpy Kid* in Irish. Leabhar Breac produced editions of Roald Dahl's most popular titles, Cló Iar-Chonnacht published *Horrid Henry* and Enid Blyton. These books proved extremely popular, but, as Mac Dhonnagáin puts it, 'there is concern among writers, publishers and funders that a better balance now needs to be struck between inward translation and original writing.'[39]

The recession and government cuts did inadvertently cause another positive development, in stimulating the creation of a new Irish language publishers' organisation, Cumann na bhFoilsitheoirí. Similarly, a writers' organisation, Aontas na Scríbhneoirí, was also born and subsequently the two groups became collaborators on a number of initiatives.

Silver Linings

Any Irish publisher surviving the pressures and turbulence of the period 2008–13 deserves a campaign medal. It was a period of difficult challenges and hard, unpleasant decisions. Yet within those years were a number of significant success stories for Irish publishing.

With considerable imagination and arduous preparation, in 2010, Dublin City Council led a bid for Dublin to be awarded UNESCO's designation 'City of Literature'. The success of this effort was announced on 26 July that year, making Dublin the world's fourth such city (following Edinburgh, Melbourne and Iowa). The literary activities associated with this designation and the raising of the international profile of Irish writers that came with it not only meant the development was a 'feel good' story, it also resulted in tangible benefits for Irish authors and publishers in the form of increased international audiences for Irish works.

Another positive story from the wider world of books was that of the Gutter Bookshop, set up in 2009 in Dublin's Temple Bar, a location that would have been out of the price range of founder Bob Johnston before the recession. 'You couldn't get a nice shop in Dublin for love nor money during the boom years.' Despite the opportunity provided by the collapse of property prices in central Dublin, with two independent bookshops folding every week in the UK at the same time, to set up a bookshop was a considerable risk. By 2013, the shop had not only survived but Johnston was able to open a new branch in Dalkey. His model has been to sell service as much as books, with customers appreciating the selection process, both in regard to the stock and also recommendations. The Gutter Bookshop won the O'Brien Press Bookseller of the Year Award in 2016 and the independent bookshop of the year (UK and Ireland) at the British Book awards in 2017.[40]

Several new publishing attempts arose in the recession era. Some, such as YBooks (2010–14), an initiative led by Chenile Keogh, former managing director of Merlin Wolfhound, soon faced liquidation. Roads Publishing, based in Dublin, is an interesting experiment in Irish publishing, concentrating on luxury books with a focus on art. Established in 2013 by Danielle Ryan (granddaughter of Tony Ryan, founder of Ryanair), Roads Publishing is part of a luxury lifestyle brand that includes a fragrance and property development company. Probably, Roads Publishing would have floundered, given losses of €484,162 in 2015 and €310,033 in 2016, but for the commitment of Ryan to provide ongoing financial support.[41]

More definitely success stories are those of two small but high-profile publishers, Little Island and Tramp. Siobhán Parkinson, publisher and editor at Little Island (and former Laureate na nÓg) explained their history:

> Little Island began as a children's list of New Island in 2010. By the end of the year, New Island decided to disband the project and I thought, we can't let this happen. So a group of us pooled some money together and bought out the name, the website and so on … The risk was terrifying. I wasn't concerned about the work: the stress was financial. Would we meet the bills? That's why it began in my house.[42]

From the outset, Parkinson looked outside Ireland, both for markets and potential titles. An agreement with Walker Books made a UK distribution possible for Little Island, but when that ended after two years, the position looked critical. Arts Council support for Little Island titles made all the difference at this time:

> Then we got Bounce. Who said, 'this is a big risk for us … but we admire what you do.' The relief was amazing. So we started again in the UK with Bounce, which was a better fit as they weren't a publisher, only a distributor, and in the long run this has worked out very well.[43]

Publishing manager and art director Gráinne Clear added: '40 per cent of our sales are in the UK, which is double that of 2017. It's very unusual for a small Irish publisher to achieve this.'[44] In the 2018 Children's Books Ireland awards, Little Island had four titles on the Book of the Year shortlist, with its highly successful *Tangleweed and Brine* by Deirdre Sullivan (author) and Karen Vaughan (illustrator) taking the prize.

Tramp Press is a publishing initiative run on a small scale but with considerable success. In 2012, Sarah Davis-Goff was working in Lilliput Press, covering the manager's sabbatical, while Lisa Coen was also there on a temporary basis, on an editorial internship. The two bonded over a shared belief that 'a certain homogeneity in publishing personnel at the top was causing a lot of interesting and important work to be overlooked in favour of conservative choices.'[45]

Sarah Davis-Goff found Donal Ryan's first novel *The Thing About December* in the Lilliput slush pile, and immediately recognised its merit, providing evidence for the validity of this outlook. Lisa Coen continues the story:

> We also didn't think literary publishing worked, on a smaller scale, if companies didn't take an arts-organisation approach to running an imprint. We structured the company to be very lean (very little capital outlay; no office and so on), and to apply for funding from bodies such as the Arts Council, so that we could make editorial decisions based on the high quality of a

> manuscript rather than on whether or not we could predict its performance in the market.[46]

Tramp Press has made successful applications to the Arts Council in every year of its existence. Although its output has been modest – three or four titles a year – it has published a number of award-winning titles, including the highly successful and Man Booker longlisted *Solar Bones* by Mike McCormack (2016).[47]

Enter the E-Book

In 2007, Amazon launched Kindle and a transformation of international publishing right at the point that publishers were already facing the challenges posed by the recession. Many publishers initially saw the e-book as a rival to their traditional print book and a great deal of energy was spent arguing the merits of a physical book format over that downloaded into a reader.

Some publishers, however, become champions of the new format, recognising that it offered a way of reaching a global audience. Kieran Devlin of Poolbeg Press, made the point that:

> The advent of the digital book has opened up the world market to small publishers like ourselves. We are now able to compete with the big publishers and exploit digital sales on the world stage. We do not need massive infrastructure or sales teams on the ground to expand our digital sales but just old fashioned creativity, enthusiasm and digital knowhow.[48]

Similarly, Ivan O'Brien told the *Sunday Independent* in 2015:

> I welcome the emarket, obviously, I mean, I've sold thousands of eBooks in Australia and New Zealand – markets I would never have cracked with just physical books. For a small independent publisher, it makes a big difference to our bottom line.[49]

Now that matters have stabilised so that e-books sit alongside physical books as an alternate format and revenue stream, no doubt most publishers would concur with these views. There is, perhaps, a touch of hindsight about them. In his Irish Publishing News blog (2010–13), Eoin Purcell was a champion and advocate of the new publishing format and his editorial features were often designed to goad Irish publishers and booksellers – whom he saw as reluctant to grasp the potential of the new format – to devote more effort to e-publishing and e-selling. Yet publishers had to wait until sufficient e-readers were sold in Ireland to make converting books to electronic formats worthwhile. Apple's iPad, for example, only went on sale in Ireland in mid 2010.

Penguin Ireland, under Michael McLoughlin was very positive about the e-book publishing opportunity, although, speaking at the Irish Branch Conference of the Booksellers Association in 2010, he revealed that only 100 e-sales had been made in 2009. By the end of March 2010, however, this figure had risen to over 1,000. Anticipating continued rapid growth, McLoughlin said that change would come to Ireland and that publishers 'can't wait another year or two, because everything is changing so fast'.[50]

The following graph demonstrates that 2010 and 2011 were indeed the key years in which Irish publishers grasped the nettle and converted hundreds of titles to that format, as well as publishing new books both in print and electronic form.

Figure 2. Total Number of e-books with ISBNs published per annum in Ireland

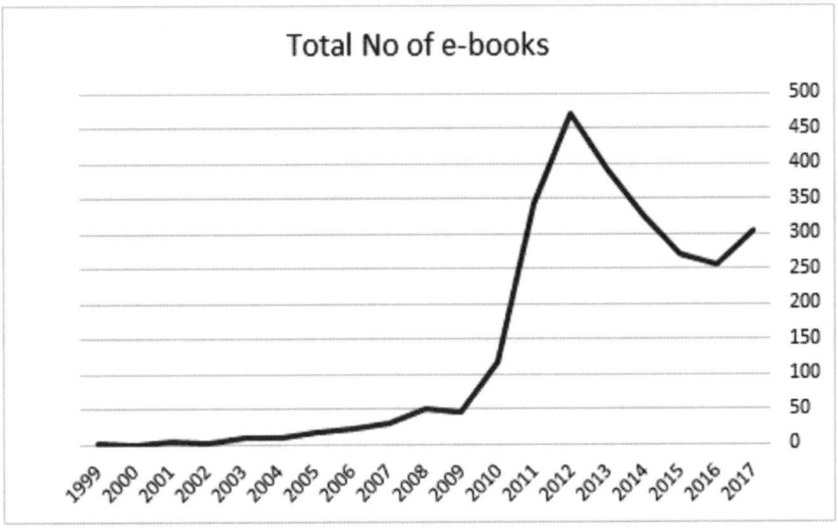

Source: Nielsen BookScan[51]

With Kindles, iPads, and other reading devices in the hands of millions of people worldwide, a new dynamic appeared: self-publishing – authors independently attempting to reach an audience by publishing an e-book through their own efforts (the best-produced ones hiring freelance editors, cover and layout designers of the same calibre and experience as those used by the traditional publishers).

Laurence O'Bryan, founder of Books Go Social and the Dublin Writers Conference explains: 'Irish authors have been reluctant to be independent authors but there are a growing community of people who have been dropped, or don't want a publisher because of the possibility of earning an income that Amazon allows.'

The independent movement was underground, little known, little heard of, but it had significant voices. Catherine Ryan Howard, a Cork writer whose self-published memoir *Mousetrapped* sold over 10,000 copies, was one of the first. (She has since moved to traditional publishing.) Other examples include J.J. Toner (History) and Gerry Kilbie (SciFi) who are successfully self-publishing.[52] For Catherine Ryan Howard, 2011 was the year self-publishing became mainstream:

> It shed its stigma. It used to be an absolute last resort. You could almost guarantee that a self-published book wasn't very good, because it would be published by an author who'd been rejected all over town. [In 2011] … it became an option. Thereby, the quality of self-published books improved. The fact we can now sell eBooks on Amazon alongside the world's bestselling authors puts us on an even keel.[53]

Quantifying the extent of this micro-side of Irish publishing is difficult, because very often the indie author prefers to use Amazon's own identifying number for new titles, rather than purchasing an ISBN. This means their sales figures are not recorded by Nielsen. O'Bryan believes the figures provided by the Publishers Association in the UK about the size of the non-traditional sector seriously and wilfully underestimate it:

> Their data excludes eBook sales by Amazon itself for its own imprints; for micro-presses who aren't part of the Publishers Association and independent authors. According to some estimates (e.g. *The Bookseller*, 13 June, 2015) these sales could be 40 per cent of the eBook sales market by volume.[54]

While traditional publishing is still the preferred route for most authors, established or aspirant, Ireland has followed the international trend in seeing the emergence of growing networks of independent authors. One measure of this is the Dublin Writers Conference, aimed at this community, which started in 2014 with fifty-five attendees (about twenty indie Irish) and by 2018 had 110 writers attending (about thirty-five indie Irish). Another is the establishment in 2018 of the Irish Independent Authors Collective, with an initial eighty indie authors as members.[55]

The issue of e-books and online resources became an important strategic one for educational publishers, who had to assess the extent to which schools would create a demand for new kinds of resources. Both Folens and Edco appreciate the point that there's more to e-formats than PDFs. Justifying a heavy investment in its digital platform Edco Learning, Edco's sales manager, Alan White told the *Sunday Business Post*:

> You have to be providing something above and beyond a simple digital version of a book. A lot of our competitors have gone down the route of providing what are basically just PDF files of a static book: the print version in digital format. In contrast, we've been conscious of the need to add value, to make sure that the digital book has all of the additional resources needed to take it to another level, such as interactive videos, animated diagrams and embedded audio clips.[56]

John Cadell, CEO with Folens, addressing the same subject, said:

> It's not easy, but all of our products are available on all platforms and that's something that is very complex and expensive to deliver, particularly for minority subjects. But it is no longer an optional part of publishing; we must give teachers access to our products anywhere, any time and in any format that they're looking for them.[57]

On the other hand, in 2011, Seamus McGuinness of Prim-Ed was not convinced that heavy investment in electronic resources had become justified:

> All the talk in our sector is about creating digital content but very few companies have managed to make money on it because the fact is that it is too soon. Teachers aren't yet sure what they want from digital content; they prefer to stay with material that is familiar to them.[58]

And a similar sentiment was expressed by Ruth Gill: 'The transition to digital has required significant investment from education publishers, with, to date, little opportunity for return on this investment.'[59]

The experience of Pearson, the world's biggest educational publisher, suggests that McGuinness and Gill are right to suggest that moving too quickly in an effort to anticipate the future direction of technology in schools is a mistake. Having sold the *Financial Times* and its half-stake in *The Economist* in 2015 to invest heavily in online and virtual courseware, for fear that textbooks would enter terminal decline, Pearson suffered a 30 per cent fall in sales in the last three months of 2016 and saw profits fall £60 million in 2017, obliging them to put their 47 per cent stake in Penguin up for sale.[60]

Supports for Irish Publishing

Throughout the period covered in this chapter, Irish publishing obtained direct or indirect support from a number of organisations, the most important of which is probably the least appreciated, the Irish Copyright Licensing Agency. It was established in 1992 by the Irish Writers Union and Clé, on an equal footing between writers and publishers, to issue licences (which are mandatory) to those bodies (educational ones especially) who make multiple copies of works protected by copyright. The ICLA redistributes the licence money paid by the users to the authors and publishers in proportion to the extent their works are being used.

This solution to the needs of schools, universities and some businesses to make heavy use of copyright-protected works has provided publishers and authors with a revenue stream that for some has been a significant proportion of their incomes. While a board member, and three times chair of the ICLA, Tony Farmar gave sophisticated strategic leadership to the organisation and made a priority of maximising the distribution-to-income ratio. (The ICLA's modest overheads are smaller than those of comparable international organisations.) Like many publishers, Farmar was concerned by some of the potential consequences of the Irish 2015 Copyright Review process and drew on the expertise of ICLA director Samantha Holman in helping to compose Publishing Ireland's submission. The main point made in that submission was that the protection of copyright, in an environment where increasingly people expect to access content without charge, especially via the Internet, is fundamental to the viability and continued economic growth of Ireland's publishing sector.[61]

The ICLA was influential in the Irish Writers Union's successful advocacy of a Public Lending Right scheme for Ireland, which was introduced in 2009.

For decades, the Arts Council of Ireland supported Irish publishers in the form of a direct subvention, the Annual Programming Grant. With considerable cuts to its budget during the recession, this policy was changed to focus reduced levels of support on a 'title-by-title' scheme. In 2009, the Arts Council saw a reduction in its budget of €9 million to €75.7 million. In order to sustain spending commitments, €2.4 million was 'borrowed' from the 2010 budget, which meant that when the axe fell again the following year, the €6.5 million cuts in 2010 were effectively €9 million. For literature, this meant a cut from €2.29 million in 2009 to €1.98 million in 2010. This is the context in which a number of publishers suffered significant reductions in funding from the Arts Council.[62]

The publisher most affected in the first instance was Mercier Press; its funding was cut from €32,000 in 2009 to €20,000 in 2010, causing a number of literary and children's projects to be cancelled or postponed. Managing director Clodagh Feehan said that the company's 'focus was on survival' in difficult economic circumstances.[63]

This precedent was followed in 2015 by the ending of O'Brien Press's Annual Programming Grant, worth €65,000 in 2014. For 2016, under the title-by-title scheme, the company was awarded €10,000 for two titles, a cut of 84 per cent. There was a public outcry at this and O'Brien had visible support from a number of leading children's writers. Some of the arguments on behalf of the publisher, however, were misplaced. The Arts Council was hardly likely to be moved by complaints that small poetry and Irish language publishers received disproportionate support in comparison to a company that employed more staff than all these put together. With the Arts Council's remit being to support poetry, arts criticism and literary fiction and not commercial fiction (or job creation) a much stronger case for a restoration of the O'Brien Press's subvention – either direct or through titles – would have rested on the 2010 strategic assessment by the Arts Council that children's literature was a form of literature falling within its remit. Unmoved by the campaign, Orlaith McBride of the Arts Council stated that, 'publishing is changing. There are other organisations and other presses emerging and the Arts Council needs to also respond their needs.'[64]

A similar public campaign, with numerous prominent authors putting their names to letters to the press, came when, in 2009, the Arts Council cut the Irish Writers Centre budget from €200,000 in 2008 to zero. From the outside, both in the UK and Ireland, this decision seemed barely believable. But what the authors who gave generous donations to keep the centre open did not appreciate was that – as accounts filed with the CRO revealed – the figure for wages and pensions in the organisation had risen rapidly. In 2005, €114,945 was allocated for salaries (and €6,250 for pension costs). In 2006, this rose to €155,424 (€9,450) and in 2007, to €199,258 (€12,950), The Arts Council wrote to the board of the centre, critical of the high proportion of its income spent on staff salaries, saying it no longer believed the centre could offer value for money and quality of service for authors. And so it pulled the plug.[65]

Forced to roll up his sleeves once more and recruit volunteers, founder Jack Harte kept the centre functioning until it could claw its way back from the brink. Under the directorship of Valerie Bistany from 2013, the centre has been revived with a particular focus on career development for authors and it has returned to annual funding.

In Northern Ireland, Blackstaff Press suffered an even more drastic cut than O'Brien Press, when, effective 1 April 2015, the Arts Council of Northern Ireland reduced the £82,200 grant of 2014 to zero. This was no doubt a major factor in the 2017 sale of Blackstaff to Colourpoint Creative, a publisher based in Newtownards which had previously grown through the production of educational and non-fiction books. Colourpoint, with nine staff, was the largest publisher in Northern Ireland and led by directors Malcolm and Wesley Johnston, made the decision to take on Blackstaff Press as a distinct imprint.[66]

Funded by Culture Ireland and the Arts Council, Literature Ireland (formerly known as Ireland Literature Exchange) promotes Irish writers and writing internationally. It does this through its translation grant, translator development, literature events and book fair programmes. For some publications, this grant has made it possible to sub-license the rights to a title to a non-English territory. In April 2013, Literature Ireland partnered with Dalkey Archive Press, the Oscar Wilde Centre and the School of Languages, Literatures and Cultures in TCD to create The Centre for Literary Translations.

Children's Books Ireland is the national children's books organisation of Ireland founded in 1997 as a result of the merger of the Irish Children's Book Trust and the Children's Literature Association of Ireland. It is a company limited by guarantee, with charitable status, and it receives funding from the Arts Council. CBI produces the magazine, *Inis*, and organises several initiatives that are very important to publishers and authors of children's literature, including an annual book award, an annual festival and collaborations with the Laureate na nÓg.

Through Poetry Ireland, the Arts Council and the Arts Council Northern Ireland run the 'Writers in Schools' scheme, which over the course of eighteen years has part-funded the visits of authors to schools, with more than 500,000 children having had the opportunity to meet authors. Not only have the – modest and below Irish Writers Union recommended rates – visiting fees helped sustain authors, but the subsequent interest in the associated titles has helped sales. The scheme is particularly helpful for Irish language authors, as Tadhg Mac Dhonnagáin of Futa Fata has noted:

> The Writers in Schools Scheme, run by Poetry Ireland, tries to service the strong demand from the Gaelscoil/Gaeltacht sector for visiting writers, and they have been very supportive. This outreach work provides extra income to writers and makes a career in the area a bit more sustainable.[67]

Recovery 2013–18

In line with the general recovery of the Irish economy, those publishers who came through the recession in reasonably good shape found themselves in an environment where publishing could not only regain the lost ground of the previous five years, but surge ahead into record levels of turnover and sales.

Based on Nielsen BookScan figures, by November 2016, book sales in Ireland were up 11 per cent to €130.8 million compared to the same point a year earlier, with volume up by 9 per cent to 10.9 million books sold. Irish-published titles comprised 24.3 per cent (€31.8 million) of the market, up from 23.2 per cent in 2015. The largest growth in the 2015/16 period was recorded in non-fiction and in children's book sales. Leading the way in market share was Penguin Random House with 22.3 per cent (€29.3 million in sales), followed by Hachette at 13.1 per cent (€9.1 in sales), Pan Macmillan 4.5 per cent (€5.9 million in sales) and Gill at 4.2 per cent (€5.5 million in sales).[68]

In the year to July 2018, the Irish book sales market increased by 6 per cent in volume and 7 per cent in value. This rapid growth compares with a sluggish 0.8 per cent increase in volume and 2.1 increase in value in the UK. The impact of these increased sales has been very evident in an upsurge in profits for the previously under-siege bookselling industry. The accounts filed by Dubray Books in 2017 show that in the year August 2015 to August 2016, the eight shops of the chain generated €1.3 million profit, up nearly half a million on the already healthy figure of €824,228 in the previous year. Managing director Maria Dickenson told the *Examiner*: 'I am certainly optimistic about the future of bookshops and the physical books, after what has been a long period of uncertainty.'[69]

During these years of recovery, the publishing landscape remained relatively stable, although the 2013 international merger of Random House with Penguin had notable repercussions for Ireland and in 2017 there was a significant increase in the strength of HarperCollins in Ireland.

One attempted change to the picture was rebuffed by the Competition Authority. In September 2012, Eason's announced that it had acquired the Argosy wholesale and distribution business, subject to a review by the Authority. That caveat proved to be significant. Having circulated a questionnaire to publishers, the Competition Authority concluded that the 'absence of credible actual and potential competitors' in Ireland meant that the acquisition might result in increased book prices. This decision was widely welcomed by publishers. The status quo was returned to only briefly, however, with Eason's subsequently announcing plans to reduce stock significantly and to move its distribution systems to Masterlink Logistics.[70]

From October 2012, the story of a possible $2.4 billion merger of Penguin and Random House began to appear in the press, although it wasn't until 1 July 2013 that the merger was finalised. While both profitable, the two companies had seen a dip in earnings and the attraction of the merger was the prospect of saving an estimated $40 million and also in allowing the companies to jump ahead of Hachette to become the biggest publishing company in the world.[71]

For Penguin Ireland, this meant a merger with Transworld Ireland (and Doubleday Ireland), creating a publisher that, based on Nielsen's 2012 figures, accounted for 22 per cent of the Irish market.[72]

The departure of Eoin McHugh and Brian Langan of Transworld four years later left Michael McLoughlin 'wearing three hats' – those of Penguin Ireland, Transworld Ireland and Penguin Random House Ireland, the latter being focused on selling the books from the other Penguin divisions into Ireland.[73]

HarperCollins in Ireland had long been an imprint of the UK-based company. Up until 2017, its actual investment in on-the-ground staff and infrastructure in Ireland was relatively modest and largely focused on PR and marketing for books it hoped would do well in Ireland. As its website puts it: 'The HarperCollins team in Ireland works to promote and sell HarperCollins titles across the whole group while placing particular emphasis on those authors on our list who are either Irish by birth or living and working in Ireland.' Late that year, however, four new appointments doubled the Irish team and Eoin McHugh – having left the merged Penguin Random House operation five months earlier – was given a newly-created position of publishing director for Ireland. This put the imprint in a much better position to rival Penguin Ireland, Hachette Ireland (which had acquired Hodder Headline in 2005) and Gill for the bestseller spots.[74]

The financial revival of Irish publishing has been accompanied by a rise in production standards across the board, but most noticeably in non-fiction. The

Royal Irish Academy perhaps deserves credit for initiating this new phrase in high production values with its *Judging Dev*, which won the Irish Book of the Year award in the 2007 Irish Book Awards. After the buyout from Macmillan, Gill rebranded and freshened up its design approach, leading to some impressive successes, such as the 2017 hit, *Oh My God What a Complete Aisling*. Another publication with notably high design values was Cork University Press's *Atlas of the Irish Revolution*. At 1,000 pages, weighing 5kg and costing €59, the title was an unusual and unexpected bestseller. Within six weeks the initial 8,000 copies (which CUP anticipated would last it a year) were all sold, and the book won a number of awards.[75]

Publishers' Relationships with Authors

Considered as a business, the publishing industry's relationship to authors is an unusual one. When a book is launched, both publisher and author embark on a shared journey that has the potential to be the making of them both. And very often for the publisher the reward of producing books is not so much the financial one, but that arising from the creation of a work of art and in knowing it has made a difference to the cultural life of a country. This sense of creative as well as commercial achievement is shared by publishers both large and small, with Michael McLoughlin of Penguin Ireland, for example, relishing the role: 'it's most important to have fun. It's great craic.'[76]

Nevertheless, there has always been a tension between publishers and authors over the question of royalties. What is a reasonable royalty? Largely, the answer to the question is one of expectation in terms of sales, but over the course of the 2002–18 period there has been a noticeable decline in royalties and correspondingly, author earnings.

According to a June 2018 survey in the UK on writers' pay (answered by 5,523 writers) conducted by the Authors' Licensing and Collecting Society (the UK's equivalent to the ICLA), writers in 2018 earned 15 per cent less in real terms than they did in 2013. The typical income for a 'professional author' in the UK was £10,437, down from £11,000 in 2013. This is a 42 per cent drop since 2005. The survey also revealed a gender bias, with average earnings of female professional authors around 75 per cent of the of males, down from 78 per cent in 2013. Philip Pullman's response to these figures was to comment: 'that publishers' profits are growing at a time when authors' incomes are falling speaks for itself.' The situation in Ireland is probably similar, with the

Irish Writers Union believing that typical royalties paid by Irish publishers are somewhat below those of their UK counterparts.[77]

When, in 2016, Liberties Press was reported by *The Irish Times* as having failed to pay monies owed to at least eleven authors and three former members of staff, Publishing Ireland – of which Liberties Press was no longer a member – revived its Code of Practice, which was first published in 1987. This action was well-received by the Irish Writers Union, and at a meeting between the two bodies Publishing Ireland accepted the validity of several of the points arising from an international campaign for fair contracts. The campaign, under the auspices of the International Authors Forum had been launched at the start of 2016 and was largely driven by the Authors Guild (USA).[78]

Ireland and the Man Booker Prize

In 2013, Donal Ryan's *The Spinning Heart* appeared on the longlist for the Man Booker Prize. In 2017, Mike McCormack's *Solar Bones* did likewise. Neither title would have been eligible to appear on the list while they were published by an Irish publisher alone. The contradiction between Ireland and the UK being treated as one book market and the Booker's rules was exposed by these examples – particularly that of *Solar Bones*, which was ineligible in 2016, when published by Tramp Press, but became eligible when Tramp sold the rights to Canongate, a discrepancy which they publicised highly effectively in the Irish and UK media.

Behind the scenes, Publishing Ireland, led by Ronan Colgan of The History Press Ireland and Ruth Hegarty of the Royal Irish Academy, had been negotiating with the committee of the Man Booker Prize. And it was agreed that, from January 2018, Irish publishers would be eligible to nominate titles for consideration.[79]

In making the decision, as the Booker Prize Foundation explained in its press release:

> [The Foundation] consulted with Publishing Ireland, the Irish Association of Book Publishers. It was agreed that given the special relationship between the UK and Irish publishing markets – whereby most Irish publishers release books simultaneously in Ireland and the UK – all Irish publishers should be eligible. The aim of the new rule is to ensure independent Irish publishers are given the same opportunity to be recognised by the prize as Irish publishers who have headquarters in the UK and are already eligible

to submit titles.[80]

Ronan Colgan, president of Publishing Ireland, stated:

> We are extremely grateful for the support shown by the Man Booker Prize and our friends and colleagues in the UK publishing industry. This announcement is wonderful news, not just for Irish publishers and Irish writers but for our intertwined literary heritage.[81]

Asked by *The Times* whether the latest rule change gave Irish authors a better chance, Colgan replied:

> I don't think it's necessarily going to increase the chances of Irish authors winning more than before because the very big Irish authors tend to go to the UK publishers and may still do that. What it means is, once these authors become very successful, they could stay with their Irish publisher because they could get the same access to the market.[82]

Antony Farrell of Lilliput offered Desmond Hogan, Rob Doyle, Orfhlaith Foyle and Elske Rahill from among its authors who could be Booker contenders, regretting he could not enter them all, while Sarah Davis-Goff of Tramp Press, said:

> The Man Booker is a hugely impressive prize, it is one of the greatest literary awards in the world. In the past, some people were not aware that books from Irish publishers were excluded and there may have been an assumption that we weren't good enough, which is absolutely not true.[83]

With the boost to Irish publishers and authors provided by Publishing Ireland's successful negotiation with the Man Booker Foundation, as well as the way in which the economy had revived and e-books had been incorporated into the world of publishing, Ivan O'Brien's' perspective on the future was positive but realistic:

> Irish publishing is currently strong but fragile: there are a lot of good companies producing beautiful, high-quality books for readers of all ages, but growing wages in other industries, Brexit, constant challenges to copyright law and many other challenges mean that this could change rapidly. The situation would be greatly helped by core public funding, in line with the

> situation in nearly every other country, for Publishing Ireland, our trade body. It currently survives on subscriptions and voluntary work. With secure funding, we could build stronger training programmes, promote the industry and help our creators to share Ireland's cultural vision with the widest possible audience.[84]

Brian Langan described the overall position of publishing in Ireland in 2018 as 'hopeful'. Langan, who left Transworld to freelance as an editor and return to novel writing, also observed that the landscape had settled down after the arrival of the big conglomerates:

> There's room for all the different models: there's room for the big conglomerate to bring out the blockbusters and some of the major literary writers; there's room for the smaller boutique publishers to bring out experimental works like *Solar Bones*, which go on to win awards and there's also room for the newer model of eBook first then the physical book, or even eBook only.[85]

Given the history of Irish book publishing, and the way in which publishing is affected by periods of rapid turbulence associated with economic shocks and sharp technological or legal shifts, this cautious optimism is probably realistic.

PART TWO

A Chronicle of Irish Book Publishing Since 1890

1890

—In March, Frederick Macmillan writes to *The Bookseller* a letter entitled 'A remedy for underselling', proposing a scheme to eliminate the destructive discounting so common in book retailing. Interviewed for the *Pall Mall Gazette* most contemporary booksellers say it can't be done. In July, Marshall's *Principles of Economics* is published as the first trade 'net' book.[1]

—The Society of Authors (founded in 1884) starts publishing *The Author* (editor Walter Besant) in response to the rapidly widening market for authorship. Some 6,500 books are recorded as published in Britain and Ireland.[2]

—Alex Thom incorporated as a new company, including Sealy, Bryers & Walker and the educational publisher Sullivan Brothers. Capital £150,000, annual profits of the pre-combined companies £16,000.[3]

—Edmund Downey, co-founder of the Irish Literary Society, splits with his partner Ward but continues to publish under the names of Ward & Downey in London until he buys the *Waterford News* in 1906.[4]

—Opening of the new National Library building. In the months preceding the move, over 100,000 volumes are transferred from their previous home in the RDS building of Leinster House.[5]

1891

—US copyright Act (the Chace Act) extends copyright protection to non-American books, subject to a manufacturing clause.
—William Morris founds the Kelmscott Press.

1892

—National Literary Society founded by W.B. Yeats and others on 24 May, following the establishment of the Irish Literary Society in London in December 1891. On 25 November, Douglas Hyde delivers his lecture 'The necessity for de-anglicising the Irish people'.[6]
—Hodges Figgis becomes a private limited company; directors: Figgis, Charles Evans, Thomas Brown.[7]
—'The old-established library, bookselling and stationery business of the late John Greene in Clare Street Dublin has been purchased by Messrs Crinion and Quinn who will carry on the business in the same name.'[8]

1893

—Linotype hot-metal typesetting is first installed in Ireland in the Dublin Steam Printing Co. of Abbey Street, Dublin. Printers are slow to invest in automatic typesetting machines, not having the requisite volume of straight setting.[9]
—The United International Bureaux for the Protection of Intellectual Property (French acronym BIRPI), the forerunner of WIPO (World International Property Organization), set up to administer the Berne Convention of 1886.
—W.B. Yeats's *Celtic Twilight* published by London firm Lawrence & Bullen.[10]
—T. Fisher Unwin (in London) commences publishing the *New Irish Library*, selected by Charles Gavan Duffy.[11]

1894

—*The Real Charlotte* by Somerville & Ross published by Ward & Downey in May as one of the very last three-decker novels, following the announcement in June by Mudie's and W.H. Smith that they will no longer buy three-volume novels at a guinea and a half (31*s* 6*d*). New novels hereafter generally published at 6*s*.[12]

1895

—In January the Associated Booksellers of Great Britain and Ireland (Booksellers' Association from 1948) is reorganised from the London Booksellers Society, which had been founded in 1890. It unanimously approves 'the net system of publishing books'.[13]

—Death of Daniel Sullivan of Sullivan Brothers educational publishers and booksellers, Marlborough Street, Dublin. The deceased founded the firm in 1855, which was well known for its schoolbook series *Sullivans Series*. He was 'prominently identified with the Masonic body'.[14]
—Oscar Wilde's *annus horribilis*: the triumphant first performance of *The Importance of Being Earnest* followed by the trial, conviction and sentencing for gross indecency.[15]
—October: Publishers Association of Great Britain and Ireland established; despite the name there are no Irish members at either inaugural meeting. The following year, the Associated Booksellers request the Publishers Association to meet with them to discuss terms. The PA refuses, stating that terms are 'a matter for arrangement by individual publishers'. As *The Bookseller* puts it, 'the instant the first trade question comes before it, the Association refuses to discuss it'.[16]

1896
—First meeting of the Dublin Booksellers Association, held in Eason's. William McGee of No. 18 Nassau Street is the first chairman. (McGee had been in business without a partner at No. 18 Nassau Street since 1859.) Members: Browne & Nolan, Christian Knowledge Association, Combridge's, Dublin Tract Repository, J. Duffy, Eason's, Educational Depository, Fannin, M.H. Gill, John Greene, Hodges Figgis, Wm McGee, E. Ponsonby, Sibley, Robert Stewart. Key resolution (29 May): 'that the Dublin bookselling trade will not alter the present practice of allowing only 2*d* in the 1/- discount to the general public.'[17]
—John Murray comes from London in an attempt to resolve the ongoing dispute of the Dublin Booksellers Association with Clerys; the department store persists in offering 3*d* in the 1*s* discount. More than 100 years before (1770–93), Murray's grandfather had been a regular visitor to Dublin with the so-called Society of Dublin Booksellers.[18]

1897
—Langston Monotype sets up an office in London to market the 1887 patented Monotype setting machine. *The Nation* reports claims that cost savings with Linotype could be about 40 per cent compared to hand-setting.[19]
—Rotunda commences 'moving picture' screenings. Marconi granted first wireless telegraphy patent.

1898
—After arbitration by W. H. Lecky Longman ceases to supply Clerys, the end of a long dispute initiated by the Dublin booksellers in 1896 as resistance to

'price cutting drapers and others'. In 1904, Clerys accepts the restrictions of the Net Book Agreement.[20]
—26 April: inaugural meeting of the Irish Text Society in London. Douglas Hyde elected president. First volume published in 1899.[21]
—A great fire destroys Sealy, Bryers & Walker's printing plant in Middle Abbey Street; several authors' stock is burned, including the stock, setting and manuscripts of Fr Edmund Hogan's latest book *Physical Characteristics of Irishmen*. The sole surviving record is a copy he had collected two days earlier. Over 100 employees thrown out of work.[22]

1899
—Net book scheme accepted by the Publishers Association (in January) 'unanimously, if not with enthusiasm', and Associated Booksellers (in February).[23]
—An tAthair Peadar Ó Laoghaire's *Séadhna*, claimed as the first Irish language novel, begins serialisation.[24]
—Gaelic League establishes a publications committee to co-ordinate the publication of creative work and education booklets.[25]
—May: first performance at the Irish Literary Theatre – W.B. Yeats's *The Countess Cathleen*. (The successor company, the Irish National Theatre Co. (the Abbey), founded in 1904.)
—Catholic Truth Society of Ireland established to provide 'a supply of reading both suitable and attractive' to counteract the influence of the 'questionably good and unquestionably bad' material imported from England. The first twenty-five pamphlets were published together in June 1900.[26]

1901
—Belfast branch of Associated Booksellers established.

1902
—The point system for describing type introduced, which has been in common use in the US since 1886. Although initially expensive, it makes typesetters' lives much easier, especially where varying sizes are used in the same setting.[27]
—Dublin Booksellers Association reconstituted, with same members, having been allowed to lapse.[28]

1903
—Harry Tempest of Dundalgan Press starts a long publishing career with *The Irish Motor Directory and Motorists Annual*. By the time of his death in 1964, he

had published over seventy English language titles and more than fifty Irish language school books.[29]

—On death of the second managing director, Michael J. Gill, M.H. Gill becomes a private limited company. Patrick Keohane, later managing director, becomes the company secretary.[30]

—August: Dun Emer Press publishes first title, *In the Seven Woods* by W.B. Yeats; 325 copies printed, 64pp, price 10*s* 6*d*.[31]

1904

—Whaley & Co. commences publishing in No. 12 Dawson Street. Among the first titles is Synge's *Well of the Saints*.[32]

1905

—Following a crucial breakdown in contract negotiations with railway companies in October, W.H. Smith in a few months replaces over 250 bookstalls with 144 high-street shops throughout England, thus creating a retail chain that is a powerful presence in English bookselling for generations. Eason's, which until a management buyout in 1886 was a subsidiary of Smith's, does not follow suit until 1963.[33]

—New publishing company Maunsel & Co. takes over Whaley's list and W.B. Yeats's *Samhain* from Sealy, Bryers & Walker. Joseph Maunsel Hone (aged 23) invests £2,000 (i.e. over €250,000 in 2015) and becomes chairman until 1913.[34]

—First series of *An Learbharlann* commences publication; it lasts until 1909.[35]

1906

—William McGee, bookseller of No. 18 Nassau Street and long-serving chairman of the Dublin Booksellers Association, dies. His shop is taken over by Fred Hanna and Walter Neale.[36]

—The first fifty titles of the *Everyman* series published by Dent.[37]

—The 'Book War' between the *Times* Book Club and the Publishers Association fought in successful defence of the Net Book Agreement.[38]

1907

—Sealy, Bryers & Walker publishes 386 titles between 1882 and 1922, peaking with thirty titles in 1907. It is a mixed list including Yeats's first title *Mosada* and titles from Samuel Ferguson, Thomas MacDonagh, Charles Gavan Duffy and Douglas Hyde, as well as poetry, fiction, directories, educational texts and issues of the *Dublin University Review*.[39]

—James Joyce sends the manuscript of *Dubliners* to Maunsel managing director George Roberts.

1908

—Gaelic League establishes An Cló-Chumann (later Clódhanna Teoranta) to deal with the growing number of circulars, pamphlets and books of all kinds in Irish.[40]

—George Bryers, MRIA, chairman of Sealy, Bryers & Walker, Alex Thom and the Dublin Steam Printing Company, dies. His obituary records how he was first employed as a boy in a Dublin printing company on 5*s* a week.[41]

1909

—Dublin Booksellers Association objects to London publishers supplying books to the Café Cairo, on the grounds that it is a café with a mere sideline in books and not a proper stockholding bookshop. London not very responsive to *Dubliners*. The Café Cairo was at 57 Grafton Street, and became notorious as the meeting place of the group of British intelligence officers killed on Bloody Sunday, 21 November 1920.[42]

—'It is generally established that 25% on the published price is the maximum royalty that a 6*s* novel will stand.' This royalty is threatened by the 'flood' of new novels published at 2*s* or less.[43]

1910

—Blackie closes its Dublin branch because of business difficulties caused by the political climate and establishes the Educational Company with a wholly Irish board, and at the same time takes over the education firm of Fallon & Co. Capital of the new company is £50,000; shareholders W.G. Lyon, C.J. Fallon, W. Fitzsimmons, William Magennis.[44]

1911

—The Copyright Act sets the period of copyright as life plus fifty years after author's death.

—*Catholic Bulletin* founded by M.H. Gill, initially as a book review vehicle before developing into an outspoken, even scurrilous, Catholic nationalist polemic. Last edition December 1939.[45]

—Padraic Colum, James Stephens, David Houston and Thomas MacDonagh found the *Irish Review*. Despite its distinguished contributor list, it gets into financial trouble and is taken over by the Plunkett family in 1913. Edited until its demise in November 1914 by MacDonagh's former Irish language pupil Joseph Mary Plunkett, who switches its emphasis from literature to Volunteer politics.[46]

1912

—Associated Booksellers of Great Britain and Ireland meet in Dublin. Charles Eason presides over the great dinner. Reporting Stephen Gwynn's speech, *The Irish Times* notes, 'we are a clever and inquisitive people but somehow booksellers and publishers have come to regard us as very indifferent customers.'[47]

—Herbert Heber Pembrey, who has worked in Combridge's since 1892, buys Greene's bookshop.[48]

1913

—M.J. Gill, third managing director of M.H. Gill, dies aged 42, and is succeeded by his brother Richard. He was author of *Public Libraries for Ireland* (1903).[49]

—Educational Company establishes Talbot Press as a separate imprint to publish 'general literature'. Blackie's and the Educational Company have published intermittently since 1894 under the imprint. More than forty titles published in 1918.[50]

—The US Supreme Court defeats, on anti-trust grounds, an attempt by the American Publishers Association and the American Booksellers Association to impose their fixed book pricing agreement on Macy's department store. The attempt by the defendants to argue that copyright books are a special case is rejected.[51]

1914

—Attention drawn to Ireland's absence from the International Book Trade Exhibition in Leipzig.[52]

1915

—Death of James Walker, the last remaining partner of Sealy, Bryers & Walker publishers, which pioneered colour printers (chromo-lithography) in Ireland. Walker, a Presbyterian, was a Home Ruler and friend of Parnell. He was also an evolutionary socialist who entertained William Morris when the latter came to Dublin to lecture.[53]

—Books published in UK (including Ireland) down on previous years. Drop mostly in fiction; war books popular. *Publishers' Circular* reports 10,615 titles in 1915, 11,5317 in 1914 and 12,379 in 1913.[54]

1916

—Commission on the Importation of Paper established by Board of Trade to control licences for the import of paper. Initially, quota levels set at one third pre-war usage. From January 1917 imports of both paper and paper-making materials reduced to half of the pre-war levels.[55]

—Eason's (incorporated as a plc in 1888) premises in Abbey Street and Sackville Street destroyed in Rising, as are other premises in Middle Abbey Street, including Sealy, Bryers & Walker, Alex Thom, Maunsel and the Monotype office. M.H. Gill, in O'Connell Street and the Educational Company/Talbot Press in Talbot Street escape damage.

—Following the Rising, an office of press censorship established in Dublin with a view to suppressing inflammatory writing. Remit includes the power to redact or suppress books.

—Books published in UK down 13 per cent on 1913 due to paper restrictions. 'Little evidence of decline in volume of rubbish,' says *The Irish Times* (10 March) unsympathetically.

1917

—Combination of capital input from Edward MacLysaght and generous compensation from the Property Losses (Ireland) Compensation Board gives Maunsel a new lease of life. George Roberts sets up Maunsel & Roberts, printers, in early 1917.[56]

1918

—Publisher Martin Lester founded in conjunction with the Candle Press (est. 1916). Directors Bulmer Hobson, James MacNeill (brother of Eoin), Colm Ó Lochlainn.[57]

—Book-burning: on 28 May infuriated local people burn copies of *The Valley of the Squinting Windows* and attack the author's father.[58]

1919

—Management buyout at the Educational Company. W.G. Lyon and William Fitsimmons acquire the financial interest of the founding company Blackie & Son of Glasgow.[59]

1920

—Eason's rebuilt as a connected set of buildings from 1920.[60]

1921

—'As a nation,' says *The Irish Times*, 'we have not yet acquired the habit of buying books. We do not class books, as we class tobacco and summer holidays, among the necessities of life.'[61]

—Nearly ninety titles published in Ireland plus fifty-five pamphlets, from Catholic Truth Society and the Irish Messenger. Top publishers: M.H. Gill (19 titles), Burns & Oates (10), Educational Co. (5), Browne & Nolan (4), Cahill and Fallon's (3 each).[62]

1922

—*Ulysses* published in Paris 2 February.

—Catholic Central Library founded by Stephen Brown SJ.

—Darrell Figgis's *The Irish Constitution Explained* published by Mellifont Press.[63]

—The existence of the new state fuels heated debate among disillusioned Gaeilgeoirí: 'The related questions of orthography and typeface were argued with a ferocity that could divide families and friends, and drive would-be sympathisers away from the revival in amazed disgust.'[64]

—Eason's formally opens its 'new and extended premises on Sackville Street'.

—Due to the disturbed state of the country the National Library closes from 28 June 1922 to 13 February 1924.[65]

1923

—Censorship of Films Act passed.

—November: trial of the 'Squinting Windows' case, as the consequences of Brinsley MacNamara's book (Maunsel 1918), including assault, public book-burning and the continuing boycott of MacNamara's father's school, work their way through the courts. The case fizzles out after the jury disagrees.[66]

—Martin Lester, publisher since 1919 of e.g. Eimar O'Duffy and Wolfe Tone's letters, closes when its principal manager Bulmer Hobson joins the civil service. Publishes a government-commissioned memorial volume paying homage to Griffith and Collins in February 1923. A wildly optimistic 25,000 copies printed, of which fewer than half had been sold six months later; by 1925, when the Talbot Press took over the title, there were still 7,800 copies in the warehouse.[67]

—Richard Gill, the fourth of the family to run M.H. Gill, dies. Patrick Keohane, the company secretary, takes over the management until 1939, paying special attention to the *Catholic Bulletin* (1911–39) briefly edited by J.J. O'Kelly and then by Keohane himself.[68]

1925

—Maunsel & Roberts, the surviving imprint of Maunsel, founded in 1905, closes. Managing director George Roberts works for Talbot for two years before moving to England.[69]

—Irish booksellers urged to stop selling immoral books, at a meeting of the Irish Vigilance Association.[70]

—Cork University Press publishes its first four titles.

—First edition of Eason's *Trade Bulletin*, advising and recommending new popular books, selling techniques, trade matters etc. for newsagent customers. The *Bulletin* runs from 1925 to 1940 and from 1945 to 1960.[71]

1926

—Wireless Telegraphy Act establishes 2RN, later Radio Éireann.

—First census in Irish Free State identifies 567 self-described 'journalists and authors'.

—February: Minister for Justice Kevin O'Higgins, reluctantly sets up Committee of Enquiry on Evil Literature. Its report, published a year later, recommends the establishment of a permanent committee to advise the minister on doubtful publications.

—May: First meeting of Coiste na Leabhar, the advisory committee to An Gúm.[72]

—In discussion in the Dáil of the Commercial and Industrial Property (Protection) Act, confirming the 1911 British Copyright Act, an attempt to make Irish copyright for Free State authors dependent on printing in Ireland (following US and Canadian precedents) defeated 34–8 as a result of concern not to violate the Berne Convention. The Act adds the National Library and the constituent colleges of the NUI to the list of deposit libraries, jumping the number from six to ten.[73]

1927

—C.J. Fallon starts publishing educational books again under his own name.

—First publication of Belfast-based Quota Press, 'the most productive publishing house in Belfast in the middle part of the century' (NIPR), run by Antrim woman Dora Kennedy; it is the first Irish commercial publishing house run by a woman. The press published more than 100 titles up to 1954.[74]

1929

—'Small demand for books by Irish writers, with the exception of Donn Byrne whose books sell by the hundreds,' says manager of Combridge's bookshop in Grafton Street.[75]

—First annual meeting of the Library Association of Ireland, President R. Lloyd Praeger. Disappointment that only 71 out of the 150 eligible librarians have become members. The following year the key topic is the demand for a 'commission' of 10 per cent on book purchases.[76]

—The egregious architect Page Dickinson, recalling his time in Dublin before the First World War, mentions his friend Joseph Hone's shortlived literary quarterly *The Shanachie* (1906–7). 'Like all such ventures of its sort in Dublin, it failed through lack of a sufficiently large educated public to support it. The standard of public taste in literary matters in Ireland, outside of Dublin, has always been a very low one, and still is so. Dublin on the contrary, one is told by publishers and booksellers, ranks very high, and in proportion to its size more first-rate books are sold there than in any English city.'[77]

—Censorship of Publications Act establishes the Censorship Board, after a last-ditch attempt to restrict censorship to 'fugitive publications', i.e. magazines and newspapers, fails; 1,200 books and 140 periodicals banned in the first ten years of operation, including works by Austin Clarke, Samuel Beckett, Colette, Daphne du Maurier, Sigmund Freud, Ernest Hemingway, Aldous Huxley, André Malraux, Somerset Maugham, Sean O'Casey, Marcel Proust and H.G. Wells. The Act also makes criminal the displaying and selling of any book advocating contraception or abortion, banned or not.[78]

1930

—Associated Booksellers of Great Britain and Ireland meets in Dublin for the first time since 1912. It is estimated that only 3 per cent of books sold in Ireland were published here.

—William Fitzpatrick, who joined Eason's in 1863, retires after sixty-seven years' service aged 80.

—Second series of *An Leabharlann*, now the official journal of the Library Association of Ireland, commences publication.

—Non-Irish-speaking Trinity graduate Letitia Dunbar-Harrison appointed to Mayo Library by the Local Appointments Commission, causing a row in which the Library Committee is accused of rejecting her on sectarian and anti-Trinity grounds.

1931

—Death of educational publisher C.J. Fallon.

—National Library records 140 Irish titles including sixty-four pamphlets mainly CTS and *Irish Messenger*. Top publishers: Browne & Nolan (twenty-four titles including five in Latin as part of a classics studies programme edited by Timothy Corcoran), M.H. Gill (20), Educational Co. (14).[79]

1932

—Tariff imposed on imported books and magazines. Imported periodicals subject to ¾*d* duty per copy (preferential rate) and novels in English 1*d* per copy. Records suggest that 700,000 books were imported every year, i.e. fewer than one per household per year. This number is perhaps understated by a proportion of those books being printed in Ireland for British publishers which avoided duty by being processed through local wholesalers and library suppliers such as Eason's.[80]
—An Gúm's annual report for 1930–31 shows that the agency had evaluated 389 manuscripts in five years, publishing 103 titles (i.e. 20 per year, equal to M.H. Gill or Browne & Nolan). Average sale 680 copies.[81]
—The incoming Cabinet decides to commit to the old Gaelic type and the traditional spelling for Irish. Department of Education abandons its plan to switch schoolbooks from Gaelic to roman type. In 1945, de Valera approved a popular edition of *Bunreacht na hÉireann* and it was published in roman type and revised spelling.[82]
—Irish Academy of Letters registered (12 September) by Yeats. Intended as 'a solid body of informed opinion that might encourage writers and discourage the Catholic Church from suppressing them' (Frank O'Connor).[83]

1933

—The Central Catholic Library, originally established in Westmoreland Street in 1921, moves to 74 Merrion Square. According to founder Stephen Brown SJ, the library had 37,000 volumes by 1937.[84]
—Women Writers Club (1933–58) founded by Blánaid Selkeld; first president Dorothy Macardle. Its 'Book of the Year' awards begin in 1936.[85]

1934

—'What Dublin is reading' feature begins in *The Irish Times* (3 November 1934).

1935

—In May Allen Lane announces in *The Bookseller* the publication of ten titles of a new series of reprints entitled 'The Penguin Books'. 'I would be the first to admit,' he writes, 'that there is no fortune in this series for anyone concerned.'
—Irish PEN, a branch of the international NGO, founded.[86]

1936

—John O'Keefe buys Duffy & Co., paying for three quarters of the stock. Duffy was formally wound up in 1996.[87]

1937

—Edmund Downey of Ward & Downey dies in Waterford.[88]

—First publication of Blánaid Salkeld's Gayfield Press which produces eight titles between then and 1945.[89]

—Monotype issues the Irish typeface Columcille designed by Karl Uhlemann and Colm Ó Lochlainn (1892–1972) of the Sign of the Three Candles. Digital version launched in 1993 by Dublin typesetting firm DOTS (founder and managing director John O'Loughlin Kennedy, also co-founder of Concern).[90]

—Browne & Nolan opens new printing plant at Richview, Clonskeagh, to replace the Fenian Street plant destroyed by fire in 1935.[91]

—Irish Young Master Printers Association established. Members include Allen Nolan of Browne & Nolan, Gerry Agnew of Cahill's, Ian and Jim Robertson of Thom's, Charlie Gibbs of Dublin University Press, Wilford and Billy Fitzsimmons of Talbot Press and George Hetherington of Hely's.[92]

1938

—Lord Mayor of Dublin confirms that, following complaints from a councillor, 'a few books that were thought undesirable' were removed from public library shelves. These books, says the Irishman's Diary in *The Irish Times*, concern 'Spain, Mexico and Russia and certain philosophical and sociological issues'.[93]

—Death of William ('Billy') Fitzsimmons of Educational Company, aged 60. Originally secretary, became chairman and managing director in 1929. Described as 'the guiding spirit of that famous Dublin firm'. He was also chairman of the Dublin Master Printers Association and president of the Golfing Union of Ireland.[94]

—After ten years of operation, writes Leon Ó Broin: 'The Gúm's publications fall under two heads, those that are described as Secondary School texts and works of general literature. Up to the present, there are 64 books in the first category with an average sale of 1,600 copies each, and 358 in the second category with an average sale of 480 copies each.' Thirteen of the textbooks and five of the general titles had repaid their costs.[95]

1939

—On the death of Senator Patrick Keohane, William Gill (1908–81) becomes managing director of M.H. Gill, the firm founded by his great-grandfather in

1856 as McGlashan & Gill; it became M.H. Gill from 1876, and M.H. Gill & Son from 1903. William Gill retired in 1976. *The Catholic Bulletin*, Keohane's pride and joy, ceases publication in December.[96]

—W.G. Lyon of Educational Company, Talbot, and Phoenix Publishing, dies, leaving his shares to his son R.H. Lyon, who takes over as managing director of the Educational Company. Estate £25,983.[97]

—D. O'Kelly, secretary of the Irish Publishers Association, writes to *The Irish Times* stating that trade book discounts are 25 to 33⅓ per cent and education 15 per cent (in response to a columnist's claim that unenterprising Irish publishers only allow 15 per cent discount on trade books as opposed to 33⅓ per cent allowed by British publishers).[98]

1940

—Elizabeth Yeats of Cuala Press dies. She ran the Dun Emer Press from its foundation in 1902 and its reincarnation as the Cuala Press in 1908. The Cuala Press published seventy-seven titles up to 1946 (thirty of which were by her brother W.B.) and then was briefly revived by Liam Miller in 1969. Day-to-day running of the press taken over by Mrs George Yeats; after the death of F. R. Higgins in 1941, Sean O'Faolain and Frank O'Connor became directors and literary advisers.[99]

—Paternoster Row, the historic centre of the British book trade since Pepys's day, bombed to extinction. Numerous firms destroyed, most notably the wholesaler Simpkin Marshall.[100]

—October: first issue of the monthly *The Bell*, edited by Sean O'Faolain.[101]

1941

—National Library records 104 titles of which 43 are pamphlets from CTS, Irish Independent and Irish Messenger. Top publishers: Browne & Nolan (15), M.H. Gill (14), Burns & Oates (8), Duffy (5).

—The first Irish Book Fair, the idea of Lennox Robinson, opened by Thomas Derrig, Minister for Education, at the Mansion House, 19 March; 6,000 visitors recorded.[102]

—The Irish Writers, Actors, Artists and Musicians Association (WAAMA) founded. Sean O'Faolain president.[103]

1942

—Second and final Irish Book Fair in this series opened by Seán MacEntee in the Mansion House.[104]

—Herbert Pembrey of Greene's bookshop dies and is succeeded by his second son Bertie (1908–2000) who had been in the business since 1928.[105]

—Second book-burning: a number of local clergy force 'The Tailor' to burn Eric Cross's book *The Tailor and Ansty* on his own hearth after a four-day Seanad debate confirms the Censorship Board's ban. Some passages from the book read into the record by Sir John Keane are deemed so shocking that they are expunged.[106]
—The Irish language journal *Comhar* founded. With a distinguished list of editors, it operated for years as the network core of the new generation of Irish language enthusiasts and writers including Máirtín Ó Cadhain, Seán Ó hÉigeartaigh, Brendan Behan, Breandán Ó hEithir etc.

1943
—Book Association of Ireland, president Stephen Brown SJ described in August as 'newly formed'; over the next seven years organises lectures, a children's book fair, a Mangan memorial poetry competition, a catalogue of works of politics, economics etc. relating to Ireland (1943), a general catalogue of Irish publications (1944) and later a monthly note to newspaper editors describing recent Irish publications. Petered out in the mid 1950s.[107]

1944
—Captain Seán Feehan (1916–91) founds Mercier Press. First title J. O'Mahony *The Music of Life*. In 1946, he publishes Dom Eugene Boylan's *This Tremendous Lover* which was reputed to have sold more than 1 million copies (the title, it was claimed, misled some purchasers). Retired from the army and became a full-time publisher in 1950. Initially achieved a world-wide reputation as a publisher of religious titles (especially translations from German); after Vatican II refocused the list to popular books on Irish history and culture.[108]
—Death of Michael O'Leary, director of Fallon's responsible for translating and publishing Macmillan titles such as Hall & Knight and Carty's *Irish History* into Irish.[109]

1945
—Dubliner Maurice Fridberg begins publishing (eponymously) in London. He comes to Dublin in 1948. Authors include Elizabeth Bowen, Stephen Bennet, Donagh MacDonagh, John Brophy and Frank O'Connor. Ceases publishing in 1954, claiming that censorship makes the job impossible.[110]

1946
—Only two Irish-published books were ever banned by the Censorship Board, both in 1946. These were Frank O'Connor's translation of *The Midnight*

Court (1945) and Norah Hoult's *Selected Stories* (1946), both published by Maurice Fridberg (Dublin & London).[111]

—First appeal to the newly formed Censorship of Publications Appeals Board dismisses Frank O'Connor's appeal against the banning of his translation of *The Midnight Court*.[112]

—David Marcus publishes the first edition of his periodical *Irish Writing*.[113]

1947

—The British Board of Trade withdraws the open licence for Irish books and periodicals, effectively preventing their sale in Britain except by mail order. David Marcus's new periodical *Irish Writing* crippled by being prohibited from selling into Britain.[114]

—Public Libraries Act establishes Library Council to accept from the Carnegie Library its Irish Central Library for Students and to assist local authorities to promote libraries.[115]

—British Publishers' Traditional Market Agreement formalises de facto practice since the early century, with some seventy countries identified as the inalienable British 'traditional markets'. This effectively splits English language world rights into two spheres, British and American. The agreement was destroyed by an anti-trust suit in 1974.[116]

—Foilseacháin Náisiúnta Teo established by taking over the *Mayo News*. Initially publishes *Inniú* and *Mayo News*; later becomes a significant publisher of Irish language books. Printed *Cré na Cille* in 1949. Finally goes into liquidation 1988.[117]

—First title (Séamus Ó Néill's *Tonn Tuile*) published by new imprint Sáirséal & Dill, founded by Department of Finance official Seán Ó hÉigeartaigh and his wife Bríghid with a £300 legacy from his aunt Lizzy Dill Smyth. He was the son of veteran IRB editor/civil servant P.S. O'Hegarty. Sáirséal was his own and his father's second name and his father's pen-name, after a Limerick hero of the 1690s. By 1981, the press had published 120 titles.[118]

1948

—Irish language book club An Club Leabhar founded by Comhdháil Náisiúnta na Gaeilge, secretary Donncha Ó Laoire; 1,116 subscribers in the first year rising to 2,000 by 1950. By 1956, the Club had distributed over 80,000 vols.[119]

1949

—Prickly exchange of letters about the British book ban between Sir Stanley Unwin and D.S. Magee, secretary of the Irish Publishers Association.[120]

—Fiftieth anniversary of the Catholic Truth Society of Ireland. The 2,000 or so pamphlets published since the first batch of twenty-five in June 1900 have sold 45 million copies in that period, typically through schools and its network of 800 'church boxes'. Sales peaked at 2.3 million copies in 1945–46.[121]
—May O'Flaherty, recently redundant from Leon's, the Grafton Street furriers, takes over Parsons in Baggot Street. The shop, built in 1916, was a general store selling hardware, pencils etc., as well as newspapers, and only gradually became a bookshop with periodicals.[122]
—Boycott of all British publications proposed (but not passed) at Librarians' Conference in Limerick. Supported by Captain Feehan (Mercier) who said that up to the imposition of import controls in 1947, 50 per cent of their sales had been to Britain. He believed that British publishers depended on the Irish market for 'the success or failure of an edition'; if there was a ban 'they would immediately go running to the Board of Trade and within a few months all bans would be lifted'.[123]
—The devastating British controls on import of Irish books finally lifted, subject to certain paper restrictions. Irish publishers reportedly dusting off long-delayed manuscripts.[124]
—December: first publication of the short-lived literary and arts magazine *Envoy* (1949–1951).[125]

1950
—March: Sáirséal & Dill publishes its most distinguished title, Máirtín Ó Cadhain's *Cré na Cille*. (The publication date is often given as 1949, as on the title page, but production delays led to postponement.)[126]

1951
—Census identifies 880 people describing themselves as 'author, editor or journalist'.
—Ben Brennan (ex Gill) starts Eblana Bookshop in Grafton Street; he is married to show-jumping legend Iris Kellett (1926–2011).
—Annual Conference of the Associated Booksellers of Great Britain and Ireland held in Dublin 22–25 June. Irish Branch President R.B. Eason acts as host, with P.T. Hughes of Browne & Nolan; 200 booksellers and 90 publishers attend including Michael Joseph and Allen Lane of Penguin. Delegates discuss the inevitable rising prices and the possibility of establishing a Book Trade Association combining booksellers and publishers.[127]
—In a pamphlet, Waterford librarian Fergus Murphy (president of the Library Association 1959) points out that Irish publishers produced 555 books in the eleven years to 1948.[128]

—Architect Liam Miller founds Dolmen Press; first title Sigerson Clifford's *Travelling Tinkers*.[129]

1952

—UNESCO records 149 titles published in the Irish Republic, a quarter of them religious.
—Sáirséal & Dill produces the first Irish language title on a Varityper, an office typesetter capable of producing justified camera-ready copy.[130]
—Geoffrey Faber admits defeat in the contest between those who prefer spine titling to read bottom to top (the European style also used in early Penguins) and those who prefer top to bottom (now canonised as ISO 6357: 1985).[131]

1953

—Reform-focused public service quarterly *Administration* starts: such was the paranoia of the service that readers were asked not to refer in public to its existence.[132]

1954

—*The Bell* ceases publication.
—Maurice James Craig's *Irish Bookbinding* published.[133]
—Last outing for the Sealy, Bryers & Walker imprint, with the biography *William Higgins Chemist* by T.S. Wheeler.[134]
—Final issue – the 28th – of *Irish Writing* as edited by David Marcus and Terence Smith. Taken over by Dolmen for six more issues.[135]

1956

—'Speaking at the Diamond Jubilee of the Booksellers Association of Great Britain and Ireland (Irish Branch) Mr Donagh MacDonagh said that the only kind of book that sold in Ireland today was a book in the Irish language. A book in Gaelic had a guaranteed sale of at least 3,000 because of the great work that Club Leabhar had done.'[136]
—Leader in *The Irish Times* describes Irish publishers as 'an unenterprising lot' willing to publish religious or educational books and not much else. In response, James Maher notes that perhaps a dozen original English language titles were published in Ireland every year.[137]
—Ken Library Service, Clare Street, closes. Managing director Maurice Fridberg claims censorship makes it impossible to run an efficient library service in Ireland.[138]

—December: Sean O'Faolain appointed director of the Arts Council; he appoints Mervyn Wall as secretary in July 1957. The two writers fail to increase the investment in literature which was less than 2 per cent in 1951–60. Music and theatre together represented 52 per cent of expenditure in that period.[139]

1957

—*Irish Book Lover*, founded 1909, ceases publication.[140]

—A total of 14,798 new books published in Britain and Ireland; the total of new books, reprints and new editions exceeds 20,000 for the first time, this figure being regarded at the time as 'a maximum high-water limit'. Fifteen Irish publishers listed in Thom's produce ninety-five trade and educational titles.[141]

1958

—*The Dublin Magazine* ceases publication.

—Last edition of the traditional combined format Thom's *Directory*; subsequent editions consist of the street directory only or a commercial directory in 1968.

—Kerry-based Irish language publisher An Sagart founded.

1959

—Ireland ratifies Universal Copyright Convention thus bringing US books into Irish copyright protection.[142]

—Joseph Hone, first chairman of Maunsel, dies.[143]

1960

—Dundalgan Press's last title published by publisher Harry Tempest, who died two years later.[144]

—Jeremy Addis becomes trade publications manager of Browne & Nolan.[145]

—In a letter *to The Irish Times* James Duffy & Co. note the difficulty of getting British booksellers to stock Irish books: 'In 1960, having just published at *9s 6d* the only up to date history of Ireland we sent to the leading bookseller in each of 200 towns in England a special circular, a jacket of the book (a striking three-colour job), and an offer to send copies at full trade terms, sale or return and carriage paid. The result was one order for two copies.'[146]

—National Library catalogue records seventy-six titles published by Irish trade and educational publishers, as follows: newcomer Allen Figgis with his first list (10), Dolmen (10), Burns Oates (10), Clonmore & Reynolds (9), Mercier (8), Folens (7), Educational Co. (5), M.H. Gill (4), Talbot (3), Browne & Nolan (3), Fallon's (3), Parkside (2), Duffy and Golden Eagle (1 each).

—Proposal to combine resources and reading rooms of the National and Trinity Libraries vetoed by Archbishop John Charles McQuaid and the Catholic bishops. Funding for both increases.[147]
—Allen Figgis, managing director of Hodges Figgis, sets up his own publishing company: first eight titles published together in December. Figgis later becomes treasurer (later administrator) of Christ Church Cathedral and ceases to publish after 1980.[148]
—While the British public are given the chance to complete their D.H. Lawrence studies with the unexpurgated *Lady Chatterley's Lover*, the Censorship Board bans thirty or forty books a month including Edna O'Brien, Muriel Spark, Nicholas Monserrat, John O'Hara and 'Hank Janson', the pseudonymous author of toughies such as *Torrid Temptress* (1959) and *She Sleeps to Kill* (1960).

1961

—State grants made available to public libraries for the first time, which eventually stimulate substantial development of the system. Public library stock stands at 2.4 million volumes; by 1983 stock is 8.7 million.[149]

1962

—Vatican II opens: its reforms eventually destroy some backlists of existing Catholic publishers (most notably Burns & Oates) but make way for great opportunities in lively Catholic publishing. Clonmore & Reynolds and Eason's Catholic prayer book publishing department (dating from 1866) close around this time.[150]
—Boom in paperback sales reported. 'A Dublin firm of distributors' is quoted as saying, 'the sale of paperbacks is becoming more and more a higher proportion of our business'; sales now estimated at a million copies a year at an average price of 3*s* 6*d*.[151]
—The Arts Council of Northern Ireland established as a successor to the Committee for the Encouragement of Music and the Arts (CEMA) which had operated since 1942.
—Alex Thom (including Sealy, Bryers & Walker) merge with Hely Group renamed Hely-Thom.
—Stephen Brown SJ dies. His *Ireland in Fiction* (1915) is reprinted by the Irish University Press in 1969, and *The Press in Ireland* (1937) in 1971 by Lemma Publishing Corp. of New York.
—Irish book trade keenly supports the British Publishers Association in its successful legal defence of the Net Book Agreement.

1963

—New Irish Copyright Act, based on 1956 UK Act.

—The Irish Publishers Association, whose key function had been liaising with the Department of Education, described as 'moribund'. Liaison function taken on by the Irish Educational Publishers Association (an entry for which appears in Thom's *Commercial Directory 1968*: Chairman R. H. Lyon, who had been MD of the Educational Company since 1939).[152]

—Despite protests from the trade, the 2.5 per cent turnover tax is applied to book sales.[153]

—Eason's opens a shop in Patrick Street, Cork, signalling a move into the high street away from the railway bookstalls; O'Connell Street extended 1965. Shops were also opened in Dún Laoghaire 1966, Limerick 1970, Belfast 1971, etc.[154]

1964

—Brendan Behan, Sean O'Casey die.[155]

1965

—London-based Australian publisher Geoffrey Chapman establishes a subsidiary in Dublin as a liturgical and religious publisher, stimulated by Alex Tarbett (later of Educational Company); ceased membership of Clé in 1973.[156]

—Irish Books & Media, an offshoot of Eoin McKiernan's Irish American Cultural Institute, begins importing Irish books into the US.[157]

—Faced with the alternative of investing in new offset litho technology, and believing the market is overcrowded, M.H. Gill's print works close in December. The hot-metal equipment is sold the following February.[158]

—Herder & Herder Dublin set up with 'a strictly academic theological programme'.[159]

—John McGahern's *The Dark* banned by the Censorship Board. McGahern refused permission to return to his teaching job after leave of absence. He believed that John Charles McQuaid, Archbishop of Dublin, had initiated this, backed by a threat to the Irish National Teachers Organisation that he would not support their forthcoming wages claim.[160]

1966

—Seamus Heaney's *Death of a Naturalist* published by Faber (on the invitation of fellow-Ulsterman Charles Monteith) after Dolmen failed to publish his first poems; that Dolmen rejected them is disputed by Thomas Kinsella, as is the report that Dolmen had also rejected a submission by Philip Larkin.[161]

—Hely-Thom acquires Educational Company of Ireland for £335,000.[162]

—Dublin's first shop specialising in paperbacks, the Paperback Centre, Suffolk Street, opened by Hodges Figgis; sold (1971) to Richard Moss.[163]
—Professor Gordon Foster of LSE creates a 9-digit SBN system for the British Publishers Association. This subsequently evolves into the 10-digit and 13-digit ISBNs. A year later he became professor of statistics at Trinity.[164]
—Censorship Reform Society established; takes the unbanning of Edna O'Brien's books as its first legal challenge.[165]
—Colin Smythe, having graduated from Trinity in 1963, founds the eponymous publishing company in London, later moving to Buckinghamshire where he meets Terry Pratchett in 1968, publishing Pratchett's first book in 1971.[166]
—Sáirséal & Dill, which had published ninety titles since its foundation in 1948, about to close, being heavily in debt, is rescued by the government after strong cries from the public.[167]

1967
—Mercier publishes *The Course of Irish History* from an RTÉ broadcast to mark the Rising; subsequent sales of half a million claimed.[168]
—Irish University Press established by James Hamilton MacMahon, ex Thomson Organisation; publisher Tadgh MacGlinchey. Staff include senior editor Tom Turley, production manager Jeremy Addis (ex Browne & Nolan), sales manager Michael Adams (ex Scepter Press).[169]
—Longman Browne & Nolan established; incorporated into the Educational Company in 1971.[170]
—Herder acquires Burns & Oates London; this firm takes over the books and production of Herder & Herder Dublin. In 1970 Herder gives up Burns & Oates, thus ending its connection with Dublin.[171]
—First edition of the Institute of Public Administration's *Yearbook*, filling the niche left by the discontinuance of Thom's *Directory*.
—Robin Montgomery (ex Hodges Figgis, Association for the Promotion of Christian Knowledge) joins Paperback Centre and sets up shop in Stillorgan Shopping Centre.
—Schoolmaster poet Michael Smith and his brother Peter found the 'non-commercial' New Writers Press; first title is Trevor Joyce's *Sole Glum Trek*. Described in 1972 as 'the foremost poetry publisher in Ireland'.[172]
—Censorship Act releases thousands of previously banned titles and considerably eases nearly forty years of the book trade's problems with censorship.[173]
—Patrick Kavanagh dies.
—Seán Ó hÉigeartaigh dies; his widow Bríghid continues to run Sáirséal & Dill for another fourteen years, finally selling the firm to Caoimhín Ó Marcaigh in 1981.[174]

—Constantine Fitzgibbon formally proposes to Mervyn Wall, secretary of the Arts Council, that artists' earnings from artistic work should be tax free. Two years later Charles Haughey's Finance Act gives authors and artists tax relief.[175]
—From September, free secondary education made available to all.
—Recruitment for the Irish University Press printing plant in Shannon commences.[176]

1968

—*Irish Press* 'New Writing' page edited by David Marcus starts with a story by John McGahern; Marcus's first choice, a story by Edna O'Brien, vetoed by editor Tim Pat Coogan as too controversial for the initial outing.[177]
—Harold Clarke, having re-animated Eason's wholesale book business from 1956, is appointed to Eason's board; he retired as chairman in 1995 and from the board in 2010.[178]
—Michael Adams's *Censorship*, the first full-length study of the system, published by Scepter Publishers (the Irish branch of the US Opus Dei house).
—Founded in Bristol in 1942, after several moves Carraig Books lands in Blackrock, Co. Dublin.
—Last recorded title of Clonmore & Reynolds (NLI records 173 titles 1945–1968). The chairman, 'Billy' Clonmore, a passionate convert and a friend of Evelyn Waugh and John Betjeman, became Earl of Wicklow in 1946. Patrick Reynolds had been manager of Eason's prayerbook publishing department.[179]
—Eileen Power, UCD librarian, commences publication of the annual *Irish Publishing Record*, identifying 424 titles published in Ireland in 1967 from 129 publishers including government and semi-state publications. Only eight firms (CTS, Gill, Dolmen, Mercier, Scepter, Educational Company, Fallon & Co. and the Stationery Office) produce ten or more. Ninety publishers produce only one title.
—Gill & Macmillan established, after Macmillan Sales Director (later MD) Nicholas Byam Shaw initially approached Gill to sell Macmillan's educational titles in Ireland. Gill retains a bare majority of the new company.[180]

1969

—Captain Feehan publishes *An Irish Publisher and his World* recording his experiences since successfully publishing his first book, James O'Mahony's *The Music of Life*, twenty-five years before in 1944.
—Irish University Press republishes Stephen Brown's *Ireland in Fiction* (first published 1915, 2nd ed. 1919). The follow-up by Stephen Brown and Desmond Clarke, *Ireland in Fiction 2,* is published in 1985 by Royal Carbery Books, an imprint of Mercier Press.

—Samuel Beckett wins the Nobel Prize for Literature.
—Catholic Truth Society (founded 1899) relaunched as Veritas, part of the Catholic Communications Institute.[181]
—Booksellers Association publishes *Trade Reference Book* noting that 'unless the bookseller states otherwise his order will be treated as firm'.
—Irish Export Board (Córas Tráchtála) sponsors the first Irish stand at Frankfurt Book Fair. Seven firms attend under the Córas Tráchtála banner (Geoffrey Chapman, Dolmen, Allen Figgis, Irish University Press, Scepter, Talbot and Gill & Macmillan); Mercier attends on its own as it had since the late 1950s.[182]

1970
—Clé, the Irish Book Publishers Association or Cumann Leabharfhoilsitheoirí Éireann, founded with seven members; Liam Miller the first president; Michael Gill treasurer; Bernard Share paid secretary.[183]
—Gallery Press, publisher Peter Fallon, first title appears: *Answers* by Des O'Mahony and Justin McCarthy.[184]
—*Books from Ireland* published by Clé; lists 230 titles (not including IUP's *British Parliamentary Papers*) published between January 1969 and December 1970. Published thereafter twice a year, edited by Bernard Share; nine issues to 1974.
—Trinity Library commences publication of *Long Room*, later described as 'Ireland's journal for the history of the book'.
—Committee on Industrial Development *Paper, Paper Products, Printing and Publishing Industry* published; warns of a 'further tendency of publishing to move into "paperback"'.[185]
—Listowel Writers Week initiated.[186]
—Michael Longley becomes literature officer of NI Arts Council.
—In January Smurfit takes over Browne & Nolan. Browne & Nolan print and retail sections merged into Smurfit Print and Retail divisons. R. Allen Nolan becomes a Smurfit main board director. In August Smurfit takes over Hely-Thom (including subsidiaries Educational Company and Talbot).[187]

1971
—Census identifies 1,264 people describing themselves as 'author, editor or journalist': up 43 per cent in twenty years.
—William Stern buys Cahill Group (including subsidiaries C.J. Fallon and Irish University Press) for £1.65 million.[188]
—Blackstaff founded by Linen Hall librarian Jim Gracey and Diane Gracey (ex Hodder editor). First title is R. Friers's *Riotous Living*. From January they publish *Irish Booklore*.[189]

—Last appearance in a Clé promotion of the venerable publisher James Duffy, founded before the Great Famine.[190]
—Five hundred delegates from forty countries attend International PEN's 38th Annual Conference in Dún Laoghaire; new chairman Heinrich Böll welcomed by the president of Irish PEN, children's book writer Meta Mayne Reid.[191]
—First O'Brien title, Michael McInerney's *The Riddle of Erskine Childers,* published by E. & T. O'Brien printers. The book is announced as the first in a 'Men of Ireland' series.[192]

1972
—Gifford Lewis and Clare Craven, ex Irish University Press, establish a small printing, publishing and design house.[193]
—Browne & Nolan (now part of Smurfit Retail) opens Ireland's first children's bookshop at No. 3 Dawson Street, Dublin. Manager Alan Hanna stocks 8,000 titles.[194]
—Arthur G. Gray, manager of APCK Bookshops, dies. Became manager of Dawson Street branch in 1942; set up branches in Belfast (1944), Limerick (1948), Cork (1961); set up first Irish campus bookshop, in Coleraine, in 1968.[195]
—The metric grams per square metre method of describing paper weights replaces the old basis weight method: a great relief to production departments.
—Thomas Kinsella's Peppercanister Press begins with publication of *Butcher's Dozen*, a protest against the Widgery Report on Bloody Sunday.[196]
—VAT on books introduced at 10 per cent, replacing turnover tax.
—Colm Ó Lochlainn sells Three Candles Press, printer and publisher, founded in 1926, and dies soon after. Three Candles is later renamed Aston.[197]
—Irish University Press presents its newly completed 1,000-volume set of British Parliamentary Papers at Frankfurt.[198]

1973
—IUP closes Shannon printing plant with the loss of the sixty jobs remaining from the initial (1968) strength of 300.[199]
—IUP editorial director Tom Turley sets up short-lived Millington imprint based in London to break into the British trade market. 'Primarily hardcover [but] with plans to bring out several paperback Irish novels.'[200]

1974

—William Stern's UK property market collapse thrusts Irish University Press, Fallon's and Cahill's printers into bankruptcy. Irish Academic Press established (with the help of English reprint publisher Frank Cass), managing director Michael Adams; takes over stock of IUP and continues to sell the *British Parliamentary Papers* for many years.[201]

—Over-expansion drives Clé's finances on to the rocks, not for the last time.[202]

—UK adopts ISO 2108 (1970) specifying the 10-digit ISBN code for books in place of the 9-digit SBN used since 1966.[203]

—Educational publisher C.J. Fallon bought from Cahill Group by senior staffers Edward White and Henry MacNicholas and outside interests. First title published by Dick and C.J. Fallon trading as Fallon & Co. appeared in 1894; after joining the Educational Company in 1910, C.J. created the eponymous C.J. Fallon in 1927, acquired by Cahill's in 1940, J.J. O'Leary (Cahill's managing director) having been joint owner since 1928. Subsequent purchasers of the company were: 1978 management buy-out of outside interests; 1988 bought by the Perigord Group; 1992 bought by the Clondalkin Group; 1998 bought by Adare plc; 2006 bought by Boundary plc.[204]

—O'Brien Press founded by Michael O'Brien and his father Thomas (who died suddenly later in the same year); first title is Éamonn MacThomáis's *Me Jewel and Darlin' Dublin*.[205]

—Appletree Press, publisher John Murphy, first title *Faces of the Past* appears on 10 December. Sells out the first run of 1,000 copies in a day.[206]

—Wolfhound founded by Seamus Cashman (ex IUP); first title *Proverbs and Sayings in Ireland* appears in August.[207]

—*Irish Printer* magazine begins publication.

1975

—Ireland's first feminist publisher Arlen House is founded by Catherine Rose: first title *The Female Experience: The Story of the Woman Movement in Ireland* by Catherine Rose; closed 1987; revived as a general press in 2000 (by a man).[208]

—Steve MacDonogh is approached by Neil Jordan and Des Hogan of the Irish Writers' Co-operative for advice on publishing. They publish first two titles in 1976 under the imprint Co-op Books.[209]

—Folens, the educational publisher established in 1957 by Albert Folens, a Flemish Legion nationalist escapee from Belgium, claims direct losses of £82,000 on preparation work, plus loss of £500,000 profits, on a sixteen-volume Irish language encyclopaedia when the Department of Education cancels its agreement to buy 5,000 copies of each volume. Eventually (1982)

awarded £57,600 with no loss of profits compensation. Folens died in 2003, his son Dirk (the only Irish publisher with his own aeroplane) having increasingly taken over since 1978.[210]
—Arts Act 1973 enables Arts Council to be more proactive, especially when Mervyn Wall is replaced as director in 1975 by Colm Ó Briain; David Collins appointed literature officer in November 1975.[211]
—Eight juveniles charged with setting fire to the APCK bookshop in Dawson Street; general manager Paddy Willis claims that over £50,000 worth of books were destroyed.[212]

1976
—*Books Ireland* first issue. Published by Jeremy Addis, edited by Bernard Share, designed by Jarlath Hayes. Clé advertisement lists twenty-eight members.
—Irish Book Fair revived, but dominated by 'Irish interest' books from British publishers.[213]
—Anti-trust suit in US brings to an end the British Publishers Traditional Market Agreement formally signed in 1947 but in de facto operation long before. In response, British firms step up involvement in US market e.g. Penguin's acquisition of Viking.[214]
—Dublin University Press, founded in 1734, moves in November from the Trinity campus and is forcibly merged with Brunswick Press in Sandymount.[215]
—Poolbeg founded by David Marcus and Philip MacDermott.[216]

1977
—Michael Adams begins to publish under the Four Courts Press imprint. Early titles include Jeremiah Newman's *The State of Ireland*. Previously he had published a few poetry and theology titles under the Michael Atteridge imprint (Atteridge being his mother's maiden name).[217]
—Irish Book Design Awards sponsored by Kilkenny Design Workshops initially run in parallel with the *Books Ireland* Publishers' Awards. Kilkenny scheme 'ground to a sudden halt' in 1987.[218]
—First edition of *Irish Library News* (ed. Alun Bevan) published by Library Council. Went online–only in 2009.[219]
—Raven Arts, publisher Dermot Bolger, publishes first titles (pamphlets and broadsheets sold around pubs); 'first real book' is *Priorities* by Sydney Bernard Smith in 1979.
—Closure of Grafton Street, Dublin, bookshop Combridge's which was an offshoot of a Birmingham firm. The Sibley family transformed the business into a fine art dealership which closed in 2012.

1978

—Hodges Figgis bought by the Pentos chain, for £210,000. The forty employees, in the stores in Stephen's Green, Dún Laoghaire, Donnybrook and UCD Belfield, are assured of their jobs. Previous year's pre-tax profits are 3.75 per cent on £800,000 sales (which represented about 5 per cent of the Irish market).[220]

—APCK bookshops close. APCK was set up in 1792 as an educational publisher. The bookselling side had been transformed in the 1940s by Arthur Gray who died in 1972. Manager Paddy Willis takes over the shops and establishes a stylish new chain with a book distribution arm (Andrews).[221]

—Poetry Ireland, founded by John F. Deane, begins poetry readings; the review *Poetry Ireland* (ed. David Marcus) first appeared in 1948; *Poetry Ireland Review* (ed. John Jordan) first appeared in 1981.[222]

—Clé invests several hundred pounds on a library of book publishing reference and how-to books for members. Poorly policed, within months there are only one or two titles left on the shelf.

—John Paul I dies within weeks of becoming pope, thus killing the quickie biography published by newcomer Villa Books, publisher Anthony Dwyer (ex E. J. Dwyer of New South Wales).

—Books Upstairs, South King Street, opened in May by Maurice Earls and Enda O'Doherty specialising in left-wing, feminist, small poetry presses etc.

1979

—Terry Prone's *Write – And Get Paid for it* it (Turoe Press in association with Arlen House) includes a list of forty current Irish publishers.

—Appletree Press premises in Belfast severely damaged by bomb. 'Out of business for a year'; further bomb damage in 1981 and 1982.[223]

—Urged by Clé's president, Michael O'Brien, the Arts Council provides a grant to enable the employment of Hilary Kennedy as secretary, with funding of £6,000 (two thirds the estimated cost).[224]

—Irish Bookhandling founded by Dolmen, O'Brien and Wolfhound.[225]

—Murray's *Report on the Irish Publishing Industry*, published by the Department of Commerce, UCD.

—Ireland joins the European Monetary System; the split with sterling causes fears for uniform book prices. To reduce exchange losses, the Booksellers Association draws up a sterling conversion chart with a series of bands. This is revised in 1990. Pricing of UK-published books remains a sensitive point.[226]

—Last title attributed to the Talbot Press appears.[227]

—Gill closes the bookshop in No. 50 O'Connell Street in June after 123 years' trading. Premises subsequently gutted in a fire started by intruders during Pope John Paul II's' visit in September when access to the street is restricted. Significant loss of stock and historical archive materials. Artwork etc. stored for Anthony Dwyer's Villa Books also destroyed.[228]

1980

—Mike and Noeleen Burns buy Blackstaff after Jim and Diane Gracey decide they (especially she) have had enough of the bombs. Anne Tannahill becomes managing director.[229]
—*The Bookseller* (2 February) devotes a seven-page article to Irish publishing.
—Dolmen gives up hot metal and letterpress for phototypesetting.[230]
—Irish language publisher Coiscéim founded by Pádraig Ó Snodaigh. First title *Cúirt Oibre* by Eithne Strong.
—Lar Cassidy succeeds David Collins as literature officer of the Arts Council.
—ÁIS, a specialist Irish language book distributor, established by Bord na Gaeilge in Fenian Street; manager Diarmaid Ó Cathasaigh.[231]
—To the distress of poetry lovers, the Eblana bookshop in Grafton Street closes (founded 1950).[232]
—*Lost Book Sales* UK market research published. Originally intended to help booksellers cope with the rising tide of titles published, it reveals that as much as 40 per cent of bookshop sales are from unplanned impulse buys. Thirty years later, the 60 per cent that are known and planned seem to render bricks and mortar shops vulnerable.[233]
—Irish Academic Press, having finally exhausted sales of the Irish University Press's *Parliamentary Papers*, sets up Round Hall, a specialist law publisher, beginning with *Irish Law Reports Monthly* edited by Bart Daly. For years its turnover exceeds the parent company. Bought by Sweet & Maxwell, a Thomson subsidiary, in 1995, following Butterworth's entry into Dublin in 1988.[234]

1981

—Aosdána scheme details announced. Scheme identifies 200 (later 250) self-elected writers and artists for honour. Original suggestion from Anthony Cronin to Charles Haughey.[235]
—VAT on books increased to 15 per cent; when it was charged at point of entry Irish booksellers' cash flow was seriously at risk.
—Death of Devin Adair Garrity who inherited the US publishing company Devin Adair in 1939 and devoted 10 per cent of his otherwise eccentric list to Irish interests and authors, including Patrick Kavanagh.[236]

—Book trade slump forces Hodges Figgis to close Stephen's Green shop after nine years and go back to Dawson Street, to No. 6, a site previously occupied by Browne & Nolan. The Donnybrook branch also closed.[237]
—Clé *Manual of Book Publishing* launched; reviewed in *Books Ireland* April 1982.
—Caoimhín Ó Marcaigh (ex Mercier) acquires Sáirséal & Dill and renames it Sáirséal Ó Marcaigh. Sáirséal Ó Marcaigh acquired in 2009 by Cló Iar-Chonnacht.[238]
—Tycooly, a contract book publisher for UN agencies, founded in Dún Laoghaire; goes into liquidation three years later owing £313,000, despite lavish UN subsidies and IDA grants.[239]
—Tyrone Guthrie Centre, Annaghmakerig, residential retreat for artists, opens.
—*Publishers Weekly* (23 January) devotes a forty-page special feature to a kindly overview of Irish publishing.
—Willis and its distribution arm Andrews go into liquidation with trade creditors of £548,000, blaming difficult trading conditions worsened by the punt's fall to less than 80 per cent of sterling, causing price rises and admin problems.[240]
—The Children's Press, an imprint of Anvil, set up.[241]

1982

—Brandon founded by Steve MacDonogh, previously of Co-op Books, with the aid of finance from Bernie Goggin of Dingle and Udarás na Gaeltachta. Dingle office formally opened by An Taoiseach Charles Haughey, 22 August.[242]
—Gill & Macmillan begins third-party distribution from new premises in Goldenbridge. First client is Brandon.
—Gill Hess resigns as sales director of Poolbeg/Ward River and sets up as an independent sales agent; quickly attracts major British publishers as clients.[243]
—The old, established Belfast bookseller Erskine Mayne sells out.
—Booksellers Association (Irish branch) gives honorary life membership to Eoin O'Keeffe, the long-time manager of James Duffy of Westmoreland Street. O'Keeffe had been the secretary of the quiescent Book Association of Ireland (fl. 1943–51) which in 1944 produced a *Catalogue of Irish Books in Print*.[244]
—Books unexpectedly rated zero for VAT; implemented some weeks after the budget. 'Sales in the general books department of Hanna's the day before amounted to some £57. Several thousand on the day.'[245]
—Irish Books Marketing Group founded to exploit the opportunity presented by the removal of VAT. Two booksellers: Harold Clarke and Fred Hanna; and two publishers: Michael Gill and Sean O'Boyle, then of Veritas (later established Columba Press).[246]

—Women in Publishing inaugural meeting.[247]
—*IBM Typography Scope and Techniques* published by Officina Typographica in UCG shows how good book design can be achieved with the IBM Composer (launched 1966), the first desktop typesetting machine, producing proportionally spaced type with a 'golfball' head; widely used for production of cheap camera-ready copy, especially for academic books.[248]
—Report by Francis Fishwick on book competition in Britain and Ireland identifies an unlikely 50 per cent real growth in the Irish retail market between 1975 and 1980. Notes that Irish buyers do not seem interested in hunting for bargains caused by the split from sterling.[249]

1983

—First edition of the *Clé Directory of the Irish Book Trade* (subsequent editions as *Clé Directory of the Irish Book World* 1985, 1990, 1991).
—Eason's O'Connell Street moves magazines to the side and back to make room in the front and centre of the ground floor for books.[250]
—Hodges Figgis sells the Dún Laoghaire shop to Irish Bookshops Ltd (trading as Book Stop), formed by John Davey, ex managing director of Hodges Figgis. The Blackrock Book Stop opens in 1984.[251]
—Book House Ireland established, combining Clé and the Irish Branch of the Booksellers Association. Successive administrators: Sheila Crowley (later of Hodder, Curtis Brown), Clara Clark and Cecily Golden. Wound up June 1992.

1984

—Anne Tannahill of Blackstaff, the first woman and first from Northern Ireland, elected president of Clé.
—Third series of *An Leabharlann* commences publication.
—Apple, Lotus and Microsoft start to spend substantial amounts on computer manual printing with the traditional book printers such as Cahill's and Mount Salus, ultimately pushing Irish book publishers out.
—Ion Mills (ex Pan) and Gemma O'Connor start to represent/publicise Dolmen, O'Brien, Wolfhound and Mercier in Britain.[252]
—Antony Farrell (ex Orbis, Hutchinson etc.) sets up the Lilliput Press in Westmeath. Moves to Arbour Hill in Dublin in 1989. First title *The Rock Garden* by Mullingar man Leo Daly.[253]
—Wholesaler Dermot McDermott's spectacular rise and collapse leaves Irish publishers with £94,000 losses.[254]

—S. & J. Cleary publishes *Irish Books in Print*, a 1,000-page listing of 9,500 English language titles and 1,000 Irish language titles 'either from or about Ireland' separately classified by author, subject matter and title.

—Róisín Conroy (ex information officer of the Irish Transport and General Workers Union) and Mary-Paul Keane of Irish Feminist Information set up Attic Press; taken over by Cork UP in 1997. Róisín Conroy died in 2007.[255]

1985

—Sean O'Boyle (ex Veritas) sets up Columba Press; first titles are *Masses with Young People*; *Disturbing the Peace;* and *Funeral Homilies.*

—Treasa Coady commences publishing with Town House/Country House imprints. Moves up a league with the investment in and launch of Deirdre Purcell in 1991.

—Inaugural meeting of the Association of Freelance Editors, Proofreaders and Indexers, founded by Pat Carroll, Anna Farmar, Helen Litton and Siobhán Parkinson. First chair Tony Farmar.

—Irish language book publisher Cló Iar-Chonnacht founded by Micheál Ó Conghaile to publish Irish language books and traditional music.

—Amstrad PCW 8256, the first widely used word processor for writers, launched at £750 for the full system. Early adopters include *The Irish Times* journalists Maeve Binchy, Marion FitzGerald and Michael Viney. The incompatibility of its disks with any other systems (for editing, typesetting) would cause problems later.[256]

—Captain Seán Feehan resigns as MD of Mercier, succeeded by John Spillane.[257]

—*Ireland in Fiction* (vol. 2) by Fr Stephen Brown and Desmond Clarke includes all novels dealing with Ireland published between 1918 and 1960. Published by Royal Carbery Books, publisher Mary Feehan of Mercier.

—Clonmel specialist typesetting firm Text Processing Ltd claims to be able to read over 150 different types of input disks/programs.[258]

—Desktop publishing begins to be available with the launch of the Apple LaserWriter printer (with PostScript fonts), early versions of PageMaker software, etc. Used in large professional offices and design bureaux in Ireland from the late 1980s.[259]

1986

—Jonathan Williams commences his literary agency, the first in the country; in 1998 the Lisa Richards Agency and the Book Bureau follow and by 2010 there are five.[260]

—Irish Bookhandling collapses. Manager Máire Block accused of fraud on behalf of her father's company Dolmen. Orphaned publishers join Attic and Brandon in Gill & Macmillan's distribution arm.[261]
—Noel Browne's *Against the Tide* published by Gill & Macmillan. Sells 42,000 copies between October and December.[262]
—Wordwell, publisher of books and magazines on archaeology and history, established. *Books Ireland* added in 2013.
—Eric Pembrey, (*Dictionary of Irish Biography sub nom* Herbert Pembrey), who had joined the business in 1954, inherits Greene's bookshop from his father.

1987
—Irish Book Sales established with the aid of CTT to promote sales and marketing initiatives especially overseas; members include Anne Tannahill of Blackstaff, Philip MacDermott of Poolbeg, John Spillane of Mercier, Michael O'Brien of O'Brien Press and Seamus Cashman of Wolfhound.
—Liam Miller, Dolmen Press and first president of Clé, dies in Our Lady's Hospice, Harold's Cross, aged 63.[263]
—Irish Writers Union set up, largely in opposition to continued censorship: chairman Jack Harte, secretary Bill McCormack (alias poet Hugh Maxton).[264]
—Francis Fishwick's report *The Market for Books in the Republic of Ireland* commissioned by the Irish Books Marketing Group; refutes legend of prodigious Irish reading.
—Dolmen Press assets sold off in liquidation; stock bought by Colin Smythe.[265]
—*Poems on the DART* edited by Jonathan Williams begin in January.[266]
—Clé issues a Code of Practice guideline for publishers in their dealings with authors based on a British Publishers Association document.[267]
—Special feature in *Books Ireland* (February) lists sixteen freelance editors, forty-seven book designers and nine miscellaneous service providers, including indexers, promotion and production specialists.
—Waterstones first Irish shop opens at No. 6 Dawson Street, where Hodges Figgis had previously been for many years. First manager Marie Fitzgerald (ex Eason's, Hodges Figgis) with Bert Wright (ex Waterstones Edinburgh). Innovatively open on Sundays and until 10.30 p.m. In 1992, Tim Waterstone says it has become one of the top twelve stores in the whole chain. Closed 2011.[268]

1988
—Clondalkin Paper Mills, the last white-paper mill in the country, closes finally after bitter industrial disputes and several unavailing attempts to

revive it. *The Irish Times*, 20 September 1989, records the final sale of the site to developers.

—Gemma and Kevin Barry take over her mother's bookshop in Bray, expanding into Grafton Street (1990), Rathmines and Kilkenny (1994), Stillorgan (1997) and Galway (1998).[269]

—*To School Through the Fields* published by Brandon Books; publisher claims 142,000 copies sold between May and November.[270]

—A year after Waterstones' arrival in Dawson Street, the Paperback Centre closes its Suffolk Street branch. [271]

—Institute of Irish Studies opens at Liverpool University.[272]

—An International Writers Conference, associated with the Dublin Millennium celebrations, culminates in a public reading in Kilmainham.[273]

—National Library of Ireland takes over publication of *Irish Publishing Record*. The edition covering 1989 is published in 1990 and identifies 923 titles from 511 publishers including the Stationery Office and several semi-state bodies. The series is discontinued after 1993.

—Mrs Anne Spicer submits the Bible to the Censorship Board as containing graphic obscenity and endorsing polygamy, slavery, sexual abuse, mutilation, ritual murder and violence. The Board declines to act, referring to its artistic and historic merit and importance.[274]

—Jeremy Addis takes over editorship of *Books Ireland* from Bernard Share.[275]

—Census of Production identifies 370 outlets involved in the selling of books and/or stationery with sales of £79 million of which Dublin outlets represent 45 per cent.

—Charles Pick *Developing Publishing in Ireland* report recommends Irish publishers do more to expand international sales, improve internal management and suggests Irish books are significantly underpriced.[276]

1989

—Louis Cullen's history of Eason's, *Eason and Son*, published by Eason's.

—Roberts Rinehart set up by Jack van Zandt of Mizen Books, Schull, Co. Cork; later concentrated on co-publishing with the US; in March 1997 set up the Irish American Book Company for sales and distribution of Irish books in the US. This collapsed in 2000, leaving Irish publishers with 'substantial losses'.[277]

—Controversy surrounds the GPA Irish Writers Award as Graham Greene, the final adjudicator, ignores the panel's choice (John Banville's *Book of Evidence*) and selects outsider Vincent McDonnell's *The Broken Commitment* as the £50,000 winner. A compromise eventually reached.[278]

—Parsons Bookshop, Baggot Street bridge, haunt of 1950s literati from Patrick Kavanagh and Brendan Behan onwards, closes after forty years. May O'Flaherty died two years later.[279]
—Samuel Beckett dies.
—Belfast bookseller Anna Crane (ex University Bookshop) moves out of new books. *Books Ireland* (May 1989) claims it was in apprehension of the promised Waterstones Belfast branch and the potential ending of the Net Book Agreement.
—Brandon Books makes an out of court settlement for £72,000 as a result of the Kerry Babies libel case.[280]
—Pat Donlon appointed director of the National Library.
—Blackwater, started by Tom Turley in 1976 with Tom Barrington's *Discovering Kerry*, before he joined Folens, revived under John O'Connor.[281]
—Mary-Paul Keane leaves Attic Press to open Síle na Gig feminist bookshop in Galway.
—Fatwa declared against Salman Rushdie; Steve MacDonogh leads Irish response.[282]

1990
—Hodges Figgis follows Pentos policy in challenging Net Book Agreement by reducing Booker prize shortlist novels by 25 per cent; soon after starts discounting Irish titles. Irish publishers retaliate by refusing to supply.[283]
—ColourBooks established to specialise in book printing, filling the gap caused by established printers concentrating on computer manuals; closed in 2011.

1991
—Bookseller Con Collins (an ex school teacher), under commercial pressure from Waterstones and others, publishes his first title *The Cork Diary*.[284]
—Census identifies 2,696 people describing themselves as 'author, editor or journalist': more than twice the number for twenty years before.
—Dublin Writers Museum and Irish Writers Centre set up in Nos 18–19 Parnell Square; office space made available to Irish Writers Union, Irish Children's Book Trust, Society of Playwrights and other bookish groups.[285]
—Hodges Figgis, 'seeking to bring terms of trading in line with suppliers in the UK', raises discounts from 35 per cent to 42.5 per cent (45 per cent for paperbacks); and propose a ninety-day credit period.[286]
—Timothy O'Keefe (born Kinsale 1926), London-based publisher of Brian O'Nolan, Patrick Kavanagh and Francis Stuart, dies.

—Captain Seán Feehan, founder of Mercier Press, dies aged 74.[287]
—The first three volumes of the *Field Day Anthology of Irish Writing* published to considerable controversy, with critics complaining of the lack of women's voices and excess of Northern men.

1992
—Cork University Press, originally founded in 1925 by Alfred O'Rahilly, revitalised; Sarah Wilbourne (ex Longman) appointed publisher.[288]
—Raven Arts folded into New Island; managing director Edwin Higel, Dermot Bolger editorial director. In 2011, Edwin's poor health forces New Island temporarily to cease publishing.[289]
—Attic Press publisher Róisín Conroy publishes her *So You Want to be Published?*
—Blackstaff named as *Sunday Times* UK Small Publisher of the Year. Also receives AIB Better Ireland Communications Award and (in 1991) the Christophe Ewart-Briggs Memorial Award.[290]
—Irish Copyright Licensing Agency set up by Clé and the Irish Writers Union. Administered by barrister Muireann Ó Briain. Orla O'Sullivan appointed administrator in January 1994; Samantha Holman full-time chief executive from November 2001.
—Hughes & Hughes (formerly incorporated as Overseas Publications in 1957) opens bookshop in the departures area of Dublin Airport. Derek Hughes was sales manager of Overseas until he succeeded Bobby Hughes as MD in 1987.[291]
—First of a series of Clé surveys of publisher activity, published in September, estimates total turnover of Irish publishers at £27.7 million of which 71 per cent is educational. Irish publishers' share of trade market is 18 per cent.
—The outcry against Madonna's *Sex* forces re-formation of Censorship Board, which had been allowed to lapse.[292]
—A. & A. Farmar established in Ranelagh by Anna and Tony Farmar.

1993
—Man Booker Prize winners: Roddy Doyle 1993; John Banville 2005; Anne Enright 2007.
—National Print Museum founded in the Garrison Chapel, Beggars Bush.[293]
—New NI publisher Colourpoint established by railway buff and lay preacher Norman Johnston and his wife Sheila. Johnston died in 2014 and his sons Malcolm (finance) and Wesley (editorial) took over.[294]

—Greene's of Clare Street celebrates 150th anniversary, having been founded in 1843. When the founder John Greene died in 1899 he was laid out in the shop.[295]

1994

—Competition Authority (28 October 1994) challenges Gill & Macmillan's distribution contract with eight publishers. After deletion of a clause relating to fixed prices, the agreements are passed.
—Fergal Tobin appointed editorial director of Gill & Macmillan.
—The last edition of *Irish Publishing Record* (actually published in 1996) identifies 1,480 titles from 329 publishers.
—After a 1992 EC court ruling, the Competition Authority declares the Net Book Agreement's aims are to prevent, restrict or distort competition, so refuses a licence.[296]
—International IMPAC award announced with £100,000 prize to the winner. First awards 1996; Irish winners Colm Tóibín 2006, Colum McCann 2011.[297]
—Ireland Literature Exchange (Literature Ireland from 2016) set up. Three directors to date: Marc Caball (1995–2003), Dara O'Hare (2003–04) and Sinéad Mac Aodha (2004 to date). From 2016, the organisation is funded by Culture Ireland and the Arts Council.[298]
—September: the Competition Authority refuses to authorise a currency conversion chart drawn up by the Booksellers Association to be applied to the cover price of books imported from the UK on the grounds that it is anti-competitive.[299]

1995

—A group of authors under the auspice of the Irish Writers Union takes children's book publisher Aran Books, run by ex Clé administrator Cecily Golden, to court. The following year the judge finds in the group's favour.[300]
—Amazon begins to sell books online. First profits announced in 2001.
—Coopers & Lybrand report *The Future of the Irish Book Publishing Industry* published in July.[301]
—September: after an extremely contentious meeting of the council of the British Publishers Association it is decided that the Association will no longer support the Net Book Agreement.[302]
—Seamus Heaney wins Nobel Prize for Literature.
—Belfast printing company W.G. Baird buys Blackstaff.[303]
—UCD Press established by Barbara and Stephen Mennell.[304]

1996

—The festival l'Imaginaire Irlandais brings writers and publishers to various venues in France.

—Ireland is the theme for the Frankfurt Book Fair. Clé publishes *Books from Ireland: Ireland and its Diaspora.*

—Copyright extended to seventy years after the death of the author. Joyce, Yeats, and other estates, having been briefly in the public domain, now have a new lease of copyright, causing some considerable transition problems.

—*Books Ireland* publishes *Irish Writers Guide 1996–7*, edited by Jeremy Addis and Shirley Kelly. Second edition for 1998–99 published in 1998.

—Columba Mercier Distribution established.[305]

—Argosy buys CK Distributors from Mercier, signalling expansionary intentions in book wholesaling.[306]

1997

—Over 500 delegates of the Booksellers Association of Great Britain and Ireland meet for their annual conference in Dublin. The Irish branch no longer maintains a separate office in Dublin and with the demise of the Net Book Agreement many members wonder if the subscription (set at 0.05 per cent of turnover) is worth it.

—Lar Cassidy, Literature Officer of the Arts Council, dies aged 47.[307]

—Dubray buys Paperback Centre in Stillorgan Shopping Centre, Dublin.

—Children's Books Ireland formed out of merger of the Children's Literature Association of Ireland and the Irish Children's Book Trust.

—December: final meeting of Brandon Book Publishers. Ownership transferred to the new imprint Mount Eagle Publications. Bernie Goggin retires.[308]

1998

—July: Colin Smythe awarded honorary LLD by Trinity.

—Michael Adams and Frank Cass separate. Irish Academic Press continues to publish with a small office in Dublin.

—Waterstones joins Hodges Figgis, facing each other across Dawson Street, as part of the HMV Group.[309]

1999

—Fred Hanna's Nassau Street shop sold to Eason's. It traced its origins to the 1840s, being purchased by Fred's grandfather in 1906. Shop first moved to Morison's Chambers and then closed in 2009.

—Penguin pays Nuala O'Faolain an advance of £500,000 for a book she claims to 'have barely begun'. In 1998, John Connolly of *The Irish Times* received £350,000 for his crime novel and a $1 million US book deal.[310]
—Steve MacDonogh's autobiography *Open Book* published.

2000
—Copyright and Related Rights Act 2000 (No. 28 of 2000) passed.
—Town House and Simon & Schuster sign joint venture agreement.[311]
—Gill & Macmillan moves to purpose-built premises at Park West.
—Herbert Pembrey and his son Eric of Greene's both die. David, Eric's son, becomes the fourth generation to own the shop.[312]
—Michael Gill becomes president of the Federation of European Publishers, 2000–01, founded in 1967. Fergal Tobin president in 2010–11.

2001
—Seamus Cashman sells Wolfhound to Merlin. It ceases trading in 2010.

2002
—Penguin Ireland set up; publisher Michael McLoughlin (ex Hodder marketer), fiction editor Brendan Barrington.[313]
—Hodder Headline Ireland set up (now Hachette); first title Sheila Flanagan *Destinations* (2003).
—Nielsen Irish Consumer Market surveys established; provide objective market data for the first time. By 2011, Nielsen claims market coverage of 70 per cent; observers think 60–64 per cent more likely.

2003
—John Davey (ex MD of Hodges Figgis) sells his Book Stop shops in Dún Laoghaire and Blackrock to Dubray. Davey invests in Ashfield Press with Susan Waine (daughter of Jarlath Hayes) and Gerry O'Connor.[314]
—Despite Michael Gill's declaration to the *Publishers Weekly* reporters in 1980 that Dublin was not an appropriate place to publish fiction, Gill & Macmillan sets up a popular fiction imprint called Tivoli (editor Alison Walsh). It publishes twenty-four titles between 2003 and 2006.
—Seán O'Keefe and Peter O'Connell set up Liberties Press.
—Clodagh Feehan, the captain's granddaughter, a software developer, joins Mercier; MD from January 2004.
—Butterworth (Ireland), established October 1977, renamed LexisNexis Butterworth.

—SPI – the Society of Publishers in Ireland – a networking organisation for the Irish publishing industry is founded by Susan Rossney (Round Hall), Rachel Pierce (then of O'Brien Press) and Emma Byrne (O'Brien Press). Over 200 staff from various publishers attend launch party in September.

2004

—Google announces its plans to scan books in major libraries.
—Judge Chin's decision in *Authors Guild v Google*, 22 March 2011.
—'Long tail' theory proposed by Chris Anderson in *Wired* (October 2004) underscores viability of Internet bookshops.

2005

—Trinity awards an honorary doctorate to Michael Adams of Four Courts for services to academic publishing; he died in 2009 aged 71.[315]
—The new Nonsuch Press first title, P. Walsh's *Images of Ireland*, published.[316]
—Institute of Chartered Accountants in Ireland (later CAI) begins business publishing.
—ISO 2108:2005 replaces the 10-digit ISBN with a new 13-digit book identifier.
—Kenny's of Galway lets its high street premises to concentrate from the beginning of 2006 on online business from an industrial estate.[317]
—Michael Gill succeeded as managing director of Gill & Macmillan by finance director Dermot O'Dwyer.[318]

2006

—Eason's makes major investment to combine its Santry and Crumlin warehouses in one 170,000ft warehouse in St Margaret's, near Dublin airport. Move causes considerable disruption to book wholesaling, and is not well timed.[319]
—November: general meeting agrees constitution of the newly formed IBBY (the Irish section of the International Board on Books for Young People founded in 1953).
—April: Ivan O'Brien succeeds his father Michael as managing director of O'Brien Press; Michael continues as publisher.
—R. & M. Loeber's magnum opus *A Guide to Irish Fiction 1650–1900* is published. Introduction identifies how Irish publishing shifted from the provinces to Dublin in the eighteenth and nineteenth centuries and then Dublin succumbed in the late nineteenth century to the dominance of British publishing.[320]
—Mercier hits new turnover high of €1.2 million.[321]
—Ex investment banker Barry O'Callaghan engineers a reverse takeover of 160-year-old US publisher Houghton Mifflin by his company Riverdeep

(founded 1995 as an e-learning company). A year later HM Riverdeep buys Harcourt from Reed Elsevier for €4 billion. The new company is then the biggest US educational publisher. In 2008, massive cuts in US educational spending force restructuring and O'Callaghan loses his 38 per cent shareholding and admits he had paid too much for both acquisitions.[322]
—Vol. III (the eighteenth century) of *The Oxford History of the Irish Book* published. Vol. IV (nineteenth century) and Vol. V (twentieth century) published in 2011.

2007
—Irish Books and Media of St Paul Minnesota closes after forty years' importing Irish books into the US.
—Amazon launches Kindle first generation e-book reader.
—Greene's bookshop closes its historic Clare Street premises and moves to Sandyford.
—Bord na Leabhar Gaeilge, which traced its existence back to 1952, closes; 2007 expenditure was €1.8 million.
—Transworld Ireland, a subsidiary of Random House, set up; publisher is Eoin McHugh, ex Hanna, Eason's.[323]

2008
—Maureen Kenny, founder of Kenny's Bookshop, Galway, dies.[324]
—Mercier acquires Anvil, which began as the book publishing arm of *The Kerryman* in 1947, specialising in memoirs relating to the national struggle 1916–24.[325]

2009
—Arts Council funding of Irish Writers Centre slashed from €200,000 to nothing following controversy about salaries paid to staff.[326]
—Irish Public Lending Right scheme established after lobbying by the Irish Copyright Licensing Agency and the Irish Writers Union and an EU legal ruling; first payments 2010.[327]
—Scottish distributor BookSource takes over Columbia Mercier Distribution.[328]

2010
—Siobhán Parkinson, publisher of Little Island books, becomes the first Laureate na nÓg, an initiative of the Arts Council in conjunction with Children's Books Ireland, the Minister for Children and Poetry Ireland.

—Dublin becomes UNESCO City of Literature.
—Alan Hanna dies.
—Joe Ardle McArdle – barrister, linguist, academic, broadcaster, author, and publisher – dies aged 76. He set up his own imprint O'Dell Adair after the collapse of the Irish Writers Co-op in 1987, with the help of Philip MacDermott of Poolbeg. NLI catalogue lists six titles.[329]
—Gill & Macmillan acquires the book publishing assets of Carroll Education.
—Nonsuch (founded in 2005 and having published eighty titles since then) rebranded as The History Press Ireland when the UK's The History Press acquires Alan Sutton's NPI Media Group.
—Eoin Purcell (ex Nonsuch, ex Mercier) launches an online newsletter Irish Publishing News.
—Clé changes its name to Publishing Ireland. Members are not consulted.
—BookSource closes CMD Book Source; Mercier to be distributed by Argosy.[330]
—Steve MacDonogh, founder of Brandon Books, dies unexpectedly, aged 61.
—Hughes & Hughes go into receivership; Eason's takes over airport outlets. Dublin's Terminal 2 slot awarded to W.H. Smith.[331]

2011

—Cahill's Printers, trading under that name since 1866, renamed Clondalkin Pharma and Healthcare (Clonshaugh) Ltd by the Dutch owners.[332]
—Fred Hanna dies. His famous rare book collection fetches €350,000 at Mealy's auction.[333]
—Census reveals that 6,721 people described themselves as 'authors, writers & journalists' – nearly three times the 1981 figure.
—At the Frankfurt Book Fair, O'Brien Press announces the acquisition of Brandon Books titles following the 2010 death of founder Steve MacDonogh.
—Waterstones close two of its five Irish shops, including the flagship Dawson Street shop and Jervis Street, after £8 million losses; fifty jobs lost. Owners HMV keep Hodges Figgis, across the road in Dawson Street.[334]

2012

—New Island revived with Eoin Purcell as editor.
—Despairing of the future of the trade, Clodagh Feehan, MD of Mercier, returns to a hi-tech job in London.
—Publishing Ireland in financial difficulties. Frank Scott-Lennon negotiates departure of staff. Public funding is cut off. Jean Harrington, appointed executive director in January, is let go.

—Irish Government Publications, first opened in 1922, closes its shop in Molesworth Street.[335]
—Competition Authority prevents Eason's taking over Argosy.[336]

2013
—Columba Press and Mercier finally join Gill & Macmillan distribution service in April.
—A print-on-demand publisher from Sligo called HardPress claims a total of 131,000 titles (ISBNs) available; the largest print publisher Gill & Macmillan has 2,400.
—The sixth generation of the Gill family joins the firm: Ruth Gill joins Gill & Macmillan.[337] The Gill family re-takes full ownership of Gill & Macmillan, buying out the Macmillan/Holtzbrink shares. By January 2016 the company is renamed M.H. Gill & Co.
—Copyright Review, proposing the establishment of an intellectual property court in Ireland, by Professor Eoin O'Dell (TCD) *et al.* published.[338]
—Pearson (47 per cent) and Bertlesman (53 per cent) combine their publishing holdings to create Penguin Random House. Irish houses Penguin Ireland, Transworld Ireland and imprints Black Swan Ireland and Doubleday Ireland affected.
—*Books Ireland* bought by Wordwell, publisher of books and magazines on archaeology and history. Jeremy Addis's final issue December 2013.
—Anonymous letter by Irish book editor to the *Guardian,* 'Problems at work', of December 2013 complains, 'publishing is dead, especially here in Ireland where the market is small and there are few jobs … I work in a dying industry.'
—Laureate for Irish Fiction, worth €150,000 for three years, launched. Supported by Arts Council, University College Dublin and New York University creative writing schools. Arts Council chair Pat Moylan says the award would 'place Irish writing at the forefront of global public thought'. Anne Enright appointed January 2015.[339]
—Roads Publishing, part of Danielle Ryan's high-end design group (including perfume and film), founded. Maeve Convery (ex The History Press Ireland) publishing director. First titles ten classics and highly designed large-format coffee-table items such as *Libraries of the World.*[340]

2014
—Liberties (in Terenure) follows Lilliput (in Arbour Hill) in opening a shop for sales of their books. The Liberties shop closes in 2018.

—April: Kevin Barry, former Central Bank economist and stockbroker, latterly of Dubray Books, dies. Dubray Books expanded rapidly after he left NCB Stockbrokers in 1993 to work in the shops full time, opening branches in Rathmines, Stillorgan, Kilkenny and Galway to add to the Bray and Grafton Street outlets.[341]
—Eoin Purcell, ex Mercier, editorial director of New Island and author/publisher of the online Irish Publishing News, always a great advocate of e-books etc., appointed 'editorial leader' of Amazon's new print publishing venture in London.[342]
—Gill & Macmillan pulls out of third level and professional publishing, citing low sales and margins.[343]
—Cló Iar-Chonnacht publishes Cian Ó hÉigeartaigh and Aoileann Nic Gearailt *Sáirséal & Dill 1947–1981*; by far the most attractive and thorough history of an Irish publishing house (available only in Irish). Reviewed in the *Times Literary Supplement* on 5 June 2015, fittingly with the first English language version of *Cré na Cille*.

2015
—Arts Council cuts regular funding to O'Brien Press from €63,000 to €10,000 and rejects most of its title-by-title applications.[344]
—After an 11.2 per cent cut in its income, the Arts Council NI cuts all its regular funding to Blackstaff after forty-four years, without discussion or notice, effective from 1 April 2015. Blackstaff's previous grant was £82,000; Blackstaff is invited to apply for title-by-title assistance.
—C.J. Fallon acquired by Levine Leichtman Capital Partners after two years in the hands of Lonsdale Capital Partners.[345]
—Sarah Bannan, literature officer with the Arts Council, publishes her first novel, with J.K. Rowling's English publisher.
—Penguin Random House Ireland established to combine sales and publicity for Penguin Ireland and Transworld under Michael McLoughlin. Gill Hess no longer involved.[346]

2016
—Irish Writers Union circulates a letter to sixteen publishers as part of the US-started Fair Contract Initiative calling for the removal of draconian provisions (habitually removed by agents) including return of rights of unsupported titles, quarterly royalty payment, sharing of legal risk, authors to retain copyright, authors to retain final say in regard to text, etc.

—First book banned for eighteen years by the Censorship Board: *The Raped Little Runaway* by Jean Martin.[347]

2017

—April: Colourpoint purchases Blackstaff from W.G. Baird.
—May: Ruth Gill, aged 38, becomes the sixth generation of the family to head up Gill. Her father Michael remains as chairman.
—August: Carraig Books, Blackrock, premises sold.
—Eoin McHugh, publisher since 2007, leaves Transworld. Some months later becomes HarperCollins publishing director for Ireland.
—June: special edition of *The Bookseller* covers Irish publishing.

2018

—Following a publicity campaign by Tramp Press and Publishing Ireland's negotiations with the committee of the Man Booker Prize, it is agreed that from January 2018 Irish publishers will be eligible to nominate titles for consideration.
—October: Anna Burns wins the Man Booker Prize for *Milkman*, published by Faber. She is the first writer from Northern Ireland to win the prize.

Appendix

An Estimate of the Number of Printed Books Published in Ireland Since 1551

The task is to provide a framework for the history by estimating the number of books published in Ireland since the very first in 1551. It will be impossible unfortunately to justify the precision of Google's estimate of 129,864,880 books ever published – but then Google could not either.[1]

As is usual with book trade statistics, the definitions, limits and boundaries to any attempt to quantify the business are legion. We can start with the basic question: what is a book, i.e. what are we counting?

UNESCO defines a 'book' as a bound non-periodical publication with at least forty-nine pages (thus excluding many favourite children's books); the US postal service limits the definition to a publication of at least twenty-four pages; the Irish VAT system says eight pages plus a cover.

Others say a book is defined by its binding, which excludes the scroll, in which the books of antiquity appeared for a thousand years or more; also boxed sets of prints, concertina folds, etc.

A customary usage also allows the use of 'book' to describe a subset of a larger volume as in the Bible or *Les Misérables*.

One title may be in multiple volumes, in multiple bindings and reprinted multiple times in multiple countries. Bibliographers distinguish an edition (substantially a new text) from an impression, printing or issue of the same basic text. Publishers have by no means been scrupulous in distinguishing the two. 'To print 750 copies of a novel and divide this into 5 "editions" of 150, announcing the exhaustion of each puny infant with a prodigious flourish is ridiculous,' complained the founder of Methuen in 1893. The advent of stereo plates in the nineteenth century confused this issue, especially after the 1890 Chace Act insisted that in order to establish copyright books must be manufactured in the US. The plates ensured that exactly the same text was printed in the US as in Britain, except for the preliminary metadata. Other variants invented by publishers to add value to the basic text include special bindings, deluxe or large paper editions, abridged editions, large print editions, school editions and even pirated editions.

Many countries, notably Soviet Russia, have not distinguished between private or commercial and official publications. For Western countries where the distinction is clear, it is customary to exclude official publications such as advance copies of Bills and Parliamentary Reports from the count. To exclude the productions of Irish state-sponsored bodies, for instance from the 1960–80 period, would significantly impoverish the reality. (Clé did not. A promotional document called *Books from Ireland January–June 1974* stoically started with the An Foras Forbartha's *Car Number Projections by County for 1985 and 1986.* The Books from Ireland series came to an end in December 1974.) In the 1980s, a new difficulty arose as the Central Statistical Office included computer manuals from Apple and Microsoft as 'book exports'.

Source

Although trade and educational book publishers are the main source of such books, there has always been enormous output from one-off publishers such as local history societies, companies, etc. all creating intellectual property, not to mention semi-state bodies. The volume of one-off publishing can be large. The last *Irish Publishing Record* that identified publishers (in 1989) discovered that 923 titles were identified from as many as 511 separate publishers. Membership of Clé at the time was no more than sixty. On the other hand, these sixty would have included the most active publishers responsible for hundreds of titles. Given that 70 per cent of Irish ISBNs issued were issued to a core group of seventy-one publishers, we might reasonably multiply the output of the core group of active publishers by 1.4 to get an estimate of the total.

Evidence for Output Since 1551

Since there is no single complete count we have to assemble data from different sources.

Sixteenth and Seventeenth Centuries

The first printed book was published in Dublin in 1551. The output in the two centuries since 1551 can be estimated from the regional data gathered for the early English Short Title Catalogue. This is a listing of titles garnered from library holdings up to 1801. It estimates 2,338 titles (including e.g. statutes and official publications) up to 1699. In the appendix to *Reading Ireland*, Raymond Gillespie estimates book production in seventeenth-century Ireland, giving a total output of 2,247 titles of which official publications (statutes, proclamations etc.) were 1,057, resulting in a balance of 1,190.

Eighteenth Century

The Eighteenth-century Short Title Catalogue (ESTC) found 8,939 titles published in the first half of the century and 14,439 in the second: a total of 23,378.

Nineteenth Century

The Nineteenth-century Short Title Catalogue (NSTC) carries on the ESTC technique up to 1919. It covers all British Isles, colonial and US titles from 1801 to 1919, and says that there were 21,000 Irish titles published in the period, of which 18,000 came from Dublin and 1,872 from Belfast.

Unfortunately, Series III of the NSTC, which covers the period from 1871 to 1919, has a serious undercounting problem. If we compare the NSTC Dublin-published data with the holdings of the National Library (which took over the stock of the Royal Dublin Society in 1890), publisher by publisher, we can see that the NSTC undercounts by an average of half, with variants favouring high-literature publishers such as Maunsel and discriminating against reference books such as those published by Thom.[2]

Table 11. Comparison of NSTC with NLI holdings, 1871–1919

Publisher	*NSTC*	*NLI*	*NSTC/NLI*
Duffy	135	373	0.36
Gill	696	1,282	0.54
Hodges	500	967	0.52
Thom	83	369	0.22
Smith/Eason	35	61	0.67
Talbot	91	164	0.55
Maunsel	279	387	0.72
Sealy Bryers	209	414	0.50
Browne & Nolan	104	382	0.27
Totals	2,132	4,399	0.48 (av.)

Twentieth Century

1900–1919: For the period 1900 to 1919 NSTC estimates for Dublin and Belfast found 2,796 titles. If we double that, as the table above suggests, we get 5,600.

1922: probably no more than 100 titles a year published in Ireland. The leading literary publisher, Talbot Press, published an average of ten titles a year between 1922 and 1970. Maunsel averaged seventeen titles a year between 1912 and 1925.

1944: A listing published in 1944 by the Book Association of Ireland identified 381 books published in Ireland between 1938 and 1943, i.e. seventy-six titles a year. Half of these titles come from three publishers: M.H. Gill, Talbot and Browne & Nolan.

1960: National Library catalogue records only thirty-eight titles published in that year by the principal Irish trade publishers, as follows: Browne & Nolan (3), Clonmore & Reynolds (9), Dolmen (10), James Duffy (1), M. H. Gill (4), Mercier (8), Talbot (3).

1968: Eileen Power, University College Dublin librarian, commences publication of the annual *Irish Publishing Record*, identifying from various libraries 424 titles published in Ireland in 1967 from 129 publishers including government and semi-state publications. Only eight firms (Catholic Truth Society, Gill, Dolmen, Mercier, Scepter, Educational Co., Fallons and the Stationery Office) produce ten or more. Ninety-three publishers produce only one title.

1969: *Irish Publishing Record* identifies 992 titles from 209 publishers, of which 349 come from Irish University Press. In 1970, 398 out of 1,043 titles come from IUP.
1970: *Books from Ireland* published by Clé, lists 230 titles (not including Irish University Press's *British Parliamentary Papers*) published between January 1969 and December 1970. First SBNs (later ISBNs) registered by Irish publishers; by 2012 Nielsen recorded 100,400 separate ISBNs.

Table 12. ISBNs issued to Irish publishers 1969–2013*

Title range	*Publishers*		*ISBNs*	
	No.	*%*	*No.*	*%*
200+	45	1.7	22,922	61.4
100–199	26	1.0	3,849	10.3
50–99	31	1.2	2,375	6.4
20–49	76	2.9	2,235	6.0
2–19	956	36.9	4,484	12.0
1	1,456	56.2	1,456	3.9
Total	2,590		37,321	

Source: Nielsen (with thanks to the Irish Copywriting Licensing Agency)
*Excludes HardPress which claimed some 130,000 titles in print.
Total ISBNs issued 37,321 (plus 130,000 from the Sligo reprinter HardPress) from 2,590 publishers. 70 per cent come from seventy-one publishers; bear in mind these are ISBNs, not titles. A single text may attract multiple ISBNs, e.g. hardback and paperback, multiple copy packs, deluxe editions, and even, as in the Harry Potter series, adult and juvenile bindings. This table suggests that the true number of publications should be 1.4 times the Clé estimate.

1981: *Irish Publishing Record* records 745 titles published in 1980 from 288 publishers.
1989: NLI take over publication of *Irish Publishing Record*. The edition covering 1989 is published in 1990 and identifies 923 titles from 511 publishers including the Stationery Office and several semi-state bodies. The series is discontinued after 1993.
1992: The last *Irish Publishing Record* lists 1,918 titles, making 26,253 in all since the first edition in 1967. The first Clé Survey is published, recording 'over 700' titles from fifty-four publishers, with 'over 6,500' titles in print.
1995: *Books Ireland* records 650 titles in its First Flush columns.
1997: Clé Survey records 841 new titles and 7,300 in print.

Twenty-first Century

2003: Clé Survey records 1,064 new titles and 8,253 in print.
2005: Clé Survey records 1,018 new titles and 9,200 in print.
2008: Publishing Ireland survey finds 1,114 new titles.

Based on the estimates above, we might tentatively extrapolate from the fragmentary records for the twentieth century as follows:

1922–1960, average titles per annum 100 = 3,800
1960–1967, say 400 per annum = 2,800
[1968–2013: 37,000 per ISBNs]
1967–1993, *Irish Publishing Record* total + 20 per cent not found = 31,800
1993–2012, average titles per annum 1,000 identified by Clé x 1.4 for others = 26,600
Total = 65,000 or between 60,000 and 70,000.

Summary of estimates of non-official publications:

Sixteenth and seventeenth centuries say 1,200
Eighteenth century 14,000
Nineteenth century 25,000
Twentieth century 65,000 (+ 1900–1921 say 5,600)
Total 105,000 (+5,600).

We have seen (in the Introduction) that Google estimated that some 130 million is the total count of books published, of which 80 per cent were published since 1922. My count suggests that in Ireland the twentieth-century total is no more than 70 per cent of the number since 1551. This finding, that our performance in the twentieth century was below average, accords well with other data showing the relatively poor Irish performance in titles per head compared to a wide range of EU and other countries, some of which are notably poorer in resources.

Notes

Part One

Introduction

1 Herbert S. Bailey Jr, *The Art and Science of Book Publishing* (University of Texas Press, 1970), p. 195.
2 M. Pollard, *Dublin's Trade in Books* (Oxford, 1989), Preface.
3 A vivid example is the drastic editing by Gordon Lish of *Esquire* of the stories of Raymond Carver. Carver has been lavishly praised for 'masterful minimalism', an effect achieved after Lish had trimmed the original texts by as much as 50 to 78 per cent. See *Times Literary Supplement*, 31 July 2009, review of The Library of America's, *R. Carver Collected Stories*.
4 R. Sher, *The Enlightenment and the Book: Scottish Authors and their Publishers in Eighteenth Century Britain, Ireland and America* (Chicago, 2005), p. 10.
5 R. Escarpit, *The Book Revolution* (London, 1966), pp. 69–7.
6 Letter to the Editor, *The Irish Times*, 25 May 1990.
7 R. Cole, *Irish Booksellers and English Writers 1740–1800* (London, 1986), p. 31. The study is based on over 200 auction catalogues. Lexicography scores unexpectedly well because of the widespread holding of Samuel Johnson's *Dictionary*.
8 J. Carter & P. Muir, *Printing and the Mind of Man* (Cambridge, 1967); B. Fanning & T. Garvin, *The Books that Define Ireland* (Dublin, 2014).
9 Lucien Febvre & Henri-Jean Martin, *The Coming of the Book* (trans. David Gerard London, 1976, first published as *L'Apparition du Livre* by Editions Albin Michel in 1958).
10 W. St Clair, 'The Political Economy of Reading', The John Coffin Memorial Lecture in the History of the Book 2005, revised 2012, www.ies.sas.ac.uk. Access date, 9 June 2018.
11 J. Carty, *A Class-Book of Irish History: Book Four* (London, 1931), p. 111. The first in the series was welcomed by the *Irish Book Lover* in March–April 1930 thus: 'At last the researches of Eoin MacNeill towards the establishment of a definite groundwork of Early Irish History are filtering down to the schools.'
12 E. Evans, *Historical and Bibliographical Account of Almanacs, Directories, etc. Published in Ireland from the Sixteenth Century* (Carraig Books: Dublin, 1976 [1897]). A total

of 5,092 years puts the Creation at 3446 BC, making the world rather younger than Archbishop Ussher's better-known contemporary estimate of 4004 BC, or Bede's 3952 BC. The execution of Mary, Queen of Scots is normally put at 1587, i.e. fifty-nine years before.

13 Royal Commission on Book Publishing *Canadian Publishers and Canadian Publishing* (Ontario, 1970), p. 10. This is a stimulating study of publishing in conditions where a sophisticated, well-financed and aggressive same-language neighbour dominates. According to Roy McSkimming, historian of modern Canadian publishing, the key influence (and indeed author of the Report) was the veteran academic publisher Marsh Jeanneret; see R. McSkimming, *The Perilous Trade* (Ontario, 2003), pp. 113–4.

14 C. Haynes, *Lost Illusions: The Politics of Publishing in Nineteenth Century France* (Harvard, 2010), p. 17.

15 Sarah Davis-Goff of Tramp Press, Dublin Book Fair, November 2015.

16 E. Lyall, *Derrick Vaughan, Novelist* (London 1889) chapter 5. This, the first title published by the new publishing house Methuen, was the author's sixth published novel, selling 25,000 copies in its first year. M. Duffy, *A Thousand Capricious Chances: A History of the Methuen list 1889–1989* (London, 1989), pp. 2–4.

17 A. Powell, *Faces in my Time* (London, 1980), p. 200.

18 C. Benson, 'The Dublin Book trade 1801–1850', (unpublished PhD thesis: Trinity College Dublin, 2000), p. 63.

19 A. Schriffen, *The Business of Books* (London, 2000), chapter 3.

20 C. Cipolla, *Literacy and Development in the West* (Penguin, 1969), pp. 113, 126.

21 J. Smith Allen, *In the Public Eye: A History of Reading in Modern France 1800–1940* (Princeton, 1991), p. 59.

22 J. Coolahan, 'Three Eras of Reading' in V. Greaney (ed.), *Studies in Reading* (Dublin, 1977), p. 16, summarising data from the 1901 Census. See also C. Hutton, 'Publishing the Literary Revival: The Evolution of Irish Textual Culture 1886–1922' (unpublished D.Phil thesis: Oxford, 1999), p. 28.

23 E. Devlin, *Speaking Volumes* (Belfast, 2000), p. 50.

24 A. Manguel, *A History of Reading* (London, 1997), p. 8.

25 F.S.L. Lyons, *Ireland Since the Famine* (London, 1973), p. 88.

26 Actually they announced an absurdly precise 129,864,880. Google Books Search official blog, 5 August 2010, posted by software engineer Leonid Taycher.

27 R. Williams, *Communications* (Harmondsworth, 1962), p. 31.

28 S. Eliot, *Some Trends and Patterns in British Publishing 1800–1919* (London, 1994), p. 14.

29 J. Phillips, *Printing and Bookselling in Dublin 1670–1800* (Dublin, 1998). Phillips's thesis was originally researched in the 1950s, but its 'astonishingly comprehensive view of the eighteenth-century Dublin trade' (as librarian and scholar Mary 'Paul' Pollard put it) is still impressive.

30 See Sher, *The Enlightenment and the Book*, especially chapter 7.

Chapter 1

1 M. Pollard, *Dictionary of Members of the Dublin Book Trade 1550–1800* (London, 2000), pp. 465–6.

2 R. Gillespie, *Reading Ireland: Print, Reading and Social Change in Early Modern Ireland* (Manchester, 2005), p. 56.

3 *Ibid.*, p. 61.

4 Pollard, *Dictionary of Members*, p. 39.

5 *Ibid*, p. 482.

6 M. Pollard, *Dublin's Trade in Books 1550–1800* (Oxford, 1990), pp. 36–9.

7 Gillespie, *Reading Ireland*, pp. 187–8. Identification based on English Short Title Catalogue (ESTC).
8 Pollard, *Dublin's Trade in Books*, pp. 42–61, Appendix.
9 V. Kinane, 'The early books trade in Galway', in G. Long (ed.), *Books Beyond the Pale* (Dublin, 1996), pp. 55–6.
10 John Dunton, *The Dublin Scuffle,* A. Carpenter (ed.) (Dublin, 2000 [1699]).
11 Quoted in Phillips, *Printing and Bookselling*, p. 26.
12 Dunton, *Dublin Scuffle* p. 121.
13 Pollard, *Dublin's Trade in Books*, pp. 69–70.
14 Sher, *The Enlightenment and the Book*, p. 448.
15 *Ibid.*, pp. 459–60.
16 Phillips, *Printing and Bookselling*, chapter 11: both contemporary criticism and (occasional) praise.
17 T. Barnard, *Brought to Book* (Four Courts: Dublin, 2017), pp. 230–1. Barnard's is a copiously referenced account of writers and readers and their books in the eighteenth century. He is sadly unsympathetic to the book trade, variously describing its participants as mendacious (p. 235), cautious (p. 208), pusillanimous (p. 347) and brutally commercial (p. 335).
18 John Rutty, quoted in Barnard, *Brought to Book*, p. 346.
19 Pollard, *Dublin's Trade in Books*, p. 193.
20 Barnard, *Brought to Book*, pp. 365–73.
21 P. Fagan, *The Second City: Portrait of Dublin 1700–1760* (Branar: Dublin, 1986), pp. 203, 208.
22 Barnard, *Brought to Book.*
23 Pollard, *Dictionary of Members*, pp. 182–3.
24 R. Munter, *Dictionary of the Print Trade in Ireland 1550–1775* (New York, 1988), p. 169.
25 These figures are based on the Eighteenth-century Short Title Catalogue (ESTC), which is derived from library holdings. Categories that tended not to be preserved in libraries (notably schoolbooks) are therefore under-represented, to an unquantifiable degree.
26 Sher, *The Enlightenment and the Book*, p. 443: Sher's rounded estimates of non-official publications enable us to guess that in the second half of the century official publications were some 7 per cent of the whole by the late eighteenth century.
27 P. Gedin, *Literature in the Market Place* (London, 1982), chapter 3.
28 ESTC, *passim.*
29 Benson, 'The Dublin Book Trade', p. 15.
30 J. Warburton, J. Whitelaw & R. Walsh, *A History of the City of Dublin* (London, 1818), vol. 2, p. 1162, quoted in Benson, 'The Dublin Book Trade'.
31 *Ibid.*, This lament was to be heard again in the 1930s.
32 *Dublin Penny Journal*, March 1833.
33 W. Carleton, *Traits and Stories of the Irish Peasantry* (Dublin, 1843), 1.xxxii.
34 T. Wall, *The Sign of Dr Hay's Head* (Dublin, 1958), chapter 1 describes Wogan's career.
35 Benson, 'The Dublin Book Trade', p. 405.
36 Wall, *The Sign of Dr Hay's Head*, p. 126.
37 J.J. O'Kelly, 'The House of Gill', unpublished ms., Appendix B, pp. vii–xxiii. This 600 pp. text (in the Trinity College Dublin Archives) was written by the retired editor of the *Catholic Bulletin* to celebrate the 100th anniversary of the firm. It is full of information about the firm and its trading conditions, especially in the early nineteenth century, much of which is now unverifiable as a result of fires in Gill's premises.
38 The book trade has traditionally used the term 'discount' to refer both to what the booksellers allowed off the advertised price to customers (later forbidden under the

Net Book Agreement) and what the publisher allowed the bookseller, representing their gross margin.

39 Obituary in *The Bookseller,* September 1871. The anonymous obituarist could not resist a little sermonising, hoping that Duffy's exemplary life (as 'a genuine Irish gentleman') would 'convince his fellow-countrymen that if instead of useless blatings (sic) about their country's wrongs and Celtic rights they will apply themselves to business, they may not only redress the former but make us respect the latter'.

40 Benson, 'The Dublin Book Trade', p. 32.

41 'Duffy, James' in J. McGuire & J. Quinn (eds), *Dictionary of Irish Biography* (Cambridge: Royal Irish Academy & Cambridge University Press, 2009).

42 Quoted in J.R.R. Adams, *The Printed Word and the Common Man* (Belfast, 1987), p. 149.

43 J.R.R. Adams, 'Simms & M'Intyre: Creators of the Parlour Library', *Linen Hall Review* 4.2 (Summer 1987).

44 J. McCulloch, *Dictionary of Commerce* (Longman: London, Second Edition: 1839), Supplement p. 20. I am grateful to my friend Professor Antoin Murphy for the loan of this fascinating reference work.

45 D. Diderot, *Lettre sur le Commerce de la Librairie* (1767), quoted in R. Escarpit, *The Book Revolution* (London, 1966), p. 115.

46 McCulloch, *Dictionary of Commerce*, p. 144.

47 See Pollard, *Dictionary of Members*, pp. 238, 291. For some reason the Hodges Figgis website claims John Milliken as the founder – a connection Pollard is silent about. Milliken had a shop in Skinner Row, then College Green; he decamped to England in the 1770s but returned in 1789 only to be judged bankrupt in 1793.

48 See Pollard, *Dictionary of Members*, p. 291 and Benson 'The Dublin Book Trade', p. 654.

49 See V. Kinane, *A History of the Dublin University Press 1734–1976* (Dublin, 1994), pp. 103–204.

50 O'Kelly, 'The House of Gill', chapter 9.

51 Kinane, *A History of the Dublin University Press*, p. 202.

52 J. Goldstrom, *The Social Content of Education 1808–1870* (Shannon, 1978) pp. 134–6; J. Goldstrom, 'Lord John Russell and the publishing trade', *Publishing History*, 20 (1986).

53 M. McNeill, *Vere Foster 1819–1900: An Irish Benefactor* (Newton Abbott, 1971), pp. 131–48, 181–84. Vere Foster was a remarkable man who spent a lifetime sponsoring Irish education, helping would-be emigrants and generally relieving Irish poverty. See also G. McIntosh, 'Marcus Ward & Co.' in J. Murphy (ed.), *Oxford History of the Book in Ireland, Vol IV: The Irish Book in English 1800–1891* (Oxford, 2011), p. 130.

54 Vere Foster, *Origin and History of Vere Foster's Writing and Drawing Copybooks and Judgement of the Master of the Rolls Delivered on Jan 28 1882* (Dublin 1883).

55 T. Farmar, 'Setting up home in Dublin in the 1850s', *Dublin Historical Record*, 54.1 (Spring 2001), pp. 25–6.

56 John Sproule, 'The Publishing Trade' in J. Sproule (ed.), *The Irish International Exhibition of 1853* (Dublin, 1854), p. 326.

57 R. Loeber & M. Loeber, *A Guide to Irish Fiction 1650–1900* (Dublin, 2006), p. lx.

58 *Ibid.*

59 *Report of the Select Committee on Industries* (Ireland), 1884/5, p. 288.

60 *Royal Commission on Technical Instruction*, 1881–4 C-3981-111, Appendix X, p. 492.

61 *Report of the Select Committee on Industries (Ireland)*, 1884/5, p. 288, questions 2904, 2905. Quoted in the *Weekly Irish Times*, 2 September 1882. The widely reported proceedings of this committee, though in themselves inconclusive, had a long-term effect on the way people thought about Ireland's industrial possibilities, supporting the idea of tariff barriers to protect native industries.

Chapter 2

1 F.S.L. Lyons, *Culture and Anarchy in Ireland 1890–1939* (Oxford, 1982), p. 38.
2 *Athenaeum*, 28 December 1889.
3 P. Blom, *Fracture: Life and Culture in the West 1918–38* (London, 2015), p. 406.
4 The aura of 'science' carefully attached to Freud's ideas gave them a spurious but incontestable authority which has, for instance among literary critics, barely waned. F. Crews, *Freud: the Making of an Illusion* (London, 2017), *passim* but especially pp. 661–6.
5 H. Jackson, *The Eighteen Nineties* (Harmsworth, 1939), p. 15. Jackson was for a while editor of *T.P.'s Weekly* and later owner of a small press. He wrote numerous books on typography, printing and bibliography.
6 R. Le Gallienne, *The Romantic '90s* (New York, 1925), p. 136.
7 *The Bookseller*, April 1892. Irish publishers such as Hodges Figgis, Sealy, Bryers & Walker, and Browne & Nolan advertised and announced new publications in its pages. Occasionally, the 'Trade Gossip' column carried items of Irish news such as the amalgamation of the educational publisher Sullivan Brothers with Alex Thom in September 1891.
8 'Books in bottles', *Times Literary Supplement*, 30 October 2015.
9 *The Irish Times*, 18 August 1894. The claims to priority of the Abbé have not been generally endorsed by English-language historians of the bicycle.
10 Digital word count from *The Irish Times*' historical database.
11 Figures from Baillère, *La Crise du Livre* (Place, 1903) quoted in D. Sassoon, *The Culture of the Europeans* (London, 2006), p. 634.
12 *The Bookseller*, May 1895.
13 S. Unwin, *The Truth About Publishing* (London, 1926), p. 222.
14 J. Flood 'Germany', in M. Suarez et al. (eds), *The Oxford Companion to the Book* (Oxford, 2010) p. 232.
15 Sales figures from A. Meiner, Reclam (Leipzig, 1942) quoted in S. Steinberg, *Five Hundred Years of Printing* (Penguin, 1955), p. 351.
16 C. Haynes, *Lost Illusions: the Politics of Publishing in Nineteenth Century France* (Harvard, 2010), p. 8. In his novel, *Lost Illusions*, Balzac describes how the town of Angoulême (population in 1830 15,000, similar to Galway) was limited to two printers' licences; Paris had 60.
17 V. Goroud, 'France' in Suarez, *The Oxford Companion to the Book*, p. 207.
18 Quoted in P. Mansell, *Paris Between Empires 1814–1852* (Murray: London, 2001), p. 308.
19 Quoted in *The Bookseller*, October, 1895.
20 R. Byrne, 'The French publishing industry and its crisis in the 1890s' in *The Journal of Modern History*, 23.3 (September 1951), p. 232.
21 Percy Russell, *The Author's Manual* (London, sixth edition, 1891), p. 84. Russell was one of the most successful authors in the new 'author's guide' market.
22 For Downey's time on *T.P.'s Weekly* see J. Mahony, 'Irish writers and their London publishers 1884–1922' (unpublished PhD thesis, TCD, 2016) pp. 188–93. For comparison, the top-selling Irish magazine in 2014 was the *RTÉ Guide* with 57,000 weekly sales.
23 J. Collins, *Life in Old Dublin* (Dublin, 1913), p. 171.
24 C.S. Andrews, *Dublin Made Me* (Dublin, 1979), pp. 45, 51, 64.
25 O'Kelly, 'The House of Gill', p. 376.
26 W. Dawson 'My Dublin Year', in *Studies* 1912. Dawson was a barrister, and later Land Commissioner. He had been one of the leading lights in the revived UCD L&H Society, becoming Auditor in 1902/3.

27 Based on NLI catalogue searches.
28 S. Eliot, *Some Patterns and Trends in British Publishing 1800–1919* (London, 1994), pp. 51, 123.
29 S. Eliot, 'Patterns and trends and the NSTC', *Publishing History*, XVIII (1998), p. 43.
30 P. Gaskell, *A New Introduction to Bibliography* (Oxford, 1972), p. 301.
31 M. Arnold, 'Copyright', *Irish Essays* (London, 1882), pp. 249, 263.
32 Frederick Nesta has pointed out that this happy outcome was by no means inevitable: F. Nesta, 'The myth of the "triple-headed monster": the economics of the three-volume novel', *Publishing History*, 62 (2007), p. 48.
33 G. Gissing, *New Grub Street* (London, 1985 [1891]), p. 168.
34 *The Bookseller*, January 1895.
35 *The Importance of Being Earnest* was first produced in February 1895, some months after the libraries announced that they would no longer buy three-deckers, pushing authors of Miss Prism's type out of the market.
36 Rudyard Kipling, 'The Three-Decker', *The Week*, 11 (1894), p. 921.
37 J. St John, *William Heinemann* (London, 1990), p. 3.
38 P. Unwin, *The Publishing Unwins* (London, 1972), p. 45.
39 J. Barnes, *Free Trade in Books: A study of the London Book Trade since 1800* (Oxford, 1964) p. 184, from Lord Cambell's judgement in the arbitration.
40 *The Bookseller*, October 1871.
41 W. Corp, *Fifty Years: A Brief Account of the Associated Booksellers of Great Britain and Ireland 1895–1945* (Oxford, 1946), p. 6.
42 J. M. Keynes, 'Alfred Marshall 1842–1924', *The Economic Journal*, 34.135 (1924), pp. 301–72.
43 C. Guillebaud, 'The Marshal–Macmillan correspondence over the net book system', *The Economic Journal*, 75.299 (1965), pp. 518–38.
44 History has not been kind to C.J. Longman. One historian of the house, Cyprian Blagden, writes: 'the Longmans who controlled the business [at this time] … provided no new publishing answers', they had provided the old answers 'over and over again under new conditions and with changing problems' (*Fire More than Water*, 1949). Asa Briggs more politely says that in running his great company Charles and his cousin Thomas were 'guided more by experience rather than abstract knowledge or imagination' (*A History of Longmans and Their Books* (London, 2008)). Towards the end of his life (he retired in 1928) Longman refused to have a telephone in his room.
45 Quoted in J. Barnes, *Free Trade in Books* (Oxford, 1964), p. 145.
46 *The Bookseller*, September 1895.
47 See for instance Gissing, *New Grub Street*, p. 106.
48 C. Sevill, 'Copyright' in D. McKitterick (ed.), *The Book in Britain, Vol VI, 1830–1914* (Cambridge, 2009), p. 222.
49 Haynes, *Lost Illusions*, p. 76.
50 The Chace Act was in fact drafted by the publisher and historian Henry C. Lea whose father had married the daughter of the Irish-born printer in Philadelphia, Matthew Carey, and succeeded to the business. Lea Brothers was one of the most successful publishing firms in the US. Henry was also an historian specialising in the later Middle Ages, with books on witchcraft, the Spanish Inquisition and sacerdotal celibacy. His anti-Catholic bias is particularly clear in the latter.
51 Eliot, *Some Trends and Patterns*, p. 14.
52 A. Birrell, *Seven Lectures on the Law and History of Copyright in Books* (London, 1899), p. 196. Birrell intriguingly adds 'and never in the world's history was the spending of a fortune so easy and so agreeable as in the England of today'.
53 Gissing, *New Grub Street*, p. 8.

54 R. Foster, *W.B.Yeats: A Life Vol. I, The Apprentice Mage* (Oxford, 1997), p. 234.
55 See for instance the figures given in J. Nelson, *Elkin Mathews: Publisher to Yeats, Joyce and Pound* (Wisconsin UP, 1989), pp. 186–7.
56 *The Nation*, 14 February 1897.
57 Gaskell, *A New Introduction to Bibliography*, pp. 54–5, 278.
58 *Belfast Newsletter*, 1 August 1889. The *Newsletter* experimented with an earlier and unreliable setting machine called a Thorne in 1892.
59 Kinane, *A History of the Dublin University Press*, p. 227.
60 Educational Company and Talbot archive in National Archives EFP/1048/1/35 letter of 19 April 1916; C. Tempest McCrea, *Tempest of Dundalgan* (Dundalk, 1988), p. 23.
61 A. Corrigan, *A Printer and his World* (London, 1944), p. 172. His firm, Corrigan & Wilson, was in Sackville Place.
62 The process can be detected as the corrected lines often print as sharper and lighter.
63 Maunsel & Roberts plant and stock list, to be sold at auction by Battersby. 22 April 1926.

Chapter 3

1 H. Balzac, *Lost Illusions* (Modern Library: New York, 1985), p. 260.
2 The draw of London to Irish writers is discussed in detail in Mahony, 'Irish Writers', chapter 2.
3 A Methodist leader who, though initially a strong supporter of Home Rule, declared that if Parnell was proved an adulterer no Methodist could support him, causing Gladstone to declare he could no longer remain Liberal leader if Parnell remained head of the Irish Parliamentary Party. This promoted the 'Parnell split' in the Party.
4 G. Allen in the *Fortnightly Review* (1891), quoted in H. Jackson, *The Eighteen Nineties* (Penguin, 1939), p. 132. Allen was of Canadian origin, though educated in England. His father was a Protestant minister, originally from Dublin. Allen's best-known work was the sex-liberation sensation *The Woman who Did*.
5 A. Powell, *At Lady Molly's* (London, 1957), p. 158.
6 Quoted in Mahony, 'Irish Writers', p. 170; for Yeats and Edmund Downey's career, see Mahony, chapter 3.
7 *Ibid*.
8 See Hutton, 'Publishing the Literary Revival', pp. 11–25 for a discussion of Lubbock and his Irish counterpart 'Historicus'.
9 A listing of Downey's publications is in Mahony, 'Irish Writers', Appendix A.
10 See Hutton, 'Publishing the Literary Revival', pp. 64–7.
11 Foster, *W.B.Yeats, Vol. I*, p. 118.
12 J. St John, *William Heinemann: A Century of Publishing 1890–1990* (London, 1990), pp. 3, 7–10; J. McAleer, *Passion's Fortune* (Oxford, 19990), pp. 15, 17; S. Hodges, *Gollancz: The Story of a Publishing House 1928–1978* (London, 1978). Gollancz left his previous employer Ernest Benn Ltd in October 1927; the first books under the new imprint appeared in April 1928.
13 Memorandum from Downey to Duffy laying out a plan for the proposed publishing house, quoted by Mahony, 'Irish Writers', pp. 175–6. Subsequent proposals are on pp. 177–9.
14 Foster, *W.B.Yeats, Vol. I*, pp. 118–24.
15 C. Hutton, 'The Promise of Literature in the Coming Days', *Victorian Literature and Culture*, 39 (2011), pp. 581–92 lists the twelve titles in this series, which were published between 1893 and 1897.
16 W.B.Yeats, *The Bookman*, August 1894.

17 Mahony, 'Irish Writers', p. 194.
18 *Ibid.*, pp. 194–5.
19 *Ibid.*, p. 172; Hutton, 'Publishing the Literary Revival', p. 70.
20 J. Feather, *A History of British Publishing* (London: Second Edition, 2006), p. 88.
21 A.H. Bullen, whose father came from Cork, was the publisher of the first collected edition of Yeats. When his first firm Lawrence & Bullen failed in 1900 he established a private press and publishing house in Stratford on Avon, taking Frank Sidgwick, later founder of Sidgwick & Jackson, as apprentice and then partner. His career as a not very effective publisher, including his tendency to amend Yeats's texts according to his own taste, is detailed in A. Baer (ed.), *Frank Sidgwick's Diary* (Oxford 1975).
22 The scale of non-professional publishing in recent decades can be gleaned from the Irish ISBNs issued in the forty-four-year period 1969–2013. Some 37,000 ISBNs were issued, 70 per cent of which were issued to professionals. This leaves nearly 11,000 books published (often as a single title only) to over 2,500 publisher organisations or self-publishing individuals.
23 O'Kelly, 'House of Gill', additional papers, sheet 16.
24 See T. Wall, *The Sign of Dr Hay's Head* (Dublin, 1956), pp. 138–9 for an extended list of authors and publications.
25 4 June 1874, 'Improvements in machines for finishing printed sheets of paper'.
26 G. McIntosh, 'M.H. Gill later Gill and Macmillan' in C. Hutton (ed.), *The Oxford History of the Irish Book, Vol. V: The Irish Book in English 1891–2000* (Oxford, 2011), p. 519.
27 *The Irish Times*, 25 September 1915.
28 *Ibid.*, 13 October 1898.
29 *Ibid.*, 10 January 1879.
30 *Ibid.*, 8 July 1890.
31 Royal Irish Academy Certificate of Candidate, 27 January 1897.
32 Obituary, *The Irish Times,* 12 December 1908.
33 P. O'Leary, *The Prose Literature of the Celtic Revival 1881–1921* (Pennsylvania State UP, 1994), p. 8.
34 E. Evans, *Historical and Bibliographical Account of Almanacks, Directories, etc., etc. Published in Ireland from the Sixteenth Century with Jottings of their Compilers and Printers* (Dublin: facsimile reprint, 1976 [1897]), pp. 137 – 42.
35 F. Higgins (ed.), *Progress in Irish Printing* (Dublin, 1936). *The Irish Book Lover* (August & September 1916) states that it was stereotype plates that were destroyed. This is unlikely. Working from plates without standing metal would require, for every corrected page, the whole page to be reset and replated. I vividly remember from the early 1970s the mighty rows upon rows of galleys full of type stored by Clays for Macmillan's *Statesman's Yearbook.*
36 Educational Company and Talbot archive, National Archives 1048/35/14.
37 *Ibid.*
38 A. Blackie, *Blackie & Son 1809–1959* (London & Glasgow, 1959), pp. 52–3.
39 *The Irish Times*, 7 January 1938.
40 J. Dunne, 'The Educational Company of Ireland and the Talbot Press 1910–1990', *Long Room,* 42 (1997), pp. 34–41.
41 Over 500 pages of relentless polemic against the influence of the Catholic Church in Ireland, this sold well, with six printings between March and November 1901.
42 J. Hagen, *Tennyson and his Publishers* (London, 1979), Chapter 2.
43 J. Nelson, *Elkin Mathews* (Wisconsin, 1989), p. 47.
44 For the period before 1900, see A. Wade, *Bibliography of the Writings of W.B. Yeats* (London: third edition, 1968).

45 See L. Miller, *The Dun Emer Press, Later the Cuala Press* (Dublin, 1973), Introduction.
46 Quoted in Hutton, 'Publishing the Literary Revival', p. 151.
47 *Freeman's Journal*, 24 May 1923.
48 C. Franklin, *The Ashendene Press* (Dallas, 1986), p. 1.
49 Quoted in Hutton, 'Publishing the Literary Revival', p. 151.
50 *Ibid.*, p. 153.
51 Miller, *The Dun Emer Press*, p. 7.
52 Hutton, 'Publishing the Literary Revival', p. 153.
53 Miller, *The Dun Emer Press*, pp. 105–131. The count of sixty-two books does not include the numerous non-book items that were so important to the press's finances such as broadsheets, private publications, hand-coloured prints and greeting cards, bookplates etc.
54 Cuala's work was highly regarded in Ireland, though one acerbic historian of the private press movement, Colin Franklin, described the press's standard designs 'as dreary visually as December in Dublin', C. Franklin, *The Ashendene Press* (Dallas, 1986). The use of a second colour (red) where another press would have used italic was eccentric.
55 F.-J. French, 'A History of the House of Maunsel' (unpublished MLitt thesis: Trinity College Dublin, 1969); Mahony, 'Irish writers and their London publishers' and C. Hutton, 'Publishing the Literary Revival'.
56 Mahony, 'Irish Writers', p. 60.
57 Hutton, 'Publishing the Literary Revival', p. 164.
58 *The Irish Times*, 4 August 1955. Double Royal is 25in x 40in (102 x 63 cm). This size would enable him to print sixteen pages to view (and so a full sheet of thirty-two pages when perfected). It is not clear where Roberts learned his print and typography, but according to the *Dictionary of Irish Biography* he learned them well enough to become later in life a typographical advisor to Victor Gollancz, a role previously associated with Stanley Morison.
59 Mahony, 'Irish Writers', p. 71.
60 Little about this saga is straightforward. Joyce's scurrilous verse, 'Gas From a Burner', suggests that the sheets were burned, but it is more likely that, if they existed at all, they were guillotined (as Roberts told Ellmann). 10,000 large pieces of paper (1,000 copies of ten sections) would be very awkward to burn, but a normal, straightforward task to guillotine. Some of the strips may have been subsequently used as paper linings on the spines of hardback law texts published by Falconer.
61 A. McCarthy, 'Publishing for Catholic Ireland' in Hutton (ed.), *The Oxford History of the Irish Book, Vol. V*, pp. 250–2.
62 CTS, *Catholic Truth Society of Ireland First Fifty Years 1899–1949* (Dublin, 1949).
63 Eason's Archive.
64 Augustine Birrell quoted in R. Altick, 'From Aldine to Everyman: Cheap Reprint Series of the English classics 1830–1906', in *Studies in Bibliography*, 11 (University of Virginia, 1958).
65 T. Basset *et al.*, 'Booksellers and Bestsellers: British Book Sales as Documented by *The Bookman* 1891–1906', *Book History* 4 (2001), p. 221.
66 *The Irish Times*, 16 June 1909.
67 *Ibid.*, leader 7 January 1911.
68 Basset, 'Booksellers and Bestsellers', pp. 215–6.
69 B. Levitas, 'Reading and the Irish Revival 1891–1922' in Hutton (ed.), *The Oxford History of the Irish Book, Vol. V*, pp. 47–8.
70 S. Brown, *Ireland in Fiction* (Dublin, 1915), pp. 25, 221.
71 *Publishers' Circular* figures reported in Eliot, *Some Trends*, p. 116.

Chapter 4

1 French, 'A History of the House of Maunsel', p. 44.
2 Dunne, 'The Educational Company of Ireland', pp. 34–41.
3 Quoted in L. Cullen, *Eason & Son* (Dublin, 1989), p. 207.
4 O'Kelly, 'The House of Gill', p. 472.
5 Personal communication, Michael Gill, longtime managing director of Gill & Macmillan.
6 *Freeman's Journal*, 2 February 1916.
7 *Irish Independent*, 31 January 1916.
8 Eliot, *Some Trends*, p. 124: *Publishers' Circular and Booksellers' Record* figures.
9 Hutton, 'Publishing the Literary Revival', p. 226.
10 *Ibid.*
11 Henry James, 'The Art of Fiction' originally published in 1884, reprinted in *Partial Portraits* (London, 1888).
12 T. Farmar, *The Versatile Profession: A History of Accountancy in Ireland Since 1850* (Chartered Accountants Ireland: Dublin, 2013), p. 45.
13 Hutton, 'Publishing the Literary Revival', p. 222.
14 French, 'A History of the House of Maunsel', p. 42.
15 *Ibid.*, chapter 4.
16 A. Dolan, *Commemorating the Irish Civil War* (Cambridge: CUP 2003), p. 104.
17 The NLI Catalogue lists 182 items between 1928 and 1974. The Press was sold in 1972. See D. Maguire, 'Colm Ó Lochlainn and the Sign of the Three Candles', *Long Room*, 41 (1996), and C. Trench, 'The Three Candles Press in the Thirties', *Long Room*, 41 (1996).
18 French, 'A History of the House of Maunsel', chapter 5.
19 *Dublin Penny Journal*, 15 December 1832.
20 W. St Clair, *The Reading Nation in the Romantic Era* (Cambridge: CUP, 2004), p. 191.
21 J. Hinks & M. Bell, 'The Book Trade in English Provincial Towns 1700–1849', *Publishing History*, LVII (2005).
22 J.R.R. Adams, *The Printed Word and the Common Man* (Belfast, 1987), pp. 159–64.
23 B. Lally, *Print Culture in Loughrea 1850–1900* (Dublin, 2008), p. 50.
24 J. Mahaffy, 'The Irish landlords', *Contemporary Review* (1882), p. 160.
25 G. Taylor, *The Emerald Isle* (London, 1952), p. 56. Taylor, born Phibbs, was from a landed Anglo-Irish family. He was, for a while, poetry editor of *The Bell*, but is best known for his disastrous involvement in a three- (or four-) cornered affair with Laura Riding and Robert Graves.
26 J.B. Howell, *A History of the Dublin Library Society 1791–1881* (Dalhousie, 1985). MacDonnell, described as a clever but lazy man, is best known as the projector of Sorrento Terrace, Dalkey, which was built on his land.
27 *Ibid.*
28 J. Kelly, E. Domville (eds.) *The Collected Letters of W.B. Yeats, Vol. 1, 1865–85* (Oxford, 1986), pp. 296–7. Yeats of course is not to be taken literally. He once wrote 'no educated man ever bought an Irish book', which, even if we assume an idiosyncratic understanding of the word 'educated', has to be nonsense, but no doubt served whatever thesis he was presenting at the time.
29 T. Zeldin, *France 1848–1945, Vol. 2* (Oxford, 1977), p. 353 .
30 S. Gwynn, *Irish Book Lover*, March 1913.
31 Edward MacLysaght quoted in Hutton, 'Publishing the Literary Revival', p. 326.
32 W. Dawson, 'My Dublin Year', *Studies* (Dublin, 1912), p. 705.

33 *The Irish Times*, 12 July 1930.
34 George Birmingham, *The Search Party* (London: Methuen, 1909), chapter 2.
35 S. O'Casey, *Inishfallen, Fare Thee Well* (London: Pan, 1973), pp. 191, 194. *Peg O' My Heart* was a novel first published in 1913 based on the successful comedy drama of the same name by J. Hartley Manners.
36 F. O'Connor, *My Father's Son* (London, 1968), p. 86.
37 P. Sheehan 'The American report on Irish education' in *The Literary Life and Other Essays* (Dublin, 1921), p. 87. Canon Sheehan's essay is based on a lengthy summary of the report in the *Times Literary Supplement*, 6 December 1910.
38 P. Kavanagh, *Tarry Flynn* (London, 1948), p. 18.
39 N. Hoult, *Coming from the Fair: Being Book Two of 'Holy Ireland'* (London, 1937).
40 S. Brown, 'The Choice of Fiction for Public Libraries' in *Libraries and Literature from a Catholic Standpoint* (Dublin, 1937), p. 104.
41 J. O'Brien, *'Dear Dirty Dublin': A City in Distress 1899–1916* (Berkeley: University of California Press, 1982), pp. 57–8.
42 Quoted in David S. Barnes, *The Making of a Social Disease: Tuberculosis in Nineteenth-Century France* (California: California UP, 1995), p. 48.
43 Val Mulkerns, *Friends with the Enemy* (Dublin, 2017), chapter 2.
44 Brown, 'The Choice of Fiction', p. 110.
45 E.M. Forster, *Abinger Harvest* (London: Deutsch, 1996), p. 73. See Forrest Reid, *The Nation*, 10 April 1920.
46 *Freeman's Journal*, 24 January 1920. Would Irish authors prefer to be pilloried as absentee landlords, as they had been in the 1840s, or pitied as migratory labourers in the 1920s?
47 E. Russell, 'Holy Crosses, Guns and Roses: Themes in Popular Reading Material' in J. Augusteijn (ed.), *Ireland in the 1930s: New Perspectives* (Dublin: Four Courts, 1999), pp. 16–21.
48 Eimar O'Duffy, *Printer's Errors* (Dublin: Martin Lester, 1922), p. 53.
49 In M. Oakeshott's 1947 essay, 'Rationalism in politics', 'the revival of Gaelic as the official language of Éire' is seen as a prime example of what he calls Rationalism, the principled application of *de novo* reason, the sworn enemy of the conservative. The rationalist combines power with romanticism and is both a perfectionist and a believer in uniformity. (*Rationalism in Politics and Other Essays* (London, 1962)).
50 J.A. Murphy, 'Censorship and the Moral Community', in B. Farrell (ed.), *Communications and Community in Ireland* (Cork, 1984), p. 52.
51 E. O'Duffy, *The Wasted Island* (London, 1929), p. 257.
52 M. Moynihan (ed.), *Speeches and Statements by Éamon de Valera* (Dublin, 1980), p. 35.
53 *Catholic Bulletin*, last issue, December 1939, Appendix. This obituary, signed Fear Faire, was written by Liam Ó Rinn, a translator in the Oireachtas, who has been described by Philip O'Leary as 'the most sophisticated and perceptive Gaelic literary critic of his time' and 'a serious and erudite man of letters' (P. O'Leary, *Gaelic Prose in the New State 1922–40* (Dublin, 2004), pp. 72, 591). Ó Rinn was, incidentally, the translator of 'The Soldiers Song' into 'Amhrán na bhFiann'.
54 *Dáil Debates*, 10 May 1928.
55 *Seanad Debates*, 7 June 1923.
56 *Ibid.*, 28 May 1928.
57 *Ibid.*, 7 December 1926.
58 *Ibid.*, 7 and 25 January 1927.
59 Quoted in Cullen, *Eason & Son*, p. 261.
60 *Ibid.*, p. 256.
61 *Irish Independent*, 20 October 1926.

62 Ironically it was Ireland, despite tough anti-contraception laws and its commitment of women to the home, that came nearest to this, as alarmed commentators noted in the 1950s, most famously J. O'Brien (ed.), *The Vanishing Irish* (London, 1954).
63 *Dáil Debates*, 18 October 1928, p. 625.
64 *Ibid.*, 29 October 1928, Professor Tierney at p. 645.
65 R. Foster, *W.B. Yeats A Life: II The Arch-Poet* (Oxford, 2003), pp. 374–7. Note Yeats's characteristic use of the word 'educated', to mean 'people who think like me'; his remarks on Aquinas particularly annoyed sophisticated Catholics such as Desmond FitzGerald.
66 *Dáil Debates*, 28 October, p. 658.
67 *Ibid.*, 29 October, p. 691.
68 *Ibid.*, 29 October, p. 700.
69 See Q. Leavis, *Fiction and the Reading Public* (London, 1932), N. Beauman, *A Very Great Profession* (London, 1983) and J. McAleer, *Passion's Fortune* (Oxford, 1999): the quote about 'pure passion' is from p. 47 of this book about the publishing firm Mills & Boon.
70 D. Ó Drisceoil, 'Irish Books Banned under the Censorship of Publications Acts 1929–67' in Hutton (ed.), *The Oxford History of the Irish Book, Vol. V*, p. 644.
71 *The Irish Times*, 12 July 1930.

Chapter 5

1 M. Adams, *Censorship: The Irish Experience* (Dublin, 1968), pp. 148–50. The Irish Association of Civil Liberties was founded in 1948. Its first three presidents were Professor Felix Hackett, Dorothy Macardle and Sean O'Faolain. Its secretary was the solicitor Christopher Gore-Grimes. Eoin Sheehy-Skeffington was a key activist.
2 Michael Gill, personal communication.
3 B. Behan, *Brendan Behan's Island* (London: Hutchinson, 1965), p. 19.
4 *Catholic Bulletin*, December 1939. For the distinguished author of the obituary see note 53 in chapter 4. *The Bulletin*, which had been losing money for years and would have lost more if the actual sales (as opposed to the print run) had been known to advertisers, ceased publication with this issue.
5 Educational Company and Talbot archive, National Archives 1048/1, November 1925.
6 *Ibid.*, 5 July 1932.
7 Q 134, *The Querist*, republished by Talbot in 1935.
8 Educational Company and Talbot archive National Archives 1048/1/, 13 May 1932.
9 *The Irish Times* supplement, Saorstát Éireann Irish Free State 1921–1931 A Decade of Progress, 21 January 1932, p. 62.
10 Frank O'Connor, *My Father's Son* (London, 1971), p. 29.
11 O. Robertson, *Dublin Phoenix* (London, 1957), p. 27.
12 P. Costello, *Dublin's Literary Pubs* (Dublin, 1998); V. Igoe, *Literary Guide to Dublin* (London, 1994), pp. 293–301.
13 H. Tracy, *Mind You, I've Said Nothing!* (London, 1953), p. 77.
14 A. Thwaite, *Edmund Gosse: A Literary Landscape* (Oxford, 1985), p. 453.
15 First described in *The Irish Times*, 7 November 1941.
16 B. O'Nolan/Myles na Gopaleen, *The Best of Myles* (London, 1968), pp. 18–22.
17 F. O'Connor, *My Father's Son* (London, 1968), p. 91.
18 National Library of Ireland, Ms 33,745.
19 *Ibid.*
20 L. Ó Broin, 'Contemporary Gaelic Literature and some of its Paradoxes', *Capuchin Annual* (1935), p. 123.
21 P. O'Leary, *The Prose Literature of the Celtic Revival, 1881–1921* (Pennsylvania, 1994), p. 1.

22 *Ibid.*, p. 8.
23 *Ibid.*
24 B. Ó Conchubhair, 'An Gúm, the Free State and the Politics of the Irish Language' in L. King & E. Sisson (eds.), *Ireland, Design and Visual Culture: Negotiating Modernity 1922–1992* (Cork, 2011), p. 95.
25 Quoted in L. Ó Broin, *Just Like Yesterday* (Dublin, 1986), p. 66.
26 Ó Broin, 'Contemporary Gaelic Literature', p. 122.
27 P. O'Leary, *Gaelic Prose in the Free State 1922–40* (Dublin, 2004), p. 25.
28 *Ibid.*, pp. 32–3.
29 *Irish Monthly*, February 1938.
30 G. Uí Laighléis, 'An Gúm: The Early Years' in S. Mac Mathúna *et al.* (eds.) *Celtic Literature in the Twentieth Century* (Belfast, 2007), pp. 199–216.
31 *Ibid.*
32 Ó Broin, *Just Like Yesterday*, p. 67.
33 Quoted in O'Leary, *Gaelic Prose*, p. 508.
34 Quoted in Uí Laighléis, 'An Gúm: The Early Years', p. 213.
35 *Irish Monthly*, February 1938. Ó Broin's sales figures refer to 422 books. The balance making up the 506 recorded by the NLI catalogue consists of music and booklets of technical terms.
36 Uí Laighléis, 'An Gúm: the Early Years'.
37 P. O'Leary, *Irish Interior: Keeping Faith with the Past in Gaelic Prose 1940–1951* (Dublin 2010), pp. 16–21.
38 *Ibid.*, p. 22.
39 J. Coolahan, *Irish Education: Its History and Structure* (Dublin, 1981), p. 34.
40 *Ibid.*, p. 40.
41 Educational Company archive, 13 February 1940.
42 Apart from an essay in Hutton (ed.), *The Oxford History of the Irish Book* (2011), there has been little or nothing written about the role of publishers in the educational system.
43 Seoirse Mac Niocaill, chief inspector of the Department of Education in 1926, quoted in T.J. McElligott, *This Teaching Life* (Westmeath, 1986), p. 29.
44 Educational Company archive, 2 April 1932.
45 *Ibid.*, 26 April 1933.
46 *Ibid.*, 11 December 1933.
47 Máirín O'Byrne, 'Libraries and Librarianship in Ireland', *Administration* (16), p. 149. Máirín O'Byrne was chief librarian for Dublin city 1961–67, and Dublin city and county librarian 1967–84.
48 Andrew MacIntyre quoted in F. Shovlin, 'Irish Reading 1939–69' in C. Hutton (ed.), *Oxford History of the Irish Book* (2011), pp. 131–2.
49 'Irishman's Diary', *The Irish Times*, 1 March 1938. The column was edited by the paper's editor R.M. Smyllie.
50 *The Bell*, vol. 1 no. 6 (March 1941).
51 Mary and Lucy Stanley, personal communication, 29 April 2016. Headquarters was in Sandford Road, in rooms now occupied by the Wild Goose Grill.
52 J. McAleer, *Passion's Fortune: The Story of Mills and Boon* (London, 1999), pp. 168, 213–6.
53 *The Irish Times*, 3 November 1934. The same reservations apply to this unquantified survey as were discussed in respect of *The Bookman*'s surveys in the 1890s (Chapter 3). Once again, local interest titles appeared more frequently than seems likely. Special circumstances must for instance account for *Caisleáin Óir* by 'Máire', originally published ten years before, being the bestselling fiction title for Three Candles in that week.

54 *The Irish Times*, 26 July 1941.
55 *The Irish Times Review and Annual* (Dublin, 1946), p. 63.
56 *The Bell*, vol. 6 (1943).
57 M. Harmon, *Sean O'Faolain* (London, 1994), p. 106.
58 *The Irish Times*, 14 March 1947.
59 D. Marcus, *Oughtobiography* (Dublin, 2001), pp. 64–7.
60 *The Bell*, vol. 15 no. 4 (January 1948).
61 G. Ivan Morris, *In Dublin's Fair City* (1947), pp. 59–60. Morris was managing director of Fodhla printers.
62 I am grateful to the UCC university archivist Catriona Mulcahy for these figures.
63 J.A. Murphy, 'Cork University Press in Context' in *75th Anniversary Catalogue of Cork University Press* (Cork, 2000), pp. 36–44. This catalogue also contains a full list of publications from 1925.
64 *Ibid.*
65 D. Brady, 'Modernist presses and the Gayfield Press', *Bibliologia* 9 (2014), pp. 113–128. It is clear that the active manager of the press was Blánaid Salkeld and not her son Cecil ffrench Salkeld who is usually credited with that role.
66 J.R.R. Adams, 'The Quota Press – a Preliminary Checklist', *Linen Hall Review*, 3.1 (Spring 1986), pp. 16–7. I am grateful to Anne Tannahill for bringing this to my attention.
67 F. Murphy, *Publish or Perish* (Mercier, 1951).
68 The twelve publishers were: Catholic Truth Society; Browne & Nolan; Clonmore & Reynolds; Dundalgan; James Duffy; Educational Publishing Company; C.J. Fallon; M.H. Gill; Hodges Figgis; Mercier; Talbot; Three Candles. Dolmen's first publication came in August 1951.
69 M. Moynihan (ed.), *Speeches and Statements by Éamon de Valera* (Dublin, 1980), p. 536.
70 J.R. Hill (ed.), *New History of Ireland 1921–84* (Oxford, 2003); N. Buttimer & M. Ní Annracháin, 'Irish Language and Literature 1921–84' in Hill (ed.) p. 558.
71 *Inniú* continued until the withdrawal of government funding in 1984 and FNT went into liquidation in 1988.
72 O'Leary, *Irish Interior: Keeping Faith with the Past.*
73 See C. Ó hÉigeartaigh & A. Nic Gearailt, *Sáirséal agus Dill, 1947–1981* (Indreabhán, 2014).
74 *The Irish Times*, 25 October 1948.
75 Quoted in P. O'Leary, *Writing Beyond the Revival: Facing the Future in Gaelic Prose 1940–51* (Cork, 2011), p. 403.
76 Adams, *Censorship: The Irish Experience*, p. 118.
77 J. Kelly, 'The Operation of the Censorship of Publications Board: the Notebooks of C.J. O'Reilly 1951–55', *Analecta Hibernica*, 38 (2004), pp. 225–369.
78 Adams, *Censorship: The Irish Experience*, pp. 171–5.
79 Kelly, 'The Operation of the Censorship of Publications Board', p. 227.
80 Adams, *Censorship: The Irish Experience*, p. 119.
81 Fr Aloysius, *The Catholic Home* (Dublin, 1951), p. 77, a Clonmore & Reynolds publication. Fr Aloysius argued elsewhere in this book that married love between Catholic and non-Catholic is impossible: it can be no more than 'the blindness of what seems love, but is no more than infatuation' (p. 24). Fr Aloysius was by this time an old man, having been 46 when he attended Pearse and MacDonagh before their deaths in 1916.
82 See Adams, *Censorship: The Irish Experience*, pp. 120–8, and D. Ferriter, *Occasions of Sin* (London, 2009), pp. 305–7.

Chapter 6

1 D. Athill, *Stet* (London, 2000), p. 117. Diana Athill was editorial director of André Deutsch for more than thirty years.
2 J. Feehan, *An Irish Publisher and his World* (Cork, 1959), pp. 113–5.
3 M. Daly, *Sixties Ireland* (Cambridge, 2016) has argued that the publicly feted sense of immediate transition, of a switch being pulled, was something of an illusion. The graduate job market, for instance, did not react immediately: of the nine graduates in 1964 of University College Dublin's BA course IXA (economics) only one stayed in Ireland.
4 *Creation*, February 1963.
5 *The Irish Times*, 13 February 1963.
6 B. Biever SJ, *Religion, Culture and Values* (New York, 1976), p. 240.
7 F. Tobin, *The Best of Decades: Ireland in the 1960s* (Dublin, 1984), p. 66. Fergal Tobin joined M.H. Gill in 1967, and became editorial director of Gill & Macmillan in 1994.
8 P. Craig, *Bookworm* (Bantry, 2016), p. 93.
9 *The Irish Times*, 1 July 1961.
10 A. Quinn, *Patrick Kavanagh: A Biography* (Dublin, 2003), pp. 139–40.
11 Jeremy Addis, personal communication, 6 June 2016. Downside is a prestigious English Catholic boarding school run by Benedictines. Nolan would have been one of twenty or thirty boys crossing the Irish Sea to attend, mostly from the Dublin area; see C. O'Neill, *Catholics of Consequence* (Oxford, 2014), p. 82.
12 N. Hudson, *How Times Changed* (Newstead, 2009), p. 23. Hudson joined Heinemann in 1957, moving to Heinemann Australia in 1958.
13 Macmillan & Co., 'Notes for Suppliers' (London, 1968). I was given a copy of this when I joined the company in 1971: it felt very old fashioned even then.
14 Committee on Industrial Progress, *Report on Paper, Paper Products, Printing and Publishing Industry* Prl 1356 (Dublin, 1970), p. 146.
15 D. Jerrold, *Georgian Adventure* (London, 1938), p. 248.
16 'Publishing in Ireland', *Hibernia*, 8 October 1971.
17 The sole reference to editing in *The Truth about Publishing* discusses marking up, which he calls 'preparing the manuscript for press'. The index makes it clear that for him, editors oversee periodicals. Unwin, *The Truth about Publishing*, p. 119. See also S. Unwin, *The Truth about a Publisher* (London, 1960), pp. 160, 194–5.
18 Educational Company and Talbot archive, letter of July 1932.
19 *The Irish Times*, 19 July 1955.
20 Educational Company and Talbot archive, letter of 1 December 1925.
21 *Ibid.*
22 *Ibid.*
23 J. Feehan, *An Irish Publisher and his World* (Cork, 1959), p. 32; P.J. Conradi *Iris Murdoch: A Life* (London, 2002) p560
24 Irish Univeristy Press, draft house style (c. 1970).
25 Feehan, *An Irish Publisher and his World*, p. 32, 53.
26 Anne Tannahill, personal communication.
27 One whole box of the seven of the IUP archive is devoted to these drafts.
28 See Diana Athill's description of her editorial work in *Stet*, p. 59 *et seq.*
29 C. Blake, *From Pitch to Publication* (London, 1999), p. 30.
30 J. Thompson, *Merchants of Culture: The Publishing Business in the Twenty-First Century* (London, 2010), p. 144. Regular complaints in the review pages suggest that this ideal is often not achieved, particularly in academic houses such as Yale and Oxford.
31 The first catalogue, issued in spring 1968, promised nearly fifty titles, not including the *British Parliamentary Papers*.

32 R. Braddon, *Roy Thomson of Fleet Street* (London, 1968), pp. 274, 280.
33 As well as being MD of Cahills, O'Leary was a director of Aer Lingus, the ICC and other companies. He died in 1978 aged 88; see *The Irish Times*, 19 January 1978.
34 M. Adams, 'The World of the Irish University Press' in C. Hutton, *The Irish Book in the Twentieth Century* (Dublin, 2004), pp. 157–77. This is a lively insider's point of view; the article also contains an appendix detailing the 'afterlife' of many of the participants. Adams's information is backed by the seven boxes of archive material presently in the hands of Seamus Cashman.
35 Peter Ford was at this time emeritus Professor of History in Southampton. Grace Ford was a close collaborator in the work who was said to have read herself over 3,000 of these reports. From the letters in the archive they seem to have been a delightful couple. The Ford Collection of British Official Publications housed at Southampton University, now digitalised, is still the major resource in the field.
36 The approach was refused by the then managing William Gill, (Michael Gill, personal communication).
37 *The Irish Times*, 17 December 1969.
38 Marilyn Nordstedt was an American librarian who was very influential in developing the expertise of Irish University Press's editors.
39 The story was covered by Andrew Whittaker in *The Irish Times*, 15 March, 7 May, 1 June, 13 November 1971.
40 *Ibid.*
41 Adams, 'The World of the Irish University Press', p. 166.
42 *The Corruption of Harold Hoskins* was described in *Kirkus Review* as 'a breezy, light-hearted romp … too good-natured to be offensive'.
43 Obituary, *The Irish Times*, 24 November 2001.
44 Interview in 1989 with Michael Smurfit, unpublished MS in Smurfit archive. The material about Smurfit is based on work done for my unpublished history of the firm.
45 Interview with Des Kilroy, uncle of Howard who became a key member of Smurfit senior management.
46 Ó hÉigeartaigh & Nic Gearailt, *Sáirséal agus Dill*, pp. 417–22. It is difficult to imagine the two companies making a comfortable or longlasting mix.
47 Jefferson Smurfit, *Annual Report and Accounts 1971*.
48 Tarbett left Smurfit in 1977 and joined Concern. After some vicissitudes, he later ran the Cathedral Bookshop in Dublin.
49 *The Irish Times*, 5 January 1967; like everything else in the book trade the numbers have exploded since: in 2009 there were 7,300 exhibitors and 400,000 books.
50 Presentation to a Clé Rights Training Course by Michael Gill.
51 'Behind the Frankfurt facade', *The Irish Times*, 5 January 1967.
52 John Horgan, 'Ireland at Frankfurt Book Fair', *The Irish Times*, 27 October 1969.
53 *Ibid.*
54 G. Doherty & G. Doherty, 'Publishing in Ireland 1939–69' in C. Hutton (ed.), *Oxford History of the Irish Book* (2011), p. 114, reports several mentions of this organisation from the Educational Company archive.
55 Irish Book Publishers' Association Minute Book; Publishing Ireland archive.
56 *The Irish Times*, 15 September 1970.
57 See T. Farmar, *A Brief History of Clé: 1970–1995* (Dublin, 1995), pp. 8–9.
58 *Report on Paper, Paper Products, Printing and Publishing Industry* Prl 1356, pp. 140, 145. National publishing statistics regularly show how the low cost of entry into the market means that it is easy for organisations, societies and individuals to produce single titles.
59 *The Irish Times*, 22 January 1962.

60 *Ibid.*, 19 January 1970; the series ran intermittently until February.
61 See L. Miller, *Dolmen XXV* (Dublin, 1976).
62 *Ibid.*, p. 7.
63 For instance, a review in *Irish Booklore*, vol. 3 no. 2 (1977), of the cumulative catalogue *Dolmen XXV*: 'the books of the press have rather often not been so well produced that one would collect them as fine books.' For *Dolmen XXV* itself, the anonymous critic commented adversely not only on the inking but also the quality of the paper, with see-through affecting the heavy black images and even some offsetting.
64 P. Fallon, 'Notes on a History of Publishing Poetry', *Princeton University Library Chronicle* (Spring 1998), p. 549.
65 John Montague in M. Harmon, *The Dolmen Press: A Celebration* (Dublin, 2001), p. 71.
66 *The Irish Times*, 8 October 1960.
67 A. Titley, 'Twentieth Century Irish Prose' in S. Mac Mathúna & Ailbhe Ó Corráin (eds), *Celtic Literatures in the Twentieth Century* (Moscow, 2007), p. 15.
68 *Hibernia*, 8 October 1971.
69 *The Irish Times*, 2 February 1970.
70 See Ó hÉigeartaigh & Nic Gearailt, *Sáirséal agus Dill*; personal interview with Cian Ó hÉigeartaigh.
71 Feehan, *An Irish Publisher*, pp. 126 – 7.
72 *Ibid.*, p. 132.
73 *The Irish Times*, 18 February 1970.
74 'Interpreting the Irish', *Books Ireland*, May 1994.
75 *Irish Independent*, 23 March 1956.
76 *The Irish Times*, 18 February 1970.
77 Internal Gill & Macmillan summary in the Farmar papers.
78 Quoted in Mahony, 'Irish Writers and their London Publishers', p. 74.
79 F. Timms, 'The Price of Books', *The Bookseller,* 11, 18 September 1971. Timms was an accountant at Cambridge University Press.
80 The marked fluctuations of the shares of printer, publisher and bookseller over the period since 1890 are discussed in T. Farmar, 'An Eye to Business' in C. Hutton (ed.), *The Oxford History of the Irish Book* (2011).

Chapter 7

1 See F. Litton *et al.* (eds), *Unequal Achievement: The Irish Experience 1957–1982* (Dublin, 1982).
2 R. Mac Cormaic, *The Supreme Court* (Dublin, 2016) chapter 8.
3 R. Hegarty, 'From Two Supersers and a Cat to a Movement for Change' (unpublished MPhil thesis: Trinity College Dublin, 2000).
4 L. Miller, *Reluctant Capitalists* (Chicago, 2006), p. 71.
5 E. de Bellaigue, *British Book Publishing as a Business Since the 1960s* (London, 2004), pp. 14–15.
6 *The Bookseller*, 1 February 1981; 'A Small Publishing House: The First Year', *Times Literary Supplement*, 2 April 1982.
7 The Booksellers Association, *Industry Reports: UK Book Sales*; Jiabo Liu, *Copyright Industries and the Impact of Creative Destruction* (London, 2013), p. 138.
8 From 1947, until it was struck down in an antitrust suit in 1976, British publishers signed an agreement reserving the seventy countries of the so-called British Publishers Traditional Market (basically the former empire) to themselves. Signatories were expected to insist that any deal with American or other publishers included this reservation. Ireland was included on the list, as was, to its irritation, Australia.

See M. Bryant, 'English Language Publication and the British Traditional Market Agreement', *The Library Quarterly*, 494 (1979), pp. 374–5.

9 *Books Ireland*, March 1979.

10 T. Caherty, *More Missing Pieces* (Dublin, 1985), p. 14.

11 *Books Ireland*, March 1979, pp. 29 – 30.

12 F. O'Mahony, 'Schedule of Statistics Relating to Three Booksellers', in the author's papers.

13 Booksellers Association, *Directory of Book Publishers and Wholesalers* (London: 12th edition, 1982).

14 *The Irish Times*, 22 September 1981.

15 From November 1977, I worked in the Irish publishing industry and was actively involved in trade matters, being a member of the Clé committee (treasurer 1980, 1990, president 2002, 2003), a regular contributor on trade affairs to *Books Ireland* and in the early 1980s Irish correspondent of *The Bookseller*.

16 J. Epstein, *Book Business: Publishing Past Present and Future* (New York, 2001), p. 4.

17 *The Irish Times*, 5 October 1982.

18 Personal interview with Seamus Cashman, October 2016.

19 Quoted in *Books Ireland*, March 1980.

20 *The Irish Times*, 23 September 1972.

21 *The Guardian*, 1 February 1980.

22 *The Bookseller*, 2 February 1980; *Publishers Weekly*, 23 January 1981. The authors of the very positive series of articles in *Publishers Weekly* accepted as true an amount of boosterism: for instance, the Irish 'passion' for book reading, the number of new bookshops opening 'in places so small Americans would call them villages' and so on.

23 In the 1970s, Gill & Macmillan received 60 per cent of sales from books published in previous years.

24 *Books Ireland*, March 1976 and NLI catalogue.

25 C. McAndrew, 'Arlen House: Early Years of an Irish Publishing House 1975–1986' (unpublished M.Phil dissertation: Trinity College Dublin, 2016).

26 A. Blond, *The Publishing Game* (London, 1971), p. 41.

27 Personal interview with Philip MacDermott, 14 September 2016; personal interview with Anne Tannahill, 15 August 2017.

28 Personal interview with Michael O'Brien, 3 August 2016.

29 Personal interview with Kieran Devlin, 27 September 2016.

30 Publishing Ireland archive, minutes of meeting of 4 November 1983.

31 Interview with John Keohane, *Books Ireland*, May 1979.

32 *Publishers Weekly*, 23 January 1981.

33 Personal communication, Michael O'Brien, 12 October 2016.

34 *The Bookseller*, 25 April 1981; liquidation accounts in the Farmar papers. These sums are in £IR.

35 *The Irish Times*, 25 June 1985.

36 This account is based on personal interviews with Michael O'Brien and Seamus Cashman, plus a contemporary account 'Irish book fraud allegations', *Hot Press*, 14 August 1986, which was a detailed insider-driven account. Other information from contemporary documents in Farmar's papers.

37 Personal interview with Peter Thew, sales director of Gill & Macmillan, 21 September 2016. Peter Thew joined Gill & Macmillan from Macmillan's in London in 1975.

38 Personal interview with Michael O'Brien, 3 August 2016.

39 See F. Fishwick, *Book Publishing and Distribution* (Commission of the European Community IV/657/82-EN, Brussels, 1982), p. 10. Trusting too far in official statistics

this report identified a 7 per cent drop in output 1970–77 and a surge in the Irish language books share of sales over the same period from 5 per cent to 28 per cent.
40 *Books Ireland*, October 1986.
41 T. Farmar (ed.), *Clé Manual of Book Publishing* (Dublin, 1981), section 5.
42 *Communications Ireland 1984/5*, p. 94. The book trade would of course have been only a small part of the business of these firms.
43 The Galway university-based typesetter/publisher Officina Typographica produced an admirable guide, *IBM Typography Scope and Techniques,* describing how to produce an attractive page with the Composer, identifying three fonts suitable for bookwork: Journal, Baskerville and Aldine (reviewed in *Irish Printer*, December 1982).
44 See T. Clark, *Bookbinding with Adhesives* (London, 1988).
45 *Books Ireland*, May 1994.
46 R. Dardis, 'Printers: A Publisher's Eye View' in *Books Ireland*, June 1981.
47 E. O'Rourke, 'On Not Buying Irish', *Books Ireland*, March 1980.
48 See T. Farmar, 'Irish Publishing: Expanding into the Uneasy '80s', *The Bookseller*, 2 February 1980. The most active trade publishers at the time are identified and described in this article.
49 *Publishers Weekly*, 23 January 1981.
50 *Ibid.*, 23 January 1981.
51 *Books Ireland*, July/August 1976.
52 Marcus, *Oughtobiography*, pp. 221–9.
53 Personal interview with Kieran Devlin, 27 September 2016.
54 P. Fallon, 'Notes on a History of Publishing Poetry', *Princeton University Library Chronicle* (Spring, 1998), p. 550.
55 *Ibid*, p. 557.
56 *The Irish Times*, 25 July 1980. Booksellers are traditionally inclined to take a pessimistic view of the future.
57 Personal interview with Robert Towers, 19 October 2016.
58 F. Fishwick, *Book Publishing and Distribution*, Commission of the European Community: Evolution of Concentration and Competition Series: Collection: 'Working Papers' IV/657/82–EN, Appendix II, Table II.3, p. 92.
59 In 1985, Kathy Sheridan credited Clé with having 'brought off such successes as the abolition of VAT in the teeth of a cheeseparing Government', but alas it wasn't true (*The Irish Times*, 22 July 1985).
60 T. Farmar, *A Brief History of Clé*, pp. 17–18.
61 *Books Ireland*, July/August 1976; December 1986. In 1982 there were bookshops in the following counties (excluding Northern Ireland): Carlow 2, Clare 1, Cork 14, Donegal 2, Dublin 34, Galway 5, Kerry 4, Kildare 2, Kilkenny 2, Limerick 3, Longford 1, Louth 1, Mayo 3, Meath 1, Offaly 1, Sligo 3, Westmeath 3, Tipperary 6, Waterford 14, Wexford 5, Wicklow 2.
62 *Business & Finance*, 16 August 1984.
63 *The Irish Times*, 22 July 1985.
64 *Business & Finance*, 14 February 1985. I worked as editorial and production manager during Tycooly's last nine months. Francis O'Kelly died in 2015.
65 S. MacDonogh, *Open Book: One Publisher's War* (Dingle, 1999), p. 38.
66 *Ibid.*, p. 40.
67 The 'grotesque, unbelievable, bizarre and unprecedented' events (as described by Conor Cruise O'Brien), a week before the opening, saw a violent and widely hunted murderer staying as a guest in the flat of the Attorney General, who had left him there while he visited New York.
68 MacDonogh, *Open Book: One Publisher's War*, pp. 62–82.

69 See, for instance, his contribution to the 26 February 1976 issue of the British Marxist publication *Red Weekly*, in which he describes activities of 'the Revolutionary Marxist Group (the Irish section of the Fourth International)' with an insider's confidence. I understand that his involvement was paid.
70 MacDonogh, *Open Book*, p. 251.
71 Interview 20 October 2016. Feature article by Kevin Myers in *The Irish Times*, 25 January 1992.
72 P. Oakeshott *et al.*, *The Current Use of Word Processors by British Publishers* (University of Leicester, 1981).
73 *The Observer*, 12 October 1986.
74 H. Oram in *Books Ireland*, 19 September 1985.
75 R. Hammond, *The Writer and the Word Processor* (London, 1984), pp. 29, 46.
76 Personal communication, Máiréad Peters of Gill & Macmillan.

Chapter 8

1 The differences are vividly displayed in two books describing the US publishing scene in 1982 and 2010 respectively: L. Coser *et al.*, *Books: The Culture and Commerce of Publishing* (New York, 1982) and J. Thompson, *Merchants of Culture* (Cambridge, 2010). In the former, the process of consolidation had only begun, the large book chains were a recent phenomenon and agents were treated with condescension. There were just 240 throughout the US, compared to one current estimate of almost 1,500 in New York alone.
2 Ian Chapman lecture to the Royal Society of Arts quoted in G. Greenfield, *Scribblers for Bread* (London, 1989), p. 144. His son, also Ian, became CEO of Simon & Schuster.
3 S. Unwin, *The Truth about a Publisher* (London, 1960), p. 98.
4 Stephanie Wolfe Murray died in June 2017 and in August her son Rupert produced an elegant memorial volume: *Stephanie Wolfe Murray: A Life in Books* (Edinburgh, 2017).
5 J. Lewis, *Grub Street Irregular* (London, 2008), p. 47. Lewis did a degree in Trinity College Dublin in the early 1960s.
6 *Books Ireland*, February 1987.
7 Interview with Peter Thew, sales director of Gill & Macmillan, 21 September 2016.
8 MacDonogh, *Open Book*, pp. 121–2.
9 F. Fishwick, *The Market for Books in the Republic of Ireland* (Dublin: Irish Books Marketing Group, 1987), pp. 8, 11.
10 *Books Ireland*, March 1987.
11 Fishwick, *The Market for Books*, p. 60.
12 *Ibid.*, pp. 60–2.
13 Interview with Jonathan Williams, 19 July 2017.
14 Fishwick, *The Market for Books*, summary.
15 *The Clé Directory of the Irish Book Trade* (ed. T. Farmar) was published in 1983 as a spin-off from the *Clé Manual of Book Publishing*. It was updated as *The Clé Directory of the Irish Book World* in 1990 and 1991, and as *The Irish Writers Guide* (eds Jeremy Addis and Shirley Kelly) in 1996 and 1998.
16 *Annual Register* for 1987, 1988 (Longmans: Harlow, 1988, 1989).
17 *The Bookseller*, 2 February 1980.
18 Greenfield, *Scribblers for Bread*, pp. 107–8. Greenfield was for many years head of the John Farquharson agency which specialised in travel and adventure tales. Greenfield probably had in mind Irish publishers based in London, such as the extraordinary Derek Verschoyle, rather than the serious-minded members of Clé.
19 Harmon (ed.), *The Dolmen Press: A Celebration*, p. 66.
20 *The Irish Times*, 29 May 2017.

21 *Ibid.*, 22 July 1985.
22 Dolmen Trading Account in the Farmar's papers.
23 J. Montague, 'Liam Dolmen' in Harmon (ed.), *The Dolmen Press: A Celebration*, p. 81.
24 *Irish Press*, 2 February 1983.
25 Royal Commission on Book Publishing *Canadian Publishers and Canadian Publishing* (Ontario, 1970), p. 11.
26 Harmon (ed.), *The Dolmen Press*, p. 15.
27 J. St John, *William Heinemann* (London, 1990), pp. 438–9.
28 *Books Ireland*, September 1988.
29 *The Irish Times*, 11 June 1988.
30 *Irish Publishing Record 1978, 1988* (University College Dublin, 1979, 1989).
31 *The Irish Times*, 11 June 1988.
32 *Ibid.*
33 *Irish Publishing Record 1988* (University College Dublin, 1989), Introduction.
34 *Irish Independent*, 23 September 2006.
35 Personal interview with Fergal Tobin. We have seen similarly skewed expectations from the eighteenth and nineteenth centuries (chapter 1). Indeed, the literature on publishing agrees with this so regularly it is in danger of becoming a truism. In 2010, a New York editor said that 'roughly half the books' an editor buys will lose money, and 'it's really the top ten per cent that make the difference' (Thompson, *Merchants of Culture*, p. 211).
36 R. Barker & G. Davies, *Books are Different* (London, 1966), pp. 921–2.
37 Miller, *Reluctant Capitalists*, p. 66.
38 B. Behan, *Hold Your Hour and Have Another* (London, 1965), p. 16.
39 Personal interview with Robert Towers, 19 October 2016.
40 *Ibid.*
41 Miller, *Reluctant Capitalists*, p. 67.
42 Book Marketing Council, *Lost Book Sales* (London, 1980), chapter 4.
43 Bowker PubTrack data reported in Thompson, *Merchants of Culture*, pp. 258–60.
44 A description of the US chain store 'co-operative advertising and promotion' practices, some of which were adopted by large Irish stores is in Miller, *Reluctant Capitalists*, pp. 99–104.
45 'Sellers, Stayers and Stickers' from P. Fitzgerald's novel, *The Bookshop* (London, 1978), especially chapter 3, based on her experience of a small shop in Southwold, Suffolk, in the 1950s.
46 Interview with Peter Thew, sales director of Gill & Macmillan, 21 September 2016.
47 Until the 1980s firm sales were the norm.
48 These sweetheart deals between publishers and booksellers undoubtedly existed, but they remained secret, even shamefaced, so hard evidence is not available.
49 M. Zifcak, 'Australia without resale price maintenance: who were the losers? The public', *Logos* 2.4 (1991), pp. 204–8.
50 *The Bookseller*, 7 March 1981.
51 *Straus & Straus v American Publishers Association* 231 US 222 (1913).
52 S. Bradley (ed.), *The British Book Trade: An Oral History* (London, 2010), p. 231.
53 Interview with Antony Farrell, August 2016.
54 See Athill *Stet*, p. 132 for one author's view: 'No doubt all writers know in their heads that their publishers, having invested much money and work in their books, deserve to make a reasonable profit; but I am sure that nearly all of them feel in their hearts that whatever their books earn *ought* to belong to them alone.' Constant suspicion is a poor basis for a relationship.
55 Coopers & Lybrand, *The Future of the Irish Book Publishing Industry* (Dublin, 1995).

Chapter 9

There are no notes for this chapter.

Chapter 10 (by Conor Kostick)

1 See Chapter 9.
2 *The Irish Times*, 15 February 2003.
3 Conor Kostick interview with Michael McLoughlin, 26 June 2018.
4 *The Irish Times*, 15 February 2003.
5 CK interview with Michael McLoughlin, 26 June 2018.
6 See 'Business profile: Hachette Ireland', *The Bookseller*, 22 July 2013.
7 Liz Thompson, 'From Clare to Here', *Publishing News*, 2003.
8 *Sunday Independent*, 29 October 2006.
9 *Ibid.*
10 *The Irish Times*, 15 February 2003.
11 *Ibid.*
12 CK interview with Michael McLoughlin, 26 June 2018.
13 *The Bookseller*, 18 December 2007.
14 *The Bookseller*, 1 January 2007; *The Bookseller*, 3 July 2008; Irish Publishing News, www.irishpublishingnews.com/2010/01/08/nonsuch-ireland-rebrands-as-the-history-press-ireland/ accessed 23 July 2018.
15 www.writing.ie/resources/eoin-mchugh-transworld-ireland-in-conversation-with-barbara-scully/ accessed 23 July 2018.
16 CK interview with Brian Langan, 19 June 2018.
17 Unemployment figures: CSO 2013: www.cso.ie/en/statistics/labourmarket/principalstatistics/, Emigration figures: CSO 2012: www.cso.ie/en/media/csoie/releasespublications/documents/latestheadlinefigures/popmig_2012.pdf, access date 17 July 2018.
18 Cited in Bob Johnston, 'Bookselling in a bankrupt country', *The Bookseller*, 16 March 2011.
19 Eoin Purcell, 'Celtic Tiger Feeling Cold', *The Bookseller*, 20 January 2010.
20 www.irishpublishingnews.com/2010/01/06/obrien-press-partner-with-kelloggs/ accessed 30 July 2018; CK digital archives, containing an image of the proposed cereal packet promotion.
21 Thanks to Ivan O'Brien for obtaining and discussing this data.
22 Personal communication, Ivan O'Brien of O'Brien Press (to CK).
23 *Sunday Business Post*, 12 September 2010.
24 www.irishpublishingnews.com/2010/08/31/merlin-wolfhound-to-cease-publishing/ accessed 19 July 2018.
25 Irish Publishing News, www.irishpublishingnews.com/2010/08/18/the-history-press-slims-down-but-retains-irish-imprint/ accessed 23 July 2018.
26 www.irishpublishingnews.com/2010/10/13/new-island-cuts-costs/ accessed 30 July 2018.
27 *The Irish Times*, 18 February 2017; Irish Publishing News, www.irishpublishingnews.com/2011/07/21/mercier-rebrands-mccaughrens-childrens-classics/ accessed 26 July 2018.
28 www.irishpublishingnews.com/2011/10/14/obrien-press-acquires-brandon-books/ accessed 30 July 2018.
29 www.irishpublishingnews.com/2011/04/01/colour-books-enters-receivership/ accessed 28 July 2018.

30 Personal communication, Ruth Gill of Gill (to CK).
31 Gill & Macmillan, *Directors' Report 2008*, CRO.
32 *Sunday Times*, 11 December 2011.
33 *Ibid.*
34 'Bookselling Business is a Real Page-Turner', *Sunday Independent*, 27 September 2015.
35 *The Bookseller*, 22 June 2018.
36 Personal communication, Seosamh Ó Murchú (to CK).
37 *Ibid.*; https://www.mykidstime.com/things-to-do/colm%C3%A1n-o-raghallaigh/ accessed 25 July 2018.
38 Personal communication, Tadhg Mac Dhonnagáin (to CK).
39 *Ibid.*
40 TheJournal.ie, 24 June 2017; *Books Ireland*, issue 361, May/June 2015.
41 https://www.solocheck.ie/Irish-Company/Ipsilon-Books-Limited-488302, accessed 30 July 2018; *The Independent*, 4 January 2018.
42 www.irishpublishingnews.com/2010/12/16/little-island-sails-clear-of-new-island/ accessed 30 July 2018; CK interview with Siobhán Parkinson and Gráinne Clear, 25 May 2018.
43 *Ibid.*
44 *Ibid.*
45 Personal communication, Lisa Coen (to CK).
46 *Ibid.*
47 Mike McCormack won the €100,000 2018 Dublin International Literary Award for *Solar Bones*.
48 Personal communication, Kieran Devlin (to CK).
49 *Sunday Independent*, 27 September 2015.
50 www.irishpublishingnews.com/2010/03/29/penguin-ireland-sold-100-ebooks-in-2009/, accessed 30 July 2018.
51 Thanks to Ivan O'Brien for obtaining and sharing this data.
52 CK interview with Laurence O'Bryan, 26 July 2018.
53 *Sunday Times*, 15 January 2012.
54 CK interview with Laurence O'Bryan, 26 July 2018.
55 *Ibid.*
56 *Sunday Business Post*, 20 January 2017.
57 *Ibid.*, 24 January 2016.
58 *Sunday Times*, 11 December 2011.
59 Personal communication, Ruth Gill (to CK).
60 *The Guardian*, 18 January 2017.
61 Publishing Ireland, *Submission to the Copyright Review*, 2015.
62 www.artscouncil.ie/News/Arts-Council-comments-on-its-Budget-allocation/ accessed 30 July 2018; www.artscouncil.ie/News/Arts-Council-announces-2010-funding-decisions/ accessed 30 July 2018; *Magill*, 26 February 2010.
63 www.irishpublishingnews.com/2010/02/11/mercier-press-cancels-or-postpones-literary-and-childrens-titles/ accessed 30 July 2018.
64 https://www.independent.ie/irish-news/education/arts-council-cut-the-end-for-kids-books-30897889.html accessed 30 July 2018; https://www.irishexaminer.com/viewpoints/yourview/cuts-in-funding-to-obrien-press-is-unfair-treatment-by-the-arts-council-302843.html accessed 30 July 2018.
65 Irish Writers Centre, *Director's Report and Financial Statements 2005, 2007*, CRO; *Books Ireland* 363 (September/October 2015); *Irish Times*, 15 January 2009; CK digital archive.
66 *Belfast Telegraph*, 5 May 2017.

67 Personal communication, Tadhg Mac Dhonnagáin (to CK).
68 *The Bookseller*, 23 November 2017; *The Irish Times*, 7 October 2016; *Irish Independent*, 19 January 2017.
69 *The Bookseller*, 23 July 2018; https://www.irishexaminer.com/business/happy-pear-help-boost-dubray-book-sales-in-2016-445872.html accessed 30 July 2018.
70 www.irishpublishingnews.com/2012/09/07/easons-acquires-argosy/ accessed 30 July 2018.
71 *The Telegraph*, 23 October 2012; 1 July 2013.
72 www.irishpublishingnews.com/2012/11/07/penguin-random-house-will-have-22-of-irish-market/ accessed 30 July 2018.
73 CK interview with Michael McLoughlin, 26 June 2018.
74 www.theeditor.ie/new-appointments-harper-collins-ireland/ accessed 30 July 2018; https://www.writing.ie/news/harpercollins-steps-up-investment-in-ireland/ accessed 30 July 2018.
75 *Sunday Times*, 15 April 2018.
76 CK interview with Michael McLoughlin, 26 June 2018.
77 *The Bookseller* , 29 June 2018; CK digital archive.
78 *The Irish Times*, 18 October 2016; https://www.internationalauthors.org/10-principles-fair-contracts-authors/ accessed 30 July 2018; CK digital archives.
79 Personal communication, Ronan Colgan (to CK).
80 https://themanbookerprize.com/resources/media/pressreleases/irish-publishers-eligible-submit-novels-man-booker-prize-2018-onwards accessed 30 July 2018.
81 *Ibid.*
82 *The Times*, 9 January 2018.
83 *Ibid.*; *Sunday Times*, 14 January 2018.
84 Personal communication with Ivan O'Brien (to CK).
85 CK interview with Brian Langan, 19 June 2018.

Part Two

A Chronicle of Irish Book Publishing since 1890

1 *The Bookseller*, March 1890; Sir Frederick Macmillan, *The Net Book Agreement 1899* (1924) pp. 5, 14–6.
2 S. Eliot, *Some Patterns and Trends in British Publishing 1800–1919*, London 1994.
3 *The Irish Times*, 9 July 1890.
4 *Dictionary of Irish Biography* (Cambridge, 2009), *sub nom* Downey, Edmund.
5 *The Irish Times,* 26 July 1890, 30 August 1890.
6 R. Ellman, *Yeats: The Man and the Mask* (Penguin, 1987), p. 107; B. Levitas 'Reading and the Irish Revival' in C. Hutton (ed.), *The Oxford History of the Irish Book Vol. V: The Irish Book in English 1891–2000* (Oxford, 2011).
7 *The Bookseller*, May 1892; Figgis's first name not given.
8 *The Bookseller*, November 1892.
9 V. Kinane, *A History of the Dublin University Press 1734–1976* (Dublin, 1994), p. 227. The first printing of this book, by Brunswick Press who took over the Dublin University Press title, was rejected by the publishers Gill & Macmillan as substandard.

10 R. Foster, *W.B. Yeats: A Life, I The Apprentice Mage* (Oxford, 1998), p. 129.
11 C. Hutton, 'The promise of literature in the coming days' in *Victorian Literature and Culture* (2011), p. 39; pp. 581–92 list the twelve titles in this series, which were published between 1893 and 1897.
12 G. Greist, *Mudie's Circulating Library and the Victorian Novel* (Bloomington: Indiana University Press, 1970), pp. 171–4; *The Bookseller Centenary Edition*, 3 May 1958, comment under 1897.
13 Macmillan, *The Net Book Agreement*, pp. 18–9.
14 *The Bookseller*, September 1895.
15 H. Montgomery Hyde (ed.), *Trials of Oscar Wilde* (London, 1948).
16 *Bookseller Centenary Edition*, 1958; W. Kingsford, *The Publishers Association*, (Cambridge: 1970) Appendix.
17 Eason's archive, 27 April; there was no reference in the minutes to the growing movement in favour of net prices, which provincial booksellers often considered a London phenomenon.
18 Eason's archive, 10 December; W. Zachs, 'John Murray and the Dublin book trade', *Long Room* 40 (1995).
19 *The Nation*, 14 February 1897, *Eye*, Autumn 2012.
20 L. Cullen *Eason and Son* Dublin 1989 p. 190.
21 P. Riggs, 'The origins of the Irish Text Society' in *History Ireland*, Spring 1998.
22 *The Irish Times*, 13 October 1898.
23 Macmillan *The Net Book Agreement* 1924 pp. 27–30; *Bookseller Centenary Edition*, 1958, under 1899.
24 R. Welch, *The Oxford Companion to Irish Literature* (Oxford, 1996).
25 Philip O'Leary, *The Prose Literature of the Celtic Revivial 1881–1921*, Pennsylvania State UP (1994) p. 8.
26 Catholic Truth Society of Ireland, *First Fifty Years 1899–1949* (Dublin, 1949).
27 Andrew Corrigan, *A Printer and his World* (London, 1944) pp. 139–2.
28 Eason's archive, 12 March.
29 C. Tempest McCrea, *Tempest of Dundalgan (*Dundalk, 1988).
30 T. Wall, *The Sign of Dr Hay's Head* (Dublin, 1958) pp. 134, 143.
31 L. Miller, *The Dun Emer Press, Later the Cuala Press* (Dublin, 1973) p. 105.
32 C. Hutton ,'"Yogibogeybox in Dawson Chambers": The Beginnings of Maunsel and Company' in C. Hutton (ed.), *The Irish Book in the Twentieth Century* (Dublin, 2004).
33 Anon, *The Story of W.H. Smith* (printed for private circulation, 1955), p. 23; C. Wilson, *First with the News* (London 1985), pp. 235–52.
34 Hutton, 'Yogibogey box'; *Dictionary of Irish Biography, sub nom* Joseph Hone.
35 S. Brown, *The Press in Ireland* (Dublin, 1937).
36 Eason's archive, 17 May 1906.
37 *Bookseller Centenary Edition*, 1958.
38 *The Irish Times* 13 October 1906; Macmillan *Net Book Agreement* 1924.
39 NLI catalogue.
40 O'Leary, *Prose Literature* (1994) p. 8.
41 Obituary, *The Irish Times*, 12 December 1908.
42 Eason's archive.
43 *The Irish Times*, 16 June 1909.
44 Agnes Blackie, *Blackie & Son 1809–1959* (Glasgow & London, 1959), pp. 52–3.
45 Wall, *Sign of Dr Hay's Head*, p. 144–5; J. J. O'Kelly, 'House of Gill' (unpublished manuscript in Trinity College Dublin archive).
46 Ed Mulhall, 'From Celtic twilight to revolutionary dawn', RTÉ's Century Ireland website.

47 *Freeman's Journal*, 8, 10 July 1912; *The Irish Times*, 8 July 1912.
48 *Dictionary of Irish Biography*, *sub nom* Pembrey.
49 Wall, *Sign of Dr Hay's Head* 1958, pp. 140–2.
50 N. Allen & T. Browne, 'Publishing after partition 1922–39' in Hutton (ed.), *The Oxford History of the Irish Book, Vol. V* 2011, pp. 71–9; NLI Catalogue.
51 *Straus & Straus v American Publishers' Association* 231 US 222, 1913.
52 *The Irish Times,* 6 April 1914.
53 *Ibid.*, 25 September 1915.
54 *Ibid.*, 28 December 1915; *Irish Independent*, 4 January 1916.
55 *Ibid.*, 17 February 1916, 30 November 1916.
56 F.-J. French, 'A history of the house of Maunsel' (unpublished MLitt thesis, Trinity College Dublin, 1969) pp. 43–9.
57 Robert Hogan, *Eimar O'Duffy* (Bucknell University Press 'Irish Writers Series', 1972) p. 28; M. Hay, *Bulmer Hobson* (Manchester, 2009) p. 217.
58 P. O'Farrell, *The Burning of Brinsley MacNamara* (Dublin, 1990) chapter 3.
59 Blackie, *Blackie & Son*, p. 53.
60 Eason's archive: Introduction by John Rooney, November 2011.
61 *The Irish Times,* 18 February 1921, leader stimulated by the stoning of an Italian.
62 NLI catalogue.
63 *The Irish Times*, 26 September 1922.
64 Philip O'Leary, *Gaelic Prose in the Irish Free State 1922–39* (Dublin, 2004), p. 25.
65 G. Long, 'The National Library of Ireland' in A. Black (ed.) *Cambridge History of Libraries in Britain and Ireland, Vol III 1850–2000* (Cambridge, 2006), p. 251.
66 O'Farrell, *Burning of Brinsley MacNamara.*
67 Hay, *Bulmer Hobson*, p. 218; A. Dolan, *Commemorating the Irish Civil War* (Cambridge, 2003.)
68 *Dictionary of Irish Biography, sub nom* M.H. Gill; Wall, *Sign of Dr Hay's Head*, pp. 144–5.
69 *Dictionary of Irish Biography*, *sub nom* George Roberts.
70 *The Irish Times*, 15 January 1925.
71 Eason's archive EAS/A/14.2 & 14.3.
72 G. Uí Laighléis, 'An Gúm: The Early Years' in S. Mac Mathúna *et al.* (eds), *Celtic Literature in the Twentieth Century* (Moscow, 2007), p. 202.
73 Dáil Debates, 7 December 1926; *The Irish Times*, 5 March 1927.
74 J.R.R. Adams in *Linen Hall Review*, vol. 3, Spring 1986, NLI catalogue, Northern Ireland Publications Resource.
75 *The Irish Times,* 7 February 1929. Donn Byrne (1889–1928), who lived near Bandon, had died in a motor accident not long before. His novel *Field of Honour* was published posthumously.
76 *The Irish Times*, 11 November 1929.
77 Page Dickinson, *The Dublin of Yesterday* (London, 1929) p. 106.
78 Michael Adams, *Censorship* (Dublin, 1968); S. 16 (4) of the Act does not make it clear whether it is a defence that the bookseller was ignorant of such advocacy.
79 NLI catalogue.
80 Adams, *Censorship.*
81 *Irish Press*, 23 November 1932.
82 *All-Party Committee on the Constitution* (Dublin, 1999) pp. 30, 34.
83 R. Foster, *W.B. Yeats A Life II: The Arch-poet* (Oxford, 2003) pp. 448–52; F. O'Connor, *My Father's Son* (London, 1968) p. 91.
84 S. Brown, *Libraries and Literature* (Dublin, 1937) chapter 2.
85 Deirdre Brady in *The Irish Times*, 7 May 2015.
86 NLI MS 49, 143, 49, 144.

87 C. Hutton, 'Publishing the literary Revival' (unpublished DPhil thesis, Oxford 1999), p. 52.
88 Obituary, *The Irish Times*, 12 February 1937.
89 D. Brady, 'Modernist presses and the Gayfield Press', *Bibliologia*, vol. 9 (2014) p. 121.
90 *Dictionary of Irish Biography, sub nom* Colm Ó Lochlainn; *Long Room* (41), 1996.
91 *Irish Press*, 8 June 1937, special feature.
92 *Long Room* (38), 1993, p. 56.
93 *The Irish Times*, 31 March, 3 May 1938.
94 *Ibid.*, 8 January 1938.
95 L. Ó Broin in *Capuchin Annual 1935*, and in *Irish Monthly*, February 1938.
96 *Dictionary of Irish Biography, sub nom* William Gill; Wall, *Sign of Dr Hay's Head.*
97 *The Irish Times*, 26 June 1939.
98 *Ibid.*, 14 January 1939.
99 *Dictionary of Irish Biography*; Miller, *Dun Emer Press.*
100 *Bookseller Centenary Editon*, 1958, under 1941.
101 F. Shovlin, *The Irish Literary Periodical 1923–58* (Oxford 2003) chapter 4.
102 *The Irish Times,* 15 March 1941.
103 *Ibid.*, September 1941.
104 *Ibid.*, 25 March 1942; Joseph Holloway's season ticket giving the programme of talks is at NLI Ephemera EPH A456.
105 *Dictionary of Irish Biography, sub nom* Herbert Pembrey.
106 O'Connor, *My Father's Son,* pp. 128–31; Seanad Debates, 12 September 1942.
107 *The Irish Times*, 13 August 1943.
108 *Dictionary of Irish Biography, sub nom* Seán Feehan; J. Feehan, *An Irish Publisher and his World* (Cork, 1969), Appendix: The story of the Mercier Press.
109 *The Irish Times*, 12 February 1944.
110 NLI catalogue; 'Irishman's Diary' *The Irish Times*, 6 July 1946.
111 D. Ó Drisceoil, 'Irish books banned under the Censorship of Publications Acts 1929–67' in Hutton (ed.), *The Oxford History of the Irish Book, Vol. V*, p. 644.
112 *The Irish Times*, 16 July 1946.
113 D. Marcus, *Oughtobiography* (Dublin, 2001).
114 *The Irish Times*, 14 March 1947, exact details of restrictions spelled out 19 September 1949; letter from Philip Rooney *The Irish Times*, 16 July 1949; Marcus *Oughtobiography* (2001), pp. 64–6.
115 Diarmaid Ferriter, 'The post-war library service: bringing books to the remotest hamlets and the hills' in McDermott (ed.), *The University of the People: Celebrating Ireland's Public Libraries*, An Comhairle Learbharlanna (2003); Mary Castelyn, *A History of Literacy and Libraries in Ireland* (Aldershot, 1984) p. 219.
116 M. Bryant, 'English language publication and the British Traditional Market Agreement' in *Library Quarterly* vol. 49, no. 4, Oct 1979.
117 Context: note to papers of Prionsias Mac an Bheatha collection G40 NUI Galway.
118 *Dictionary of Irish Biography*; Cian Ó hÉigeartaigh agus Aoileann Nic Gearailt *Sáirséal & Dill 1947–1981* Indreabhán Co. Galway 2014, Aguisín 4: Amlíne.
119 *Irish Press* 11 March 1950; *The Irish Times*, 25 October 1948, 6 October 1956, 20 December 1958.
120 *Irish Independent*, September 1949.
121 Catholic Truth Society of Ireland, *First Fifty Years 1899–1949* (Dublin, 1949).
122 B. Lynch, *Parsons Bookshop* (Dublin, 2006); *The Irish Times*, 11 June 1991.
123 *The Irish Times*, 30 September 1949.
124 *Ibid.*, 12 October 1949

125 F. Shovlin, *The Irish Literary Periodical 1923–58* (Oxford, 2003) chapter 5.
126 Ó hÉigeartaigh and Nic Gearailt, *Sáirséal & Dill* 2014, Aguisín 4: Amlíne.
127 *Irish Press*, 26 June 1951.
128 F. Murphy, *Publish or Perish* (Mercier, 1951).
129 *Dictionary of Irish Biography, sub nom* Liam Miller, a biography which resolutely evades controversial matters such as the failure to pay royalties and the financial irregularities.
130 *Sunday Independent*, 7 September 1952.
131 *Bookseller Centenary Edition*, 1958, under 1952.
132 *Administration*, vol. 1 no. 1.
133 *The Irish Times*, 1 May 1954.
134 NLI catalogue.
135 Marcus, *Oughtobiography*, 2001, pp. 98–9.
136 *The Irish Times*, 27 April 1956.
137 *Ibid.*, 6, 9 October 1956.
138 *Ibid.*, 18 January 1956.
139 B. Kennedy, *Dreams and Responsibilities* (Dublin, 1991) pp. 118, 123, 242.
140 *Long Room* (41), 1996.
141 *Bookseller Centenary Edition*, 3 May 1958, under 1957; NLI catalogue.
142 *The Irish Times*, 25 March 1959.
143 *Ibid.*, 27 March 1959.
144 McCrea, *Tempest of Dundalgan*, 1988, p. 126.
145 Pat Donlon, 'Books for Irish children' in Hutton (ed.), *The Oxford History of the Irish Book Vol. V*, p. 385.
146 *The Irish Times*, 20 October 1964, 2 May 1959.
147 *Long Room* (46), 2001, pp. 20–21.
148 *The Irish Times*, 8 October, 2 December 1960.
149 Máirín O'Byrne, 'Libraries and Librarianship in Ireland', *Administration*, Summer 1968.
150 Feehan, *An Irish Publisher*, 1969; Cullen *Eason & Son*, 1989; M. Gill, *The Irish Times*, 12 November 2005.
151 *The Irish Times*, 22 January 1962.
152 Hutton (ed.), *The Oxford History of the Irish Book, Vol. V*, p. 114, footnote 18.
153 *The Irish Times*, 16 July 1963; Finance Act 1963 S. 53.
154 Cullen, *Eason & Son*, p. 381.
155 *The Irish Times*, 21 March 1964, 21 Sept 1964.
156 *Books from Ireland*, successive issues.
157 *Books Ireland*, December 1985.
158 G. McIntosh, 'M.H. Gill, later Gill & Macmillan' in Hutton (ed.), *The Oxford History of the Irish Book, Vol. V*, p. 524; Kinane, *History of Dublin University Press*, p. 344.
159 Information from Herder.
160 J. Cooney, *John Charles McQuaid* (Dublin, 1999), pp. 369–70.
161 D. O'Driscoll, *Stepping Stones: Interviews with Seamus Heaney* (London, 2009), pp. 80–4; Peter Fallon, 'Notes on a History of Publishing Poetry', *Princeton University Library Chronicle* (Spring 1998).
162 *The Irish Times*, 5 January 1966.
163 'Dublin's Bookshops', a pamphlet produced by O'Brien Press *c.* 1980, in Farmar papers.
164 T. Stiphas, *Late Age of Print* (New York, 2006); Informatics Development Institute website.
165 *The Irish Times*, 5 December 1966.
166 www.colinsmythe.co.uk.
167 *Dictionary of Irish Biography, sub nom* Seán Ó hÉigeartaigh.

168 Hutton (ed.), *The Oxford History of the Irish Book, Vol. V*, p. 311.
169 M. Adams, 'The world of Irish University Press' in C. Hutton (ed.) *The Irish Book in the Twentieth Century* (Dublin, 2004); Michael Gill's presentation to Society of Publishers in Ireland, 24 April 2004 (in Farmar's papers).
170 *The Irish Times*, 2 February 1967; *Jefferson Smurfit Annual Report 1971*.
171 Information from Herder.
172 *Books from Ireland*, 4 January–July 1972; *The Irish Times*, 27 January 1972; M. Smith's obituary, *The Irish Times*, 6 December 2014.
173 Harold Clarke interview, *Publishing News*, 10 February 1995; *The Bookseller* 21 January 1978.
174 *The Irish Times*, 16 June 1967.
175 Arts Council archive 'origins of tax exemption for artists' proposal dated 6 November 1967.
176 *The Irish Times*, 26 September 1967.
177 Marcus, *Oughtobiography*, chapter 21.
178 Clarke interview, *Publishing News*, 10 February 1995.
179 NLI catalogue.
180 M. Gill, presentation to SPI, 2004.
181 *The Irish Times*, 3 October 1969.
182 *Ibid.*, 27 October 1969; James Mongey, *Books Ireland*, March 1976.
183 T. Farmar, *A Brief History of Clé*, Dublin 1995; *The Irish Times*, 14, 15 September 1970.
184 Fallon, 'Notes on a History of Publishing Poetry'.
185 Prl 1356: chapter vii deals with publishing.
186 *The Irish Times*, 1 June 1971.
187 J. H. Dunne, 'History of Educational Company and Talbot', *Long Room* (42), 1997; Jefferson Smurfit Annual Accounts 1971.
188 *The Irish Times*, 13 November 1971; M. Adams, 'The world of Irish University Press' in Hutton (ed.), *The Irish Book*.
189 Anne Tannahill, 'Blackstaff Press: Publishing "a local row"' in Hutton (ed.), *The Irish Book*; *Books Ireland*, December 1981; Eamonn Hughes, 'The Blackstaff Press' in Hutton (ed.), *The Oxford History of the Irish Book, Vol. V*.
190 *Books from Ireland*, 3 July/December 1971: James Duffy is mentioned under 'publishers not listed' as having been listed in previous issues but does 'not appear in this issue'.
191 *The Irish Times*, 15 September 1971.
192 Michael O'Brien in *Books Ireland*, April 1976.
193 Gifford Lewis, 'Gifford and Craven', *Long Room* (39), 1994.
194 *The Irish Times,* 14 June 1972.
195 *Ibid.*, 20 March 1971.
196 D. Tubridy, 'Thomas Kinsella and the Peppercanister Press' in Hutton (ed.), *The Irish Book*.
197 *Long Room* (41), 1996.
198 Advertisement in *The Irish Times*, 23 September 1972.
199 *The Irish Times*, 23 May 1973.
200 *Ibid.*, 1 August 1973.
201 Adams in Hutton (ed.), *The Irish Book* includes details of what happened afterwards to various Irish University Press staff.
202 Farmar, *Brief History*, p. 12.
203 www.isbn.org.
204 L. Ruiséal, *Liam Ruiséal Remembers* (Cork: Tower Books, 1978. I believe this is the only published autobiography of an Irish bookseller. It deals very little with the book trade, concentrating on the author's involvement with the Volunteers and the

Legion of Mary. Incorporation reported *The Irish Times*, 4 January 1928; subsequent information from Brian Gilsenan MD of Fallon's, 2013.

205 Personal communication, Michael O'Brien.
206 Interview with publisher John Murphy, *Linen Hall Review*, vol. 2 no. 1 (Spring 1985). The article wrongly cites 1976 as the date of the first title (personal communication, John Murphy; NLI catalogue).
207 Documents issued for 'Thirty Years a-publishing', 2003.
208 R. Phelan, *Two Irelands: Literary Feminisms North and South* (New York, 2005).
209 Steve MacDonogh, *Open Book* (Dingle, 1999).
210 *The Irish Times*, 9 December 1975, 5 October 1982, 20 September 2003; RTÉ documentary on Folens's career with the Waffen-SS 'Flemish Legion' during the war, broadcast January 2007; *Dictionary of Irish Biography*, *sub nom* Albert Folens.
211 No. 33 of 1973; Kennedy, *Dreams and Responsibilities*, chapter 9.
212 *The Irish Times*, 22 January 1975.
213 *Ibid.*, 9 November 1976, 7 April 1977.
214 M. Bryant, 'English language publication and the British Traditional Market Agreement', *The Library Quarterly* vol. 49 no. 4 (University of Chicago).
215 Kinane, *History of the Dublin University Press*, p. 352.
216 Marcus, *Oughtobiography*, chapter 24; *Books Ireland*, April 1995: in this interview Philip MacDermott says the press started in 1979 – but the NLI has several 1976 titles.
217 Adams in Hutton (ed.), *The Irish Book*.
218 *Books Ireland*, July 1977, September 1988.
219 *Ibid.*, May 1988.
220 *The Irish Times*, 28 July 1978.
221 *Ibid.*, 28 April 1978; *Books Ireland*, June 1978.
222 Information from Poetry Ireland.
223 Interview with publisher John Murphy, *Linen Hall Review*, vol. 2 no. (1 Spring 1985).
224 *Books Ireland*, January–February 1979; Farmar, *Brief History*, p. 13; copy of letter of 5 June from David Collins in the Farmar papers.
225 *Books Ireland*, July 1979.
226 'Publishing and the punt', *Books Ireland*, May 1979; Competition Authority decision 348 of 2 September 1994.
227 NLI catalogue.
228 Personal communication, Michael Gill.
229 Anne Tannahill in Hutton (ed.), *The Irish Book*.
230 *Books Ireland*, January–February 1980.
231 *Books Ireland*, October 1986.
232 *The Irish Times*, 3 April 1980.
233 Book Marketing Council and the Booksellers Association, *Lost Book Sales*, October 1980.
234 Adams in Hutton (ed.), *The Irish Book*; *The Irish Times*, 16 April 1988.
235 There are also suggestions that the idea came from Colm Ó Briain.
236 *New York Times*, January 1981; *Books Ireland*, February 1981.
237 *The Irish Times*, 22 September 1981.
238 Ó hÉigeartaigh and Nic Gearailt, *Sáirséal agus Dill*, Aguisín 4: Amlíne.
239 *Business & Finance*, 14 February 1985.
240 *The Irish Times*, 25 April 1981.
241 Pat Donlon, 'Books for Irish Children' in Hutton (ed.), *The Oxford History of the Irish Book, Vol. V*, p. 386.
242 *Irish Press*, 20 June 1982; *Aspect*, 17 June 1982.

243 *Books Ireland*, February 1982.
244 *Ibid.*, September 1982.
245 Personal communication, Robert Towers.
246 Farmar, *Brief History*.
247 Farmar papers.
248 Reviewed in *Irish Printer*, December 1982.
249 F. Fishwick, *Book Publishing and Distribution*, Commission of the European Community IV/657/82-EN.
250 'Trade Winds', *Books Ireland*, June 1983.
251 Personal communication, John Davey.
252 *Books Ireland*, June 1984.
253 *Books from Ireland*, 1995; personal information.
254 *Books Ireland*, July/August and September 1985.
255 *Irish Literary Supplement*, March 1988; Attic Press/Róisín Conroy Collection, Boole Library, University College Cork.
256 *The Observer*, 12 October 1986.
257 *Books Ireland*, June 1985; *The Irish Times*, 27 May 1991.
258 *Books Ireland*, June 1985.
259 *The Irish Times*, 16 June 1988.
260 *Books Ireland*, November 1986; *The Irish Times*, 4 March 1999; Jonathan Williams 'Minding Other People's Business' in Hutton (ed.), *The Oxford History of the Irish Book, Vol. V*.
261 *Hot Press*, 14 August 1986: this accurate and well-informed article was based on insider information.
262 Personal communication, Michael Gill.
263 *The Irish Times*, 18 May 1987.
264 *Books Ireland*, June 1987.
265 *Sunday Tribune*, 25 October 1987; *Books Ireland*, December 1987.
266 Personal communication, Jonathan Williams.
267 *Books Ireland*, September 1987; Farmar papers.
268 *The Irish Times*, 25 & 31 July 1987, 17 October 1992; *Books Ireland*, November 1987.
269 Obituary of Helen Clear, *The Irish Times*, 13 June 2009.
270 MacDonogh, *Open Book*, p. 224.
271 Personal communication, Robin Montgomery.
272 *The Irish Times*, 10 February 1989.
273 *Ibid.*, 11 June 1988; *Books Ireland*, June 1988.
274 *Ibid.*, 8 March 1988.
275 *Books Ireland*, February 1988.
276 *The Irish Times*, 12 August 1988; summarised in *Books Ireland*, September 1988.
277 *Books Ireland*, February 1997, February 2000.
278 *Ibid.*, October 1995.
279 Lynch, *Parsons Bookshop*, chapter 18.
280 *Books Ireland*, December 1989.
281 *Books from Ireland*, 1996.
282 *The Irish Times*, 15 Februry 1989; MacDonogh, *Open Book*, chapter 10.
283 *Ibid.*, 20 October 1990; *Books Ireland*, December 1990.
284 *Books Ireland*, May 1997; Mary N. Harris 'The concerns of Irish regional publishing' in Hutton (ed.), *The Oxford History of the Irish Book, Vol. V*, p. 319.
285 *Books Ireland*, Summer 1990, Summer 1995.
286 *Ibid.*, April 1991.
287 *The Irish Times*, 27 May 1991.

288 *Books Ireland*, September 1994; John A. Murphy in Cork University Press *75th Anniversary Catalogue*, 2000, and *The Irish Times*, 31 May 2004.
289 *Books Ireland*, May 1994; May 1996.
290 *Books Ireland*, April 1992; Hughes 'The Blackstaff Press' in Hutton (ed.), *The Oxford History of the Irish Book, Vol. V, p.* 623.
291 *The Irish Times* supplement, 10 June 1992.
292 *Ibid.*, 24 November 1992.
293 *Books Ireland*, May 1993.
294 *Belfast Telegraph*, 5 May 2015; press release May 2017 announcing Colourpoint's purchase of Blackstaff from Bairds.
295 'Long Room' 1993, *The Irish Times*, 26 May 2007.
296 Competition Authority decision of 10 June 1994 reported in *Iris Oifigiúil*, 24 June 1994.
297 *Books Ireland,* May 1995.
298 Information from Sinéad Mac Aodha.
299 Competition Authority Decision 348 of 2 September 1994.
300 *Books Ireland*, February 1997.
301 Coopers & Lybrand, July 1995; *Books Ireland*, September 1995.
302 S. Bradley (ed.), *The British Book Trade: An Oral History* (London, 2010), chapter 14.
303 Hughes 'The Blackstaff Press' in Hutton (ed.), *The Oxford History of the Irish Book, Vol. V,* 2011.
304 *Books Ireland*, October 1995.
305 Information from Trish Lowth, Columba Press; *The Irish Times*, 27 July 2010.
306 *Books Ireland*, May 1999.
307 *Ibid.*, May 1997.
308 MacDonogh, *Open Book*, p. 247.
309 Waterstones website.
310 *The Irish Times*, 20 February 1999.
311 *Books Ireland*, April 2000.
312 *The Irish Times*, 18 March, 10 October 2000 .
313 *Ibid.*, 18 January 2003.
314 Personal communication, John Davey.
315 Trinity College Dublin Citation; *The Irish Times*, 14 February 2009.
316 NLI catalogue.
317 *The Irish Times*, 28 September 2005; magazine feature, 7 January 2006.
318 *Ibid.*, 12 November 2005.
319 *Ibid.*, 3 August 2006.
320 R. & M. Loeber, *A Guide to Irish Fiction 1650–1900* (Dublin, 2006) p. xci.
321 *The Irish Times*, 26 February 2010.
322 *Ibid.*, 15 January 2010.
323 *Ibid.*, 7 July 2007.
324 *Ibid.*, 29 March 2008.
325 *The Irish Times*, 26 February 2010; Harris, 'The concerns of Irish regional publishing' in Hutton (ed.), *The Oxford History of the Irish Book, Vol. V*.
326 *The Irish Times*, 15 January 2009.
327 Library Council website.
328 *The Irish Times*, 27 July 2010.
329 *Ibid.*, 24 April 2010.
330 *Ibid.*, 27 July 2010.
331 *Ibid.*, 27 February 2010.

332 Letter of 9 June 2011 from the company in Farmar papers.
333 *The Irish Times*, 3 June 2011, 20 July 2011.
334 *Ibid.*, 2 February 2011, 5 February 2011.
335 *Ibid.*, 24 November 2012.
336 Competition Authority statement, 1 October 2012.
337 *Irish Independent*, 15 August 2013.
338 *The Irish Times*, 29 October 2013.
339 *Ibid.*, 14 December 2014, 29 January 2015.
340 *Sunday Independent*, 18 August 2013.
341 Obituary, *The Irish Times*, 17 May 2014.
342 *Irish Independent*, 9 August 2014.
343 *The Irish Times*, 2 September 2014.
344 *Irish Independent*, 11 January 2015.
345 *The Irish Times*, 26 March 2015.
346 *The Bookseller*, 20 September 2015.
347 *The Irish Times*, 12 March 2016.

Appendix

1 Google Books Search official blog, 5 August 2010, posted by software engineer Leonid Taycher.
2 The NSTC is a commercial database run by ProQuest, and neither I nor the book trade historian Simon Eliot have been able to identify how or why this undercount has occurred.

Select Bibliography

Unpublished Manuscripts and Theses

Anon. *The Story of W.H. Smith* (printed for private circulation, 1955)

Benson, C. 'The Dublin Book Trade 1801–1850' (unpublished thesis: Trinity College, 2000)

French, F.-J. 'A History of the House of Maunsel' (unpublished MLitt thesis: Trinity College, 1969)

Hegarty, R. 'From Two Supersers and a Cat to a Movement for Change' (unpublished MPhil in Creative Writing: Trinity College, 2000)

Hutton, C. 'Publishing the Irish Revival: The Evolution of Irish Textual Culture 1886–1922' (unpublished DPhil: Oxford, 1999)

McAndrew, C. 'Arlen House: Early Years of an Irish Publishing House 1975–1986' (unpublished MPhil in Creative Writing: Trinity College, 2016)

Macmillan & Co. 'Notes for Suppliers' (London, 1968)

Mahony, J. 'Irish Writers and their London Publishers 1884–1922' (unpublished PhD thesis: Trinity College, 2016)

O'Kelly, J. J. 'The House of Gill', Trinity College archive

Archives, Reports and Other Sources

Booksellers Association *Directory of Book Publishers and Wholesalers* (London: 12th edition, 1982)

Booksellers Association and Book Marketing Council *Lost Book Sales: A Nationwide Survey of Book Buyers and their Bookshop Purchases* (London, 1980)

Committee on Industrial Progress *Paper, Paper Products, Printing and PublishingIndustry* Prl 1356 (Dublin, 1970)

Coopers & Lybrand *The Future of the Irish Book Publishing Industry* (Dublin, 1995)

Dáil Debates

Eason's archive

Educational Company and Talbot archive

Farmar papers

Fishwick, F. *Book Publishing and Distribution* (Commission of the European Community IV/657/82-EN, 1982)

—*The Market for Books in the Republic of Ireland* (Irish Books Marketing Group, 1987)
Irish Times: *Saorstát Éireann Irish Free State 1921–1931* (supplement, Dublin, 1932)
Irish University Press archive
Iris Oifigiúil
Murray, J.A. *et al. The Irish Publishing Industry* (Dublin: University College Dublin, 1979)
National Library of Ireland
Northern Ireland Publications Resource
Pick, C. *Developing Publishing in Ireland* (Dublin: Arts Council, 1987)
Publishing Ireland *Submission to the Copyright Review* (2015)
Publishing Ireland archive
Royal Commission on Technical Instruction, 1881–4 C-3981-111 (1884)
Royal Commission on Book Publishing *Canadian Publishers and Canadian Publishing* (Ontario, 1970)
Seanad Debates
Select Committee on Industries (Ireland) 1884/5 Report (Prl 288)

Periodicals

Administration
Analecta Hibernica
Annual Register
Aspect
Athenaeum
Author
Belfast Newsletter
Belfast Telegraph
Bell, The
Bibliologia
Booklover
Bookman
Books from Ireland
Books Ireland
Bookseller, The
Bookseller Centenary Edition
Business & Finance
Capuchin Annual
Catholic Bulletin
Contemporary Review
Creation
Dublin Historical Record
Dublin Penny Journal
Economic Journal
Fortnightly Review
Freeman's Journal
Guardian
Hibernia
History Ireland
Hot Press
Inniú
Irish Booklore
Irish Book Lover
Irish Independent
Irish Literary Supplement
Irish Monthly
Irish Press
Irish Printer
Irish Publishing Record
Irish Times, The
Irish Times Review and Annual
Journal of Modern History
Kirkus Review
Library Quarterly
Linen Hall Review
Logos
Long Room
Nation
Observer
Princeton University Library Chronicle
Publishers' Circular
Publishers Weekly
Publishing History
Publishing News
Studies
Sunday Business Post
Sunday Independent
Sunday Times
Sunday Tribune
Telegraph
Times Literary Supplement
T.P.'s Weekly
Week, The
Weekly Irish Times

Books and Articles

Adams, J.R.R. *The Printed Word and the Common Man* (Belfast, 1987)
—'The Quota Press – a Preliminary Checklist', *Linen Hall Review*, 3.1 (Spring 1986)
—'Simms & M'Intyre: Creators of the Parlour Library', *Linen Hall Review*, 4.2 (Summer 1987)
Adams, M. *Censorship: The Irish Experience* (Dublin, 1968)
—'The World of the Irish University Press' in C. Hutton (ed.), *The Irish Book in the Twentieth Century* (Dublin 2004)
Addis, J. and Kelly, S. (eds) *The Irish Writers Guide* (Dublin, 1996, 1998)
Allen, J.S. *In the Public Eye: A History of Reading in Modern France 1800–1940* (Princeton, 1991)
Allen, N. and Browne, T. 'Publishing after Partition 1922–39' in C. Hutton (ed.), *The Oxford History of the Irish Book, Vol. V* (Oxford, 2011)
Aloysius, Fr. *The Catholic Home* (Dublin, 1951)
Altick, R. 'From Aldine to Everyman: Cheap Reprint Series of the English Classics 1830–1906' in *Studies in Bibliography*, 11 (University of Virginia, 1958)
Andrews, C.S. *Dublin Made Me* (Dublin, 1979)
Arnold, M. 'Copyright', *Irish Essays* (London, 1882)
Athill, D. *Stet* (London, 2000)
Augusteijn, J. *Ireland in the 1930s: New Perspectives* (Dublin, 1999)
Baer, A. (ed.), *Frank Sidgwick's Diary* (Oxford, 1975)
Bailey, H.S., *The Art and Science of Book Publishing* (University of Texas Press, 1970)
Balzac, H. *Lost Illusions* (New York, 1985)
Barker, R. and Davis G. *Books are Different: An Account of the Defence of the Net Book Agreement* (London, 1966)
Barnard, T. *Brought to Book* (Dublin, 2017)
Barnes, D. S. *The Making of a Social Disease: Tuberculosis in Nineteenth-Century France* (California, 1995)
Barnes, J. *Free Trade in Books: A Study of the London Book Trade Since 1800* (Oxford, 1964)
Basset, T. *et al.*, 'Booksellers and Bestsellers: British Book Sales as Documented by *The Bookman* 1891–1906', *Book History* 4 (2001)
Beauman, N. *A Very Great Profession* (London, 1983)
Behan, B. *Brendan Behan's Island* (London, 1965)
—*Hold Your Hour and Have Another* (London, 1965)
Berkeley, G. *The Querist* (Dublin: Talbot edition 1935)
Biever, B. *Religion, Culture and Values* (New York, 1976)
Birmingham, G. *The Search Party* (London, 1909)
Birrell, A. *Seven Lectures on the Law and History of Copyright in Books* (London, 1899)
Blackie, A. *Blackie & Son 1809–1959* (London & Glasgow, 1959)
Blagden, C. *Fire More than Water* (London, 1949)
Blake, C. *From Pitch to Publication* (London, 1999)
Blom, P. *Fracture: Life and Culture in the West 1918–38* (London, 2015)
Blond, A. *The Publishing Game* (London, 1971)
Braddon, R. *Roy Thomson of Fleet Street* (London, 1968)
Brady, D. 'Modernist presses and the Gayfield Press', *Bibliologia*, 9 (2014)
Briggs, A. *A History of Longmans* (London, 2008)
Brown, S. *Ireland in Fiction* (Dublin, 1915)
—*Libraries and Literature from a Catholic Standpoint* (Dublin, 1937)
—*The Press in Ireland* (Dublin, 1937)

—'The Choice of Fiction for Public Libraries' in *Libraries and Literature from a Catholic Standpoint* (Dublin, 1937)
Bryant, M. 'English language publication and the British Traditional Market Agreement' *The Library Quarterly*, vol. 49 no. 4 (University of Chicago: 1979)
Buttimer, N. and Ní Annracháin, M. 'Irish Language and Literature 1921–84' in J. Hill (ed.), *New History of Ireland 1921–84* (Oxford, 2003)
Byrne, R. 'The French Publishing Industry and its Crisis in the 1890s' in *The Journal of Modern History*, 23.3 (September 1951)
Butcher, J. *Copy-editing: The Cambridge Handbook* (Cambridge, 1975)
Caherty, T. *More Missing Pieces* (Dublin, 1985)
Carleton, W. *Traits and Stories of the Irish Peasantry* (Dublin, 1843)
Carter, J. and Muir, P. *Printing and the Mind of Man* (Cambridge, 1967)
Carty, J. *A Class-Book of Irish History: Book Four* (London, 1931)
Castelyn, M. *A History of Literacy and Libraries in Ireland* (Aldershot, 1984)
Cheney, O.H. *Economic Survey of the Book Industry 1930–31* (New York, 1948)
Cipolla, C. *Literacy and Development in the West* (Penguin, 1969)
Clark, T. *Bookbinding with Adhesives* (London, 1988)
Cole, R. *Irish Booksellers and English Writers 1740–1800* (London, 1986)
Collins, J. *Life in Old Dublin* (Dublin, 1913)
Coolahan, J. *Irish Education: Its History and Structure* (Dublin, 1981)
—'Three Eras of Reading' in V. Greaney (ed.), *Studies in Reading* (Dublin, 1977)
Cooney, J. *John Charles McQuaid* (Dublin, 1999)
Cork University Press *75th Anniversary Catalogue* (Cork, 2000)
Corp, W. *Fifty Years: A Brief Account of the Associated Booksellers of Great Britain and Ireland 1895–1945* (Oxford, 1946)
Corrigan, A. *A Printer and his World* (London, 1944)
Coser, L. *et al. Books: The Culture and Commerce of Publishing* (New York, 1982)
Costello, P. *Dublin's Literary Pubs* (Dublin, 1998)
Craig, P. *Bookworm* (Bantry, 2016)
CTS, *Catholic Truth Society of Ireland: First Fifty Years 1899–1949* (Dublin, 1949)
Cullen, L. *Eason & Son* (Dublin, 1989)
Daly, M. *Sixties Ireland* (Cambridge, 2016)
Dardis, R. 'Printers: A Publisher's Eye View' in *Books Ireland* (June 1981)
Dawson, W. 'My Dublin Year', in *Studies* (1912)
de Bellaigue, E. *British Book Publishing as a Business Since the 1960s* (London, 2004)
Devane, R.S. *The Imported Press* (Dublin, 1950)
Devlin, E. *Speaking Volumes* (Belfast, 2000)
Dickinson, P. *The Dublin of Yesterday* (London 1929)
Doherty, G. and Doherty, G. 'Publishing in Ireland 1939–69' in C. Hutton (ed.), *The Oxford History of the Irish Book, Vol V* (Oxford 2011)
Dolan, A. *Commemorating the Irish Civil War* (Cambridge, 2003)
Donlon, P. 'Books for Irish Children' in C. Hutton (ed.), *The Oxford History of the Irish Book, Vol. V* (Oxford, 2011)
Duffy, M. *A Thousand Capricious Chances: A History of the Methuen List 1889–1989* (London, 1989)
Dunne, J.H. 'The Educational Company of Ireland and the Talbot Press 1910–1990' *Long Room*, 42 (1997)
Dunton, J. *The Dublin Scuffle* (Carpenter, A. (ed.), Dublin, 2000 [1699])
Eliot, E. 'Patterns and trends and the NSTC', *Publishing History*, XVIII (1998)
Eliot, S. *Some Trends and Patterns in British Publishing 1800–1919* (London, 1994)

Epstein, J. *Book Business: Publishing Past Present and Future* (New York, 2001)
Escarpit, R. *The Book Revolution* (London, 1966)
Evans, E. *Historical and Bibliographical Account of Almanacks, Directories, etc, etc Published in Ireland from the Sixteenth Century with Jottings of their Compilers and Printers* (Dublin, 1976 [1897])
Fagan, P. *The Second City: Portrait of Dublin 1700–1760* (Dublin, 1986)
Fallon, P. 'Notes on a History of Publishing Poetry', *Princeton University Library Chronicle* (Spring 1998)
Fanning, B. and Garvin, T. *The Books that Define Ireland* (Dublin, 2014)
Farmar, T. *A Brief History of Clé: 1970–1995* (Dublin, 1995)
—(ed.) *Clé Manual of Book Publishing* (Dublin, 1981)
—'An Eye to Business' in C. Hutton (ed.) *The Oxford History of the Irish Book, Vol. V* (Oxford, 2011)
—(ed.) *The Directory of the Irish Book World* (Dublin 1985, 1990, 1991)
—'Irish Publishing: Expanding into the Uneasy '80s', *The Bookseller* (2 February 1980)
—'Setting up Home in Dublin in the 1850s', *Dublin Historical Record*, 54.1 (Spring 2001)
—*The Versatile Profession: A History of Accountancy in Ireland since 1850* (Dublin, 2013)
Farrell, B. (ed.) *Communications and Community in Ireland* (Cork, 1984)
Feather, J. *A History of British Publishing* (London: second edition, 2006)
Febvre, L. and Martin, H.-J. *The Coming of the Book* (trans. David Gerard, London, 1976, first published as *L'Apparition du Livre* by Editions Albin Michel, Paris, 1958)
Feehan, J.M. *An Irish Publisher and his World* (Cork, 1959)
Ferriter, D. 'The post-war library service: bringing books to the remotest hamlets and the hills' in McDermott (ed.) *The University of the People: Celebrating Ireland's Public Libraries* (Dublin, 2003)
—*Occasions of Sin* (London, 2009)
Fitzgerald, P. *The Bookshop* (London, 1978)
Flood, J. 'Germany' in M. Suarez *et al.* (eds), *The Oxford Companion to the Book* (Oxford, 2010)
Forster, E. M. *Abinger Harvest* (London, 1996)
Foster, R., *W.B. Yeats: A Life, Vol I The Apprentice Mage* (Oxford, 1997)
—*W.B. Yeats: A Life, Vol II The Arch-Poet* (Oxford, 2003)
Franklin, C. *The Ashendene Press* (Dallas, 1986)
Gaskell, P. *A New Introduction to Bibliography* (Oxford, 1972)
Gedin, P. *Literature in the Market Place* (London, 1982)
Gillespie, R. *Reading Ireland: Print, Reading and Social Change in Early Modern Ireland* (Manchester, 2005)
Gissing, G. *New Grub Street* (London, 1891)
Goldstrom, J. 'Lord John Russell and the Publishing Trade', *Publishing History*, 20 (1986)
—*The Social Content of Education 1808–1870* (Shannon, 1978)
Goroud, V. 'France' in M. Suarez *et al.* (eds.) *The Oxford Companion to the Book* (Oxford, 2010)
Greaney, V. (ed.) *Studies in Reading* (Dublin, 1977)
Greenfield, G. *Scribblers for Bread* (London, 1989)
Greist, G. *Mudie's Circulating Library and the Victorian Novel* (Bloomington: Indiana University Press, 1970)
Guillebaud, C. 'The Marshal–Macmillan Correspondence over the Net Book System', *The Economic Journal*, 75.299 (1965)
Hagen, J. *Tennyson and his Publishers* (London, 1979)
Hammond, R. *The Writer and the Word Processor* (London, 1984)

Harmon, M. *Sean O'Faolain* (London, 1994)
—*The Dolmen Press: A Celebration* (Dublin, 2001)
Harris, M.N. 'The Concerns of Irish Regional Publishing' in C. Hutton (ed.) *The Oxford History of the Irish Book, Vol. V* (Oxford, 2011)
Hart, H. *Rules for Compositors and Readers at the University Press Oxford* (London, 37th edition, 1967)
Hay, M. *Bulmer Hobson* (Manchester, 2009)
Haynes, C. *Lost Illusions: The Politics of Publishing in Nineteenth-Century France* (Harvard, 2010)
Higgins, F. (ed.), *Progress in Irish Printing* (Dublin, 1936)
Hill, J. (ed.) *New History of Ireland 1921–84* (Oxford, 2003)
Hinks, J. and Bell, M. 'The Book Trade in English Provincial Towns 1700–1849', *Publishing History*, LVII (2005)
Hodges, S. *Gollancz: The Story of a Publishing House 1928–1978* (London, 1978)
Hogan, R. *Eimar O'Duffy* (Lewisburg, Penn., 1972)
Hoult, N. *Coming from the Fair: Being Book Two of 'Holy Ireland'* (London, 1937)
Howell, J.B. *A History of the Dublin Library Society 1791–1881* (Dalhousie, 1985)
Hughes, E. 'The Blackstaff Press' in C. Hutton (ed.) *The Oxford History of the Irish Book, Vol. V* (Oxford, 2011)
Hutton, C. '"Yogibogeybox in Dawson Chambers": The Beginnings of Maunsel and Company' in C. Hutton (ed.) *The Irish Book in the Twentieth Century* (Dublin, 2004)
Hutton, C. (ed.) *The Irish Book in the Twentieth Century* (Dublin, 2004)
—(ed.) *Oxford History of the Irish Book, Vol V: The Irish Book in English 1891–2000* (Oxford, 2011)
—'The Promise of Literature in the Coming Days', *Victorian Literature and Culture*, 39 (2011)
Hyde, H.M. (ed.) *Trials of Oscar Wilde* (London, 1948)
Igoe, V. *Literary Guide to Dublin* (London, 1994)
Jackson, H. *The Eighteen Nineties* (Harmsworth, 1939)
James, H. 'The Art of Fiction' in *Partial Portraits* (London, 1888).
Jerrold, D. *Georgian Adventure* (London, 1938)
Kavanagh, P. *Tarry Flynn* (London, 1948)
Kelly, J. and Domville, E. (eds) *The Collected Letters of W.B. Yeats, Vol 1 1865–85* (Oxford, 1986)
Kelly, J. 'The Operation of the Censorship of Publications Board: the Notebooks of C.J. O'Reilly 1951–55', *Analecta Hibernica*, 38 (2004)
Kennedy, B. *Dreams and Responsibilities* (Dublin, 1991)
Keynes, J.M. 'Alfred Marshall 1842–1924', *The Economic Journal*, 34.135 (1924)
Kinane, V. *A History of the Dublin University Press 1734–1976* (Dublin, 1994)
—'The Early Books Trade in Galway' in G. Long (ed.) *Books Beyond the Pale* (Dublin, 1996)
Kingsford, W. *The Publishers Association* (Cambridge, 1970)
Kipling, R. 'The Three-Decker', *The Week*, 11 (1894)
Lally, B. *Print Culture in Loughrea 1850–1900* (Dublin, 2008)
Le Gallienne, R. *The Romantic '90s* (New York, 1925)
Leavis, Q. *Fiction and the Reading Public* (London, 1932)
Levitas, B. 'Reading and the Irish Revival 1891–1922' in C. Hutton (ed.) *The Oxford History of the Irish Book, Vol. V* (Oxford, 2011)
Lewis, G. 'Gifford and Craven', *Long Room*, 39 (1994)
Litton, F. *et al.* (eds) *Unequal Achievement: The Irish Experience 1957–1982* (Dublin, 1982)

Liu, J. *Copyright Industries and the Impact of Creative Destruction* (London, 2013)
Loeber, R. & M. *A Guide to Irish Fiction 1650–1900* (Dublin, 2006)
Long, G. (ed.) *Books Beyond the Pale* (Dublin, 1996)
—'The National Library of Ireland' in A. Black (ed.) *Cambridge History of Libraries in Britain and Ireland, Vol. III 1850–2000* (Cambridge, 2006)
Lyall, E. *Derrick Vaughan, Novelist* (London, 1889)
Lynch, B. *Parsons Bookshop* (Dublin, 2006)
Lyons, F.S.L. *Culture and Anarchy in Ireland 1890–1939* (Oxford, 1982)
—*Ireland since the Famine* (London, 1973)
McAleer, J. *Passion's Fortune* (Oxford, 1999)
McCarthy, A. 'Publishing for Catholic Ireland' in C. Hutton (ed.) *The Oxford History of the Irish Book, Vol. V* (Oxford, 2011)
MacCormaic, R. *The Supreme Court* (Dublin, 2016)
McCrea, C. *Tempest of Dundalgan* (Dundalk, 1988)
McCulloch, J. *Dictionary of Commerce* (London, 1839)
McDermott, N. (ed.) *The University of the People: Celebrating Ireland's Public Libraries* (Dublin, 2003)
MacDonogh, S. *Open Book: One Publisher's War* (Dingle, 1999)
McElligott, T.J. *This Teaching Life* (Westmeath, 1986)
McGuire, J. and Quinn J. (eds) *Dictionary of Irish Biography* (Cambridge: Royal Irish Academy & Cambridge University Press, 2009)
McIntosh, G. 'M. H. Gill, later Gill & Macmillan' in C. Hutton (ed.) *The Oxford History of the Irish Book, Vol. V* (Oxford, 2011)
—'Marcus Ward & Co.' in J. Murphy (ed.) *Oxford History of the Book in Ireland, Vol IV* (Oxford, 2011)
McKitterick, D. (ed.), *The Book in Britain, Vol VI, 1830–1914* (Cambridge, 2009)
Mac Mathúna, S. *et al.* (eds) *Celtic Literature in the Twentieth Century* (Moscow, 2007)
Macmillan, F. *The Net Book Agreement 1899* (Glasgow, 1924)
McNeill, M. *Vere Foster 1819–1900: An Irish Benefactor* (Newton Abbott, 1971)
McSkimming, R. *The Perilous Trade: Publishing Canada's Writers* (Ontario, 2003)
Mahaffy, J. 'The Irish landlords', *Contemporary Review* (1882)
Manguel, A. *A History of Reading* (London, 1997)
Mansell, P. *Paris Between Empires 1814–1852* (London, 2001)
Marcus, D. *Oughtobiography* (Dublin, 2001)
Miller, L. *Reluctant Capitalists* (Chicago, 2006)
Miller, L. *Dolmen XXV* (Dublin, 1976)
—*The Dun Emer Press, Later the Cuala Press* (Dublin, 1973)
Montague, J. 'Liam Dolmen' in M. Harmon (ed.) *The Dolmen Press: A Celebration* (Dublin, 2001)
Morris, G.I. *In Dublin's Fair City* (Dublin, 1947)
Moynihan, M. (ed.) *Speeches and Statements by Éamon de Valera* (Dublin, 1980)
Mulkerns, V. *Friends with the Enemy* (Dublin, 2017)
Munter, R. *Dictionary of the Print Trade in Ireland 1550–1775* (New York, 1988)
Murphy, F. *Publish or Perish* (Cork, 1951)
Murphy, J.A. 'Censorship and the Moral Community', in B. Farrell (ed.), *Communications and Community in Ireland* (Cork, 1984)
—'Cork University Press in Context' in *75th Anniversary Catalogue of Cork University Press* (Cork, 2000)
Murphy, J.H. (ed.) *Oxford History of the Book in Ireland, Vol IV* (Oxford, 2011)
Nelson, J. *Elkin Mathews: Publisher to Yeats, Joyce and Pound* (Wisconsin, 1989)

Nesta, F. 'The Myth of the "triple-headed monster": the economics of the three-volume novel', *Publishing History*, 62 (2007)
Oakeshott, P. and Meadows, J. *The Current Use of Word Processors by British Publishers* (University of Leicester, 1981)
O'Brien, J. (ed.) *The Vanishing Irish* (London, 1954)
O'Brien, J.V. *Dear Dirty Dublin: A City in Distress 1899–1916* (Berkeley, 1982)
Ó Broin, L. 'Contemporary Gaelic Literature and some of its Paradoxes', *Capuchin Annual* (1935)
—*Just Like Yesterday* (Dublin, 1986)
O'Byrne, M. 'Libraries and Librarianship in Ireland' *Administration*, 16, (Summer 1968)
O'Casey, S. *Inishfallen, Fare Thee Well* (London, 1973)
Ó Conchubhair, B. 'An Gúm, the Free State and the Politics of the Irish Language' in L. King and E. Sisson (eds.) *Ireland, Design and Visual Culture: Negotiating Modernity 1922–1992* (Cork, 2011)
O'Connor, F. *My Father's Son* (London, 1968)
Ó Drisceoil, D. 'Irish Books Banned under the Censorship of Publications Acts 1929–67' in C. Hutton (ed.) *The Oxford History of the Irish Book, Vol. V* (Oxford, 2011)
O'Driscoll, D. *Stepping Stones: Interviews with Seamus Heaney* (London, 2008)
O'Duffy, E. *Printer's Errors* (Dublin, 1922)
—*The Wasted Island* (London, 1929)
Officina Typographica *IBM Typography Scope and Techniques* (Galway, 1982)
Ó hÉigeartaigh, C. and Nic Gearailt A., *Sáirséal agus Dill 1947–1981* (Indreabhán, 2014)
O'Leary, P. *Gaelic Prose in the Irish Free State 1922–39* (Dublin, 2004)
—*Irish Interior: Keeping Faith with the Past in Gaelic Prose 1940–1951* (Dublin, 2010)
—*The Prose Literature of the Celtic Revival 1881–1921* (Pennsylvania, 1994)
—*Writing Beyond the Revival: Facing the Future in Gaelic Prose 1940–51* (Cork, 2011)
O'Neill, C. *Catholics of Consequence* (Oxford, 2014)
O'Nolan, B. (Myles na Gopaleen), *The Best of Myles* (London, 1968)
O'Rourke, E. 'On Not Buying Irish', *Books Ireland*, March 1980
Phelan, R. *Two Irelands: Literary Feminisms North and South* (New York, 2005)
Phillips, J. *Printing and Bookselling in Dublin 1670–1800* (Dublin, 1998)
Pollard, M. *Dictionary of Members of the Dublin Book Trade 1550–1800* (London, 2000)
—*Dublin's Trade in Books* (Oxford, 1989)
Powell, A. *At Lady Molly's* (London, 1957)
—*Faces in my Time* (London, 1980)
Quinn, A. *Patrick Kavanagh: A Biography* (Dublin, 2003)
Rees, H. *Rules of Printed English* (1970)
Reid, F. in *The Nation* (10 April 1920)
Riggs, P. 'The Origins of the Irish Text Society' in *History Ireland* (Spring 1998)
Robertson, O. *Dublin Phoenix* (London, 1957)
Ruiséal, L. *Liam Ruiséal Remembers* (Cork, 1978)
Russell, E. 'Holy Crosses, Guns and Roses: Themes in Popular Reading Material' in J. Augusteijn (ed.) *Ireland in the 1930s: New Perspectives* (Dublin, 1999)
Russell, P. *The Author's Manual* (London: sixth edition, 1891)
St Clair, W. *The Reading Nation in the Romantic Era* (Cambridge, 2004)
St John, J. *William Heinemann: A Century of Publishing 1890–1990* (London, 1990)
Sassoon, D. *The Culture of the Europeans* (London, 2006)
Schriffen, A. *The Business of Books* (London, 2000)
Sevill, C. 'Copyright' in D. McKitterick (ed.) *The Book in Britain, Vol VI, 1830–1914* (Cambridge, 2009)

Sheehan, P. *The Literary Life and Other Essays* (Dublin, 1921)
Sher, R. *The Enlightenment and the Book: Scottish Authors and their Publishers in Eighteenth Century Britain, Ireland and America* (Chicago, 2005)
Shovlin, F. *The Irish Literary Periodical 1923–58* (Oxford, 2003)
—'Irish Reading 1939–69' in C. Hutton (ed.) *The Oxford History of the Irish Book, Vol. V* (Oxford, 2011)
Sproule, J. (ed.) *The Irish International Exhibition of 1853* (Dublin, 1854)
—'The Publishing Trade' in J. Sproule (ed.) *The Irish International Exhibition of 1853* (Dublin, 1854)
Steinberg, S. *Five Hundred Years of Printing* (Penguin, 1955)
Stiphas, T. *Late Age of Print* (New York, 2006)
Suarez, M. *et al.* (eds) *The Oxford Companion to the Book* (Oxford, 2010)
Tannahill, A. 'Blackstaff Press: Publishing "a local row"' in C. Hutton (ed.) *The Irish Book in the Twentieth Century* (Dublin, 2004)
Taylor, G. *The Emerald Isle* (London, 1952)
Thompson, J. *Merchants of Culture: The Publishing Business in the Twenty-First Century* (London, 2010)
Thwaite, A. *Edmund Gosse: A Literary Landscape* (Oxford, 1985)
Timms, F. 'The Price of Books', *The Bookseller*, 11, 18 September 1971
Titley, A. 'Twentieth Century Irish Prose' in S. Mac Mathúna & A. Ó Corráin (eds.) *Celtic Literatures in the Twentieth Century* (Moscow, 2007)
Tobin, F. *The Best of Decades: Ireland in the 1960s* (Dublin, 1984)
Tracy, H. *Mind You, I've Said Nothing!* (London, 1953)
Trench, C. 'The Three Candles Press in the Thirties' *Long Room*, 41 (1996)
Tubridy, D. 'Thomas Kinsella and the Peppercanister Press' in C. Hutton (ed.) *The Irish Book in the Twentieth Century* (Dublin, 2004)
Uí Laighléis, G. 'An Gúm: The Early Years' in S. Mac Mathúna *et al.* (eds) *Celtic Literature in the Twentieth Century* (Belfast, 2007)
University of Chicago Press *A Manual of Style* (Chicago and London 12th edition, 1969)
Unwin, Stanley *The Publishing Unwins* (London, 1972)
— *The Truth About a Publisher* (London, 1960)
— *The Truth About Publishing* (London, 1926)
Wade, A. *Bibliography of the Writings of W.B. Yeats* (London, 1968)
Walker, G. *Soviet Book Publishing Policy* (Cambridge, 1978)
Wall, T. *The Sign of Dr Hay's Head* (Dublin, 1958)
Warburton, J. *et al.* *A History of the City of Dublin* (London, 1818)
Welch, R. *The Oxford Companion to Irish Literature* (Oxford 1996)
Williams, J. 'Minding Other People's Business' in C. Hutton (ed.) *The Oxford History of the Irish Book, Vol. V* (Oxford, 2011)
Williams, R. *Communications* (Harmondsworth, 1962)
Wilson, C. *First with the News* (London 1985)
Wolfe Murray, R. *Stephanie Wolfe Murray: A Life in Books* (Edinburgh, 2017)
Zachs, W. 'John Murray and the Dublin Book Trade' *Long Room*, 40 (1995)
Zeldin, T. *France 1848–1945* (Oxford, 1977)
Zifcak, M. 'Australia Without Resale Price Maintenance: Who Were the Losers? The Public', *Logos*, 2.4 (1991)

Index

Note: page numbers in **bold** refer to tables.